THE STATE OF THE WORLD'S CHILDREN 2013

ACKNOWLEDGEMENTS

This report is the result of collaboration among too many individuals and institutions to acknowledge here. The editorial and research team thanks all who gave so willingly of their time, expertise and energy, in particular:

Vesna Bosnjak (International Social Services); Shuaib Chalklen (UN Special Rapporteur on Disability); Maureen Durkin (University of Wisconsin); Nora Groce and Maria Kett (Leonard Cheshire Disability and Inclusive Development Centre, University College London); Nawaf Kabbara (Arab Organization of Disabled People); Lisa Jordan (Bernard van Leer Foundation); Connie Laurin-Bowie (International Disability Alliance); Barbara LeRoy (Wayne State University); Charlotte McClain-Nhlapo (United States Agency for International Development); Helen Meekosha (Women with Disabilities Australia); Peter Mittler (University of Manchester); Roseweter Mudarikwa (Secretariat of the African Decade on Persons with Disabilities); David Mugawe (African Child Policy Forum); Ghulam Nabi Nizamani (Pakistan Disabled Peoples' Organization); Victor Santiago Pineda (Victor Pineda Foundation); Tom Shakespeare (World Health Organization); Aleksandra Posarac (World Bank); Shantha Rau Barriga (Human Rights Watch); Eric Rosenthal (Disability Rights International); Albina Shankar (Mobility India); and Armando Vásquez (Pan American Health Organization) for serving on the External Advisory Board.

Judith Klein (Open Society Foundations); Gerrison Lansdown (independent); Malcolm MacLachlan and Hasheem Mannan (Trinity College Dublin); Susie Miles (independent); Daniel Mont (Leonard Cheshire Disability); and Diane Richler (International Disability Alliance) for authoring background papers.

Sruthi Atmakur (City University of New York); Parul Bakshi and Jean-Francois Trani (Washington University in St. Louis); Nazmul Bari and Amzad Hossain (Centre for Disability in Development); Simone Bloem and Mihaylo Milovanovitch (Organization for Economic Co-operation and Development); Johan Borg (Lund University); Megan Burke, Stephane De Greef and Loren Persi Vicentic (Landmine and Cluster Munition Monitor); James Conroy (Center for Outcome Analysis); Audrey Cooper, Charles Reilly and Amy Wilson (Gallaudet University); Alexandre Cote (International Disability Alliance); Marcella Deluca, Sunanda Mavillapalli, Alex Mhando, Kristy Mitchell, Hannah Nicolls and Diana Shaw (Leonard Cheshire Disability/Young Voices); Avinash De Souza (De Souza Foundation); Catherine Dixon (Handicap International); Fred Doulton (Secretariat of the Convention on the Rights of Persons with Disabilities); Natasha Graham (Global Partnership for Education); Jean Johnson (University of Hawaii); Chapal Khasnabis and Alana Officer (World Health Organization); Darko Krznaric (Queen's University); Gwynnyth Llewellyn (University of Sydney); Mitch Loeb (Centers for Disease Control and Prevention/National Center for Health Statistics); Rosemay McKay (Australian Agency for International Development); Amanda McRae (Human Rights Watch); Sophie Mitra (Fordham University); David Morissey, Sherzodbek Sharipoo and Andrea Shettle (United States International Council on Disabilities); Zelda Mycroft (The Chaeli Campaign); Emma Pearce (Women's Refugee Commission); Natalia Raileanu (Keystone Human Services); Richard Rieser (World of Inclusion); Marguerite Schneider (Stellenbosch University); Morsheda Akter Shilpi (Organization for the Poor Community Advancement); Silje Vold (Plan Norway) for writing background material or providing advice and information.

Tracy Achieng; Grace Okumu Akimi; Sophia Rose Akoth; Abeida Onica Anderson; Washinton Okok Anyumba; Beatrice Atieno; Ssentongo Deo; Ivory Duncan; Argie Ergina; Mary Charles Felix; Michael Salah Hosea; Amna Hissein Idris; Tiffany Joseph; Hannah Wanja Maina; Saitoti Augustin Maina; Dianne Mallari; Modesta Mbijima; Shida Mganga; Nicole Mballah Mulavu; Joseph Kadiko Mutunkei; Ann Napaashu Nemagai; Rachael Nyaboke Nyabuti; Alice Akoth Nyamuok; Sarah Omanwa; Benson Okoth Otieno; Nakafu Phiona; Shalima Ramadhani; Rosemarie Ramitt; Nambobi Sadat; Veronicah Shangutit Sampeke; Ladu Michel Seme; Josephine Kiden Simon; Muhammad Tarmizi bin Fauzi; Elizabeth Mamunyak Tikami; Shemona Trinidad; and the 20 other young people who participated anonymously in surveys and focus groups conducted specially for this report by facilitators from the Leonard Cheshire Disability Young Voices network.

Bora Shin and Matthew Manos (veryniceDesign) for the infographic on universal design published online at <www.unicef.org/sowc2013>.

UNICEF country and regional offices and headquarters divisions contributed to this report or to related online content or advocacy materials by submitting findings or photographs, taking part in formal reviews or commenting on drafts. Many UNICEF offices and national committees arranged to translate or adapt the report for local use.

Programme, policy, communication and research advice and support were provided by Yoka Brandt, Deputy Executive Director; Geeta Rao Gupta, Deputy Executive Director; Gordon Alexander, Director, Office of Research and colleagues; Nicholas Alipui, Director, Programme Division and colleagues; Ted Chaiban, Director, Office of Emergency Operations and colleagues; Colin Kirk, Director, Office of Evaluation and colleagues; Jeffrey O'Malley, Director, Division of Policy and Strategy and colleagues; and Edward Carwardine, Deputy Director, Division of Communication and colleagues. This edition also benefited from the close cooperation of Rosangela Berman-Bieler, Chief, and colleagues in the Disability Section of UNICEF's Programme Division.

Special thanks to David Anthony, Chief, Policy Advocacy Section; Claudia Cappa, Statistics and Monitoring Specialist; Khaled Mansour, Director of Communication until January 2013; and Julia Szczuka, deputy editor of this report until September 2012, for their generosity of intellect and spirit.

REPORT TEAM

EDITORIAL AND RESEARCH

Abid Aslam, Editor
Christine Mills, Project Manager
Nikola Balvin, Sue Le-Ba, Ticiana Maloney, Research Officers
Anna Grojec, Perspectives Editor
Marc Chalamet, French Editor
Carlos Perellon, Spanish Editor
Hirut Gebre-Egziabher (Lead), Lisa Kenney, Ami Pradhan, Research Assistants
Charlotte Maitre (Lead), Carol Holmes, Pamela Knight, Natalie Leston, Kristin Moehlmann, Copy Editors
Anne Santiago, Nogel S. Viyar, Judith Yemane, Editorial support

PUBLISHING AND DISSEMINATION

Catherine Langevin-Falcon, Chief, Publications Section; Jaclyn Tierney, Production Officer; Germain Ake; Christine Kenyi; Maryan Lobo; Jorge Peralta-Rodriguez; Elias Salem

STATISTICAL TABLES

Tessa Wardlaw, Associate Director, Statistics and Monitoring Section, Division of Policy and Strategy; David Brown; Claudia Cappa; Liliana Carvajal; Archana Dwivedi; Anne Genereux; Elizabeth Horn-Phathanothai; Priscilla Idele; Claes Johansson; Rouslan Karimov; Rolf Luyendijk; Colleen Murray; Jin Rou New; Holly Newby; Khin Wityee Oo; Nicole Petrowski; Tyler Porth; Chiho Suzuki; Andrew Thompson; Danzhen You

Design by Prographics, Inc.
Printed by Hatteras Press, Inc.

FOREWORD

Is there a child who does not dream of being counted and having her or his gifts and talents recognized? No. All children have hopes and dreams – including children with disabilities. And all children deserve a fair chance to make their dreams real.

This edition of *The State of the World's Children* includes contributions by young people and parents who show that, when given that chance, children with disabilities are more than capable of overcoming barriers to their inclusion, of taking their rightful place as equal participants in society and of enriching the life of their communities.

But for far too many children with disabilities, the opportunity to participate simply does not exist. Far too often, children with disabilities are among the last in line for resources and services, especially where these are scarce to begin with. Far too regularly, they are the objects simply of pity or, worse, discrimination and abuse.

The deprivations faced by children and adolescents with disabilities are violations of their rights and the principle of equity, at the heart of which lies a concern for the dignity and rights of *all* children – including the most vulnerable and marginalized members of society.

As this report documents, the inclusion of children with disabilities in society is possible – but it requires first a change of perception, a recognition that children with disabilities hold the same rights as others; that they can be agents of change and self-determination, not merely the beneficiaries of charity; that their voices must be heard and heeded in our policymaking and programmes.

We contribute to their exclusion by failing to gather enough data to inform our decisions. When we fail to count these children, we are failing to help them count for all they should in their societies.

Fortunately, progress is being made – albeit unevenly. This report not only examines the challenges involved in ensuring that children with disabilities have the fair access to services that is their right. It also explores initiatives that show promise in such areas as health, nutrition, education and emergency programming – and in the data collection and analysis needed to improve policies and operations in all these fields. Other chapters also discuss principles and approaches that can be adapted to advance these children's inclusion.

Somewhere, a child is being told he cannot play because he cannot walk, or another that she cannot learn because she cannot see. That boy deserves a chance to play. And we all benefit when that girl, and all children, can read, learn and contribute.

The path forward will be challenging. But children do not accept unnecessary limits. Neither should we.

Anthony Lake
Executive Director, UNICEF

CONTENTS

FOCUS

PERSPECTIVE

Additional Focus and Perspective essays are available online at
<www.unicef.org/sowc2013>.

FIGURES

REFERENCES

STATISTICAL TABLES

A NOTE ON TERMS

Victor, a 13-year-old with cerebral palsy, has fun in the water in Brazil. © Andre Castro/2012

CHAPTER 1

INTRODUCTION

Reports such as this typically begin with a statistic designed to highlight a problem. The girls and boys to whom this edition of *The State of the World's Children* is dedicated are not problems.

Rather, each is a sister, brother or friend who has a favourite dish, song or game; a daughter or son with dreams and the desire to fulfil them; a child with a disability who has the same rights as any other girl or boy.

Given opportunities to flourish as others might, children with disabilities have the potential to lead fulfilling lives and to contribute to the social, cultural and economic vitality of their communities – as the personal essays in this volume attest.

Yet surviving and thriving can be especially difficult for children with disabilities. They are at greater risk of being poor than peers without disabilities. Even where children share the same disadvantages – of poverty or membership in a minority group, say – children with disabilities confront additional challenges as a result of their impairments and the many barriers that society throws in their way. Children living in poverty are among the least likely to enjoy the benefits of education and health care, for example, but children who live in poverty and have a disability are even less likely to attend their local school or clinic.

In many countries, responses to the situation of children with disabilities are largely limited to institutionalization, abandonment or neglect. These responses are the problem, and they are rooted in negative or paternalistic assumptions of incapacity, dependency and difference that are perpetuated by ignorance. Unless this changes, children with disabilities will continue to have their rights neglected; to experience discrimination, violence and abuse; to have their opportunities restricted; to be excluded from society.

What is needed is a commitment to these children's rights and their futures, giving priority to the most disadvantaged – as a matter of equity and for the benefit of all.

From exclusion to inclusion

Children with disabilities encounter different forms of exclusion and are affected by them to varying degrees, depending on factors such as the type of disability they have, where they live and the culture or class to which they belong.

Gender is also a crucial factor: Girls are less likely than boys to receive care and food and are more likely to be left out of family interactions and activities. Girls and young women with disabilities are 'doubly disabled'. They confront not only the prejudice and inequities encountered by many persons with disabilities, but are also constrained by traditional gender roles and barriers. [1] Girls with disabilities are also less likely to get an education, receive vocational training or find employment than are boys with disabilities or girls without disabilities. [2]

At the heart of these differing forms and degrees of exclusion, however, lies the shared experience of being defined and judged by what one lacks rather than by what one has. Children with disabilities are often regarded as inferior, and this exposes them to increased vulnerability: Discrimination based on disability has manifested itself in marginalization from resources and decision-making, and even in infanticide.[3]

Exclusion is often the consequence of invisibility. Few countries have reliable information on how many of their citizens are children with disabilities, what disabilities they have or how these disabilities affect their lives. In some countries, families raising children with disabilities face ostracism. Because of this, even loving parents and family members can be reluctant to report that a child of theirs has a disability – whether because they are trying to avoid being shunned, because they are being overprotective of the

child, or both. If the child is born with an impairment, its birth might not even be registered. Children excluded in this way are unknown to, and therefore cut off from, the health, education and social services to which they are entitled.

Childhood deprivations can have lasting effects – by limiting access to gainful employment or participation in civic affairs later in life, for example. Conversely, access to and use of supportive services and technology can position a child with a disability to take her or his place in the community and contribute to it.

Indeed, the future is far from grim. Effective means are available to build inclusive societies in which children with and without disabilities can enjoy their rights equally. Physical, attitudinal and political barriers are being dismantled, although the process is uneven and has far to go.

Rahmatuallah, 14, who lost his leg in a landmine explosion, takes part in a training workshop for electricians at a centre for war-affected children in Kandahar, Afghanistan. © UNICEF/AFGA2007-00420/Noorani

Under the Convention on the Rights of the Child (CRC) and the Convention on the Rights of Persons with Disabilities (CRPD), governments around the world have taken upon themselves the responsibility of ensuring that all children, irrespective of ability or disability, enjoy their rights without discrimination of any kind. As of February 2013, 193 countries had ratified the CRC and 127 countries and the European Union had ratified the CRPD.

These two Conventions bear witness to a growing global movement dedicated to the inclusion of children with disabilities in community life. Concern for inclusion is rooted in the recognition that all children are full members of society: that each child is a unique individual who is entitled to be respected and consulted, who has skills and aspirations worth nurturing and needs that demand fulfilment and whose contributions are to be valued and encouraged. Inclusion requires society to make physical infrastructure, information and the means of communication accessible so all can use them, to eliminate discrimination so none is forced to suffer it and to provide protection, support and services so every child with a disability is able to enjoy her or his rights as do others.

Inclusion goes beyond 'integration'. The latter implies that children with disabilities are to be brought into a pre-existing framework of prevailing norms and standards. In the context of education, for example, integration might be attempted simply by admitting children with disabilities to 'regular' schools. This would fall short of inclusion, which is possible only when schools are designed and administered so that all children can experience quality learning and recreation together. This would entail providing students with disabilities with such needed accommodations as access to Braille, sign language and adapted curricula that allow them equal opportunity to learn and interact.

Inclusion benefits everyone. To continue with the example of education, ramps and wide doorways

On the numbers

By one widely used estimate, some 93 million children – or 1 in 20 of those aged 14 or younger – live with a moderate or severe disability of some kind.

Such global estimates are essentially speculative. They are dated – this one has been in circulation since 2004 – and derived from data of quality too varied and methods too inconsistent to be reliable. In order to provide a context for and illustrate the issues under discussion, this report presents the results of national surveys and independent studies, but even these must be interpreted with caution and should not be compared to one another. This is because definitions of disability differ by place and time, as do study design, methodology and analysis. These issues, and promising initiatives aimed at improving the quality and availability of data, are discussed in Chapter 6 of this report.

can enhance access and safety for all children, teachers, parents and visitors in a school, not just those who use wheelchairs. And an inclusive curriculum – one that is child-centred and that includes representations of persons with disabilities in order to reflect and cater to a true cross section of society – can broaden the horizons not only of children whose disabilities would otherwise limit their ambitions or options, but also of those without disabilities who stand to gain an appreciation of diversity and of the skills and preparedness necessary to build a society inclusive of all. Where educational attainment leads to a job or other means of earning a living, the child with a disability is able to advance and to take her or his place as a full and equal member of the adult world, one who produces as well as consumes.

A framework for action

Children with disabilities should not be treated or regarded simply as the recipients of charity. They have the same rights as others – among these, the right to life and to the opportunities that flow from good health care, nutrition and education,

(continued on p. 9)

From pioneer to advocate for inclusion

By Nancy Maguire

Nancy Maguire is a disability activist from the United Kingdom. She is a qualified social worker but, after travelling abroad, decided to campaign for the rights of people with disabilities, especially young women. She has worked with disabled people's organizations in Asia and Southern Africa, and hopes to obtain a Master's degree in policy and development.

I was born in London in 1986 and have a condition called osteogenesis imperfecta, commonly known as brittle bones. Many children with brittle bones grow up protected – overprotected, some might say – from any possibility of hurting themselves. My parents wanted me to be safe, but they also wanted me to have the opportunity to play, make friends and lead as normal a childhood as possible.

In the 1980s, inclusive education was still a fairly new concept. Like most parents of a disabled child, mine were advised to send me to a special school. My mother is a teacher, and after visiting the recommended school she was convinced that it would provide a substandard education. My parents have always used my older sister Katy, who did not have a disability, to gauge what is acceptable for me: If they thought something wasn't good enough for Katy, then it wasn't good enough for me.

I was the first child with a disability to attend my primary school, and in many ways I felt like a guinea pig for inclusion. For example, despite having a positive attitude towards including me in all aspects of school life, my teachers lacked experience in how to adapt physical education so that I could get involved in a meaningful way.

Like most childhoods, mine wasn't always easy. I spent a lot of time in hospital, and even within an 'inclusive' mainstream education system, there were times when I was excluded. For example, I wasn't allowed to go to my nursery Christmas party because the teachers were worried I would break a bone.

Also, at high school they had a separate table in the canteen for children with disabilities and the teachers could not understand why I refused to sit at it. Despite setbacks and obstacles, however, I managed to flourish both educationally and socially.

I was always encouraged to try new things. My extracurricular activities included swimming, ballet, wheelchair tennis, drama and singing. In many of these, I was also the only child with a disability. Interestingly, I often found these groups more inclusive than school in terms of how much I could participate and contribute. I felt wanted and people found creative ways for me to get involved. Nonetheless, there were many things I found difficult to do because of my limited mobility. I would sometimes feel upset because I couldn't do things as well as the other children, and as I grew older and more self-conscious, I became reluctant to put myself in situations where my difficulties were on show.

In my teenage years a lot of my friends went through phases of being a 'goth' or a 'rude girl', which involved dressing or behaving in ways designed to attract attention. Whilst they were doing everything they could to stand out and be different, I was desperate to be 'normal' and fit in. Growing up with a disability, I received a lot of attention. People in the street would often stare at me, make comments and ask my parents, "What's wrong with her?" I had days when I was able to brush it off, but no amount of resilience or family support can stop that from affecting you.

I developed extremely low self-esteem and poor body image, made worse because I was significantly overweight. I found exercise difficult, and like many girls my age, I ate to comfort myself. I had also internalized the medical terminology that was used to describe me – in particular the word 'deformed' (I had a curvature of the spine, since corrected). When I was 14, I developed an eating disorder, partly because I wanted to lose weight – but also because my weight felt like one aspect of my physical appearance that I could actually control.

Although I had incredibly supportive family and friends, being disabled was never something I viewed as a positive thing. I thought I had to overcome it, like adversity. I became obsessed with being as 'undisabled' as possible, and I was convinced that if I could walk, my life would be a lot better. Ironically, although I no longer use a wheelchair, in many ways I feel more aware of my disability than ever. People still make comments about me because I have small stature, and make assumptions about my life and ability; I always have to prove myself, particularly in the workplace. Though I am not defined by my disability, it has been pivotal in shaping who I am and what I have achieved. Having a disability is now something I embrace: I no longer see it as a negative thing or something I should be embarrassed about. In many ways being disabled has worked to my advantage and created opportunities that might never have been available to me – like writing this article.

Every child's experience is different. I come from a lower-middle-class family in the United Kingdom, where I had access to free health care and a good education. But I strongly believe that the issues of belonging, self-esteem and aspiration transcend such distinctions as gender, class and nationality. To develop a greater sense of self-worth, children with disabilities need the opportunity to participate and contribute in all aspects of their lives.

People with disabilities are becoming more visible in many walks of life – in politics and the media, for example. This is instrumental in improving children's perceptions of what they can achieve. When I was growing up, the only role model I had was Stevie Wonder. I admired him because he was a successful and respected musician despite being blind. However, it would have helped me to see people with disabilities doing everyday jobs – as teachers, doctors or shopkeepers. I think that would also have helped my parents. My mum said that when I was a child, she tried not to think about my future because it made her scared. She knew that I was capable but feared that my options would be limited.

As it turns out, my disability has not prevented me from achieving any of the important things. I am a qualified social worker, passed my driving test when I was 16, left home when I was 19 and have lived and worked in Asia and Africa. In the future I hope to be an advocate for children with disabilities on an international level, as I passionately believe in the inalienable human rights and untapped potential of these children.

Living with albinism, discrimination and superstition

By Michael Hosea

Michael Hosea was born in 1995. He is the eldest of six children and one of three persons with albinism in his immediate family. He lives in Dodoma, United Republic of Tanzania, and is about to graduate from school. He advocates for the rights of young people with disabilities, particularly those with albinism, through the Leonard Cheshire Disability Young Voices network.

I was born in Mwanza, the second largest city in the United Republic of Tanzania. I am the eldest son and live with my siblings and parents in Dodoma, the capital. There are six children in our family; one of my sisters and one of my brothers are also albinos.

The impairments caused by my condition make life very difficult. I always have trouble with the sun and have to cover up with heavy, long-sleeved clothing and wear sunglasses to protect my eyes. I also have troubles at school. Sometimes I can't see the blackboard, and I always have to sit in the shade. This country does not have sufficient vision-enhancing technology, such as glasses, magnifiers and special computer equipment, and without it children with albinism have a hard time graduating from school and finding employment. My family is poor, so getting money for school fees is also difficult.

Life is complicated even more by the way people treat us. There is a lot of discrimination against people with albinism, and I sometimes lack the company of friends. Some people also believe horrible myths about us: that we are not human and never die, that albinism is a curse from the gods and that anyone who touches us will be cursed.

Worst of all, practitioners of witchcraft hunt and kill us to use our hair, body parts and organs in charms and potions. For centuries some people have believed that if they go to a witch doctor with albino

Education is the key to stopping the murder, abuse and discrimination. It is important that others – even members of my extended family – learn that we are people just like them.

body parts, they will become rich and prosperous. Even though it is illegal to kill people with albinism, it still happens – it's greed that makes people do it. But it's all based on lies: There are people who have done these terrible things, yet their lives have remained the same.

A few months ago, thanks to a friend of my father, my siblings and I escaped being the victims of murder for witchcraft. My father's friend came to warn him that his three albino children were in danger of being hunted, and he begged my father to leave Mwanza. This wasn't easy because my parents' financial situation was not good, but we packed up everything and left at 3 a.m. that night.

We travelled over 500 kilometres to Dodoma and after two days received news from home that people had broken into our house in Mwanza looking to kill us.

When these people found that we had escaped, they went to our next-door neighbour's house. He was our local albino representative and had done so much to help us and advocate for albino rights in our community. They cut off his genitals and arms, and left him there to die. We later received a phone call from another neighbour telling us what they did to him. This news hurt me so much that I cried a lot, but what could I do? This is the way things are.

I don't understand why people do such things to fellow human beings. But I think education is the key to stopping the murder, abuse and discrimination. It is important that others – even members of my extended family – learn that we are people just like them. We are all the same.

To escape life's difficulties, I love to write songs and sing. I have just written a song about albinos and our struggle. My dream is to one day be able to record my music in a studio and spread my message. I pray that people around the world can one day understand that albinos are no different from them. We are all human beings and deserve to be treated with love and respect.

Note:

Albinism is a rare, genetically inherited condition found in all ethnicities. People with albinism have little or no pigmentation in their eyes, hair and skin owing to a lack of melanin. They are sensitive to bright light and have a higher than average risk of skin cancer from sun exposure. Most people with albinism are also visually impaired. Under the Same Sun, a Canadian non-governmental organization, estimates that albinism affects 1 in 2,000 Tanzanians. Although the medical condition itself does not affect life expectancy, in the United Republic of Tanzania the average lifespan of a person with albinism is around 30 years.

I want good memories

By Nicolae Poraico

Nicolae Poraico and his brother Grisha spent several years in a residential home for children with mental disabilities in the Republic of Moldova. Nicolae was diagnosed with a moderate intellectual disability and his brother with a severe intellectual disability. In 2010 Nicolae and Grisha reunited with their mother in the village of Lapusna. This was made possible with the assistance of the Community for All – Moldova programme, which is implemented by the Keystone Human Services International Moldova Association with financial support from the Open Society Mental Health Initiative and the Soros Foundation Moldova.

I was 11 when I went to the institution with my brother Grisha. I am now 16. Our mother sent us there because we did not have enough money to buy or rent a house, and she had to work nights. She came to see us often.

I do not remember the day I went to the institution. I even forgot some of my memories of being there, and I hope in time I will forget the other ones. I want new memories, good memories.

At holidays the food was good. It was also good on other days; we were fed four times a day. After eating I cleaned the kitchen.

The teachers taught us to recite poems and sing songs and showed us different games. I know a poem about Gigel and two about Mother.

We had naptime from 1 to 4 p.m. I would not sleep: I laughed, talked to other boys. I put my head on the pillow, kept my eyes open and looked at the boys. We were all living in one room, all 16 boys from my class.

There was one boy, Victor. He worked in the kitchen. We went to the stadium nearby. He took just me to the stadium; he had bread and sour milk, and we ate together. When my mother took me and my brother home, Victor did not know as he was sleeping. He gave me his picture so I would not forget him, but I forgot it there.

Sometimes the staff beat us. I do not know why. They beat me so much with different sticks that my back was injured. I was not the only one. Other boys were injured, too. And some boys had knives. Some boys hit others, and sometimes I fought with them, with fists. What could I do? If I did not defend myself, they could kill me. They beat Grisha, but I defended him.

I didn't want to stay there. If my mother had left us there, the administration could have sent us to different families and my mother would never find us. But I want to visit the institution, just to see Victor and take his phone number.

At home, it is very good. I now play with Colea, Igor and Dima. Here, nobody beats me. Sometimes we discuss problems with our mother and ask for advice. We get along very well and I go to school every day. I like physical education and Romanian language classes. I am glad I came here. I am happy that I am in Lapusna.

(continued from p. 3)

the right to express their views and participate in making decisions, and the right to enjoy equal protection under the law. They belong at the centre of efforts to build inclusive and equitable societies – not only as beneficiaries, but as agents of change. After all, who is in a better position to comprehend their needs and evaluate the response?

In any effort to promote inclusion and fairness, children with disabilities should be able to enlist the support of their families, disabled people's organizations, parents' associations and community groups. They should also be able to count on allies further afield. Governments have the power to help by aligning their policies and programmes with the spirit and stipulations of the CRPD, CRC and other international instruments that address or affect child disability. International partners can provide assistance compatible with the Conventions. Corporations and other entities in the private sector can advance inclusion – and attract the best talent – by embracing diversity in hiring.

The research community is working to improve data collection and analysis. Their work will help to overcome ignorance and the discrimination that often stems from it. Furthermore, because data help to target interventions and gauge their effects, better collection and analysis helps in ensuring an optimal allocation of resources and services. But decision-makers need not wait for better data to begin building more inclusive infrastructure and services: As some have already found, inclusion involves and benefits entire communities, and its elements can be applied to new projects across the board. All that is needed is for these efforts to remain flexible so they can be adapted as new data come to light.

The next chapter of this report discusses exclusion and the factors that propagate it, along with some philosophical and practical fundamentals of inclusion. Subsequent chapters – each of which applies the same approach of exploring barriers as well as solutions that show

promise – are dedicated to specific aspects of the lives of children with disabilities. Chapter 3 examines the health, nutritional and educational services that can provide a strong foundation on which children with disabilities can build full and fulfilling lives. Chapter 4 explores the opportunities and challenges of ensuring legal recognition and protection against exploitation or abuse. Chapter 5 discusses inclusion in the context of humanitarian crises.

Many of the deprivations endured by children with disabilities stem from and are perpetuated by their invisibility. Research on child disability is woefully inadequate, especially in low- and middle-income countries. The resulting lack of evidence hinders good policymaking and service delivery for children who are among the most vulnerable. Therefore, Chapter 6 of this report examines the challenges and opportunities confronting researchers – and ways in which children with disabilities can be rendered visible through sound data collection and analysis. Chapter 7, which concludes this edition of *The State of the World's Children*, outlines necessary and feasible actions that will enable governments, their international partners, civil society and the private sector to advance equity through the inclusion of children with disabilities.

Wenjun, 9, walks with her foster mother in China.
© UNICEF/China/2010/Liu

Children with and without disabilities participate in school festivities in Bangladesh. © UNICEF/BANA2007-00655/Siddique

CHAPTER 2

FUNDAMENTALS OF INCLUSION

Adopting an approach grounded in respect for the rights, aspirations and potential of all children can reduce the vulnerability of children with disabilities to discrimination, exclusion and abuse.

The Convention on the Rights of the Child (CRC) and the Convention on the Rights of Persons with Disabilities (CRPD) challenge charitable approaches that regard children with disabilities as passive recipients of care and protection. Instead, the Conventions demand recognition of each child as a full member of her or his family, community and society. This entails a focus not on traditional notions of 'rescuing' the child, but on investment in removing the physical, cultural, economic, communication, mobility and attitudinal barriers that impede the realization of the child's rights – including the right to active involvement in the making of decisions that affect children's daily lives.

It is often said that when *you* change, the world changes. Underestimation of the abilities of people with disabilities is a major obstacle to their inclusion. It exists not only in society at large but also in the minds of professionals, politicians and other decision-makers. It can also occur in families, among peers and in individuals with a disability, especially in the absence of evidence that they are valued and supported in their development. Negative or ill-informed attitudes, from which stem such deprivations as the lack of reasonable accommodation for children with disabilities, remain among the greatest obstacles to achieving equality of opportunity.

Negative social perceptions may result in children with disabilities having fewer friends and being isolated or bullied, their families experiencing additional stress, and their communities treating them as outsiders. Early studies of the way children with disabilities are treated by their peers have found that even at the preschool level, they may be overlooked as friends or playmates, sometimes because other children believe that they are not interested or able to play and interact.[4] A survey of families of children with disabilities in the United Kingdom found that 70 per cent thought that understanding and acceptance of disability among their community was poor or unsatisfactory, and almost half encountered problems in accessing such support services as childcare.[5] According to a 2007 UK study involving children with special educational needs, 55 per cent said that they had been treated unfairly because of their disability.[6] In Madagascar, one study found that ignorance about disability was common among parents – and that even among the presidents of parents' associations, 48 per cent believed, mistakenly, that disability is contagious.[7] A 2009 study in the Vietnamese city of Da Nang reported that although the community adopted generally tolerant attitudes towards children with disabilities and their families, instances of stigmatization and discrimination persisted. The appearance of children with disabilities in public on such holidays as Tet, which marks the new lunar year, was considered detrimental to good fortune.[8]

It is no wonder, then, that children with disabilities are among the most vulnerable to low self-esteem and feelings of isolation. No child should be defined by a disability. Each child is unique and has the right to be respected as such. When societies embrace inclusive principles and demonstrate this support for equity in practice, children with disabilities are able to enjoy the same rights and choices as other children. Enabling participation in the community and providing educational, cultural and recreational options is of paramount importance for the healthy physical and intellectual development of every child. Where specialized support – for communications or mobility, for example – is needed to facilitate interaction and promote self-reliant participation in everyday activities, access should be free and available to all.

Changing attitudes

Little will change in the lives of children with disabilities until attitudes among communities, professionals, media and governments begin to change. Ignorance about the nature and causes of impairments, invisibility of the children themselves, serious underestimation of their potential and capacities, and other impediments to equal opportunity and treatment all conspire to keep children with disabilities silenced and marginalized. Major public awareness campaigns that are sponsored by governments, include children as key presenters and are supported by all civil society stakeholders can inform, challenge and expose these barriers to the realization of rights. Furthermore, parents and disabled persons' organizations can – and often do – play pivotal roles in campaigning for acceptance and inclusion.

Bringing disability into political and social discourse can help to sensitize decision-makers and service providers, and demonstrate to society at large that disability is 'part of the human condition'.[9] The importance of involving children with disabilities cannot be overstated. Prejudice can be effectively reduced through interaction, and activities that bring together children with and without disabilities have been shown to foster more positive attitudes.[10] Social integration benefits everyone. It follows that if societies seek to reduce inequalities, they should start with children who are best fitted to build an inclusive society for the next generation. Children who have experienced inclusive education, for example, can be society's best teachers.

Inclusive media also have a key part to play. When children's literature includes children and adults with disabilities, it sends out positive messages that they are members of families and neighbourhoods. It is important for members of all groups, and especially those that may be discriminated against on the grounds of race, gender, ethnicity or disability, to be included in stories and textbooks for children – not necessarily as the main protagonists but simply to note their presence and participation. Books, film and media portrayal play an important role in teaching children about social norms. Just as the portrayal of girl characters in mainstream children's media carries implicit notions of gender

Estimated rates of primary school completion

with disability 51%

without disability 61%

with disability 42%

without disability 53%

Source: World Health Organization, based on surveys in 51 countries.

hierarchy and traditional expectations of gender, so the routine absence, misrepresentation or stereotyping of people with disabilities creates and reinforces social prejudices and leads to the underestimation of the roles and place of people with disabilities in society.

Similarly, participation in social activities helps to promote a positive view of disability. Sport, in particular, has helped overcome many societal prejudices. Physical activity can be a powerful means of promoting respect – it is inspirational to see a child surmount the physical and psychological barriers to participation, including lack of encouragement and support or limited adaptive equipment. In one study, physically active children with disabilities were rated as more competent than their non-disabled counterparts.[11] However, care must be taken not to create an artificial atmosphere in which children with disabilities who demonstrate physical heroism are deemed worthy and those who do not are made to feel inferior.

Sport has also been helpful in campaigns to reduce stigma. Athletes with disabilities are often among the most recognized representatives of people with disabilities, and many use such platforms as the Paralympics and Special Olympics to campaign and to become role models for children with physical or intellectual impairments. Moreover, experiences in Bosnia and Herzegovina, the Lao People's Democratic Republic, Malaysia and the Russian Federation show that access to sport and recreation is not only of direct benefit to children with disabilities but also helps to raise their standing in the community as they are seen to participate alongside other children in activities valued by society.[12]

Encouraging children with disabilities to take part in sport and recreation in company with all their peers is more than a matter of changing attitudes. It is a right and a specific requirement of the CRPD, which instructs States parties to "ensure that children with disabilities have equal access with other children to participation in play,

It's about ability

Montenegro's 'It's About Ability' campaign was launched in September 2010 and has had an impact on the public's knowledge of and attitudes and practices towards children with disabilities. The campaign brings together a broad coalition of 100 national and international organizations ranging from the Government of Montenegro to the European Union, the Council of Europe, the Organization for Security and Co-operation in Europe, United Nations agencies, embassies, associations of parents of children with disabilities, print and electronic media, the private sector, local officials and children with and without disabilities. One of the campaign's strategies involved the use of billboards all over the country to show children with disabilities as active members of society, portraying them as athletes, friends, musicians, dancers, students, daughters, sons, brothers and sisters.

A November 2011 survey measuring the impact of the campaign reported that it contributed to an 18 per cent increase in the number of people who consider children with disabilities as equal members of society. Behaviour toward children with disabilities and communication between them and people without disabilities were also seen to improve.

recreation and leisure and sporting activities, including those activities in the school system."

Supporting children and their families

The CRPD underlines the role of the family as the natural unit of society and the role of the State in supporting the family. It says that "persons with disabilities and their family members should receive the necessary protection and assistance to enable families to contribute towards the full and equal enjoyment of the rights of persons with disabilities."[13]

The process of fulfilling the rights of a child with a disability – of including that child in community

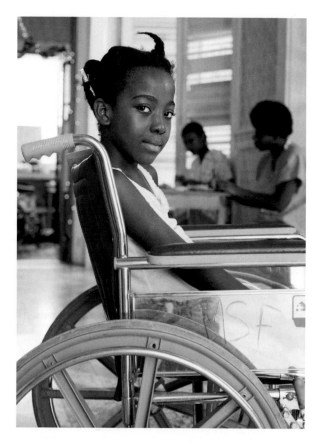

Marmane, 8, looks over her shoulder in a rehabilitation centre run by the international non-governmental organization Médecins sans Frontières in Port-au-Prince, Haiti. © UNICEF/HQ2005-1970/LeMoyne

Social protection for children with disabilities and their families is especially important because these families often face a higher cost of living and lost opportunities to earn income.

Estimates of the additional costs of disability borne by families range from 11–69 per cent of income in the United Kingdom to 29–37 per cent in Australia, 20–37 per cent in Ireland, 9 per cent in Viet Nam and 14 per cent in Bosnia and Herzegovina.[14] Costs associated with disability include such direct expenses as medical treatment, travel, rehabilitation or assistance with care, and such opportunity costs as the income forgone when parents or family members give up or limit their employment to care for a child or children with disabilities.[15]

The International Labour Organization has estimated that in 10 low- and middle-income countries, the economic costs of disability amount to 3–5 per cent of gross domestic product.[16] A review of 14 developing countries found that people with disabilities were more likely to experience poverty than those without disabilities.[17] People with disabilities tended to be less well off in terms of education, employment, living conditions, consumption and health. In Malawi and Uganda, households with members who have disabilities have been found more likely to be poorer than similar households without disabled members.[18] Households with members with disabilities generally have lower incomes than other households and are at greater risk of living below the poverty line.[19] In developing countries, households with a member or members who have disabilities spend considerably more on health care.[20] This means that even a household that technically stands above the poverty line but includes a member or members with disabilities can actually have a standard of living equivalent to that of a household below the poverty line but without members with disabilities.

The evidence is clear that childhood disability diminishes a person's life chances. Children with disabilities grow up poorer, have less access

life – begins with establishing a home setting conducive to early intervention. It involves stimulation and interaction with parents and caregivers from the first days and weeks of life through the different stages of the child's educational and recreational development. Inclusion is important at all ages but the earlier children with disabilities are given the chance to interact with peers and the larger society, the greater the likely benefits for all children.

Under the CRPD, children with disabilities and their families have the right to an adequate standard of living, including adequate food, clothing and housing. Children with disabilities and those responsible for their care are also entitled to such subsidized or free support services as day care, respite care and access to self-help groups.

to education and health-care services, and are worse off on a host of measures including the likelihood of family break-up and abuse.

States can tackle the consequent, increased risk of child poverty with such social protection initiatives as cash transfer programmes. These programmes are relatively easy to administer and provide for flexibility in meeting the particular needs of parents and children. They also respect the decision-making rights of parents and children.

Cash transfer programmes have been shown to benefit children,[21] although it can be difficult to gauge the extent to which they are used by and useful to children with disabilities and those who care for them.[22] A growing number of low- and middle-income countries are building on promising results from these broader efforts and have launched targeted social protection initiatives that include cash transfers specifically for children with disabilities. These countries include Bangladesh, Brazil, Chile, India, Lesotho, Mozambique, Namibia, Nepal, South Africa,

Turkey and Viet Nam, among others. The type of allowances and criteria for receiving them vary greatly. Some are tied to the severity of the child's impairment. Routine monitoring and evaluation of the transfers' effects on the health, educational and recreational attainment of children with disabilities will be essential to make sure these transfers achieve their objectives.

Another tool governments can use is disability-specific budgeting. For instance, a government that has committed to ensuring that all children receive free, high-quality education would include specific goals regarding children with disabilities from the outset and take care to allocate a sufficient portion of the available resources to covering such things as training teachers, making infrastructure and curricula accessible, and procuring and fitting assistive devices.

Effective access to services including education, health care, habilitation (training and treatment to carry out the activities of daily living), rehabilitation (products and services to help restore

A young boy with albinism reads Braille at school in the town of Moshi, United Republic of Tanzania.
© UNICEF/HQ2008-1786/Pirozzi

function after an impairment is acquired) and recreation should be provided free of charge and be consistent with promoting the fullest possible social integration and individual development of the child, including cultural and spiritual development. Such measures can promote inclusion in society, in the spirit of Article 23 of the CRC, which states that a child with a disability "should enjoy a full and decent life, in conditions which ensure dignity, promote self-reliance and facilitate the child's active participation in the community." [23]

States parties to the CRPD have obligated themselves to take action to eliminate discrimination against children with disabilities and to make their inclusion in society a priority. Comprehensive national strategies with measurable outcomes will make it more likely for all children to realize their rights. International cooperation and exchange of information and technical assistance – including advances in teaching or community-based approaches to early intervention – could further these aims. Development assistance programmes focusing on children can help by taking into account the needs of children with disabilities and their families, particularly in low-income settings where systems to protect and promote the rights of children with disabilities may be weak.

Services for children with disabilities are delivered by a range of government and non-governmental institutions. Appropriate multi-sectoral coordination involving family members would help to avoid gaps in provision and should be attuned to changes in the child's capacities and needs as she or he grows and experiences life.

Community-based rehabilitation

Community-based rehabilitation (CBR) programmes are designed and run by local communities. CBR seeks to ensure that people with

Community-based rehabilitation

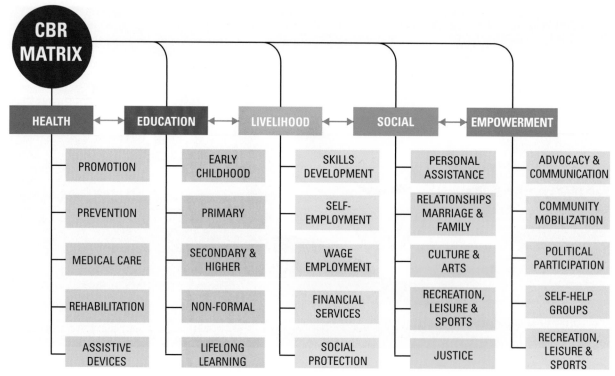

CBR MATRIX				
HEALTH	**EDUCATION**	**LIVELIHOOD**	**SOCIAL**	**EMPOWERMENT**
PROMOTION	EARLY CHILDHOOD	SKILLS DEVELOPMENT	PERSONAL ASSISTANCE	ADVOCACY & COMMUNICATION
PREVENTION	PRIMARY	SELF-EMPLOYMENT	RELATIONSHIPS MARRIAGE & FAMILY	COMMUNITY MOBILIZATION
MEDICAL CARE	SECONDARY & HIGHER	WAGE EMPLOYMENT	CULTURE & ARTS	POLITICAL PARTICIPATION
REHABILITATION	NON-FORMAL	FINANCIAL SERVICES	RECREATION, LEISURE & SPORTS	SELF-HELP GROUPS
ASSISTIVE DEVICES	LIFELONG LEARNING	SOCIAL PROTECTION	JUSTICE	RECREATION, LEISURE & SPORTS

Source: World Health Organization.

An inclusive kindergarten in Nizhny Novgorod, Russian Federation. © UNICEF/RUSS/2011/Kochineva

disabilities have equal access to rehabilitation and other services and opportunities – health, education, livelihoods. Developed by the World Health Organization (WHO) in the late 1970s and early 1980s, it is practised in more than 90 countries and represents a move away from the concentration of care in institutions and at the hands of specialists towards community self-reliance, collaboration and ownership in addressing the particular needs of people with disabilities – critically, with their own active participation.[24]

CBR can prove effective in addressing multiple deprivations. Children with disabilities who live in rural and indigenous communities contend with multiple disadvantages: They have disabilities, they belong to a marginalized group and they live in remote locations. They have little or no access to services that could ensure their development, protection and participation in community life.[25] An outreach initiative led

by the Centre for Research and Post-Secondary Studies in Social Anthropology (CIESAS) in Oaxaca, Mexico, provides an example of CBR for indigenous children with disabilities, their families and community. In collaboration with UNICEF and with financing from the state welfare agency DIF-Oaxaca, CIESAS used CBR to advance the inclusion of children with disabilities in four remote rural communities[26] with large indigenous populations and low Human Development Index scores. Teams – made up of a doctor, a physical or occupational therapist, an educator and two community activists fluent in local indigenous languages – were trained and sent into the communities to conduct workshops on discrimination, inclusion and children's rights. They promoted the formation of local support networks among the families of children with disabilities and, where appropriate, provided referrals to medical treatment or therapy. During the three-year period 2007–2010, the initiative led to increased acceptance of indigenous children with disabilities by their own families and communities. Benefits also included improved provision of social services, community-led construction of wheelchair ramps to make public spaces accessible, agreement by state and federal hospitals to provide services free of charge to children with disabilities referred by the project – and 32 new enrolments of children with disabilities in mainstream schools.[27]

Assistive technology

Depending on the type of disability, a child may need any of a number of assistive devices and services (*see next page*). According to the World Health Organization, however, in many low-income countries only 5–15 per cent of the people who need assistive technology are able to obtain it.[28] Reasons for this include costs, which can be especially prohibitive in the case of children, who need their assistive devices replaced or adjusted from time to time as they grow.[29] Children are often less likely than adults to access assistive

technology.[30] The provision and uses of assistive technology are discussed in a Focus article published online at <www.unicef.org/sowc2013>.

Universal design

Inclusive approaches are built around the concept of accessibility, with the aim of making the mainstream work for everyone rather than creating parallel systems. An accessible environment is essential if children with disabilities are to enjoy their right to participate in the community. For instance, access to all schools is necessary if children with disabilities are to take part in education. Children who are educated alongside their peers have a much better chance of becoming productive members of their societies and of being integrated in the lives of their communities.[31]

Accessibility can refer to the design of an environment, product or structure. Universal design is defined as the design of products

Liban, 8, uses crutches after losing a leg to a bomb explosion in Mogadiscio, Somalia. © UNICEF/HQ2011-2423/Grarup

Assistive technology products

Category	Examples of products
Mobility	• Walking stick, crutch, walking frame, manual and powered wheelchair, tricycle • Artificial leg or hand, caliper, hand splint, club foot brace • Corner chair, special seat, standing frame • Adapted cutlery and cooking utensils, dressing stick, shower seat, toilet seat, toilet frame, feeding robot
Vision	• Eyeglasses, magnifier, magnifying software for computer • White cane, GPS-based navigation device • Braille systems for reading and writing, screen reader for computer, talking book player, audio recorder and player • Braille chess, balls that emit sound
Hearing	• Headphone, hearing aid • Amplified telephone, hearing loop
Communication	• Communication cards with texts, communication board with letters, symbols or pictures • Electronic communication device with recorded or synthetic speech
Cognition	• Task lists, picture schedule and calendar, picture-based instructions • Timer, manual or automatic reminder, smartphone with adapted task lists, schedules, calendars and audio recorder • Adapted toys and games

Source: Johan Borg; International Organization for Standardization (2008), <http://www.iso.org/iso/home/store/catalogue_tc/catalogue_tc_browse.htm?commid=53782>.

and environments to be usable by all people, to the greatest extent possible, without the need for adaptation or specialized design. The approach focuses on design that works for all people regardless of age, ability or situation.

The principles of universal design were developed by architects, product designers, engineers and environmental design researchers. They cut across design disciplines and may be applied to guide the design process or evaluate existing designs. There are seven principles: equitable use; flexibility in use; simple and intuitive use; perceptible information; tolerance for error; low physical effort; and size and space for approach and use.

In practice, universal design can be found in the form of curb cuts or sidewalk ramps, audio books, Velcro fastenings, cabinets with pull-out shelves, automatic doors and low-floor buses.

The cost of integrating accessibility into new buildings and infrastructure can be negligible, amounting to less than 1 per cent of the capital development cost.[32] However, the cost of making adaptations to completed buildings can be much higher, especially for smaller buildings, where it can reach 20 per cent of the original cost.[33] It makes sense to integrate accessibility considerations into projects at the early stages of the design process. Accessibility should also be a consideration when funding development projects.

For deaf young people, language is the key

By Krishneer Sen

Krishneer Sen, a deaf youth activist from Suva, Fiji, and recipient of the World Deaf Leadership scholarship, is studying information technology at Gallaudet University, United States. In 2012, he served as an intern with UNICEF Fiji.

Access to information and means of communication are essential for anyone to realize their rights as a citizen. Without ways to gather knowledge, express opinions and voice demands, it is impossible to obtain an education, find a job or participate in civic affairs.

In my country, Fiji, lack of access to information and means of communication are the biggest issue facing deaf children. Information and communication technology (ICT), which I am studying at university, is helping deaf people around the world, creating opportunities that simply would not have been possible a generation ago. Where available, ICT provides deaf people with the chance to communicate and connect with friends, reduces their isolation and opens up avenues for their participation in political, economic, social and cultural life. Those who lack access – because they live in rural areas, are poor or lack education, or for whom appropriately adapted devices are not yet available – experience frustration and exclusion.

Deaf Fijians like me have limited access to the media,

emergency services – and even simple telephone conversations. In the absence of such assistive technology as captioned telephones, we must rely on people who can hear to serve as interpreters, or resort to text messaging. This will not change until ICT and media policy for people with disabilities become a top government priority.

Deaf people can succeed and contribute to society just like hearing people. Developing their abilities begins with education and language. Because deaf children grow up in a hearing world, quality education necessarily means bilingual education. In Fiji, deaf children should be taught Fiji Sign Language in addition to the languages commonly taught to hearing Fijian children (English, Fijian and Hindi), and this should start at birth. Bilingual education helps deaf children develop their ability to communicate using the languages of hearing people: Deaf children who can communicate effectively in sign language will find it easier to learn other languages, like English. I believe that bilingualism will give deaf children better access to the

We need to make media more accessible to deaf children by captioning or interpreting television programmes and developing children's programmes that use sign language.

education they need to function as equal citizens.

As a kid, I used to watch cartoon programmes on Fijian TV with no subtitles or sign language interpreters. My family didn't know sign language well. Later on, I realized that the reason I was still struggling with my English was that I had not been exclusively taught using signs at home. Parents have an important role in facilitating deaf children's ability to communicate and access information; along with other people who interact with deaf children, they need to take the initiative and use sign language to communicate in their daily lives, at home and school.

We need to make media more accessible to deaf children by captioning or interpreting television programmes and developing children's programmes that use sign language. We need an environment free of communication barriers. I would like to see Fijian Sign Language used in a range of programmes, from news to cartoons. In addition to television, social media can provide powerful tools to enhance knowledge about Fiji and

international affairs and ensure that everyone, including people with disabilities, has access to information about the political situation and can cast an informed vote during elections.

Making ICT available to deaf children can facilitate their social and emotional development, help them learn in mainstream schools and prepare them for future employment. I took a basic computer class at a special school, and it changed my life for the better: It was through the Internet that I learned about Gallaudet University, where I now study.

In addition to enhancing education, ICT provides deaf and other young people with disabilities to learn about their rights and band together to campaign for their realization. By facilitating activism, ICT may thus help increase the profile of persons with disabilities within society at large and allow them to participate actively.

My dream is to see deaf people communicate freely with hearing people through the use of assistive technologies. Once I graduate, I plan to start a

project to set up communication technologies in Fiji in order to facilitate communication between hearing and deaf people, using sign language interpreters as well as video calling. I will be working with the Fiji Association for the Deaf, of which I have been a member for many years, to advocate for human rights, opportunities and equality.

If the government is to consider the needs of deaf people a priority, deaf people must advocate on our own behalf. To facilitate activism among deaf people, we must educate deaf children to use both sign language and the languages of the hearing communities they live in, and we must work to expand access to technologies through which they can find information and communicate with others, deaf and hearing.

A teacher with a hearing impairment teaches a class of hearing-impaired children in Gulu, Uganda. © UNICEF/UGDA2012-00108/Sibiloni

CHAPTER 3

A STRONG FOUNDATION

Good health, nutrition and a solid education: These are the building blocks of life that children and their parents want, and to which all children are entitled.

Inclusive health

Under the Convention on the Rights of the Child (CRC) and the Convention on the Rights of Persons with Disabilities (CRPD), all children have the right to the highest attainable standard of health. It follows that children with disabilities are equally entitled to the full spectrum of care – from immunization in infancy to proper nutrition and treatment for the ailments and injuries of childhood, to confidential sexual and reproductive health information and services during adolescence and into early adulthood. Equally critical are such basic services as water, sanitation and hygiene.

Ensuring that children with disabilities actually enjoy these rights on a par with others is the objective of an inclusive approach to health. This is a matter of social justice and of respecting the inherent dignity of all human beings. It is also an investment in the future: Like other children, those with disabilities are tomorrow's adults. They need good health for its own sake, for the crucial role it plays in facilitating a happy childhood and for the boost it can give their prospects as future producers and parents.

Immunization

Immunizations are a critical component of global efforts to reduce childhood illness and death. They are among the most successful and cost-effective of all public health interventions, with the strong potential to reduce the burden of morbidity and mortality, particularly for children under 5 years of age. For this reason, immunization has been a cornerstone of national and international health initiatives. More children than ever before are being reached. One consequence has been that the incidence of polio – which can lead to permanent muscle paralysis – fell from more than 350,000 cases in 1988 to 221 cases in 2012.[34]

There is still a considerable way to go. In 2008, for example, over a million children under 5 died from pneumococcal disease, rotavirus diarrhoea and Haemophilus influenzae type B. Vaccination can actually prevent a large number of these deaths.[35]

The inclusion of children with disabilities in immunization efforts is not only ethical but imperative for public health and equity: Goals of universal coverage can only be achieved if children who have disabilities are included in immunization efforts.[36]

While immunization is an important means of pre-empting diseases that lead to disabilities, it is no less important for a child who already has a disability to be immunized. Unfortunately, many children with disabilities are still not benefiting from increased immunization coverage, though they are at the same risk of childhood diseases as all children. If they are left unimmunized or only partially immunized, the results can include delays in reaching developmental milestones, avoidable secondary conditions and, at worst, preventable death.[37]

It will help to bring children with disabilities into the immunization fold if efforts to promote immunization include them. Showing children with disabilities alongside others on campaign posters and promotional materials, for example, can help to promote awareness. Enhancing popular understanding of the importance of immunizing each child also involves reaching out to parents through public health campaigns, civil society and disabled peoples' organizations, schools and mass media.

Nutrition

About 870 million people worldwide are thought to be undernourished. Among them, some 165 million under-fives are believed to be stunted, or chronically malnourished, and more than 100 million are considered underweight. Insufficient food or a poorly balanced diet short of certain vitamins and minerals (iodine, vitamin A, iron and zinc, for example) can leave infants and children vulnerable to specific conditions or a host of infections that can lead to physical, sensory or intellectual disabilities.[38]

Between 250,000 and 500,000 children are considered to be at risk of becoming blind each year from vitamin A deficiency, a syndrome easily prevented by oral supplementation costing just a few cents per child.[39] For a similarly minute amount – five cents per person per year – salt iodization remains the most cost-effective way of delivering iodine and preventing cognition damage in children in iodine-deficient areas.[40] These low-cost measures help not only children with disabilities but also their mothers as they labour to raise infants and children in strained circumstances.

Doing homework in Bangladesh. © Broja Gopal Saha/Centre for Disability in Development

Early childhood stunting, which is measured as low height for age, is caused by poor nutrition and diarrhoea. A multi-country study showed that each episode of diarrhoea in the first two years of life contributes to stunting,[41] which is estimated to affect some 28 per cent of children younger than 5 in low- and middle-income countries.[42] The consequences of stunting, such as poor cognitive and educational performance, begin when children are very young but affect them through the rest of their lives. However, community-based efforts to improve basic health practices have been shown to reduce stunting among young children.[43]

Malnutrition in mothers can lead to a number of preventable childhood disabilities. Approximately 42 per cent of pregnant women in low- and middle-income countries are anaemic, and more than one in two pregnant women in these countries suffer iron deficiency anaemia.[44] Anaemia also affects more than half of pre-school aged children in developing countries. It is one of the most prevalent causes of disability in the world – and therefore a serious global public health problem.[45] Malnutrition in lactating mothers can also contribute to poorer infant health,[46] increasing the risk of diseases that can cause disability. Healthy mothers can help reduce the incidence of some disabilities and are better prepared to minister to their children's needs.

While malnutrition can be a cause of disability, it can also be a consequence. Indeed, children with disabilities are at heightened risk of malnutrition. For example, an infant with cleft palate may not be able to breastfeed or consume food effectively. Children with cerebral palsy may have difficulty chewing or swallowing.[47] Certain conditions, such as cystic fibrosis, may impede nutrient absorption. Some infants and children with disabilities may need specific diets or increased calorie intake in order to maintain a healthy weight.[48] Yet they may be hidden away from community screening and feeding initiatives. Children with disabilities who do not attend school miss out on school feeding programmes.

A combination of physical factors and attitudes may adversely affect child nutrition. In some societies, mothers may not be encouraged to breastfeed a disabled child. Stigma and discrimination may also result in a child with a disability being fed less, denied food or provided with less nutritious food than siblings without disabilities.[49] Children with some types of physical or intellectual disabilities may also have difficulty in feeding themselves, or need additional time or assistance to eat. It is probable that in some cases what is assumed to be disability-associated ill health and wasting may in fact be connected with feeding problems.[50]

Water, sanitation and hygiene

It is a widely acknowledged but little documented fact that throughout the developing world, persons with disabilities routinely face particular difficulties in accessing safe drinking water and basic sanitation. Children with physical impairments may be unable to collect water or carry it for long distances; others may find well walls and water taps too high. Hardware and washroom doors can be difficult to manipulate and there may be nowhere to rest the water container while filling it, or there may be nothing to hold on to for balance to avoid falling into a well, pond or toilet. Long or slippery paths and poor lighting also limit the use of latrines by children with disabilities.

Barriers to persons with disabilities extend beyond physical and design issues. Social barriers vary in different cultures. Children with disabilities often face stigma and discrimination when using household and public facilities. Wholly inaccurate fears that children with disabilities will contaminate water sources or soil latrines are frequently reported. When children or adolescents, and particularly girls, with disabilities are forced to use different facilities than other members of their households, or are compelled to use them at different times, they are at increased risk of accidents and physical attack, including rape. Issues preventing disabled children from accessing water and sanitation in such settings may vary depending on cultural and geographical context, as well as by the type of disability a child may have: A child with a physical impairment may face significant difficulties in using a hand pump or an outdoor latrine; a child who is deaf or who has an intellectual disability may have little physical difficulty but be vulnerable to teasing or abuse, which can render these facilities inaccessible.

Children with disabilities might not attend school for want of an accessible toilet. Children with disabilities often report that they try to drink and eat less to cut down the number of times they need to go to the toilet, especially if they have to ask someone to help them. This adds to the risk that these children will be poorly nourished. It is also cause for concern that in some places, new water, sanitation and hygiene (WASH) facilities are still being designed and built without adequate concern for children with disabilities. Low-tech, low-cost interventions for persons with disabilities

Beatriz, a 10-year-old girl with cerebral palsy, blows soap bubbles in Brazil. © Andre Castro/2012

are increasingly available – new step latrines and easy-to-use water pumps, for example. This information has yet to be widely disseminated among WASH professionals or incorporated into WASH policies and practice.[51]

Sexual and reproductive health and HIV/AIDS

Children and young people who live with a physical, sensory, intellectual or psychosocial disability have been almost entirely overlooked in sexual and reproductive health and HIV/AIDS programmes. They are often – and incorrectly – believed to be sexually inactive, unlikely to use drugs or alcohol, and at less risk of abuse, violence or rape than their non-disabled peers, and therefore to be at low risk of HIV infection.[52] In consequence, children and young people who have disabilities are at increased risk of becoming HIV-positive.

People with disabilities of all ages who are HIV-positive are less likely to receive appropriate services than peers without disabilities. Treatment, testing and counselling centres are very rarely adapted to their needs, and healthcare personnel are seldom trained to deal with children and adolescents with disabilities.[53]

Many young people with disabilities do not receive even basic information about how their bodies develop and change. Structured education about sexual and reproductive health and relationships is seldom a part of the curriculum and even where it is, children with disabilities may be excluded. Many have been taught to be silent and obedient and have no experience of setting limits with others regarding physical contact.[54] The risk of abuse is thus increased, as illustrated by a study in South Africa that suggests deaf youth are at heightened risk of HIV infection.[55]

Early detection and intervention

Children develop rapidly during the first three years of life, so early detection and intervention are particularly important. Developmental screening is an effective means of detecting disability in children.[56] It can take place in primary-health-care settings, for example, during immunization visits or growth monitoring check-ups at community health centres. The purpose of screening is to identify children at risk, to refer them for further assessment and intervention as needed, and to provide family members with vital information on disability. Screening involves vision and hearing examinations as well as assessments of children's progress against such developmental milestones as sitting, standing, crawling, walking, talking or handling objects.

Health-care systems in high-income countries provide numerous opportunities to identify and manage developmental difficulties early in a child's life. But interventions to improve young children's development are becoming increasingly available in low- and middle-income countries. These include such interventions as treating iron deficiency, training caregivers and providing community-based rehabilitation.[57]

Recent studies in high- and low-income countries have shown that up to 70 per cent of children and adults newly diagnosed with epilepsy can be successfully treated (i.e., their seizures completely controlled) with anti-epileptic drugs. After two to five years of successful treatment, drugs can be withdrawn without danger of relapse in about 70 per cent of children and 60 per cent of adults. However, approximately three quarters of people with epilepsy in low-income countries do not get the treatment they need.[58] The treatments exist – efficient dissemination is often lacking.

The detection and treatment of impairments is not a separate area of medicine but an integral aspect of public health. Nevertheless, policymakers and researchers typically characterize these measures as being in competition for resources with measures to promote the health of people without disabilities.[59] This merely serves to perpetuate discrimination and inequity.

Children with disabilities who overcome the discrimination and other obstacles that stand between them and health care may yet find that the services they access are of poor quality. Children's feedback should be invited so facilities and services can be improved to meet their needs. In addition, health workers and other professionals dealing with children stand to benefit from being educated about the multiple issues of child development and child disability and from being trained to deliver integrated services – where possible, with the participation of the extended family. International cooperation can play an important role in efforts to make higher-quality services available to children identified as having or at risk of developing disabilities, and in changing the competitive approach to allocating resources described in the preceding paragraph.

Inclusive education

Education is the gateway to full participation in society. It is particularly important for children with disabilities, who are often excluded. Many of the benefits of going to school accrue over the long run – securing a livelihood in adult life, for example – but some are almost immediately evident. Taking part at school is an important way for children with disabilities to correct misconceptions that prevent inclusion. And when these children are able to attend school, parents and caregivers are able to find time for other activities including earning a living and resting.

In principle, all children have the same right to education. In practice, children with disabilities are disproportionately denied this right. In consequence, their ability to enjoy the full rights of citizenship and take up valued roles in society – chiefly, through gainful employment – is undermined.

Household survey data from 13 low- and middle-income countries show that children with disabilities aged 6–17 years are significantly less likely to be enrolled in school than peers without disabilities.[60] A 2004 study in Malawi found that a child with a disability was twice as likely to have never attended school as a child without a disability. Similarly, a 2008 survey in the United Republic of Tanzania found that children with disabilities who attended primary school progressed to higher levels of education at only half the rate of children without disabilities.[61]

As long as children with disabilities are denied equal access to their local schools, governments cannot reach the Millennium Development Goal of achieving universal primary education (MDG 2), and States parties to the Convention on the Rights of Persons with Disabilities cannot fulfil their responsibilities under Article 24.[62] A recent monitoring report of the Convention on the Rights of the Child acknowledged that "the challenges faced by children with disabilities in realizing their right to education remain profound" and that they are "one of the most marginalized and excluded groups in respect of education."[63]

Although the Conventions make a powerful case for inclusive education, they can also sometimes be misused to justify the perpetuation of segregated education. For example, children in residential special schools may be said to be accessing their right to be 'included' in education – even though their right to live with their families and to be a part of their own community is being violated.

Inclusive education entails providing meaningful learning opportunities to all students within the regular school system. Ideally, it allows children with and without disabilities to attend the same age-appropriate classes at the local school, with additional, individually tailored support as needed. It requires physical accommodation – ramps instead of stairs and doorways wide enough for wheelchair users, for example – as well as a new, child-centred curriculum that includes representations of the full spectrum of people found in society (not just persons with disabilities) and reflects

Students learning mathematics use Braille in West Bengal, India. © UNICEF/INDA2009-00026/Khemka

the needs of all children. In an inclusive school, students are taught in small classes in which they collaborate and support one another rather than compete. Children with disabilities are not segregated in the classroom, at lunchtime or on the playground.

Studies across countries show a strong link between poverty and disability [64] – one that is in turn linked to gender, health and employment issues. Children with disabilities are often caught in a cycle of poverty and exclusion: Girls become caregivers to their siblings rather than attend school, for example, or the whole family may be stigmatized, leading to their reluctance to report that a child has a disability or to take the child out in public.[65] The education of those who are excluded or marginalized, however, brings about poverty reduction.[66]

Inclusive approaches to education have received numerous global endorsements, including at the 1994 World Conference on Special Needs Education[67] and, since 2002, through the global Education for All initiative on the right to education for persons with disabilities.[68] These approaches are by no means luxuries available only to the privileged or in high-income countries. Examples of inclusion in education are to be found in all regions of the world. To optimize the potential to include the excluded, all such efforts should apply the principles of universal design to learning systems and environments. An example of this is provided by the infographic published online at <www.unicef.org/sowc2013>.

Starting early

The first steps towards inclusion are taken at home during the early years. If children with disabilities do not receive the love, sensory stimulation, health care and social inclusion to which they are entitled, they can miss important developmental milestones and their potential may be unfairly limited, with significant social and economic implications for themselves, their families and the communities in which they live.

Ashiraff plays with friends at school in Togo after a local disabled people's organization and international partners helped to realize his right to education.
© UNICEF/Togo/2012/Brisno

A child whose disability or developmental delay is identified at an early stage will have a much better chance of reaching her or his full capacity. Early childhood education, whether it is public, private or provided by the community, should be designed to respond to the child's individual needs. Early childhood is important precisely because approximately 80 per cent of the brain's capacity develops before the age of 3 and because the period between birth and primary school provides opportunities to tailor developmental education to the child's needs. Studies suggest that the children who are at greatest disadvantage stand to benefit the most.[69]

Early childhood education is not limited to preschools and other childcare facilities – the home environment plays a fundamental role in stimulating and facilitating the development of the child. Studies from Bangladesh,[70] China,[71] India[72] and South Africa[73] have shown that enhanced interaction between mother and child and increased developmental activities benefit cognitive development in young children across a variety of settings, from home to health centre.[74]

(continued on p. 32)

My son Hanif

By Mohammad Absar

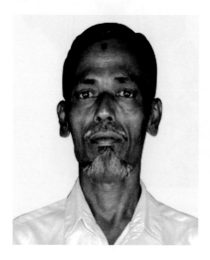

Mohammad Absar lives in the village of Maddhyam Sonapahar in Mirershorai Province, Bangladesh. He has three sons and three daughters and supports his family by running a small tea stall.

My son Hanif is 9 years old and attends the second grade. When he was 4, he got injured while playing. He started complaining about pain in his leg, which became red and swollen. We took him to Chittagong Medical Hospital. The doctors there tried to save Hanif's leg, but it was severely infected, and eventually they decided to amputate it.

After Hanif lost his leg, other children used to torment him: They called him 'lame' or 'legless creep' and pushed him to the ground when he tried to play with them. They also used to tease his brother, who suffers from mental illness. This always made me sad, and it used to drive my wife crazy. She would quarrel with people who said bad things about her children. As for Hanif – he became very reluctant to go out. He was miserable.

Things began to improve after the local, non-governmental Organization for the Poor Community Advancement (OPCA) started conducting meetings in our area to raise awareness about disability and encourage people to have a positive approach towards those with special needs.

A rehabilitation worker from OPCA visited our home along with a teacher from the primary school. They encouraged us to enrol Hanif in school. Because the local primary school is half a kilometre away from our home, I had to carry my son to school every morning. I started a small shop near the school so I could be there to carry him home at the end of the day. At first, Hanif had a lot of trouble at school. His classmates, just like his peers in the neighbourhood, mocked him and called him names.

One day, the rehabilitation worker informed us that the Centre for Disability in Development (CDD), a nationwide non-governmental organization based in Dhaka, would provide my son with an artificial leg. We travelled to the capital, where Hanif was fitted for the prosthesis and given several days of training. He also received a pair of crutches. His stump is quite small and this makes it a bit difficult for him to climb stairs. Other than that, he can now do almost everything on his own.

When he first got the new leg, people stared – it was very surprising to see him walking again. I myself had never imagined it would be possible. Some of our neighbours came to visit our home just to see the prosthesis.

Now that my son can walk again and participate in all sorts of activities, other children have stopped calling him names. They don't push him to the ground anymore. I no longer have to carry Hanif to school – he walks himself, and his classmates are eager to walk with him. The most important thing is that Hanif is happier and more confident. His artificial leg allows him to be independent, and he no longer feels inferior to the other children. He is doing better in his classes and

Look at Hanif and you will see that with proper support and encouragement, people with disabilities can be effective in society.

can now enjoy sports like cricket and soccer along with his peers.

A rehabilitation worker has visited Hanif's school several times to conduct awareness meetings on disability and the importance of inclusive education. Hanif's surrounding environment is more disability-friendly than ever before. His school works to accommodate his needs. For example, Hanif has trouble climbing stairs, so when one of his classes was scheduled on the first floor, the principal agreed to move it downstairs to make it easier for Hanif to attend.

While he's in school, Hanif enjoys drawing pictures. Outside of school and during breaks, he loves to play. He wants to be a teacher when he grows up, just like his role models – his schoolteachers Mr. Arup and Mr. Shapan. They love Hanif very much and support him in every way they can. Because our family is very poor, my son's artificial limb and associated expenses were provided by CDD through the Promoting Rights for Persons with Disabilities project funded by the Manusher Jonno Foundation. If Hanif has any problem with the prosthesis, rehabilitation workers visit our

home and take care of it. As Hanif has grown, they have adjusted his artificial limb.

Hanif also receives a disability allowance of 300 Bangladesh taka each month from our district's Department of Social Services. I take him to the local bank to receive his allowance. Hanif will need additional support to ensure that he can continue his education without interruption.

Above all, I want my son to be well educated. An education will empower him and help guide him so that he can build a

meaningful life. I think it would be best for Hanif to get a desk job so he doesn't have to walk or stand too much. Perhaps he might work in an organization like CDD, where the environment is very disability-friendly. I saw people with various disabilities working there. Such an environment would help my son work to the best of his capacity, while at the same time securing an honourable position for him. He can become an example: Look at Hanif and you will see that with proper support and encouragement, people with disabilities can be effective in society.

Hanif taking part in class. © Centre for Disability in Development

(continued from p. 29)

Age-old biases and low expectations with regard to children with disabilities should not stand in the way of early childhood development. It is clear that with family and community support from the earliest days of their lives, children with disabilities are better placed to make the most of their school years and to prepare themselves for adulthood.

Working with teachers

Teachers are a – and perhaps *the* – key element in a child's learning environment, so it is important that they have a clear understanding of inclusive education and a strong commitment to teaching all children.

All too often, however, teachers lack appropriate preparation and support in teaching children with disabilities in regular schools. This is a factor in the stated unwillingness of educators in many countries to support the inclusion of children with disabilities in their classes.[75] For example, one study of prospective teachers of special education in Israel found they held unhelpful preconceptions about people with disabilities, and that some discriminated between different types of disability.[76] Resources for children with disabilities tend to be allocated to segregated schools rather than to an inclusive mainstream education system. This can prove costly as well as inappropriate: In Bulgaria, the budget per child educated in a special school can be up to three times higher than that for a similar child in a regular school.[77]

A review of the situation of children with intellectual disabilities in 22 European countries highlighted the lack of training of regular teachers to work with children with disabilities as a major concern. Most of the time, these students were taught by support staff rather than certified teachers. Teacher training has proved effective in fostering commitment to inclusion. A 2003 study found that school principals who had taken more courses on disability expressed more inclusive views. And shifting attitudes benefit students:

Positive views on inclusion translated into less restrictive placements for specific students with disabilities.[78] Another study from 2001 found that a course on inclusion for those studying to be teachers was effective in changing their attitudes, so that they favoured including children with mild disabilities in the classroom.[79]

The greatest opportunity appears to exist among teachers who are still fresh in the profession. A recent systematic literature review of countries as diverse as China, Cyprus, India, Iran, the Republic of Korea, the State of Palestine, the United Arab Emirates and Zimbabwe found that teachers with the least general teaching experience had more positive attitudes than those with longer service. Teachers who had received training in inclusive education had more positive attitudes than those who had received no training, and those who had the most positive attitudes were those with actual experience of inclusion.[80]

Yet pre-service training rarely prepares teachers to teach inclusively. Where training exists, it is of variable quality. Although numerous toolkits exist, these are not always geared to a specific context, and so will frequently contain foreign concepts. Group learning is one example. Teachers have responded negatively to pictures of children with and without disabilities seated in groups, as this is at odds with the way students interact in more traditional classrooms.[81]

Another challenge is the lack of diversity among teaching personnel. Teachers with disabilities are quite rare and in some settings considerable obstacles exist for adults with disabilities to qualify as teachers. In Cambodia, for example, the law states that teachers must be "free of disabilities."[82]

Partnerships with civil society are providing encouraging examples of ways to enhance teacher training and diversity. In Bangladesh, the Centre for Disability in Development (CDD), a national non-governmental organization (NGO), employs a group of inclusive education trainers who run 10-day training sessions during school terms for 20 schools at a time, with training provided to one teacher from each school.[83] Several of the CDD trainers are visually impaired or have other disabilities, so they are important role models for teachers and students with and without disabilities. And in Mozambique, Ajuda de Desenvolvimento de Povo para Povo, a national NGO, has worked closely with the national disabled people's organization known as ADEMO to train student teachers to work with children with disabilities and to train student teachers who have disabilities.[84]

Teachers tend to work in isolation, which means they are often unsupported in the classroom, and are often under pressure to complete a narrow syllabus imposed from above. Inclusive education requires a flexible approach to school organization, curriculum development and pupil assessment. Such flexibility would allow for the development of a more inclusive pedagogy, shifting the focus from teacher-centred to child-centred to embrace diverse learning styles.

Teachers need to be able to call on specialist help from colleagues who have greater expertise and experience of working with children with disabilities, especially children with sensory or intellectual impairments. For example, specialists can advise on the use of Braille or computer-based instruction.[85] Where such specialists are relatively few, they can travel between schools as needed. Even these itinerant specialist teachers can be in short supply in such low-income areas as sub-Saharan Africa.[86] This presents an opportunity for appropriate support from providers of financial and technical assistance from the international to the local level.

Involving parents, communities and children

Inclusive education programmes that focus only on classroom practices fail to harness parents' potential to contribute to inclusive education – and to prevent such violations as the confinement of children with disabilities to separate rooms.

Parents can play many roles, from providing accessible transport to raising awareness, getting involved in civil society organizations and liaising with the health sector so that children have access to appropriate equipment and support and with the social sectors to access grants and credit schemes to reduce poverty. In many countries, schools have community committees that are engaged in a wide range of activities to support inclusion. For example, in Viet Nam, Community Steering Committees have been involved in advocacy, local training, securing assistive devices, providing financial support and developing accessible environments.[87] It is important that parents and community members realize that they have contributions to make and that their contributions are used.

Although the importance of child participation and child agency is well documented, they sit uncomfortably within the existing structures and

(continued on p. 36)

Boys play football at the Nimba Centre in Conakry, Guinea. The centre provides training for people with physical disabilities. © UNICEF/HQ2010-1196/Asselin

The new normal

By Claire Halford

Claire Halford lives in Melbourne, Australia, with her partner and their two children. She worked in fashion and the visual arts before becoming a full-time caregiver for her son Owen.

Everybody hopes for a healthy baby when expecting a child. When asked, "What are you having?" expectant mums and dads respond, "Oh, we don't mind, as long as it's healthy."

I remember the first-trimester milestone with my first-born son, Owen: I told the midwife that I had stopped smoking and drinking, ate a healthy diet, exercised moderately and felt pretty good about carrying a child. "That's great," she said in a reassuring tone. "After all, what can go wrong with a healthy female in a first-world country in professional medical care?" Little did I know that in about six months I would find out exactly what could go wrong.

My son's birth, at full term, was incredibly traumatic. When he finally entered the world, he could not breathe. His brain was deprived of oxygen. He was resuscitated and ventilated, and for two weeks he was swapped between intensive care and special care. He had his first seizure at 1 day old. Until he was 2 years old, epilepsy invaded our lives all day, every day.

My son was diagnosed with cerebral palsy (CP) at 5 months. Cerebral palsy is a broad term describing a brain injury that can occur in utero, during birth or in early childhood. In Australia, CP is the most common cause of physical disability in childhood, and it is a disability that affects children in all countries whether they are affluent or poor. The condition mostly affects movement and muscle tone. Owen has severe CP: He cannot sit, roll, walk or speak.

Following his diagnosis, correspondence from doctors arrived in the post on an almost weekly basis. Initial letters delivered brutal realities, using medical-speak like 'spastic quadriplegic', 'cortical visual impairment' and 'globally developmentally delayed' – terms that were completely foreign. Every online search ended in 'prognosis poor'.

In those early days, the only shining light in all this shocking darkness was Owen's beautiful personality, infectious laugh, obvious engagement with the world around him and emerging handsome looks.

The first year was very hard. Anger – no, rage – and disappointment, devastation, loneliness and disbelief lurked at every corner. As the midwife had suggested, this wasn't supposed to happen to me, to him, to us – this was a mistake! Friends and family could say or do nothing right, so I sought out others who were in a similar position, through support groups in my area and on the Internet.

Around the time of Owen's diagnosis, I received a phone call from the university at which I had once worked, asking if I'd like to return to teach life drawing and design part-time. This job was to have been my ticket out of employment in retail; it was to have been something meaningful I could sink my teeth into. I declined. I had new work: Now I was a full-time caregiver.

It turned out that Owen had intractable seizures that did not respond to epilepsy medication. So we started 2-year-old Owen on a medical diet for epilepsy. The ketogenic diet is an incredibly strict high-fat, low-carbohydrate diet. In a bizarre, unexpected stroke of grace, it worked. My poor suffering son went from having up to 200 seizures a day to almost none in the first three months. He has been virtually seizure-free since.

My partner and I have since had another son, a healthy toddler whom we love as dearly as we do Owen. He has brought us another perspective on life. Our family life has come to define us. The connection we have makes us stronger – to us, our lifestyle is normal; we carry on. It's normal to drive all over town to do physical therapy many times a week; it's normal to haul heavy equipment like standing frames and bath chairs from room to room every day. We know the children's hospital like the backs of our hands and are familiar with many of the top specialists in various fields of paediatric medicine.

I call myself my son's 'personal assistant' because he has a never-ending stream of paperwork, funding applications, doctor's appointments, therapy sessions, check-ups and blood tests. I do most of his personal care, such as feeding and bathing. My partner helps when he can, but he works very long hours to keep us all afloat financially – so that I can care for Owen and we can have a comfortable life. We try to keep busy on the weekends, doing family things

like visiting the farmer's market, going out for Vietnamese food or checking out a kids' show. Owen has a pretty fun and busy life for a 5-year-old. Yet no matter how good things can be, he has a long and difficult journey ahead of him.

We are hoping to place Owen in a mainstream primary school with the support of the Cerebral Palsy Education Centre, an early intervention programme. Owen has shown vast improvement in communication and movement since he started going there. He also attends activities at the Riding for the Disabled Association, which we both love. Over the years we have spent so much money and time on therapies and services – some of them good, others not that helpful. We're learning as we go, and we're getting better at making practical rather than emotional decisions. It's still hard for us, though; I'm always fighting or waiting for something he desperately needs, sometimes for years.

The hardest battles have to do with people's perceptions of Owen. I just want him to be treated and spoken to like a regular kid – but I also want him to receive special attention, and for people to be more patient. I want my friends and family to help him and engage with him more. Many of them tend to focus on how I am doing or on something else that's less challenging than Owen's very real problems. It's hard for them,

too – with everything he has going on, I sometimes think he should come with an instruction manual.

I've often feared that the things that defined me before I became a caregiver – work, creative interests and a social life – have been lost down a well of grief and exhaustion. More often than not, however, I feel like my life before Owen was born was comparatively superficial. Becoming a caregiver for my own child has been an overwhelmingly profound and joyful experience. We celebrate small accomplishments feverishly, and my expectations of what success entails have been smashed and rebuilt into something beautifully simple: Owen sitting unaided for five seconds, or, as he watches the Paralympics on television, hearing the words 'cerebral palsy' and 'champion' in the same sentence. I have grown through caring for Owen – above all, perhaps, in my ability to empathize.

I have learned that no matter what a child can't do, she or he will still always have an identity and a character that will leave a distinctive brushstroke on this world. If we want to be an enlightened society, our job is to believe and encourage. Only then can children who have such difficult limitations grow. And then we can all come to see that things that 'go wrong' are sometimes just different – and often amazing.

(continued from p. 33)

system of education. This is true for all children, with or without disabilities: Few are involved in making decisions about their education and lives. Involving children with disabilities in such decisions can be particularly challenging, not least because of ingrained thinking and behaviour that perceives them as passive victims. As the 2011 Report of the Secretary-General on the Status of the Convention on the Rights of the Child noted, "It remains difficult for children with disabilities to have their voices heard. Initiatives such as school councils and children's parliaments, consultative processes to elicit children's views, as well as judicial proceedings, commonly fail to ensure the inclusion of children with disabilities, or acknowledge their capacities for participation."[88]

The most underused resource in schools and communities all over the world is the children themselves. The Child-to-Child Trust in the United Kingdom has worked for many years to promote children's involvement in health education, and in some countries this approach has been used to good effect as part of inclusive education and community-based rehabilitation programmes.[89] In participatory research, for example, children frequently highlight the importance of a clean environment and hygienic toilets, and for children with disabilities, the issues of privacy and accessibility are paramount.[90] It stands to reason that children with disabilities can and must guide and evaluate efforts to advance accessibility and inclusion. After all, who better to understand the means and impact of exclusion?

Lines of responsibility

As in other fields of endeavour, it will help to realize aspirations for inclusive education if governments and their partners are clear about who is to do what and how, and to whom they are expected to report. Otherwise, the promise of inclusion risks becoming a matter of lip service.

One study of countries engaged in what was once known as the Education For All Fast Track Initiative (FTI) and is now called the Global Partnership for Education found that "a number of FTI-endorsed countries, particularly those which are approaching universal primary education, do now have national education sector plans which address the inclusion of disabled children. [...] However, in a number of countries, policies and provision for disabled children remain cursory or have not been implemented."[91] The report notes that in five FTI-endorsed countries there was no mention at all of children with disabilities.

Sometimes, the problem is one of divided or unclear mandates: In Bangladesh there is some confusion about which ministries are responsible for children with disabilities of school age. The mandate for implementing Education For All lies with the Ministry of Education and the Ministry of Primary and Mass Education, but the education of children with disabilities is managed by the Ministry of Social Welfare and is seen as a matter of charity, not a human rights issue.[92] Since 2002, children with disabilities and those with special educational needs have been included in primary education through the Primary Education Development Programme[93] under the Ministry of Education. But managing integrated educational provision for children with visual impairments and running primary schools for children with hearing, visual or intellectual impairments remains the responsibility the Ministry of Social Welfare.[94]

Ministries of Education should be encouraged to take responsibility for all children of school age. Coordination with partners and stakeholders can play a strong supporting role in this process. In Bangladesh, the National Forum of Organizations Working with the Disabled promotes networking between the government and NGOs, and has been instrumental in encouraging greater educational inclusion as well as a gradual shift of ministerial responsibility from social welfare to education. As a consequence, the Campaign for Popular Education, a national network, has committed to ensuring that all children with

Reading Braille at a school in Uganda. © UNICEF/UGDA2012-00112/Sibiloni

disabilities have access to basic and quality education, and the non-governmental Bangladesh Rural Advancement Committee, which is committed to achieving Education For All and poverty reduction, now includes learners with disabilities in its schools.

Exclusion denies children with disabilities the lifelong benefits of education: a better job, social and economic security, and opportunities for full participation in society. In contrast, investment in the education of children with disabilities can contribute to their future effectiveness as members of the labour force. Indeed, a person's potential income can increase by as much as 10 per cent with each additional year of schooling.[95] But inclusive education can also reduce current and future dependence, freeing other household members from some of their caring responsibilities, and allowing them to resume productive activity – or simply to rest.[96]

Basic reading and writing skills also improve health: A child born to a mother who can read is 50 per cent more likely to survive past the age of 5.[97] Lower maternal education has been linked to higher rates of stunting among children in the urban slums of Kenya,[98] Roma settlements in Serbia,[99] and in Cambodia.[100] Better-educated Bangladeshi parents decreased their child's risk of stunting by up to 5.4 per cent (4.6 per cent in the case of mothers, and between 2.9 and 5.4 per cent for fathers), and better-educated Indonesian parents accounted for up to a 5 per cent decrease (between 4.4 and 5 per cent for mothers, and 3 per cent for fathers) in their child's odds of stunting.[101]

Education is both a useful instrument and a right, the purpose of which, as stated in the Convention on the Rights of the Child, is to promote "the development of the child's personality, talents and mental and physical abilities to their fullest potential."[102]

Adjusting, adapting and empowering

By Yahia J. Elziq

Yahia J. Elziq is a Technical Advisor for Handicap International in Ramallah, State of Palestine.

Saja was 7 years old when I met her.

At that time I was working in one of the three national rehabilitation centres in the West Bank as an occupational therapist. Although this centre is not set up to handle Saja's needs and demands as a child with cerebral palsy, we were able to provide therapy sessions to prevent deterioration in her condition. The two main obstacles that still prevent her from reaching appropriate rehabilitation services are the absence of referral mechanisms and coordination between services in the West Bank, and the restrictions on movement that are imposed on Palestinians under occupation. The specialized rehabilitation centre for such conditions is based in East Jerusalem, but Saja's family was refused permission to enter the city.

In addition, children with disabilities in the West Bank, as elsewhere, confront a general lack of knowledge and skills about disability throughout the public and private sec-

tors. They are also faced with a dominant perspective that regards people with disabilities as pitiable and as worthy to receive charity – but not as individuals with rights who have the same entitlements as others, and who can and do contribute to society.

In this context Saja has been lucky. After an extensive evaluation, our team developed a plan to support and improve her participation in the community. The priority for her and her family was to have her enrolled in regular school. However, in order to attend a mainstream school, she needed various environmental changes – among them, the school premises had to be physically accessible, and she needed to have a suitable wheelchair. Full collaboration from her family, school and community were absolute necessities. Saja needed integrated activities involving many stakeholders, starting from her own parents, who tended to use available resources in favour of her brother, who has the same

Saja opened my eyes to my own ability to adjust and adapt as a professional – and to the positive impact that we therapeutic professionals can have if we adopt empowering attitudes.

condition, leaving her without the opportunity to develop to her full potential.

Tackling all these issues was made difficult because of the absence of adequate national policy. There is no inclusive education programme for children with disabilities, for example, and disability-inclusive policies are not priorities for decision-makers. For these reasons, the fate of children with disabilities relies heavily on the willingness of community members to recognize that these children have the same rights as all children. When these rights are recognized, many issues can be solved – often simply by mobilizing existing community resources.

Fortunately, in Saja's case, negotiations with the school principal succeeded and her classroom was moved from the second to the ground floor. The teachers accepted the idea of having her in their class. By using our own networks of professional and personal contacts, we were able to get

her a suitable wheelchair and, thanks to some local doctors and a health centre, her family was able to obtain free treatment to improve her eyesight. Social workers helped raise awareness of her particular situation within her family, and a psychologist supported her in overcoming her experience of discrimination.

Over just a couple of years, Saja's situation improved dramatically as some of her health issues were addressed, her mobility improved and her self-esteem and confidence improved along with her social interactions, knowledge and life skills. As a person, I was overjoyed at seeing Saja's progress. As a rehabilitation professional, it was highly rewarding.

Saja opened my eyes to my own ability to adjust and adapt as a professional – and to the positive impact that we therapeutic professionals can have if we adopt empowering attitudes. More importantly, she helped me to understand the value and importance of taking

a holistic view of the individual child and of taking a comprehensive approach in working with persons with disabilities and their community. This is the only way to ensure that children with disabilities can have the same opportunities as other children to participate in community life.

I want to share this realization with policymakers so they can take a more empowering, holistic approach to their work. Good policies – made with the involvement of children with disabilities and disabled persons' organizations, and properly implemented – will help to ensure that when the next Saja comes to us, she and her family will know what she is entitled to, and what she might expect to achieve – which is what every other girl of her age in her community can expect to achieve. This is the message that the Convention on the Rights of Persons with Disabilities and the Convention on the Rights of the Child give us, and that we want to promote every day.

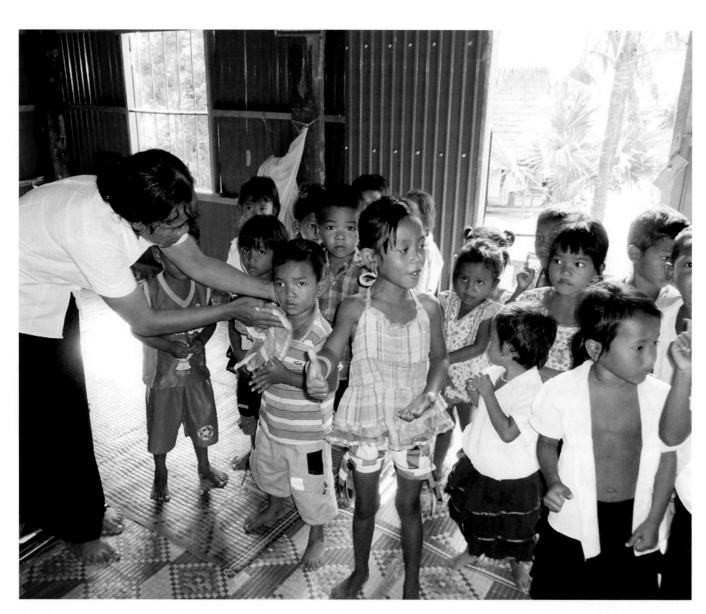

A teacher trained in inclusive education checks on 5-year-old Sok Chea, who is deaf and mute, at a preschool in Cambodia.
© UNICEF/Cambodia/2011/Mufel

CHAPTER 4

ESSENTIALS OF PROTECTION

Children with disabilities are among the most vulnerable members of society. They stand to benefit the most from measures to count them, protect them against abuse and guarantee them access to justice.

Obtaining protection can be a particular challenge for children with disabilities. In societies where they are stigmatized and their families are exposed to social or economic exclusion, many children with disabilities are not even able to obtain an identity document. Their births go unregistered: They might not be expected to survive,[103] their parents might not want to admit to them, or they might be considered a potential drain on public resources. This is a flagrant violation of these children's human rights and a fundamental barrier to their participation in society. It can seal their invisibility and increase their vulnerability to the many forms of exploitation that result from not having an official identity.

States parties to the Convention on the Rights of Persons with Disabilities (CRPD) have given themselves the clear obligation to guarantee effective legal protection for children with disabilities. They have also embraced the principle of 'reasonable accommodation', which requires that necessary and appropriate adaptations be made so that children with disabilities can enjoy their rights on an equal basis with others. For resulting legislation and efforts to change discriminatory social norms to be meaningful, it is also necessary to make certain that laws are enforced and children with disabilities are informed about their right to protection from discrimination and about how to exercise this right. Separate systems for children with disabilities would be inappropriate. As with

the other aspects of life and society discussed in this report, equity through inclusion is the goal.

Abuse and violence

Discrimination against and exclusion of children with disabilities renders them disproportionately vulnerable to violence, neglect and abuse. Studies from the United States have shown that children with disabilities who are in preschool or younger are more likely to be abused than peers without disabilities.[104] A national survey of deaf adults in Norway found that girls were twice as likely to experience sexual abuse, and boys three times as likely, as peers who had no disability.[105] Children who may already be suffering stigma and isolation have also been shown to be more likely to suffer physical abuse.

Some forms of violence are specific to children with disabilities. For example, they may be subject to violence administered under the guise of treatment for behaviour modification, including electroconvulsive treatment, drug therapy or electric shocks.[106] Girls with disabilities endure particular abuses, and in many countries are subject to forced sterilization or abortion.[107] Such procedures are defended on grounds of avoidance of menstruation or unwanted pregnancy, or even ascribed to a mistaken notion of 'child protection', given the disproportionate vulnerability of girls with disabilities to sexual abuse and rape.[108] As of the beginning of

2013, the World Health Organization was developing guidance designed to combat the human rights abuse of forced sterilization.

Institutions and inappropriate care

In many countries, children with disabilities continue to be placed in institutions. It is rare for these facilities to provide the individual attention that children need to develop to their full capacity. The quality of educational, medical and rehabilitative care provided in institutions is often insufficient because standards of appropriate care for children with disabilities are lacking or, where such standards exist, because they are not monitored and enforced.

Under the Convention on the Rights of the Child (CRC), children with and without disabilities have the right to be cared for by their parents (Article 7) and to not be separated from their parents unless this is deemed by a competent authority to be in the child's best interest (Article 9). The

CRPD reinforces this in Article 23, which states that where the immediate family is unable to care for a child with disabilities, States parties must take every measure to provide alternative care within the extended family or community.

In many countries, foster families are a frequent form of alternative care. Foster families may feel reluctant to take on the care of a child with a disability because of the perceived extra burden of care and additional physical and psychological demands. Organizations tasked with placing children in families can encourage them to consider fostering children with disabilities, and provide them with appropriate training and support.

Where authorities have come to see the perils of institutional care and have moved to return children to their families or communities, children with disabilities have been among the last to be removed from institutions and transferred to alternative care. In many countries of Central and Eastern Europe and the Commonwealth of

Children with disabilities and secondary education

▶*Armenia, 2011*

Children with disabilities who live with their families generally obtain their secondary education in mainstream schools. Children with disabilities who live in orphanages tend to not attend secondary school at all.

The main reason children with disabilities who are in the care of their families do not attend school is because their parents think their children cannot study at school.

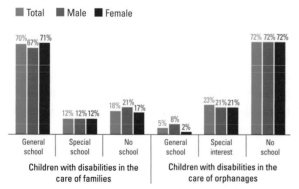

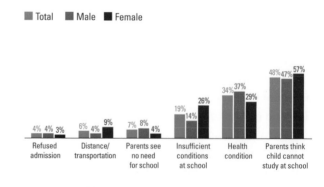

Source: Ministry of Labour and Social Issues of the Republic of Armenia and UNICEF, *It's About Inclusion: Access to education, health and social protection services for children with disabilities in Armenia.* UNICEF/Yerevan, 2012, <http://www.unicef.org/ceecis/UNICEF_Disability_Report_ENG_small.pdf>.
Sample sizes: 5,707 children in total sample; 5,322 children with disabilities in the care of families; 385 children with disabilities in the care of orphanages.
Age range: Total sample: 0–18 years old. Secondary education questions: 6–18 years old.

Independent States, institutionalized care is being reformed and children are being moved from large facilities to smaller group homes or family-based care. Serbia, for example, began wholesale reforms in 2001. Deinstitutionalization was given priority and fostering, which had an established history in the country, was given a boost. A new family law was adopted and a fund was established to help develop community-based social services. Progress ensued, but close examination revealed that children without disabilities had been released from institutions at a much faster rate than children with disabilities – about 70 per cent of whom had been committed to care directly from a maternity ward. This revelation served to demonstrate the importance of ensuring that reforms are designed and implemented so no children are excluded from progress, and it has since led to a renewed commitment to deinstitutionalization.[109]

Inclusive justice

A State's responsibility to protect the rights of all children under its jurisdiction extends equally to children with disabilities who are in contact with the law – whether as victims, witnesses, suspects or convicts. Specific measures can help: Children with disabilities can be interviewed in appropriate languages, whether spoken or signed. Law enforcement officers, social workers, lawyers, judges and other relevant professionals can be trained to work with children who have disabilities. Systematic and continuous training of all professionals involved in the administration of justice for children is vital, as is the establishment of regulations and protocols that enhance equal treatment of children with disabilities.

It is also important to develop alternative solutions to formal judicial proceedings, taking into account the range of individual capacities of children who have disabilities. Formal legal procedures should only be used as a measure of last resort, where this is in the interest of public order, and care should be taken to explain the process and the child's rights.

Last to benefit

Under Serbia's welfare reforms, children with disabilities were released from institutions at a slower rate than children without disabilities.

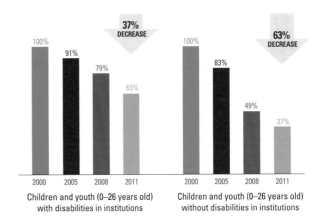

Source: Republican Institute for Social Protection, Serbia.
Sample sizes: Children and youth (0–26 years old) with disabilities: 2,020 in 2000, 1,280 in 2011. Children and youth (0–26 years old) without disabilities: 1,534 in 2000, 574 in 2011.

Children with disabilities should not be placed in regular juvenile detention facilities, neither when awaiting nor following a trial. Any decisions resulting in deprivation of liberty should be aimed at appropriate treatment to address the issues that led the child to commit a crime. Such treatment should be carried out in the context of appropriate facilities with adequately trained staff, with human rights and legal safeguards fully respected.[110]

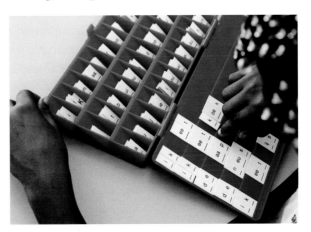

A child learns the Dutch alphabet at a school for children with learning disabilities in Curaçao, Netherlands.
© UNICEF/HQ2011-1955/LeMoyne

Violence against children with disabilities

By Lisa Jones, Mark A. Bellis, Sara
Wood, Karen Hughes, Ellie McCoy,
Lindsay Eckley, Geoff Bates
Centre for Public Health, Liverpool
John Moores University

Christopher Mikton, Alana Officer,
Tom Shakespeare
Department of Violence and Injury
Prevention and Disability, World
Health Organization

Children with disabilities are three to four times more likely to be victims of violence.

Children and adults with disabilities often face a wide range of physical, social and environmental barriers to full participation in society, including reduced access to health care, education and other support services. They are also thought to be at significantly greater risk of violence than their peers without disabilities. Understanding the extent of violence against children with disabilities is an essential first step in developing effective programmes to prevent them from becoming victims of violence and to improve their health and the quality of their lives. To this end, research teams at Liverpool John Moores University and the World Health Organization conducted the first systematic review, including meta-analysis, of existing studies on violence against children with disabilities (aged 18 years and under).

Seventeen studies, all from high-income countries, met the criteria for inclusion in the review. Prevalence estimates of violence against children with disabilities ranged from 26.7 per cent for combined measures of violence to 20.4 per cent for physical violence and 13.7 per cent for sexual violence. Estimates of risk indicated that children with disabilities were at a significantly greater risk of experiencing violence than peers without disabilities: 3.7 times more likely for combined measures of violence, 3.6 times more likely for physical violence and 2.9 times more likely for sexual violence. The type of disability appeared to affect the prevalence and risk of violence, although the evidence on this point was not conclusive. For instance, children with mental or intellectual disabilities were 4.6 times more likely to be victims of sexual violence than their non-disabled peers.

This review demonstrated that violence is a major problem for children with disabilities. It also highlighted the absence of high-quality studies on the topic from low- and middle-income countries, which generally have higher population rates of disability, higher levels of violence and fewer support services for those living with a disability. This gap in the research urgently needs to be filled.

A number of explanations have been put forward to account

Children with disabilities are at greater risk of experiencing physical or sexual violence than peers without disabilities.

for why children with disabilities are at much greater risk of violence than children without disabilities. Having to care for a child with a disability can put extra strain on parents or households and increase the risk of abuse. Significant numbers of children with disabilities continue to be placed into residential care, which is a major risk factor for sexual and physical abuse. Children with disabilities that affect communication may be particularly vulnerable to abuse, since communication barriers can hamper their ability to disclose abusive experiences.

The Convention on the Rights of Persons with Disabilities aims to protect the rights of individuals with disabilities and guarantee their full and equal participation in society. In the case of children with disabilities, this includes ensuring a safe and stable progression through childhood and into adulthood. As with all children, a safe and secure childhood provides the best chance of achieving a healthy, well-adjusted adulthood. Adverse childhood experiences, including violence, are known to be related to a wide range of negative health and social outcomes in later life. The extra

demands placed on children with disabilities – who must cope with their disabilities and overcome societal barriers that increase their risk of poorer outcomes in later life – mean that a safe and secure childhood is particularly important.

Children placed away from home need increased care and protection, and institutional cultures, regimes and structures that exacerbate the risk of violence and abuse should be addressed as a matter of urgency. Whether they live in institutions or with their families or other caregivers, all children with disabilities should be viewed as a high-risk group in which it is critical to identify violence. They may benefit from interventions such as home visiting and parenting programmes, which have been demonstrated to be effective for preventing violence and mitigating its consequences in children without disabilities. The effectiveness of such interventions for children with disabilities should be evaluated as a matter of priority.

Segregation and abuse in institutions

By Eric Rosenthal and Laurie Ahern

Eric Rosenthal, JD, is founder and Executive Director of Disability Rights International (DRI). Laurie Ahern is its President. Through investigations of orphanages and other institutions in more than two dozen countries, DRI has brought international attention to the human rights of people with disabilities.

Throughout the world, millions of children with disabilities are separated from their families and placed in orphanages, boarding schools, psychiatric facilities and social care homes. Children who survive institutions face the prospect of lifetime segregation from society in facilities for adults. According to the Convention on the Rights of Persons with Disabilities (CRPD), segregating children on the basis of their disability violates the rights of every such child. Article 19 of the Convention requires governments to establish the laws, social policies and community support services needed to prevent isolation or segregation from the community.

Over the course of 20 years, Disability Rights International (DRI) has documented the conditions of children with disabilities in institutions in 26 countries around the world. Our findings are surprisingly consistent. We have interviewed heartbroken mothers and fathers who wish to keep their children at home but receive inadequate support from governments and cannot afford to stay home from work to take care of a child. Doctors often tell parents to place their daughter or son in an orphanage before they become too attached to the child.

Raising children in congregate settings is inherently dangerous. Even in clean, well-managed and well-staffed institutions, children encounter greater risks to their life and health compared to those who grow up in families. Children who grow up in institutions are likely to acquire developmental disabilities, and the youngest among them also face potentially irreversible psychological damage.

Even in institutions with adequate food, we often observe children who are emaciated because they simply stop eating – a condition called 'failure to thrive'. Infants and children with disabilities may starve or lack adequate nutrients because staff do not or cannot take the extra time to feed them. Sometimes staff will prop a bottle on the chest of a bedridden child, in theory allowing her to grasp it and drink – but in practice, the child may be unable to pick it up.

Many children are left to languish. A DRI investigator came to the horrific realization, in 2007, that a child who looked to be 7 or 8 years old was, according to a nurse, 21 years old and had never been out of his crib in 11 years.

Without any movement, physical disabilities worsen, and children can develop life-threatening medical complications. Some children's arms and legs atrophy and have to be amputated.

Without emotional attention and support, many children become self-abusive, rocking back and forth, banging their heads against walls, biting themselves or poking their own eyes. Most facilities lack trained staff who can help children stop such behaviour. Instead, children are sometimes tied permanently to beds or held in cages – whether to prevent self-abuse or to help overwhelmed staff cope with the demands of the many children in their care. The United Nations Committee against Torture and the United Nations Special Rapporteur on Torture have said that the prolonged use of restraints may constitute torture.

For a child who has already been institutionalized, falling ill can be a death sentence. Staff members at facilities in more than one country have said that children with disabilities are routinely denied medical treatment. Institution staff have also told us – incorrectly – that children with developmental disabilities lack the ability to feel pain. So, in some cases, medical procedures are conducted without anaesthesia. In one facility, children's teeth were extracted with pliers; elsewhere, children received electro-convulsive therapy with no anaesthesia or muscle relaxants.

Children have been given electric shocks, physically restrained for long periods and isolated with the express purpose of causing pain, on the theory that this 'aversive therapy' would extinguish behaviour deemed

inappropriate. A teacher in the United States described one girl – blind, deaf and non-verbal – who was shocked for moaning. It turned out she had a broken tooth.

Without oversight and human rights protections, children have, in effect, disappeared in institutions. Human rights monitoring and enforcement programmes to protect against violence, exploitation and abuse – as required by Article 16 of CRPD – are absent in most of the facilities we have visited. In some cases, authorities do not keep track of the names or numbers of children detained in these places.

Official statistics are unreliable and often understate reliance upon segregated service systems. The numbers are often limited to orphanages and do not include children detained in other types of institutions, such as boarding schools, health-care or psychiatric facilities, criminal justice systems or homeless shelters. Private or religious institutions, which may be much larger than government orphanages, are often not counted.

The entrances to some orphanages and other institutions are emblazoned with the logos of governments, corporate donors,

churches or private charities. Even when financial assistance from international donors or technical assistance agencies makes up a small portion of an institution's operating budget, this support can provide an apparent 'seal of approval'. DRI has found bilateral and multilateral support – both official and from voluntary donations by staff – for such amenities as playgrounds at orphanages where children die for want of medical care and where they are tied to beds. These donors may be well intentioned but this support runs counter to the intent of the CRPD and other rights instruments that protect people from segregation.

No child should ever be taken away from her or his family on the basis of disability. DRI is calling on every government and international donor agency to commit to preventing any new placements in orphanages. It is much harder to protect children and provide them with an opportunity for a life in society when their ties to family have already been broken. The detention of children in institutions is a fundamental human rights violation. We can bring it to an end, on a worldwide scale, through a moratorium on new placements.

Fadi, 12, walks past houses destroyed by airstrikes in Rafah, State of Palestine, where ongoing violence has had substantial psychological impact, especially on children. © UNICEF/HQ2012-1583/El Baba

CHAPTER 5

HUMANITARIAN RESPONSE

Humanitarian crises, such as those stemming from warfare or natural disasters, pose particular risks for children with disabilities. Inclusive humanitarian response is urgently needed – and feasible.

Armed conflict and war affect children in direct and indirect ways: directly in the form of physical injuries from attack, artillery fire and landmine explosions or in the form of psychological conditions derived from these injuries or from witnessing traumatic events; indirectly through, for example, the breakdown of health services, which leaves many illnesses untreated, and food insecurity, which leads to malnutrition.[111] Children are also separated from their families, their homes or their schools, sometimes for years.

The nature of armed conflict, a major cause of disabilities among children, is changing. Fighting is increasingly taking the form of recurring civil wars and fragmented violence characterized by the indiscriminate use of force and weapons. At the same time, natural disasters are expected to affect increasing numbers of children and adults in coming years, especially in hazardous regions such as low-lying coastal zones, particularly as climate change-related disasters grow in frequency and severity.[112]

Children with disabilities face particular challenges in emergencies. They may be unable to escape during a crisis because of inaccessible evacuation routes; for example, a child in a wheelchair may be unable to flee a tsunami or gunfire and may be abandoned by her or his family. They may be dependent on assistive devices or caregivers, and in the face of the loss of a caregiver, may be extremely vulnerable to physical violence or to sexual, emotional and verbal abuse. Children with disabilities may also be made invisible by family and community beliefs – for example, a child with a mental impairment might be kept in the house because of stigma surrounding her or his condition.

In addition, children with disabilities may be excluded from or unable to access mainstream support services and assistance programmes such as health services or food distribution because of the physical barriers posed by inaccessible buildings or because of negative attitudes. Or they may be forgotten in the establishment of targeted services. For example, landmine survivors may not be able to access physical rehabilitation services because of distance, the high cost of transport or criteria for admission to treatment programmes. Furthermore, children with disabilities may be disregarded in early warning systems, which often do not take into account the communication and mobility requirements of those with disabilities.

Disability-inclusive humanitarian action is informed by and grounded in:
- A rights-based approach, based on the Convention on the Rights of the Child (CRC) and the Convention on the Rights of Persons with Disabilities (CRPD). Article 11 of the CRPD

specifically calls on duty bearers to take all necessary measures to ensure the protection and safety of persons with disabilities in situations of conflict, emergency and disaster, signifying the importance of the issue.

- An inclusive approach that recognizes that children with disabilities, in addition to their disability-specific needs, have the same needs as other children, disability being only one aspect of their situation: They are children who happen to have disabilities. Such an inclusive approach also addresses the social, attitudinal, informational and physical barriers that impede participation and decision-making by children with disabilities in regular programmes.
- Ensuring accessibility and universal design of infrastructure and information. This includes making the physical environment, all facilities, health centres, shelters and schools, and the organization of health and other services, including communication and information systems, accessible for children with disabilities.
- Promoting independent living so that children with disabilities can live as independently as possible and participate as fully as possible in all aspects of life.
- Integrating age, gender and diversity awareness, including paying special attention to the double or triple discrimination faced by women and girls with disabilities.

Disability-inclusive humanitarian response ensures that children and adults with disabilities, as well as their families, survive and live with dignity, even as it benefits the population as a whole. This approach calls for holistic and inclusive programmes, rather than just isolated projects and policies targeting disabilities. Key

Vijay, 12, survived a landmine explosion and has gone on to become a mine risk educator in Sri Lanka.
© UNICEF/Sri Lanka/2012/Tuladar

Explosive remnants of war (ERW) on display at a school in Ajdabiya, Libya. Students collected the objects from around the city. © UNICEF/HQ2011-1435/Diffidenti

intervention areas for disability-inclusive humanitarian action include:

- Improving data and assessments in order to have an evidence base for the distinct needs and priorities of children with disabilities.
- Making mainstream humanitarian services accessible for children with disabilities and involving them in planning and design.
- Designing specialized services for children with disabilities and ensuring that recovery and reintegration proceed in environments that foster well-being, health, self-respect and dignity.
- Putting measures in place to prevent injuries and abuse and promote accessibility.
- Partnering with community, regional and national actors, including disabled persons' organizations, to challenge discriminatory attitudes and perceptions and promote equity.

- Promoting participation of children with disabilities by consulting them and creating opportunities for their voices to be heard.

Parties to conflict have an obligation to protect children from the effects of armed violence and to provide them with access to appropriate health and psychosocial care to aid their recovery and reintegration. The Committee on the Rights of the Child has recommended that States parties to the CRC add explicit reference to children with disabilities as part of their broader commitment not to recruit children into armed forces.[113] Governments should also take care to address the recovery and social reintegration of children who acquire disabilities as a result of armed conflict. This is explored in greater detail in the following Focus article.

Risk, resilience and inclusive humanitarian action

By Maria Kett
Assistant Director, Department of
Epidemiology and Public Health,
Leonard Cheshire Disability and
Inclusive Development Centre,
University College London

Article 11 of the Convention on the Rights of Persons with Disabilities compels States parties to "ensure the protection and safety of persons with disabilities in situations of risk, including situations of armed conflict, humanitarian emergencies and the occurrence of natural disasters."

In an emergency – whether armed conflict or a natural or human-made disaster – children are among those most vulnerable to the loss of food, shelter, health care, education and age-appropriate psychosocial support services. This vulnerability can be even more acute for children with disabilities: Even where basic supplies and relief services are available, they may not be inclusive or accessible.

Knowing how many children with disabilities live in an area affected by an emergency is extremely challenging, because accurate numbers may not have existed even before the emergency. Parents or communities may hide such children because of stigma, for example. The resulting exclusion is of particular concern because even the most rudimentary reporting systems can unravel in humanitarian situations, since registration and reporting points or centres may not be accessible.

At the same time, increasing numbers of children may sustain disabling injuries as a result of chronic or sudden emergencies. In an earthquake, children may be disabled by falling objects or when buildings collapse. They may receive crushing injuries and undergo psychological trauma during floods and landslides. Conflict increases the likelihood that children will become disabled as a result of fighting, because of landmines, or through exposure to other explosive remnants of war (ERW). Because children are smaller and at earlier stages in their development, they often sustain more seriously disabling injuries than adults and require continuing physiotherapy, prostheses and psychological support.

The challenges facing children with disabilities and their families are rarely acknowledged when the impact of an emergency is assessed. These challenges include new environmental barriers such as collapsed ramps; damaged or lost assistive devices; and the loss of previously established services (sign language interpreters or visiting nurses) or support systems (social security payments or social protection schemes).

There are other risks. If family members die, there may be no one left who knows how to care for a child with a physical disability or who can communicate with a child with a sensory impairment. If families are forced to flee, especially if they face a long journey by foot, they may leave behind children who are unable to walk or are in frail health. Families may also leave behind children with disabilities because they fear they will be refused asylum in another country if one of their family members has a disability. Several countries practise such discrimination. Institutions and residential schools may close or be abandoned by staff, leaving few people – or no one – to help the children in their charge.

Children with disabilities, especially those with learning disabilities, can also be directly involved in conflict. They may be pressed into service as fighters, cooks or porters precisely because they are considered to be less valuable, or less likely to resist, than children without disabilities. In theory disarmament, demobilization and reintegration programmes include all child ex-combatants, but resources or programmes for children with disabilities are often non-existent. These children therefore remain marginalized and excluded, leaving them poor, vulnerable and often having to beg, as has been the case in Liberia and Sierra Leone.

The risk of violence, including sexual violence, increases when family protection and social structures break down as they do during conflict and disasters. While girls with disabilities are at particular risk in such situations, boys with disabilities are also at risk and are even less likely to be helped in the aftermath of violence.

Recovery and reconstruction come with their own challenges for children with disabilities. As is the case with all crisis-affected children, those with disabilities require a range of services, including but not limited to targeted ones. Disability-specific needs are extremely important, but they are only part of the picture. During recovery operations after the 2004 Indian Ocean tsunami, for example, one girl with a disability was given five wheelchairs – but no one asked her if she needed food or clothes.

Resilience and inclusion
Children have repeatedly demonstrated their resilience. Measures can be taken to support their participation and inclusion. These measures should be specific to particular groups and contexts: Boys and girls have different experiences of conflict, as do young children and adolescents. Similarly, emergencies can affect urban and rural areas differently.

As a starting point, children with disabilities should be given the opportunity to take part in the planning and implementation of disaster risk reduction and peace-building strategies as well as in recovery processes. Ignorance and incorrect assumptions that they are unable to contribute have often barred them from doing so, but this has begun to change. In Bangladesh, for example, Plan International learned to challenge such misconceptions through partnerships with disability organizations and by working directly with communities in undertaking child-centred disaster risk reduction.

Similarly, provision for children with disabilities is increasing in disaster response. In Pakistan, Handicap International (HI) and Save the Children built child-friendly inclusive spaces and developed sector-wide guidance on inclusion of persons with disabilities, especially in protection projects. In Haiti, HI and the faith-based development organization CBM lobbied the government to increase the inclusion of persons with disabilities in food distribution and other efforts. The United Nations often uses emergencies as an opportunity to 'build back better', an approach that can yield opportunities for children with disabilities because it offers all stakeholders a chance to work together.

Disability is also being mainstreamed in such guidelines as the Sphere Project's *Humanitarian Charter and Minimum Standards in Humanitarian Response*, framed by a group of international organizations to improve the quality and accountability of humanitarian response. The availability of emergency guidelines on how to include people with disabilities – and children in particular – is increasing. These gains need to be consolidated and extended to such areas as child nutrition and protection.

Also needed is a unified approach to data collection. Collaboration with local and national disabled people's organizations should be emphasized, and these groups' capacity to address issues specific to children should be built up where necessary. And the extent to which children with disabilities are included in humanitarian response must be audited to monitor and improve results.

Clear standards and inclusion checklists that can be applied across the range of emergencies will be essential – but to be put into practice, they must be accompanied by resource allocations.

Explosive remnants of war

By the Victim Assistance Editorial Team at the Landmine and Cluster Munition Monitor.

The Landmine and Cluster Munition Monitor provides research for the International Campaign to Ban Landmines and the Cluster Munition Coalition. It is the de facto monitoring regime for the Mine Ban Treaty and the Convention on Cluster Munitions.

Explosive remnants of war (ERW) and anti-personnel landmines have a devastating impact on children and represent a significant contributing factor to child disability. Since the signing of the 1997 Mine Ban Treaty, however, vast tracts of land have been cleared of these munitions and returned to productive use.

The 1997 treaty; the 1996 Amended Protocol II and 2003 Protocol V to the 1980 Convention on Certain Conventional Weapons; and the 2008 Convention on Cluster Munitions have all had a positive impact in terms of protecting the lives of people living in areas contaminated by ERW and landmines. The global movement to ban landmines and cluster munitions is a testament to the importance of strong political will among key stakeholders in fostering global change.

Mine action programming, which seeks to address the impact of landmines and ERW, is understood to be made up of five pillars – clearance, ERW/ mine risk education, victim assistance, stockpile destruction and advocacy. Despite the great successes in many of these pillars, as indicated by a significant global decline in ERW and landmine casualties, victim assistance continues to stand out as a key area of weakness. This is especially so in the case of children affected by ERW or landmines.

In contrast with the other four pillars of mine action, victim assistance requires a cross-cutting response that includes medical and paramedical interventions to ensure physical rehabilitation, as well as social and economic interventions to promote reintegration and the livelihood of victims.

To date the bulk of mine action assistance and funding has been dedicated to clearance activities. In 2010, 85 per cent of global funds related to mine action were allocated to clearance, while only 9 per cent were allocated to victim assistance interventions. While the International Mine Action Standards – the standards in

force for all UN mine action operations – address the mine action programming pillars of clearance, ERW/mine risk education and stockpile destruction, they do not tackle the issue of victim assistance. Moreover, the right to age- and gender-appropriate physical rehabilitation and social and economic reintegration for survivors of landmines and ERW is enshrined in international human rights and humanitarian law. However, few survivor assistance programmes have taken into consideration the specific needs of children, whether they are direct survivors or victims in the broader sense.

The impact on children
There has been a significant decrease in the numbers of people killed or injured by landmine blasts. Between 2001 and 2010, the number of new landmine and ERW casualties reported through the Landmine and Cluster Munitions Monitor, the monitoring arm of the Mine Ban Treaty and the Convention on Cluster Munitions, fell from 7,987 to 4,191. The chart on the next page demonstrates a significant reduction in the total number of civilian deaths and injuries from landmines and ERW in the five-year period between 2005 and 2010.

Since monitoring began in 1999, there have been at least 1,000 child casualties every year. Many casualties go unrecorded, so the real number is likely much higher.

Nevertheless, the percentage of total casualties represented by child casualties has increased. Annually, since 2005, children have accounted for approximately 20–30 per cent of all casualties from landmines, remnants of cluster munitions and other ERW. Since monitoring began in 1999, there have been at least 1,000 child casualties every year. The number of child casualties of landmines and ERW in 2010 surpassed 1,200, and children accounted for 55 per cent of all civilian deaths – children are now the civilian group for whom landmines and ERW are most deadly. Given that numerous casualties go unrecorded in many countries, the total number of child casualties annually is likely much higher, and in some of the world's most mine-affected countries, the percentage of casualties represented by children is higher still: In 2011, children constituted 61 per cent of all civilian casualties in Afghanistan. In the same year, they were 58 per cent of civilian casualties in the Lao People's Democratic Republic, 50 per cent in Iraq and 48 per cent in the Sudan.

If children now constitute the majority of casualties caused by landmines, remnants of cluster munitions and other ERW, since 2008, boys have made up the single largest casualty group, approximately 50 per cent of all civilian casualties. In 2006, the first year in which the Landmine Monitor began disaggregating casualty data by both age and gender, boys represented 83 per cent of child casualties and made up the largest single casualty group among civilians in 17 countries. In 2008, boys represented 73 per cent of child casualties, and were the largest casualty group in 10 countries. In many contaminated countries, boys are more likely than girls to come across mines or ERW, because they are more involved in outdoor activities such as herding livestock, gathering wood and food, or collecting scrap metal. Children in general are more likely to deliberately handle explosive devices than adults, often unknowingly, out of curiosity or by mistaking them for toys. Boys are more likely than girls to tamper with the explosive devices they come across. These factors,

Monica and Luis, both 14 in this 2004 photograph from Colombia, sit at poolside. Monica lost a foot when a younger cousin brought home a grenade. It exploded, killing the cousin. © UNICEF/HQ2004-0793/DeCesare

as well as a tendency towards engaging in risk-taking behaviour, make well-planned risk education especially important for children.

Assistance for child survivors

ERW and landmine incidents affect children differently than they do adults, whether they are directly killed or injured, or become victims as a result of the death or injury of family and community members. Child survivors who are injured have specific needs that must be taken into consideration, in terms of both physical rescue and rehabilitation and social and economic reintegration. Smaller than adults, children are more likely to die or suffer serious injuries from a blast, including severe burns, shrapnel wounds, damaged limbs and other injuries that can lead to blindness or deafness.

Their height means that their vital organs are closer to the detonation, and children have a lower threshold for substantial blood loss than adults. If an anti-personnel landmine is stepped on, its blast will invariably cause foot and leg injuries, with secondary infections that usually result in amputation, causing lifelong disabilities and requiring long-term rehabilitation support.

More than one third of all survivors require amputation, and while data concerning the exact percentage of affected children requiring amputation are lacking, the percentage can be expected to be higher for children, given their smaller size. When children survive their injuries, their physical rehabilitation is more complex than that of adult survivors. Children whose injuries result in amputated limbs require

more complicated rehabilitation and, because their bones grow more quickly than their soft tissue, several re-amputations may be required. They also need to have prostheses made as they grow. Few countries affected by landmines and ERW have the capacity necessary to address the specific, complex medical and physical rehabilitation needs of child survivors.

In addition to the physical trauma, the psychological consequences of surviving an ERW or landmine blast are often devastating for the development of the child. They include a sense of guilt, loss of self-esteem, phobias and fear, sleep disorders, inability to speak and trauma that if left untreated can result in long-term mental disorder. Such psychological effects of war on children are difficult to document, and they are not limited to children who have sustained physical injuries.

The social and economic reintegration needs of child survivors also vary considerably from the needs of adults. Addressing the psychosocial impacts outlined above relies heavily on age-appropriate psychosocial support and access to education. In many countries, child survivors are forced to cut short their education because of the time needed for recovery, and because

Child casualties in countries heavily affected by mines and explosive remnants of war, 2011*

Country	Total civilian casualties	Child casualties	Child casualties as percentage of total casualties
Afghanistan	609	373	61%
Democratic Republic of the Congo	22	15	68%
Iraq	100	50	50%
Lao People's Democratic Republic	97	56	58%
Sudan	62	30	48%

* Includes only casualties for which the civilian/security status and the age was known.

Source: Landmine and Cluster Munition Monitor.

Child casualties in the most affected countries*

Percentage of children among civilian casualties (1999–2011)

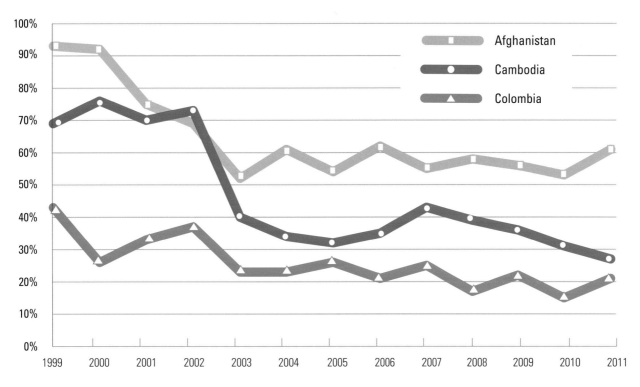

* The three States parties to the Mine Ban Treaty with the highest annual casualty rates.

Source: Landmine and Cluster Munition Monitor.

rehabilitation represents a financial burden for families. Access to free education for children with disabilities as a result of a landmine or ERW injury is necessary both to promote a sense of normalcy in their lives, enabling them to recover from the psychosocial distress of their injury, and to reintegrate them with their peer group and allow them to fully participate in society. Yet children left with a disability following a landmine or ERW blast are more vulnerable than others to the denial of this right: They may no longer be

able to walk to school, and other transportation alternatives are seldom in place. Even when they are able to get to school, classrooms may not be accessible for children with disabilities, and their teachers may not be trained in adapting to the needs of children with disabilities.

Opportunities for income generation and livelihood support are especially necessary to support children and adolescents left with a disability as a result of landmines or ERW. Unfortunately, such

opportunities seldom if ever take age considerations into account. Where age has been considered, as it was during a 2008–2010 project in Cambodia, the challenges to ensuring age-appropriate interventions for children and adolescents were such as to exclude those under 18 from victim assistance livelihood interventions altogether.

This failure to address the specific needs of and risks to children and adolescents is reflected in the livelihood and economic strengthening sector more generally: A 2011 review of 43 studies on the impact of economic strengthening programmes in crisis contexts in low-income countries found that some of these efforts had, paradoxically, increased the risk that children would be pulled out of school and put to work or that girls would be subject to violence. The programmes studied featured such initiatives as microcredit, skills training, and agricultural interventions. The review called on economic strengthening practitioners to "build children's protection and well-being into the assessment, design, implementation, monitoring and evaluation of economic strengthening programs." In addition, livelihood and income generation opportunities for children and adolescents must take into account not only their age but also their sex and the cultural context in which they live. Because children with disabilities are among those most vulnerable to deprivation, violence, abuse and exploitation, there is an urgent need to ensure that victim assistance programmes take the specific needs of child survivors into consideration.

Meanwhile, children who are victims of landmines and other ERW as a result of the death or injury of caregivers and family members, including family breadwinners, also have needs that differ from those of adults. Like child survivors, they too may be more vulnerable to the

loss of education opportunities, separation from their families, child labour and other forms of exploitation or neglect.

Despite the particular victim assistance needs of children, few victim assistance programmes take age- and gender-specific considerations into account. While research has been conducted on victim assistance in general, and guidance has been developed on what such programmes should look like, to date there has been little if any focus on children and adolescents. Meanwhile, while States parties to the Mine Ban Treaty, Protocols II and V of the Convention on Certain Conventional Weapons, and the Convention on Cluster Munitions must regularly report on national-level implementation of these international instruments, they do not report on their efforts to address the specific needs of survivors according to their age. It is not surprising then that in a 2009 survey of more than 1,600 survivors from 25 affected countries conducted by Handicap International, almost two thirds of respondents reported that services for children were "never" or "almost never" adapted to address their specific needs or ensure that services were age appropriate.

Child victims, including those directly and indirectly affected, have specific and additional

needs in all aspects of assistance. However, the information available about efforts to address these needs is limited. Most children involved in mine or ERW incidents are injured. Yet most data collection systems do not record their needs.

As children account for an increasing percentage of the total civilian casualties from ERW and landmines, it is essential to implement specific policy and programmatic recommendations on victim assistance that meets the needs of child survivors. These recommendations include:

- Supporting and promoting the establishment of national injury surveillance systems able to provide systematic and continuous information on the magnitude and nature of ERW and landmine injuries (and other types of injuries if appropriate), including age- and gender-disaggregated data about child casualties.
- Integrating a victim assistance component into the International Mine Action Standards, including through technical notes and best-practices guidelines, with specific guidance and considerations on child-specific survivor and victim assistance.
- Developing and promoting the establishment of victim assistance databases able to provide systematic data

Child casualties by type of explosive*

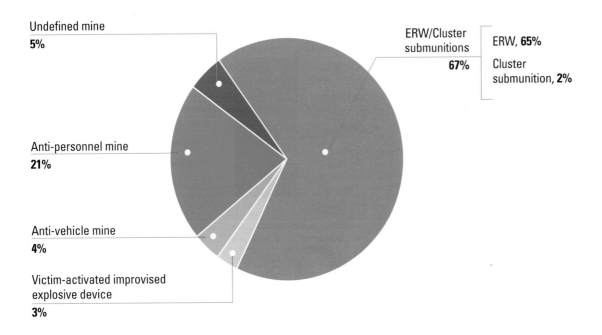

Undefined mine
5%

ERW/Cluster submunitions
67%

ERW, **65%**

Cluster submunition, **2%**

Anti-personnel mine
21%

Anti-vehicle mine
4%

Victim-activated improvised explosive device
3%

*Not including unknown explosive item types.

Source: Landmine and Cluster Munition Monitor.

to monitor the rehabilitation, psychosocial and socio-economic needs of each child and adult survivor appropriately and across time.

- Sensitizing governments, mine action actors, donors and other relevant stakeholders, through both international and national forums, on the importance of prioritizing victim assistance (including for child survivors and the children of people killed by victim-activated explosives) as a key pillar of mine action and international laws.
- Making government, humanitarian and developmental actors and service providers

aware of the importance of ensuring the availability of age- and gender-specific health and physical rehabilitation, psychosocial support, protection, education and livelihood support services for child survivors and victims of ERW and landmines.

- Training health professionals, including emergency response personnel, surgeons and ortho-prosthetic service providers, in the specific considerations and special needs of child survivors.
- Training education service providers, including school management, teachers and

educators, in providing accessible and appropriate education for child survivors and victims.

- Formulating national laws, plans and policies responding to the needs of survivors and victims of ERW and landmines, or of persons with disabilities in general, so that they integrate and respond to the age- and gender-specific needs of child survivors and victims.
- Integrating a strong victim assistance component into the draft UN Inter-Agency Mine Action Strategy, including specific child-survivor assistance considerations.

PERSPECTIVE
One bite of the elephant at a time

By Chaeli Mycroft

Chaeli Mycroft, recipient of the 2011 International Children's Peace Prize, is an ability activist and avid wheelchair dancer. She is preparing to study politics and philosophy at the University of Cape Town, South Africa.

Some people see disability as a burden, others as a gift. My disability has given me very unique opportunities and experiences that would not have happened if I were not disabled. I am happy and grateful for my disability because it has moulded me into the person that I am today.

I am in no way saying that having a disability is an easy thing to deal with. It is a very complex situation, and it affects almost every aspect of your life. But I hope, throughout my life, to inspire other young people to see their disabilities as an opportunity to focus on ability, not just on their limitations.

My family has always challenged me to focus on my abilities and has never viewed or treated me with pity. For this, I will be eternally grateful because it made me see myself as equal to any able-bodied person. I was also raised knowing that my contribution is of equal importance to anyone else's, and to stand up (metaphorically) for my rights. My friends view me as an equal and accept that my disability sometimes makes it difficult for me to do things in the same manner as they do, so we just have to be slightly more creative to include me in whatever we're doing – playing cricket when we were younger, for example. I would be the scorer.

The incredible support I received enabled me to work with children with disabilities in South Africa. For this I won the International Children's Peace Prize in 2011 – an event that has changed my life in an amazing way. The KidsRights Foundation, which awards this prize annually, has given me the opportunity to spread my message through a worldwide platform and to meet people I would otherwise never meet. They also pay for my education and are making it possible

If people with disabilities can't believe in themselves or if others don't believe in them, I will believe in them – and hopefully my positivity will spread and encourage more positivity.

for me to go to university next year with all the adjustments I need.

So many children with disabilities are not celebrated for their capabilities and are hidden away from the world because of fear and ignorance. We need to realize that people with disabilities are crucial in our population. People with disabilities are often the ones who think outside the box – because we have to. We have to make our disabilities work for us and not against us, and teach others to be caring and empathetic. Empathy, something the world desperately needs.

I believe that there are two main issues to be tackled on a worldwide level – accessibility and attitudes. These issues are interconnected and cannot be dealt with one by one. If people can change the worldwide attitude towards disability from one of pity, shame and inferiority to one of abundance, acceptance and equality, then we will see amazing progress. Positive attitudes can lead to improved accessibility – just as inaccessibility is an expression of the view that the needs of people with disabilities are less important than those of able-

bodied people, an attitude that has negative consequences for people with and without disabilities.

Improved attitudes should also help address other major issues, such as our experiences of education. I have been in every form of education that a person with a disability can do: special needs school, mainstream state primary and high school, mainstream private high school. I wouldn't say I'm an expert, but there's a lot to be said for experience. It was certainly not always easy and simple. Often it was a struggle, and at times I was incredibly unhappy. I worked really hard to be included and to make it easier for the people who are going to come after me. I am finishing my school career in a place where I am fully included and accepted. When I think about it, all I feel is relief – relief that I don't have to fight so hard for my own happiness anymore. Now I can fight harder for other people with disabilities and their right to happiness.

It may seem that I am always a super-positive person. This is not the case. I have had my struggles, and I am sure that

they are not over. The thing that tips the scale towards positivity is the fact that I am surrounded by people who believe in my ability and are positive about my contribution to society – people who counter my negative days. I really love them for that.

My lifetime goal is to have disability become something that is completely accepted and embraced by the global community. It may be a big task, and it may have many facets, but I believe it's entirely possible.

It starts with believing. I believe in my abilities; I believe wholeheartedly that I can make change happen – that I can change lives. If people with disabilities can't believe in themselves or if others don't believe in them, I will believe in them – and hopefully my positivity will spread and encourage more positivity. This might seem insignificant to some but it's still change.

One bite of the elephant at a time.

A health worker assesses a boy at the Atfaluna Society for Deaf Children, State of Palestine. The organization offers education and vocational training, free health care, psychosocial services and job placement. © UNICEF/HQ2008-0159/Davey

CHAPTER 6

MEASURING CHILD DISABILITY

A society cannot be equitable unless all children are included, and children with disabilities cannot be included unless sound data collection and analysis render them visible.

Measuring child disability presents a unique set of challenges. Because children develop and learn to perform basic tasks at different speeds, it can be difficult to assess function and distinguish significant limitations from variations in normal development.[114] The varying nature and severity of disabilities, together with the need to apply age-specific definitions and measures, further complicate data collection efforts. In addition, the poor quality of data on child disability stems, in some cases, from a limited understanding of what disability is in children and, in other cases, from stigma or insufficient investment in improving measurement. The lack of evidence that results from such difficulties hinders the development of good policies and the delivery of vital services. As discussed below, however, efforts to improve data collection are under way – and the very act of gathering information is sparking positive change.

Evolving definitions

While there is general agreement that definitions of disability should incorporate both medical and social determinants, the measurement of disability is still predominantly medical, with a focus on specific physical or mental impairments.

Estimates of disability prevalence vary depending on what definition of disability is used.

Narrow, medical definitions are likely to yield lower estimates than broader ones that take into account social barriers to functioning and participation.[115]

One framework for seeing health and disability within a broader context of social barriers is the International Classification of Functioning, Disability and Health (ICF), developed by the World Health Organization.[116] This classification regards disability in two main ways: as a matter of the body's structure and functions, and in terms of the person's activity and participation. Disability, as defined by the ICF, is an ordinary part of human existence. ICF's definition effectively mainstreams disability, shifting the focus from cause to effect and acknowledging that every person can experience some degree of disability. The ICF definition also recognizes that functioning and disability occur in context, and therefore it is meaningful to assess not only bodily but also societal and environmental factors.

While the ICF was principally designed for adult disability, a classification derived from it, the International Classification of Functioning, Disability and Health for Children and Youth (ICF-CY) takes a step towards incorporating the social dimension by capturing not only the impairment but also its effect on children's functioning and participation in their environment. The classification covers four main areas: body structures (e.g., organs, limbs and structures of the nervous, visual, auditory and musculoskeletal systems), body functions (physiological functions of body systems, such as listening or remembering), limitations on activity (e.g., walking, climbing, dressing) and restrictions on participation (e.g., playing with caregivers or other children, performing simple chores).[117]

Putting disability in context

Data should be interpreted in context. Estimates of disability prevalence are a function of both incidence and survival, and the results should be interpreted with caution, particularly in countries where infant and child mortality rates are high.[118] A low reported prevalence of disability may be the consequence of low survival rates for young children with disabilities, or it may reflect the failure to count children with disabilities who are confined to institutions, who are hidden away by families fearful of discrimination, or who live and work on the streets.

Culture also plays an important role. The interpretation of what may be considered 'normal' functioning varies across contexts and influences measurement outcomes. The attainment of certain milestones may not only vary among children, but differ also by culture. Children may be encouraged to experiment with new activities at different stages of development. For instance, in one study, 50 per cent of children were 'able to use a cup' at about 35 months of age in urban India, while the corresponding milestone was reached around 10 months of age in Thailand.[119] It is therefore important to assess children against reference values appropriate to local circumstances and understanding.

For these reasons, assessment tools developed in high-income countries, such as the Wechsler Intelligence Scale for Children and Griffith's

Four case studies:
Percentage of population reporting some form of disability

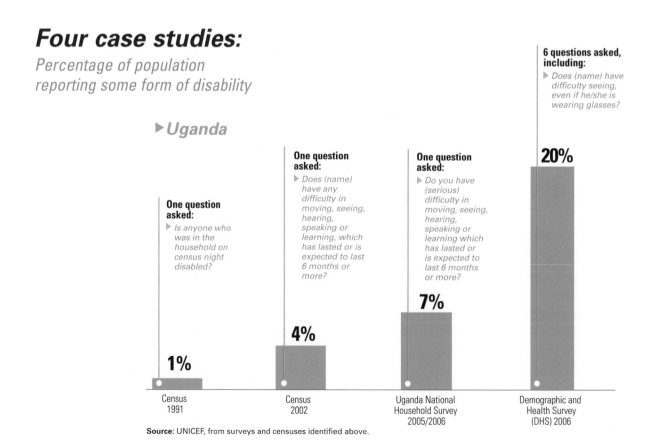

Source: UNICEF, from surveys and censuses identified above.

Mental Development Scale,[120] cannot be indiscriminately applied in other countries or communities, as their capacity to detect and accurately measure disability in different sociocultural contexts is often untested. Frames of reference may vary, and survey tools may fail to sufficiently capture local customs, cultural understanding, languages or expressions. For example, questionnaires that evaluate child development on the basis of such 'standard' activities as preparing breakfast cereal or playing board games may be appropriate in some places but not in those where children do not routinely engage in these activities.[121]

Data collection

The specific objectives of the data collection are likely to influence the definition of what constitutes 'disability', the questions asked and the resulting figures. The measurement of disability type and prevalence is frequently tied to specific political initiatives, such as social protection schemes. Results may be used to determine benefit entitlement or to plan and determine support provision. For example, the criteria used to define eligibility for a disability benefit are likely to be more restrictive than criteria for a survey conducted to identify all persons with a functional limitation, yielding dramatically different numbers.[122]

Many children are identified as having a disability when they come into contact with education or health-care systems. However, in low-income countries or communities, school and clinic staff may not be able to routinely recognize or register the presence of children with disabilities. The resulting paucity of information about children with disabilities in low-income countries has contributed to a misconception that disability does not merit global priority.[123]

Where schooling or other formal services for children with disabilities are lacking, other methods

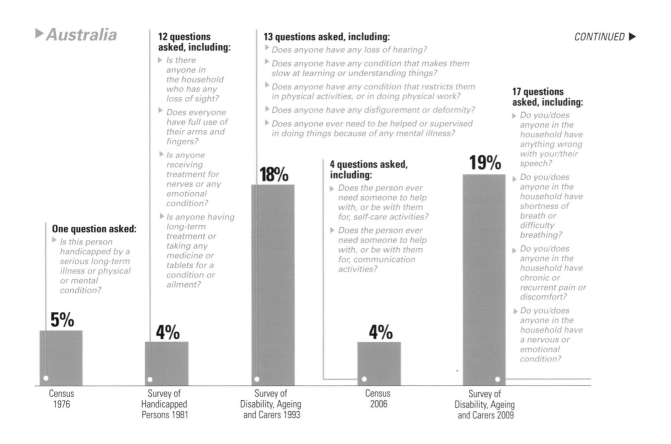

▶ *Australia*

One question asked:
▶ *Is this person handicapped by a serious long-term illness or physical or mental condition?*

5%
Census 1976

12 questions asked, including:
▶ *Is there anyone in the household who has any loss of sight?*
▶ *Does everyone have full use of their arms and fingers?*
▶ *Is anyone receiving treatment for nerves or any emotional condition?*
▶ *Is anyone having long-term treatment or taking any medicine or tablets for a condition or ailment?*

4%
Survey of Handicapped Persons 1981

13 questions asked, including:
▶ *Does anyone have any loss of hearing?*
▶ *Does anyone have any condition that makes them slow at learning or understanding things?*
▶ *Does anyone have any condition that restricts them in physical activities, or in doing physical work?*
▶ *Does anyone have any disfigurement or deformity?*
▶ *Does anyone ever need to be helped or supervised in doing things because of any mental illness?*

18%
Survey of Disability, Ageing and Carers 1993

4 questions asked, including:
▶ *Does the person ever need someone to help with, or be with them for, self-care activities?*
▶ *Does the person ever need someone to help with, or be with them for, communication activities?*

4%
Census 2006

CONTINUED ▶

17 questions asked, including:
▶ *Do you/does anyone in the household have anything wrong with your/their speech?*
▶ *Do you/does anyone in the household have shortness of breath or difficulty breathing?*
▶ *Do you/does anyone in the household have chronic or recurrent pain or discomfort?*
▶ *Do you/does anyone in the household have a nervous or emotional condition?*

19%
Survey of Disability, Ageing and Carers 2009

of enumeration, such as censuses, general and targeted household surveys, and interviews with key informants, have been used to estimate disability prevalence.

General data collection instruments are likely to underestimate the number of children with disabilities.[124] They typically employ a generic or filter question, such as whether anyone in the household 'is disabled', or use the same questions for all household members regardless of their age. Children in particular are likely to be overlooked in surveys that do not specifically ask about them.[125]

Targeted household surveys that specifically address the issue of child disability or include measures specifically designed to evaluate disability in children have produced more accurate results than household surveys or censuses that ask about disability in general.[126] Such surveys tend to report higher prevalence rates because

they usually include more numerous and detailed questions.

Questionnaire design

Even well-designed surveys can misreport disability if a single set of questions is applied to children across the age spectrum. The choice of questions must be tailored to a child's age in order to reflect the developmental stages and evolving capacities of children.[127] Some domains, such as self-care (e.g., washing and dressing), will not be appropriate for very young children. Given the complexity of developmental processes that take place over the first two years of life, it can be difficult to distinguish disability from variations in normal development without specialized tools or assessment.[128]

Questions designed to assess disability in the adult population are not always applicable to children, yet many survey instruments use a

FOUR CASE STUDIES (Continued)

▶ *Cambodia*

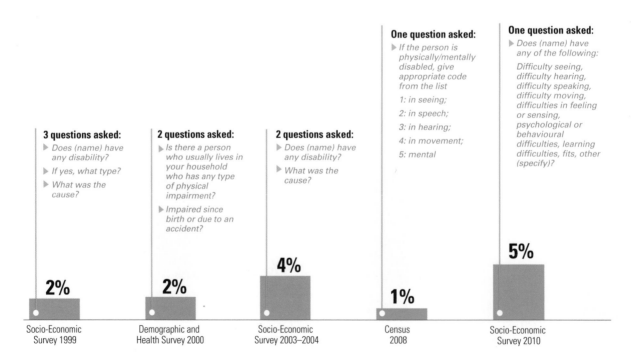

3 questions asked:
▶ Does (name) have any disability?
▶ If yes, what type?
▶ What was the cause?

2%
Socio-Economic Survey 1999

2 questions asked:
▶ Is there a person who usually lives in your household who has any type of physical impairment?
▶ Impaired since birth or due to an accident?

2%
Demographic and Health Survey 2000

2 questions asked:
▶ Does (name) have any disability?
▶ What was the cause?

4%
Socio-Economic Survey 2003–2004

One question asked:
▶ If the person is physically/mentally disabled, give appropriate code from the list
1: in seeing;
2: in speech;
3: in hearing;
4: in movement;
5: mental

1%
Census 2008

One question asked:
▶ Does (name) have any of the following:
Difficulty seeing, difficulty hearing, difficulty speaking, difficulty moving, difficulties in feeling or sensing, psychological or behavioural difficulties, learning difficulties, fits, other (specify)?

5%
Socio-Economic Survey 2010

single set of questions for both groups. Examples of questions with limited relevance to children include those about falling down or memory loss, as well as questions about tasks children may be too young to accomplish independently. Questions that link disability with an elderly population are not only irrelevant to child assessment but may also introduce a bias in the respondent's mind as to which should be considered disability and thus affect the nature and quality of the response.[129] In order to accurately assess disability in children, care must be taken to use questionnaires specifically designed for the purpose.

Many data collection instruments, including household surveys and censuses, are based on parental responses only, with caregivers normally expected to assess and report the disability status of children under their care. While parents and other caregivers are often very well placed to identify difficulties that their children may experience in performing specific tasks, their responses alone are not sufficient to diagnose disabilities or establish a prevalence of disability. Accurate assessment of disability in a child requires a thorough understanding of age-appropriate behaviours. Survey respondents may have limited knowledge of specific benchmarks used for evaluating children at each stage of development and may not be in a position to adequately detect manifestations of particular types of disability. Certain temporary conditions, such as an ear infection, may cause acute difficulties in performing certain tasks and be reported as a form of disability. At the same time, parents may overlook certain signs, or hesitate to report them, because of a lack of acceptance or stigma surrounding disability in their culture. The choice of terminology used in questionnaires can either reinforce or correct such statistically distorting and socially discriminatory phenomena.

Purpose and consequences

Efforts to measure child disability represent an opportunity to link assessment with intervention strategies. Often an assessment provides the first chance for a child with a disability to be identified and referred to or receive some form of immediate care. Unfortunately, capacity and resources for follow-up assessment and support for those children who screen positive for disability are often scarce.[130] Recognizing the critical role of early intervention, the possibility of linking screening and assessment with simple interventions should be explored, especially in low- and middle-income settings.

Data that capture the type and severity of children's disabilities as well as the barriers to the functioning and community participation of children with disabilities, when combined with relevant socio-economic indicators, help to inform decisions about how to allocate resources, eliminate barriers, design and provide services and meaningfully evaluate such interventions. For instance, data can be used to map whether income, gender or minority status affects access

▶ *Turkey*

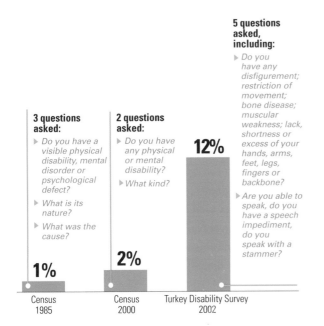

3 questions asked:
▶ *Do you have a visible physical disability, mental disorder or psychological defect?*
▶ *What is its nature?*
▶ *What was the cause?*

2 questions asked:
▶ *Do you have any physical or mental disability?*
▶ *What kind?*

5 questions asked, including:
▶ *Do you have any disfigurement; restriction of movement; bone disease; muscular weakness; lack, shortness or excess of your hands, arms, feet, legs, fingers or backbone?*
▶ *Are you able to speak, do you have a speech impediment, do you speak with a stammer?*

1% — Census 1985
2% — Census 2000
12% — Turkey Disability Survey 2002

to education, immunization or nutritional supplementation for children with disabilities. Regular monitoring makes it possible to assess whether initiatives designed to benefit children are meeting their goals.

There is a clear need to harmonize child disability measurement in order to produce estimates that are reliable, valid and internationally comparable. This would facilitate appropriate policy and programmatic responses by governments and their international partners, and thus fulfil a requirement of the Convention on the Rights of Persons with Disabilities. However, the currently fragmented state of child disability data collection is no excuse to defer meaningful action towards inclusion. As new data and analyses emerge, they will present opportunities to adapt existing and planned programmes for children with disabilities and their families.

A way forward

UNICEF is holding consultations to improve the methodology used to measure child disability in Multiple Indicator Cluster Surveys and other data collection efforts. This work is taking place in partnership with the Washington Group on Disability Statistics, national statistical offices and data collection agencies, academics, practitioners, disabled people's organizations and other stakeholders. Partnership is seen as essential to achieving a reliable and globally relevant monitoring and reporting system on child disability.

The Washington Group was established in 2001 under United Nations sponsorship to improve the quality and international comparability of disability measures. It has developed or endorsed questions on disability in adults that have been used by several countries in censuses and surveys and, in 2010, began work on developing a set of questions to measure functioning and disability among children and youth.

Work by UNICEF and the Washington Group to develop a screening tool that reflects current thinking on child functioning and disability is based on the conceptual framework of the World Health Organization's International Classification of Functioning, Disability and Health for Children and Youth. The screening tool under development focuses on limitations to activity and is intended to serve the purposes of any individual country in identifying those children at risk of social exclusion and reduced social participation in family life or education, for example. The collaborative effort aims to develop a survey module on child functioning and disability that would produce nationally comparable figures and promote the harmonization of data on child functioning and disability internationally. The module covers children aged 2–17 years and assesses speech and language, hearing, vision, learning (cognition and intellectual development), mobility and motor skills, emotions and behaviours. In addition to these relatively basic types of activity, the screening tool also includes aspects of children's ability to participate in a range of activities and social interactions. Rather than rely on a simple yes/ no approach, these aspects are to be assessed against a rating scale, to better reflect the degree of disability.

Also in development is a standardized overall methodology for a more in-depth assessment of disability in children. This will consist of data collection protocols and assessment tools, as well as a framework for the analysis of findings. Recognizing that specialists may be in short supply in some areas, a toolkit is being designed to enable teachers, community workers and other trained professionals to administer the new methodology. This will serve to strengthen local capacity to identify and assess children with disabilities.

Lessons learned

Since 1995, UNICEF has supported countries in tracking progress in key areas of children's and women's well-being through the Multiple Indicator Cluster Surveys (MICS). These nationally representative household surveys have been conducted in more than 100 low- and middle-income countries, and some have included a module designed to screen child disability. This information is now being built upon to design an improved measurement tool to assess child disability.

Disability became part of the MICS questionnaires in 2000–2001 (MICS2). Since then, data on disability have been collected through more than 50 surveys, making the MICS the largest source of comparable data on child disability in low- and middle-income countries.

The standard disability module included in MICS surveys conducted between 2000 and 2010 is the Ten Questions Screen (TQ), which was developed as part of the International Pilot Study of Severe Childhood Disability in 1984. Its design reflects how disability was understood and measured at the time.

The TQ process starts with an interview with the primary caregivers of children aged 2–9 years, who are asked to provide a personal assessment of the physical and mental development and functioning of the children under their care. Questions include whether the child appears to have difficulty hearing; whether she or he seems to understand instructions, has fits or loses consciousness; and whether she or he was delayed in sitting, standing or walking compared to other children. Response categories do not accommodate nuances, and children are classified as screening positive or negative to each question.

The validity of the Ten Questions approach has been widely tested, but results must be interpreted with caution. The TQ is a screening tool, and requires follow-up medical and developmental assessment in order to yield a reliable estimate of the number of children in a given population who have disabilities. Children who have a serious disability are very likely to screen positive, but some who screen positive may be found to have no disability on further evaluation. Some children who screen positive

may do so because of temporary health conditions that can be easily treated. Although the TQ comes with a recommendation that it be followed by an in-depth assessment, few countries have had the budgets or capacity to conduct the second-stage clinical assessment to validate results, and they have been further hampered by the lack of a standardized methodology for conducting the assessment.

Applying the Ten Questions Screen during the 2005–2006 MICS yielded a wide range of results across participating countries: The percentage of children who screened positive for disability ranged from 3 per cent in Uzbekistan to 48 per cent in the Central African Republic. It was not clear whether this variance reflected true differences among the populations sampled or additional factors. For instance, the low reported rate in Uzbekistan might have reflected, among other things, a large population of children with disabilities living in institutions, which are not subject to household surveys.

FOCUS
From screening to assessment

Child disability measurement experts agree that screening efforts, such as interviews using the Ten Questions Screen (TQ), need to be followed by in-depth assessments. These allow the initial screening results to be validated, and make possible a better understanding of the extent and nature of child disability in a country. Cambodia, Bhutan and the former Yugoslav Republic of Macedonia are three countries to have undertaken such assessments. Their experiences provide important lessons for the measurement of child disability and adaptation of methodology to local context. They also testify to the transformative power of data collection.

In Cambodia, all children who screened positive under the Ten Questions and a randomly selected 10 per cent who screened negative were referred for further assessment by a multi-professional team consisting of doctors, hearing and vision specialists, and psychologists. The team was trained and dispatched around the country to conduct child disability assessments in local health centres and similar facilities. The decision to use a mobile team of specialists was made to ensure consistent quality of screening across the country and to minimize the lag between screening and assessment.

The same sampling approach was employed in Bhutan, where the screening stage identified 3,500 children at risk, out of a sample of 11,370 children. A core team of seven professionals received two weeks of training in how to conduct the assessment. In turn, they were responsible for training another 120 health and education professionals. These professionals were then split into two groups. The first consisted of 30 supervisors recruited from among general-practice physicians, paediatricians, eye specialists, physiotherapists and special educators. The second group of 90 field surveyors and assessors was made up largely of primary school teachers and health workers.

The methodology used in the former Yugoslav Republic of Macedonia was derived from that used in Cambodia, with some adaptations shaped by the technical expertise and tools available in the local context. Two studies were conducted: a national study and one focusing on the Roma population. The assessment consisted of one hour with a physician and psychologist and a 10–15 minute assessment with an ophthalmologist and audiologist.

Experiences in all three countries demonstrate the importance of partnerships in mobilizing limited resources and ensuring high response rates, which in turn provide for robust findings. These partnerships involved government agencies and their international partners, disabled people's organizations and other civil society organizations. In the former Yugoslav Republic of Macedonia, for example, partners made it possible to conduct assessments in local kindergartens during

A strategy for intervention on behalf of children identified as having a disability should be incorporated in the assessment from the earliest stages of planning.

weekends, which was convenient for children and their families.

It is also important to adapt the composition of the core assessment team and the type of tools used to local capacity. At the time of the study, both Cambodia and Bhutan faced a shortage of qualified assessors. In Cambodia this was overcome by employing a mobile assessment team, while in Bhutan emphasis was put on training mid-level professionals. The availability of specialists cannot be taken for granted – in the case of Cambodia, the lead hearing specialist was brought in from abroad.

Assessment tools – questionnaires and tests – should be locally validated and culturally appropriate. Careful attention must be paid to language. One of the challenges encountered in Cambodia pertained to translating assessment instruments from English to Khmer, and especially finding linguistic equivalents for the concepts of impairment and disability.

The diagnostic assessment form used in the Cambodian study was revised to suit the former Yugoslav Republic of Macedonia and the local Chuturich test was utilized for the psychological component of the assessment.

Assessment leads to action

With assessment comes the potential for immediate intervention. In Cambodia, some children who screened positive for hearing impairment were found to have an ear infection or a build-up of ear wax. This limited their hearing and in many cases also their participation in school, but, once identified, their conditions were easily treated and more serious secondary infections and longer-term impairments were thus prevented.

Assessment can also aid awareness raising and spark change even while the processes of collecting and analysing data are still under way. When clinical assessments in Bhutan showed a higher incidence

of mild cognitive disabilities among children from poorer households and those whose mothers had less education, the government decided to focus on early childhood development and childcare services in rural areas, where income and education levels are lower. And in the former Yugoslav Republic of Macedonia, findings that revealed unequal access to education have spurred plans to improve school participation and fight discrimination against children with disabilities.

A strategy for intervention on behalf of children identified as having a disability should be incorporated in the assessment from the earliest stages of planning. Such a strategy should include a mapping of the available services, the development of referral protocols and the preparation of informative materials for families on how to adjust children's surroundings to enhance functioning and participation in home and community life.

From invisibility to inclusion for indigenous children with disabilities

By Olga Montufar Contreras

Olga Montufar Contreras is the president of the Step by Step Foundation, a multicultural organization that promotes the social mainstreaming of indigenous people with disabilities in Mexico. The daughter of a deaf woman, she was trained as an engineer and has a Master's degree in development and social policy.

Indigenous people have long had to live with extreme poverty, discrimination and exclusion from society and social services. Within our communities, girls and boys with disabilities are the most vulnerable and fare the worst. Their marginalization persists even though three international human rights instruments – the Convention on the Rights of Persons with Disabilities, the United Nations Declaration on the Rights of Indigenous Peoples and the Convention on the Rights of the Child – afford us a historic opportunity to address the challenges faced by indigenous children with disabilities.

I grew up with physical disability, brought on by poliomyelitis, in an indigenous community and I have seen that despite the passing of the years, the situation has changed little – if at all. Today, just as when I was little, children with disabilities are ostracized and their rejection by the community extends to parents and siblings, because the disability is considered as divine punishment and a child with a disability is seen as a liability for the community. Now as then, it is extremely difficult to access services and meet the additional expenses generated by a family member with a disability. Grinding poverty, geographic isolation and political marginalization sustain and are reinforced by discrimination and prejudice. The consequences can be severe: Many mothers, weak and lacking the power to change things, remain silent about our condition or resort to infanticide.

My family is one of few that show solidarity towards their sons and daughters who have disabilities. In our case, this was partly because we had migrated to the city and could obtain housing closer to services. But in the desperate circumstances under which most of our families live, violations of our human rights are common and fail to spark concern among others. This is why it is necessary to mobilize the will and resources to take meaningful action.

One of the most pressing problems to be addressed is the lack of data on indigenous communities in general and our children with disabilities in particular. Data can be hard to gather: Indigenous

Data can be hard to gather: Indigenous households can be scattered, often in remote areas. There might not be enough interviewers who speak indigenous languages.

households can be scattered, often in remote areas. There might not be enough interviewers who speak indigenous languages. In many cases, families deny our existence to the people who conduct surveys. Even where parents acknowledge and want to support us, they can end up providing insufficient information because they have little of it to begin with, as there are few if any screening or diagnostic services. Because the lack of such services contributes to our invisibility, it is a threat to our physical and intellectual condition. Adding to the problems, girls and boys with disabilities often go unregistered at birth, and this is one of the main obstacles to the recognition of our citizenship and our right to public services. This should motivate research into disability among indigenous populations – and the results can serve as a starting point for developing public policies and services that address our needs and guarantee our rights.

The lack of access to the mainstream education system must also be corrected. The inclusion of indigenous children with disabilities is required under the Convention on the Rights of Persons with Disabilities, but in practice, inclusion is often beyond the reach of children from our communities: The distances they must travel daily to get to school can be prohibitive. Few schools have the minimum services and facilities to make learning accessible. And again, traditional community practices contribute to the lack of educational inclusion. Clan chiefs determine the roles of boys and girls from birth and if a child has a disability, it is generally thought that sending her or him to school is a waste of time as well as an undue economic burden on the family. Many people think that those of us who have a disability are broken objects that will not be useful even if we are patched up. The situation is even worse for girls, as it is harder for us to obtain permission to study than it is for boys with disabilities.

Even when the community's stigmas are overcome and we manage to attend school, our teachers face two obstacles: insufficient knowledge of indigenous languages and inadequate teacher training in inclusive education. This lack of training makes it more difficult to include children with disabilities. As a consequence, we are forced to rely on the goodwill of individual teachers to accept the challenge of including indigenous children with disabilities in their classrooms.

In Mexico as elsewhere, governments, international agencies and community groups are striving to eliminate the gap between what is ideal and what is currently possible. We must continue to work together to ensure more just and equitable childhoods, to transform the lives of indigenous girls and boys with disabilities with hope and opportunity – so they, too, can be free to let their dreams take flight.

Nguyen, who has autism, attends a class specifically tailored to his needs at the Da Nang Inclusive Education Resource Centre in Viet Nam. Such centres were set up to help children prepare for admission to inclusive mainstream schools. © UNICEF/Viet Nam/2012/Bisin

CHAPTER 7

AN AGENDA FOR ACTION

The nations of the world have repeatedly affirmed their commitment to building more inclusive societies. As a result, the situation of many children with disabilities and their families has improved.

Progress has varied between and within countries, however. Too many children with disabilities continue to face barriers to their participation in the civic, social and cultural affairs of their communities. This is true in situations that may be considered normal as well as during humanitarian crises. The following recommendations apply equally urgently in humanitarian situations, and their application in that context is detailed in Chapter 5. Realizing the promise of equity through inclusion will require action in the areas and by the actors identified below and throughout this report.

Ratify and implement the Conventions

The Convention on the Rights of Persons with Disabilities (CRPD) and the Convention on the Rights of the Child (CRC) provide detailed guidance for the development of inclusive societies. As this year began, 127 countries and the European Union had ratified the CRPD and 193 had ratified the CRC. They have thus shown a commitment to all their citizens. Others have yet to join the global movement that these countries represent.

Ratification alone will not be enough. The process of honouring commitments in practice will require effort on the part of national governments, local authorities, employers, disabled people's organizations and parents' associations. In addition, international organizations and donors can align their assistance with these international instruments. Making good on the promises of the Conventions will require not only diligent enforcement but also rigorous monitoring and an unflagging commitment by all to accountability and adaptation.

Fight discrimination

Discrimination lies at the root of many of the challenges confronted by children with disabilities and their families. The principles of equal rights and non-discrimination should be reflected in law and policy and need to be complemented by efforts to enhance awareness of disability among the general public, starting with those who provide essential services for children in such fields as health, education and protection. To this end, international agencies and their government and community partners can increase efforts to provide officials and public servants at all levels of seniority with a deeper understanding of the rights, capacities and challenges of children with disabilities so that policymakers and service providers are able to prevail against prejudice – be it society's or their own.

When communities are accepting of disability as part of human diversity, when generic systems like education and recreation are available and inclusive, and when parents are not forced to carry the entire additional costs associated with disability, the families of children with disabilities can cope and thrive much like other families. Parents' organizations can play a pivotal role and should be reinforced so that children with disabilities are valued, cherished and supported by their families and communities.

States parties to the CRPD and the United Nations and its agencies have committed themselves to conducting awareness-raising campaigns to change attitudes towards children with disabilities and their families. Among other things, this will involve highlighting their abilities and capacities, and promoting community engagement with and by children with disabilities. States parties are also required to provide information to families on how to avoid, recognize and report instances of exploitation, violence and abuse.

Discrimination on the grounds of disability is a form of oppression. The establishment of a clear, legal entitlement to protection from

Convention on the Rights of Persons with Disabilities and Optional Protocol: Signatures and ratifications

155	**128**	**91**	**76**	**27**
COUNTRIES HAVE **SIGNED THE CONVENTION***	COUNTRIES HAVE **RATIFIED THE CONVENTION***	COUNTRIES HAVE **SIGNED THE PROTOCOL**	COUNTRIES HAVE **RATIFIED THE PROTOCOL**	COUNTRIES HAVE **NOT SIGNED**

●● Afghanistan
●● Albania
●●● Algeria
●● Andorra
● Angola
●● Antigua and Barbuda
●●●● Argentina
●●● Armenia
●●● Australia
●●●● Austria
●●●● Azerbaijan
● Bahamas
●● Bahrain
●●● Bangladesh
● Barbados
● Belarus
●●●● Belgium
●● Belize
●●●● Benin
● Bhutan

●●●● Bolivia (Plurinational State of)
●●●● Bosnia and Herzegovina
● Botswana
●●●● Brazil
● Brunei Darussalam
●●● Bulgaria
●●●● Burkina Faso
●● Burundi
●●● Cambodia
●● Cameroon
●● Canada
●● Cape Verde
●● Central African Republic
●● Chad
●●●● Chile
●● China
●● Colombia
● Comoros
●● Congo
●● Cook Islands

●●●● Costa Rica
●● Côte d'Ivoire
●●●● Croatia
●● Cuba
●●●● Cyprus
●●● Czech Republic
● Democratic People's Republic of Korea
● Democratic Republic of the Congo
●● Denmark
●● Djibouti
●●● Dominica
●●●● Dominican Republic
●●●● Ecuador
●● Egypt
●●●● El Salvador
● Equatorial Guinea
● Eritrea
●●● Estonia

●● Ethiopia
●● Fiji
●● Finland
●●●● France
●●● Gabon
● Gambia
●● Georgia
●●●● Germany
●●● Ghana
●●●● Greece
● Grenada
●●● Guatemala
●●●● Guinea
● Guinea-Bissau
● Guyana
●● Haiti
●●●● Honduras
●●●● Hungary
●● Iceland
●● India

*Includes the European Union.
Source: UN Enable; United Nations Treaty Collection. For notes on terms used, see p.154.

discrimination is vital in reducing the vulnerability of children with disabilities. Legislation is made more meaningful when children with disabilities are informed of their right to protection from discrimination and are shown how to exercise this right. Where legislation banning discrimination on the basis of disability does not exist, disabled people's organizations and civil society as a whole will continue to have a crucial role to play in pressing for such laws – as they do in providing services and promoting transparency and accountability.

Dismantle barriers to inclusion

All children's environments – early childhood centres, schools, health facilities, public transport, playgrounds and so on – can be built to facilitate access and encourage the participation of children with disabilities alongside their peers. Universal design – the idea that all products, built environments, programmes and services should be usable to the greatest extent possible by all people, regardless of their ability, age or social status – should be applied in the construction of

(continued on p. 80)

● Signed Convention   ● Ratified Convention   ● Signed Protocol   ● Ratified Protocol   ● Not signed

Indonesia	Mauritius	Romania
Iran (Islamic Republic of)	Mexico	Russian Federation
Iraq	Micronesia (Federated States of)	Rwanda
Ireland	Monaco	Saint Kitts and Nevis
Israel	Mongolia	Saint Lucia
Italy	Montenegro	Saint Vincent and the Grenadines
Jamaica	Morocco	Samoa
Japan	Mozambique	San Marino
Jordan	Myanmar	Sao Tome and Principe
Kazakhstan	Namibia	Saudi Arabia
Kenya	Nauru	Senegal
Kiribati	Nepal	Serbia
Kuwait	Netherlands	Seychelles
Kyrgyzstan	New Zealand	Sierra Leone
Lao People's Democratic Republic	Nicaragua	Singapore
Latvia	Niger	Slovakia
Lebanon	Nigeria	Slovenia
Lesotho	Niue	Solomon Islands
Liberia	Norway	Somalia
Libya	Oman	South Africa
Liechtenstein	Pakistan	South Sudan
Lithuania	Palau	Spain
Luxembourg	Panama	Sri Lanka
Madagascar	Papua New Guinea	Sudan
Malawi	Paraguay	Suriname
Malaysia	Peru	Swaziland
Maldives	Philippines	Sweden
Mali	Poland	Switzerland
Malta	Portugal	Syrian Arab Republic
Marshall Islands	Qatar	Tajikistan
Mauritania	Republic of Korea	Thailand
	Republic of Moldova	

The former Yugoslav Republic of Macedonia
Timor-Leste
Togo
Tonga
Trinidad and Tobago
Tunisia
Turkey
Turkmenistan
Tuvalu
Uganda
Ukraine
United Arab Emirates
United Kingdom
United Republic of Tanzania
United States
Uruguay
Uzbekistan
Vanuatu
Venezuela (Bolivarian Republic of)
Viet Nam
Yemen
Zambia
Zimbabwe

Open the doors to education – and employment

By Ivory Duncan

Born in 1991, Ivory Duncan is pursuing a degree in Communications Studies from the University of Guyana. She advocates for the rights of youth with disabilities through the Leonard Cheshire Disability Young Voices network and volunteers at the National Commission on Disability in Guyana.

Like me, countless other young people with disabilities are striving towards a future that cannot be taken for granted. Will we overcome the physical and financial barriers to higher education? If we make it through to graduation from university or vocational school, what jobs await us? Will we have equal opportunity, or face discrimination? Will we get the chance to prove ourselves in the competitive world of employment? And if not, how are we to be full citizens and producers, members of society in equal standing with those who do not have disabilities?

I lost my right leg following a traffic accident when I was 15 years old. My parents, people of humble means, persevere in helping to meet my expenses so I can pursue a university education, even as they try to raise two other children with disabilities. Life can be hard, but I am grateful for my good fortune: I have a loving family and am working to accomplish my dream of getting a degree and having a career.

Fulfilling our dreams takes effort not required of young people without disabilities. To get from home to the university, I have no option but to go by taxi because the only other way would be to take a boat or cross the Demerara Harbour Bridge, neither of which I can do in my wheelchair. Paying for a taxi is expensive, and my parents struggle to make ends meet. Attending university is also a physical challenge. It is difficult making my way to classes because the classrooms are often not accessible to wheelchair users. There are long flights of stairs, and when I finally manage to get to a class, I am tired and frustrated and find it hard to focus on the lectures. But I am trying because I know it is better to try and fail than to fail to try.

The challenges begin long before reaching higher education. Children with disabilities can easily become shut-ins, hidden away from society and unable to attend school or make a meaningful contribution to society. They should be encouraged to attend mainstream schools if possible, while special schools that include vocational training and support services should also be available. Special-needs schools should offer a

I would like to be confident that when I graduate and look for a job, I will not be discriminated against because of my disability, but instead be recognized for my abilities, qualifications and potential.

complete curriculum for students with disabilities, to help to develop their minds and give them opportunities to achieve academic excellence. Many children and young people with disabilities want to go on to higher education, so it is very important that they be included in schools and other learning institutions and given the same options as other students in terms of choosing courses and activities. It is up to educational institutions and governments to accommodate and support students like me, so that we are able to pursue the education we need to achieve whatever goals we may have.

Accommodating children and young people with disabilities includes things like adjusting the entry requirements and criteria for passing, and making sure that learning materials, examinations and class schedules take our needs into account. Teachers need to be properly trained and given a chance to pursue additional overseas instruction in order to improve the quality of education. Schools should teach Braille and other forms of communication where necessary, and there is also a great need

for special equipment, which many schools in Guyana do not have. Making educational institutions disability-friendly also means setting up facilities and transportation services that persons with disabilities can use; there should be ramps for wheelchair users, accessible toilets and elevators for people who cannot take the stairs. All aspects and all levels of education, from elementary school to university, need to be made accessible.

The ministries for education and public service should also work together to assist academically inclined students with disabilities who wish to go beyond secondary school. Because financial difficulties are a major reason why young people with disabilities are unable to continue their education, this assistance should include grants, loans and scholarships.

Governments also need to make sure that education opens the same doors for students with disabilities as for everybody else. My parents have put in a lot of effort and more money than they can really afford to help me to get

through school and to university – and now I am working hard, in spite of the challenges, to come to classes and learn, because I know that is what I need to do to get the best out of life. So I would also like to be confident that when I graduate and look for a job, I will not be discriminated against because of my disability, but instead be recognized for my abilities, qualifications and potential. As a young person with a disability who has worked hard to educate herself, I deserve as much as anyone else the opportunity to fulfill my dreams, make a good living for myself and contribute to our society.

(continued from p. 77)

public and private infrastructure. When children interact and understand each other across levels of ability, they all benefit.

The principles of universal design also apply to the development of inclusive school curricula and vocational training programmes as well as child protection laws, policies and services. Children need access to systems designed to equip them with the educational and life skills to see them into and through their adult years, and those that protect them from neglect, abuse and violence on their way to adulthood. If protection fails, they need to be able to make complaints and seek justice. Governments have the decisive role to play in introducing and implementing the legislative, administrative and educational measures necessary to protect children with disabilities from all forms of exploitation, violence and abuse in all settings. It is not appropriate to create separate systems for children with disabilities – the goal must be inclusive, high-quality child protection mechanisms suitable for and accessible to all children. One such mechanism is birth registration. Although not a guarantee in itself, it is an essential element of protection. Efforts to register children with disabilities – and thereby render them visible – deserve priority.

End institutionalization

All too often, invisibility and abuse are the fate of children and adolescents with disabilities who are confined to institutions. Facilities are poor substitutes for a nurturing home life even if they are well run, responsive to children's needs and subject to inspection. Immediate measures to reduce overreliance on institutions could include a moratorium on new admissions. This should be accompanied by the promotion of and increased support for family-based care and community-based rehabilitation. Additionally, there is a need for broader measures that reduce the pressure for children to be sent away in the first place. These include the development of public services, schools and health systems accessible and responsive to children with disabilities and their families.

Children with hearing and visual impairments learn the craft of pottery at an orphanage in Moscow Oblast, Russian Federation. © UNICEF/RUSS/2011/Kochineva

Support families

The CRC states that children should grow up in a family environment. It follows that the families of children and adolescents with disabilities must be adequately supported to provide the best possible environment and quality of life for their children. Support for families and caregivers – subsidized day care, for example, or by grants to offset the increased costs and reduced income that come with caring for a child with a disability – can prove critical in reducing the pressure to admit children with disabilities to institutions in the first place. Such support can also improve the prospects for children who return to the community after living in an institution.

Disability in the family is often associated with higher costs of living and lost opportunities to earn income, and thus may increase the risk of becoming or remaining poor. Children with disabilities who live in poverty can find it especially difficult to obtain such services as rehabilitation and assistive technology. To leave them and their families to fend for themselves would be to dangle the promise of inclusion just beyond their reach.

Social policies should take into account the monetary and time costs associated with disability. These costs can be offset with social grants, subsidies for transportation or funding for personal assistants or respite care. Cash benefits are easier to administer and more flexible at meeting the particular needs of children with disabilities and their families. They also respect the decision-making rights of parents and children. Where cash transfer programmes for families living in difficult circumstances already exist, they can be adapted so that the families of children with disabilities are not unintentionally left out or offered inadequate support. These recommendations would be urgent under any circumstances but are especially so in these straitened times: Aid and social budgets are being cut, unemployment remains high, goods and services grow increasingly expensive. Families around the world face an increased risk of poverty.

Move beyond minimum standards

Existing supports and services should be continuously assessed with a view to achieving the best possible quality. The aim must be to move beyond minimum standards. Attention needs to be focused on serving the individual child with a disability as well as on transforming entire systems or societies. The ongoing involvement of children with disabilities and their families in evaluating services will help to guarantee adequate and appropriate provision as children grow and their needs change. The importance of this participation cannot be overstated. Children and young people with disabilities are among the most authoritative sources of information on what they need and whether their needs are being met.

Coordinate services to support the child

Because the effects of disability cut across sectors, services can be coordinated to take into account the full range of challenges confronting children with disabilities and their families. A coordinated programme of early intervention across the health, education and welfare sectors would help to promote the early identification and management of childhood disabilities. Across all sectors, early childhood interventions should be strengthened. Studies have shown that gains in functional capacity can be largest when interventions occur early in a child's development. When barriers are removed earlier in life, the compounding effect of the multiple barriers faced by children with disabilities is lessened. As children advance through their early years, their ability to function can be enhanced through rehabilitation. Improvements in ability will have greater impact if school systems are willing and able to accept them and meet their educational needs. Moreover, acquiring an education would be more meaningful if there were also inclusive school-to-work transition programmes and economy-wide efforts to promote the employment of people with disabilities.

(continued on p. 84)

End the 'book famine' with better technology, attitudes and copyright law

By Kartik Sawhney

Kartik Sawhney is a national-award-winning high school student in New Delhi, India. He is active in advocating for the rights of persons with disabilities and is a member of the Leonard Cheshire Disability Young Voices network.

Visually impaired people face what at least one writer has called a 'book famine'. This is not news to us: The visually challenged and print-impaired have been struggling for accessibility for a long time. 'Accessibility' is an all-encompassing term that includes access to the physical environment, transportation, information and communication technology, education and other facilities. In my view, it is crucial that accessible material be readily available. The urgency is even greater when we consider the situation in developing nations.

When I conducted an informal survey of nearly 60 visually challenged students in primary and secondary grades in mainstream schools in India, I found that less than 20 per cent of them had access to material in their preferred format, and less than 35 per cent to material in any format. Being visually challenged, I've had several experiences where lack of accessibility has impeded me from availing myself of the same opportunities as others. The effort needed to make reading material acces-

sible is monumental. Thanks to advances in optical character recognition (OCR) – a technology that converts printed, handwritten or typewritten text into machine-encoded text, making it possible for computerized voices to read the text aloud – there has been some improvement. However, technical content remains inaccessible. I spend around two hours a day typing out the printed material from my science and math classes, for example, because OCR software cannot read diagrams and special symbols with sufficient accuracy. The plight of rural students is even worse: They depend on humans to read volumes of information aloud to them. For instance, my friends in a small village have no option but to rely completely on volunteers who come by weekly.

Even much online content cannot be read by standard screen reading utilities, primarily as a result of the varying standards and platforms used by authors and designers. Although the World Wide Web Consortium (W3C) has produced guidelines for websites to follow in order to ensure a wonderful experience for all, this vision is far from achieved. I come across websites daily that are not W3C-standard compliant. This calls for greater scrutiny by not only governments, but also civil society, academia and international organizations. The Government of India has taken steps to bring about a positive change on this front; it now offers a National Award for the Empowerment of Persons with Disabilities in the category of 'Best Accessible Website'. This incentive drives organizations to make their websites accessible. If applied by enough countries, such measures could usher in a revolution.

This is not just a matter for governments: Anyone can make a positive difference. I recall a historic achievement made in 2011 by a group of visually challenged youth in Bangalore, India. Preparing for the entrance exams to prestigious business schools in the country, they contacted the well-known educational publisher Pearson Education and requested that they publish their material in an accessible format. Pearson agreed and has since then made much of

their material available for the visually challenged. However, not all publishers are as sensitive and understanding. Lack of awareness and insensitivity are two of the biggest challenges. Unless – until – there is a paradigm shift in attitudes towards people who are visually challenged, it will be difficult to overcome the challenges that plague the print-impaired community today.

But there is another barrier to access – a political and legal, not technical or attitudinal, one. Currently, only 57 countries have amended their copyright laws to provide concessions for people with visual impairments. Thus, providing e-books for the visually challenged is unfortunately still considered an infringement of copyright in many countries – and this prevents local publishers from helping out within the community. For a young student, these facts are extremely disturbing: Since most countries have pledged to provide maximum support and cooperation for the welfare and empowerment of persons with disabilities, there turns out to be a vast difference between the laws on paper and

actual, real-world implementation. The need of the hour is to translate words into action. I suggest an international body to oversee implementation of international disability legislation, to the extent that it does not violate national sovereignty.

Copyright law must be amended. I hope that countries will continue to work on the legal framework, and that the United Nations will take action towards a referendum on this issue. With concerted effort, I believe we will secure this inalienable right for all people with disabilities, everywhere: the right to access all material!

(continued from p. 81)

Involve children with disabilities in making decisions

Children and adolescents with disabilities belong at the centre of efforts to build inclusive societies – not just as beneficiaries, but as agents of change. States parties to the CRPD have affirmed the right of children with disabilities to express their views freely on all matters affecting them. In so doing, governments have reaffirmed the principles of the CRC and have obligated themselves to consult children with disabilities when developing and implementing legislation and policies that concern them. This is in States' interest, for children and young people with disabilities can enrich policymaking and service provision with their daily experiences and are uniquely qualified to provide information on whether their needs are being met and their contributions utilized across the full spectrum of issues and interventions: from health and nutrition to sexual and reproductive health, education and services for the transition to adulthood.

The right to be heard applies to all children, regardless of type or degree of disability, and even children with profound disabilities can be supported to express their choices and desires. A child who is able to express herself or himself is a child who is much less likely to be abused or exploited. Conversely, abuse and exploitation thrive where children lack the means to challenge their oppression. Participation is especially important for such marginalized groups as children who live in institutions.

To recognize that children and adolescents with disabilities are the holders of rights, not the recipients of charity, is not to eliminate the need for appropriate rehabilitation, medical treatment or aids and appliances. It does mean, however, that children's rights, perspectives and choices must be respected. In turn, this will entail decision-makers communicating in ways and by means that are easily accessed and used by children with disabilities, so their views can be incorporated in the

Children play netball at Ojwina Primary School in Lira, Uganda. © UNICEF/UGDA2012-00120/Sibiloni

Six-year-old Nemanja (far left) sits with classmates in Novi Sad, Serbia. His primary school was the first to integrate children with disabilities under a law aimed at reducing institutionalization. © UNICEF/HQ2011-1156/Holt

design, implementation and evaluation of policies and services.

Global promise, local test

In order to fulfil the promises of the CRPD and CRC, international agencies and donors and their national and local partners can include children with disabilities in the objectives, targets and monitoring indicators of all development programmes. Reliable and objective data are important to assist in planning and resource allocation, and to place children with disabilities more clearly on the development agenda. The necessary statistical work will take time but would be given vital impetus were international donors to promote a concerted global research agenda on disability. In the meanwhile, planning and programming will have to continue; denying or delaying services to children with disabilities because more data are needed would be unacceptable. Rather, plans, programmes and budgets can be designed to allow for modifications as additional information is made available.

The ultimate proof of all global and national efforts will be local, the test being whether every child with a disability enjoys her or his rights – including access to services, support and opportunities – on a par with other children, even in the most remote settings and the most deprived circumstances.

Children with disabilities and universal human rights

By Lenín Voltaire Moreno Garcés

Lenín Voltaire Moreno Garcés, Vice-President of the Republic of Ecuador from 2007 until May 2013, was Latin America's only holder of high office with a physical disability. The statistics in this essay were drawn from national programme documents.

There can be no such thing as the universal exercise of human rights unless these rights are enjoyed by all people – including the most vulnerable. Spurred by this conviction, the Office of the Vice-President of the Republic of Ecuador has focused on ascertaining and improving the situation of people with disabilities – starting with children.

Beginning in July 2009, we conducted surveys throughout Ecuador under a project known as the Manuela Espejo Solidarity Mission. By visiting 1,286,331 households in the country's 24 provinces and 221 cantons, we were able to identify 293,743 persons with disabilities. Of this total, some 24 per cent had intellectual disabilities and the remaining 76 per cent had physical or sensory disabilities. We estimated the prevalence of major disabilities at over 2 per cent of the national population, as measured by the 2010 census.

We found that about 55,000 boys and girls under 18 years of age had disabilities, accounting for about 19 per cent of all persons with disabilities in Ecuador. As of June 2012, these children had received 87,629 technical assistance donations consisting of such items as wheelchairs, walkers, anti-bedsore mattresses, walking sticks, hearing aids and visual kits, depending on the need or needs identified. Three new prosthetics shops were established and expected to deliver 1,960 prosthetic and orthopaedic devices to the country's children in 2012 alone.

We also found that many families live in extremely difficult circumstances. The care of children with severe disabilities can be particularly expensive, forcing mothers to abandon them in order to earn money. So the Joaquín Gallegos Lara Subsidy was established and provides the equivalent of US$240 per month in financial assistance to the primary caregiver of a child or adult with a disability. Training in first-aid services, hygiene and rehabilitation is also provided. Ecuador is thus recognizing, for the first time, the labour of love performed by families who care for persons with disabilities. As of June 2012, the subsidies had benefited 6,585 children, 43 per cent of them girls.

In addition to support, our approach attaches importance

> *We [in government] must understand that disability is not a problem but rather a circumstance. . . . [We must] assist our youngest citizens in entering the mainstream.*

to early detection and intervention. By 2012, some 1.1 million children under age 9 had been screened to detect hearing impairments and promote early intervention. To this end, 1,401 diagnostic and aural screening service units were set up in the Ministry of Public Health network; 1,500 health professionals were trained; 30 speech therapy service units were established; and 1,508 hearing aids were provided.

In 2013, 714,000 children will have been screened at 24 impaired-sight service centres and we expect that some 2,500 children will receive aids to help them improve their vision or function with blindness.

We have also set up a national programme to screen newborns for congenital conditions that can be treated. By December 2011, this effort, known as 'Right Foot Forward: The Footprint of the Future', had screened 98,034 newborns and found 30 cases of congenital hypothyroidism, galactosaemia, congenital adrenal hyperplasia or phenylketonuria. Each of these 30 girls and boys has received treatment for conditions that, if left untreated in the first few weeks or

months of life, place children at increased risk of low cognition, speech impairment and tremors, among other impairments.

Beyond bio-social support and early intervention, we are pursuing social and cultural inclusion. Under the banner of 'An Ecuador of Joy and Solidarity', 70,000 children and young people with and without disabilities have participated in inclusive fairs held throughout the country. Play and games are being promoted as means of creating space for integration. At these fairs, persons with disabilities take the lead as instructors in physical exercise, arts and crafts, games and storytelling.

Some 7,700 marginalized or vulnerable children and young people are advancing their personal development, self-esteem and social integration through such pursuits as dance, music, painting and literature. They include 1,100 children and young people who are involved in the Social Circus, an initiative run in collaboration with the Canadian entertainment company Cirque du Soleil.

These innovations have awakened interest among Ecuador's neighbours, a number of whom

are seeking to learn more about our experience. The first thing to note is that there is no time to lose. No child should have to wait for the services and supports that are rightfully hers or his, but this is especially the case for children with disabilities, because their vulnerability can increase with age.

We in government must tackle the tasks at hand without delay. We must understand that disability is not a problem but rather a circumstance. It is up to us, regardless of the place or the role we have to play, to assist our youngest citizens in entering the mainstream. We cannot even dream of a country with social justice, one that abides by the principles of good living, unless we guarantee that persons with disabilities, especially children and adolescents, can fully exercise their rights.

Disability does not mean incapability: It is the wonderful diversity that enriches humankind.

REFERENCES

Chapter 1 Introduction

1 World Health Organization, 'Community-based Rehabilitation Guidelines', WHO, Geneva, 2010, <www.who.int/disabilities/cbr/guidelines/en/index.html>, accessed 31 January 2013.

2 Groce, Nora Ellen, 'Adolescents and Youth with Disabilities: Issues and challenges', *Asia Pacific Disability Rehabilitation Journal*, vol. 15, no. 2, July 2004, pp. 13–32.

3 Committee on the Rights of the Child, Convention on the Rights of the Child General Comment No. 9 (2006): The rights of children with disabilities, CRC/C/GC/9, Geneva, 27 February 2007, pp. 2, 9; Jones, Lisa, et al., 'Prevalence and Risk of Violence against Children with Disabilities: A systematic review and meta-analysis of observational studies', *The Lancet*, vol. 380, no. 9845, 8 September 2012, pp. 899–907; World Health Organization and the World Bank, *World Report on Disability*, WHO, Geneva, 2011, p. 59.

BOX: On the numbers

World Health Organization, *The Global Burden of Disease: 2004 update*, WHO, Geneva, 2008; United Nations, Department of Economic and Social Affairs, Population Division, *World Population Prospects: The 2010 revision*, United Nations, New York, 2011.

Chapter 2 Fundamentals of inclusion

4 Bruce Marks, Susan, 'Reducing Prejudice against Children with Disabilities in Inclusive Settings', *International Journal of Disability, Development and Education*, vol. 44, no. 2, 1997, pp. 119–120.

5 Contact a Family, 'What Makes My Family Stronger: A report into what makes families with disabled children stronger – socially, emotionally and practically', London, May 2009, <http://89.16.177.37/professionals/research/researchandreports.html>, accessed 31 January 2013.

6 United Kingdom Government, 'The Consolidated 3rd and 4th Periodic Report to UN Committee on the Rights of the Child', United Kingdom, July 2007, p. 31, <www.ofmdfmni.gov.uk/uk_uncrc-2.pdf>, accessed 31 January 2013.

7 D'Aiglepierre, Rohen, Focus Development Association and United Nations Children's Fund, 'Exclusion Scolaire et Moyens D'Inclusion au Cycle Primaire a Madagascar', February 2012, p. 67, <www.unicef.org/madagascar/EXCLUSION-INCLUSIONweb.pdf>, accessed 31 January 2013.

8 TNS and United Nations Children's Fund, 'Research Report on Children with Disabilities and their Families in Da Nang: Knowledge – attitudes – practices', Viet Nam, November 2009, p. 14.

9 World Health Organization and the World Bank, *World Report on Disability*, 2011, p. 3.

10 Maras, Pam, and Rupert Brown, 'Effects of Contact on Children's Attitudes Towards Disability: A longitudinal study', *Journal of Applied Social Psychology*, vol. 26, no. 23, December 1996, pp. 2113–2134, cited in Maras, Pam, and Rupert Brown, 'Effects of Different Forms of School Contact on Children's Attitudes toward Disabled and Non-Disabled Peers', *British Journal of Educational Psychology*, vol. 70, no. 3, September 2000, p. 339.

11 Barg, Carolyn J., et al., 'Physical Disability, Stigma, and Physical Activity in Children', *International Journal of Disability, Development and Education*, vol. 57, no. 4, December 2010, p. 378.

12 International Disability in Sport Working Group and the United Nations Office of the Special Advisor to the Secretary-General on Sport for Development and Peace, 'Sport in the United Nations Convention on the Rights of Persons with Disabilities', IDSWG, Northeastern University, Boston, 2007.

13 Convention on the Rights of Persons with Disabilities (CRPD) Preamble.

14 World Health Organization and the World Bank, *World Report on Disability*, 2011, p. 43.

15 Mont, Daniel M., and Nguyen Viet Cuong, 'Disability and Poverty in Vietnam', *World Bank Economic Review*, vol. 25, no. 2, 2011, pp. 323–359.

16 Buckup, Sebastian, 'The Price of Exclusion: The economic consequences of excluding people with disabilities from the world of work', International Labour Office Employment Working Paper No. 43, International Labour Organization, Geneva, 2009.

17 Mitra, Sophie, Aleksandra Posarac and Brandon Vick, 'Disability and Poverty in Developing Countries: A snapshot from the World Health Survey', Social Protection Discussion Paper No. 1109, The World Bank, Washington, D.C., April 2011.

18 Groce, Nora, et al., 'Disability and Poverty: The need for a more nuanced understanding of implications for development policy and practice', *Third World Quarterly*, vol. 32, no. 8, 2011, pp. 1493–1513.

19 Loeb, M. E., and Arne H. Eide, eds., 'Living Conditions among People with Activity Limitations in Malawi: A national representative study', SINTEF Health Research, Oslo, 26 August 2004, <www.safod.com/LCMalawi.pdf>, accessed 31 January 2013; Hoogeveen, Johannes G., 'Measuring Welfare for Small but Vulnerable Groups: Poverty and disability in Uganda', *Journal of African Economies*, vol. 14, no. 4, 1 August 2005, pp. 603–631.

20 World Health Organization and the World Bank, *World Report on Disability*, 2011, pp. 10, 39–40.

21 Gertler, Paul J., and Lia C. Fernald, 'The Medium Term Impact of *Oportunidades* on Child Development in Rural Areas', Instituto Nacional de Salud Pública, Cuernavaca, Mexico, 30 November 2004; Behrman, Jere R., and John Hoddinott, 'Programme Evaluation with Unobserved Heterogeneity and Selective Implementation: The Mexican *PROGRESA* impact on child nutrition', *Oxford Bulletin of Economics and Statistics*, vol. 67, no. 4, August 2005, pp. 547–569; Hoddinott, John, and Emmanuel Skoufias, 'The Impact of PROGRESA on Food Consumption', *Economic Development and Cultural Change*, vol. 53, no. 1, October 2004, pp. 37–61; Maluccio, John A., et al., 'The Impact of an Experimental Nutritional Intervention in Childhood on Education among Guatemalan Adults', Food Consumption and Nutrition Division Discussion Paper 207, International Food Policy Research Institute, Washington, D.C., June 2006.

22 Groce, Nora, et al., 'Poverty and Disability: A critical review of the literature in low and middle-income countries', Working Paper Series No. 16, Leonard Cheshire Disability and Inclusive Development Centre, University College London, London, September 2011.

23 Office of the United Nations High Commissioner for Human Rights, Convention on the Rights of the Child, article 23.

24 World Health Organization, 'Community-Based Rehabilitation', WHO, Geneva, <www.who.int/disabilities/cbr/en/>, accessed 31 January 2013.

25 Allen-Leigh, Betania, et al., *Iniciativa Evaluation: Evaluación externa de diseño y resultados del proyecto piloto 'Atención Integral a Niños y Niñas con Discapacidad en Comunidades Rurales en Oaxaca'*, Instituto Nacional de Salud Pública, Cuernavaca, Mexico, 2010, as cited in Secretariat for the Convention on the Rights of Persons with Disabilities (SCRPD), 'Compilation of best practices for including persons with disabilities in all aspects of development efforts', Working document in response to General Assembly Resolution A/65/186 and with the intention of facilitating the discussions leading up to the envisaged High Level Meeting on disability and development at the 67th session of the General Assembly in 2012.

26 Municipalities of Santa Maria Guienagati, San Martín Peras, Coicoyan de las Flores and San José Tanago.

27 Allen-Leigh, Betania, et al., *Iniciativa Evaluation: Evaluación externa de diseño y resultados del proyecto piloto 'Atención Integral a Niños y Niñas con Discapacidad en Comunidades Rurales en Oaxaca'*, 2010.

28 World Health Organization, 'Assistive Devices/Technologies: What WHO is doing', WHO, Geneva, <www.who.int/disabilities/technology/activities/en/#>, accessed 31 January 2013.

29 Borg, Johan, Anna Lindström and Stig Larsson,'Assistive Technology in Developing Countries: National and international responsibilities to implement the Convention on the Rights of Persons with Disabilities', *The Lancet*, vol. 374, no. 9704, 28 November 2009, pp. 1863–1865.

30 François, Isabelle, et al., 'Causes of Locomotor Disability and Need for Orthopaedic Devices in a Heavily Mined Taliban-Controlled Province of Afghanistan: Issues and challenges for public health managers', *Tropical Medicine & International Health*, vol. 3, no. 5, May 1998, pp. 391–396; Matsen, S. L., 'A Closer Look at Amputees in Vietnam: A field survey of Vietnamese using prostheses', *Prosthetics and Orthotics International*, vol. 23, no. 2, August 1999, pp. 93–101; May-Teerink, Teresa Lynn, 'A Survey of Rehabilitative Services and People Coping with Physical Disabilities in Uganda, East Africa', pp. 311–316; Bigelow, Jeffrey, et al., 'A Picture of Amputees and the Prosthetic Situation in Haiti', *Disability & Rehabilitation*, vol. 26, no. 4, 2004, pp. 246–252; Lindsay, Sally, and Irina Tsybina, 'Predictors of Unmet Needs for Communication and Mobility Assistive Devices among Youth with a Disability: The role of socio-cultural factors', *Disability and Rehabilitation: Assistive Technology*, vol. 6, no. 1, January 2011, pp. 10–21.

31 Steinfeld, Edward, 'Education for All: The cost of accessibility', Education Notes, The World Bank, Washington, D.C., August 2005, <http://siteresources.worldbank.org/EDUCATION/Resources/Education-Notes/EdNotes_CostOfAccess_2.pdf>, accessed 31 January 2013

32 Based on evaluations by the Department of Public Works in South Africa, Accessible Design Case Studies, 2004, in Metts, Robert, 'Disability and Development', Background paper prepared for the disability and development research agenda meeting, 16 November 2004, The World Bank, Washington, D.C., pp. 15–45.

33 South African Disability Institute, Special Housing for Disabled People, data provided by Philip Thompson, Africa Chair, International Commission on Technology and Accessibility, as cited in Metts, Robert, 'Disability and Development', p. 17; Metts, Robert, 'Disability and Development', pp. 15–45.

BOX: It's about ability

United Nations Children's Fund Montenegro, '"It's about Ability" Campaign Honoured for the Best Humanitarian Action in Montenegro', UNICEF Montenegro, Podgorica, Montenegro, 15 February 2011, <www.unicef.org/montenegro/media_16505.html>, accessed 31 January 2013.

Perovic, Jelena, 'Survey: It's about ability campaign results in positive change for children with disability in Montenegro', UNICEF Montenegro, Podgorica, Montenegro, 14 December 2011, <www.unicef.org/montenegro/15868_18773.html>, accessed 31 January 2013.

Chapter 3 A strong foundation

34 World Health Organization, 'Fact Sheet: Poliomyelitis', WHO, Geneva, 2011; Polio News, Global Polio Eradication Initiative, January 2013.

35 World Health Organization, 'Global Immunization Data', WHO, Geneva, October 2012.

36 United Nations Department of Economic and Social Affairs, 'Disability and the Millennium Development Goals: A review of the MDG process and strategies for inclusion of disability issues in Millennium Development Goal efforts', United Nations, New York, December 2011.

37 World Health Organization and the World Bank, World Report on Disability, 2011, pp. 58–60.

38 Gakidou, Emmanuela, et al., 'Improving Child Survival through Environmental and Nutritional Interventions: The importance of targeting interventions toward the poor', Journal of the American Medical Association, vol. 298, no. 16, October 2007, pp. 1876–1887.

39 World Health Organization, Nutrition for Health and Development: A global agenda for combating malnutrition – Progress report, WHO, Geneva, 2000, pp. 14–15.

40 World Health Organization, 'Micronutrient deficiencies: Iodine deficiency disorders', WHO, Geneva, 2012, <www.who.int/nutrition/topics/idd/en>, accessed 31 January 2013

41 Checkley William, et al., 'Multi-Country Analysis of the Effects of Diarrhoea on Childhood Stunting', International Journal of Epidemiology, vol. 37, no. 4, August 2008, pp. 816–830.

42 Walker, Susan P., et al., 'Inequality in Early Childhood: Risk and protective factors for early child development', The Lancet, vol. 378, no. 9799, 8 October 2011, pp. 1325–1338.

43 United Nations Children's Fund, Tracking Progress on Child and Maternal Nutrition: A survival and development priority', UNICEF, New York, November 2009, p. 16.

44 Walker, Susan P., et al., 'Inequality in Early Childhood: Risk and protective factors for early child development', pp. 1325–1338.

45 World Health Organization, 'Medical Devices: Anaemia prevention and control', WHO, Geneva, 2012, <www.who.int/medical_devices/initiatives/anaemia_control/en/>, accessed 31 January 2013.

46 Scholl, Theresa O., 'Maternal Iron Status: Relation to fetal growth, length of gestation, and iron endowment of the neonate', Nutrition Reviews, vol. 69, no. 11, November 2011, S23–S29; Vaughan, Owen R., et al., 'Environmental Regulation of Placental Phenotype: Implications for fetal growth', Reproduction, Fertility and Development, vol. 24, no. 1, 6 December 2011, pp. 80–96.

47 Adams, Melanie S., et al., 'Feeding Difficulties in Children with Cerebral Palsy: Low-cost caregiver training in Dhaka, Bangladesh', Child: Care, Health and Development, vol. 38, no. 6, November 2012, pp. 878–888.

48 National Institutes for Health (NIH), MedlinePlus, 'Cystic Fibrosis – Nutritional Considerations', <www.nlm.nih.gov/medlineplus/ency/article/002437.htm>, accessed 31 January 2013; O'Brien, S., et al., 'Intestinal Bile Acid Malabsorption in Cystic Fibrosis', Gut, vol. 34, no. 8, August 1993, pp. 1137–1141.

49 United Nations Children's Fund, 'Violence against Disabled Children: UN Secretary-General's report on violence against children – Summary report', UNICEF, New York, 28 July 2005, pp. 6–7; World Bank, May 2004, "Disability in Bangladesh: A situation analysis" The Danish Bilharziasis Laboratory for the World Bank, People's Republic of Bangladesh <http://siteresources.worldbank.org/DISABILITY/Resources/Regions/South%20Asia/DisabilityinBangladesh.pdf>, p. 15, accessed 31 January 2013

50 World Health Organization, Developmental Difficulties in Early Childhood: Prevention, early identification, assessment and intervention in low- and middle-income countries – A review, WHO, Geneva, 2012; Thommessen, M., et al., 'Feeding Problems, Height and Weight in Different Groups of Disabled Children', ActaPaediatrica, vol. 80, no. 5, May 1991, pp. 527–533; Sullivan, Peter B., ed., Feeding and Nutrition in Children with Neurodevelopmental Disability, Mac Keith Press, London, 2009, p. 61; Adams, Melanie S., et al., 'Feeding Difficulties in Children with Cerebral Palsy', pp. 878–888.

51 Groce, N., et al., 'Water and Sanitation Issues for Persons with Disabilities in Low- and Middle-Income Countries: A literature review and discussion of implications for global health and international development,' Journal of Water and Health, vol. 9, no. 4, 2011, pp. 617–627.

52 Human Rights Watch, 'Fact Sheet: HIV and disability', Human Rights Watch, New York, June 2011. Also, see World Health Organization and the World Bank, World Report on Disability, 2011, p. 77 for misconceptions on sexual activity, p. 59 for drug/alcohol use and p. 147 for risk of abuse.

53 United Nations Children's Fund, 'Towards an AIDS-Free Generation: Promoting community-based strategies for and with children and adolescents with disabilities', UNICEF, July 2012.

54 World Health Organization and United Nations Population Fund, Promoting Sexual and Reproductive Health for Persons with Disabilities: WHO/UNFPA guidance note, WHO, 2009, pp. 5–9, 12, <http://www.who.int/reproductivehealth/publications/general/9789241598682/en>, accessed 31 January 2013; United Nations Educational, Scientific and Cultural Organization, Sexuality Education in Asia and the Pacific: Review of policies and strategies to implement and scale up, UNESCO Bangkok, Bangkok, 2012, p. 2, <http://unesdoc.unesco.org/images/0021/002150/215091e.pdf>, accessed 31 January 2013.

55 Willemse, Karin, Ruth Morgan and John Meletse, 'Deaf, Gay, HIV Positive, and Proud: Narrating an alternative identity in post-Apartheid South Africa', Canadian Journal of African Studies, vol. 43, no. 1, April 2009, pp. 83–104.

56 Sices, Laura, 'Developmental Screening in Primary Care: The effectiveness of current practice and recommendations for improvement', The Commonwealth Fund, New York, December 2007, pp. v and 6; Johnson-Staub, Christine, 'Charting Progress for Babies in Child Care Project: Promote access to early, regular, and comprehensive screening', CLASP, Washington, D.C., February 2012, p. 1.

57 Ertem, Ilgi O., et al., 'A Guide for Monitoring Child Development in Low- and Middle-Income Countries', Pediatrics, vol. 121, no. 3, March 2008, pp. e581–e589; World Health Organization, Developmental Difficulties in Early Childhood: Prevention, Early Identification, Assessment and Intervention in low-and middle income countries, WHO 2012pp.1

58 World Health Organization, 'Epilepsy: Fact sheet No. 999', WHO, Geneva, October 2012, <www.who.int/mediacentre/factsheets/fs999/en/index.html>, accessed 31 January 2013.

59 Metts, Robert, 'Disability and Development', pp. 15–45.

60 Filmer, Deon, 'Disability, Poverty, and Schooling in Developing Countries: Results from 14 household surveys', World Bank Economic Review, vol. 22, no. 1, 2008, pp. 141–163, as cited in World Health Organization and the World Bank, World Report on Disability, 2011.

61 United Nations Educational, Scientific and Cultural Organization, EFA Global Monitoring Report 2010: Reaching the marginalized, UNESCO and Oxford University Press, Paris and Oxford, UK, 2010, <http://unesdoc.unesco.org/images/0018/001866/186606E.pdf>, accessed 31 January 2013; Loeb, M. E., and Arne H. Eide, eds., 'Living Conditions among People with Activity Limitations in Malawi: A national representative study', SINTEF Health Research, Oslo, 26 August 2004, <www.safod.com/LCMalawi.pdf>, 31 January 2013; Government of the United Republic of Tanzania, '2008 Tanzania Disability Survey', United Republic of Tanzania National Bureau of Statistics, Dar es Salaam, United Republic of Tanzania, 2009, p. 19, <nbs.go.tz/tnada/index.php/ddibrowser/5/download/24>, 31 January 2013.

62 World Health Organization and the World Bank, World Report on Disability, 2011, p. 206.

63 United Nations, Report of the Secretary-General on the Status of the Convention on the Rights of the Child, A/66/230, United Nations, New York, 3 August 2011, p. 8.

64 For review, see World Health Organization and the World Bank, World Report on Disability, 2011, pp. 39–40; Filmer, Deon, 'Disability, Poverty, and Schooling in Developing Countries: Results from 14 household surveys', pp. 141–163; Sundrum, Ratna, et al., 'Cerebral Palsy and Socioeconomic Status: A retrospective cohort study', Archives of Disease in Childhood, vol. 90, no. 1, January 2005, pp. 15–18; Newacheck, Paul W., et al., 'Disparities in the Prevalence of Disability between Black and White Children', Archives of Pediatrics & Adolescent Medicine, vol. 157, no. 3, March 2003, pp. 244–248.

65 United Nations Children's Fund, *Promoting the Rights of Children with Disabilities*, Innocenti Digest No. 13, UNICEF Innocenti Research Centre, Florence, October 2007, p. 15, box 5.1, <www.un.org/esa/socdev/unyin/documents/children_disability_rights.pdf>, accessed 31 January 2013.

66 van der Berg, Servaas, *Poverty and Education*, United Nations Educational, Scientific and Cultural Organization, Paris, 2008.

67 United Nations Children's Fund, *Promoting the Rights of Children with Disabilities*, Innocenti Digest No. 13, p. 27, box 5.1.

68 UNICEF, *The Right of Children with Disabilities to Education: A rights-based approach to inclusive education*, 2012, p. 8; United Nations Educational, Scientific and Cultural Organization, 'The Right to Education for Persons with Disabilities: Towards inclusion – An Education for All flagship', Paris, <http://unesdoc.unesco.org/images/0013/001322/132277e.pdf>, accessed 31 January 2013.

69 United Nations Educational, Scientific and Cultural Organization, 'Inclusion of Children with Disabilities: The early childhood imperative', UNESCO Policy Brief on Early Childhood No. 46, UNESCO, Paris, April–June 2009, <http://unesdoc.unesco.org/images/0018/001831/183156e.pdf>, accessed 31 January 2013.

70 Nahar, Baitun, et al., 'Effects of Psychosocial Stimulation on Growth and Development of Severely Malnourished Children in a Nutrition Unit in Bangladesh', *European Journal of Clinical Nutrition*, vol. 63, no. 6, June 2009, pp. 725–731.

71 Jin, X., et al., '"Care for Development" Intervention in Rural China: A prospective follow-up study', *Journal of Developmental and Behavioral Pediatrics*, vol. 28, no. 3, 2007, pp. 213–218.

72 Nair, M. K., et al., 'Effect of Child Development Centre Model Early Stimulation among At Risk Babies: A randomized controlled trial', *Indian Pediatrics*, vol. 46, supplement, January 2009, pp. s20–s26.

73 Potterton, Joanne, et al., 'The Effect of a Basic Home Stimulation Programme on the Development of Young children Infected with HIV', *Developmental Medicine & Child Neurology*, vol. 52, no. 6, June 2010, pp. 547–551.

74 Walker, Susan P., et al., 'Inequality in Early Childhood: Risk and protective factors for early child development', pp. 1325–1338.

75 Forlin, Chris, et al., 'Demographic Differences in Changing Pre-Service Teachers' Attitudes, Sentiments and Concerns about Inclusive Education', *International Journal of Inclusive Education*, vol. 13, no. 2, March 2009, pp. 195–209. Felicia Wilczenski's 'Attitudes toward Inclusive Education Scale' (ATIES), developed in 1992, has been particularly influential in studies of teacher attitudes: Wilczenski, Felicia L., 'Measuring Attitudes toward Inclusive Education', *Psychology in the Schools*, vol. 29, no. 4, October 1992, pp. 306–312. For a review, see Kuyini, Ahmed Bawa, and Ishwar Desai, 'Principals' and Teachers' Attitudes and Knowledge of Inclusive Education as Predictors of Effective Teaching Practices in Ghana', *Journal of Research in Special Educational Needs*, vol. 7, no. 2, June 2007, pp. 104–113.

76 Tur-Kaspa, Hana, Amatzia Weisel and Tova Most, 'A Multidimensional Study of Special Education Students' Attitudes towards People with Disabilities: A focus on deafness', *European Journal of Special Needs Education*, vol. 15, no. 1, March 2000, pp. 13–23.

77 Latimier, Camille, and Jan Šiška, 'Children's Rights for All!: Implementation of the United Nations Convention on the Rights of the Child for children with intellectual disabilities', Inclusion Europe, Brussels, October 2011, p. 21.

78 Praisner, Cindy L., 'Attitudes of Elementary School Principals toward the Inclusion of Students with Disabilities', *Exceptional Children*, vol. 69, no. 2, 2003, pp. 135–145.

79 Shade, Richard A., and Roger Stewart, 'General Education and Special Education Preservice Teachers' Attitudes towards Inclusion', *Preventing School Failure*, vol. 46, no. 1, 2001, pp. 37–41.

80 de Boer, Anke, Sip Jan Pijl and Alexander Minnaert, 'Regular Primary Schoolteachers' Attitudes towards Inclusive Education: A review of the literature', *International Journal of Inclusive Education*, vol. 15, no 3, April 2011, pp. 345–346.

81 Miles, Susie, and Ian Kaplan, 'Using Images to Promote Reflection: An action research study in Zambia and Tanzania', *Journal of Research in Special Educational Needs*, vol. 5, no. 2, June 2005, pp. 79–80.

82 Kalyanpur, Maya, 'Paradigm and Paradox: Education for All and the inclusion of children with disabilities in Cambodia', *International Journal of Inclusive Education*, vol. 15, no. 10, December 2011, p. 1058.

83 Miles, Susie, et al., 'Education for Diversity: The role of networking in resisting disabled people's marginalisation in Bangladesh', *Compare: A Journal of Comparative and International Education*, vol. 42, no. 2, 2012, p. 293.

84 Schurmann, Erik, 'Training Disabled Teachers in Mozambique', Enabling Education No. 10, Enabling Education Network, Manchester, UK, 2006, <www.eenet.org.uk/resources/docs/enabling_education10.pdf >, accessed 31 January 2013.

85 United Nations Children's Fund, *Promoting the Rights of Children with Disabilities*, Innocenti Digest No. 13, p. 30.

86 Lynch, Paul, et al., 'Inclusive Educational Practices in Uganda: Evidencing practice of itinerant teachers who work with children with visual impairment in local mainstream schools', *International Journal of Inclusive Education*, vol. 15, no. 10, December 2011, pp. 1119–1134; Miles, Susie, and Sue Stubbs, '*Inclusive Education and Children with Disabilities*', UNICEF background discussion paper written for *The State of the World's Children 2013*, 2012, p. 23.

87 Prag, Anat, 'Fostering Partnerships for Education Policy and Reform: Vietnam', Enabling Education No. 8, Enabling Education Network, Manchester, UK, 2004, <www.eenet.org.uk/resources/docs/eenet_news8.pdf>, accessed 31 January 2013.

88 Report of the Secretary-General on the Status of the Convention on the Rights of the Child, 3 August 2011.

89 Stubbs, Sue, 'Inclusive Education: Where there are few resources', The Atlas Alliance, Oslo, September 2008, p. 36, <www.child-to-child.org/about/index.html>, accessed 31 January 2013; Fosere, Mamello, 'Mamello's Story', Enabling Education No. 5, Enabling Education Network, Manchester, UK, 2001, p. 10, <www.eenet.org.uk/resources/eenet_newsletter/news5/page10.php>.

90 Lewis, Ingrid, 'Water, Sanitation, Hygiene (WASH) and Inclusive Education', Enabling Education No. 14, Enabling Education Network, Manchester, UK, 2010, pp. 9–13, <www.eenet.org.uk/resources/docs/Enabling%20Education~issue%2014~2010.pdf>, accessed 31 January 2013.

91 Bines, Hazel, 'Education's Missing Millions: Including disabled children in education through EFA FTI processes and national sector plans – Main report of study findings', World Vision UK, Milton Keynes, UK, September 2007, p. 3.

92 Munir, Shirin Z., and Sultana S. Zaman, 'Models of Inclusion: Bangladesh experience', ch. 19 in *Inclusive Education across Cultures: Crossing boundaries, sharing ideas*, edited by Mithu Alur and Vianne Timmons, Sage Publications India, New Delhi, 2009, p. 292.

93 Ahsan, Mohammad Tariq, and Lindsay Burnip, 'Inclusive Education in Bangladesh', *Australasian Journal of Special Education*, vol. 31, no. 1, April 2007, p. 65.

94 Miles, Susie, et al., 'Education for Diversity: The role of networking in resisting disabled people's marginalisation in Bangladesh', *Compare: A Journal of Comparative and International Education*, vol. 42, no. 2, 2012, pp. 283–302.

95 United Nations Educational, Scientific and Cultural Organization, *Building Human Capacities in Least Developed Countries to Promote Poverty Eradication and Sustainable Development*, UNESCO, Paris, 2011, p. 8.

96 Lansdown, Gerison, '*Vulnerability of Children with Disabilities*', UNICEF background research paper written for *The State of the World's Children 2013*, 2012, p. 8.

97 United Nations Educational, Scientific and Cultural Organization, *Education Counts: Towards the Millennium Development Goals*, UNESCO, Paris, 2011, p. 17.

98 Abuya, Benta A., James Ciera and Elizabeth Kimani-Murage, 'Effect of Mother's Education on Child's Nutritional Status in the Slums of Nairobi', *BMC Pediatrics*, vol. 12, no. 80, June 2012.

99 Janevic, Teresa, et al., 'Risk Factors for Childhood Malnutrition in Roma Settlements in Serbia', *BMC Public Health*, vol. 10, August 2010.

100 Miller, Jane E., and Yana V. Rodgers, 'Mother's Education and Children's Nutritional Status: New evidence from Cambodia', *Asian Development Review*, vol. 26, no. 1, 2009, pp. 131–165.

101 Semba, Richard D., et al., 'Effect of Paternal Formal Education on Risk of Child Stunting in Indonesia and Bangladesh: A cross-sectional study', *The Lancet*, vol. 371, no. 9609, January 2008, pp. 322–328.

102 Convention on the Rights of the Child, article 29.

Chapter 4 Essentials of protection

103 Cody, Clare, *Count Every Child: The right to birth registration*, Plan Ltd., Woking, UK, 2009.

104 Algood, C. L., et al., 'Maltreatment of Children with Developmental Disabilities: An ecological systems analysis,' *Children and Youth Services Review*, vol. 33, no. 7, July 2011, pp. 1142–1148; Stalker, K., and K. McArthur, 'Child Abuse, Child Protection and Disabled Children: A review of recent research,' *Child Abuse Review*, vol. 21, no. 1, January/February 2012, pp. 24–40.

105 Kvam, Marit Hoem, 'Sexual Abuse of Deaf Children: A retrospective analysis of the prevalence and characteristics of childhood sexual abuse among deaf adults in Norway', *Child Abuse & Neglect*, vol. 28, no. 3, March 2004, pp. 241–251; Lansdown, Gerison, '*Vulnerability of Children with Disabilities*', p. 6.

106 Mental Disability Rights International, 'Behind Closed Doors: Human rights abuses in the psychiatric facilities, orphanages and rehabilitation centers of Turkey', MDRI, Washington, D.C., 28 September 2005, pp. 1, 23, 72, <www.disabilityrightsintl.org/wordpress/wp-content/uploads/turkey-final-9-26-05.pdf>, accessed 31 January 2013; Mental Disability Rights International, 'Torture Not Treatment: Electric shock and long-term restraint in the United States on children and adults with disabilities at the Judge Rotenberg Center', MDRI, Washington, D.C., 2010, pp. 1–2, <www.disabilityrightsintl.org/wordpress/wp-content/uploads/USReportandUrgentAppeal.pdf>, accessed 31 January 2013.

107 Human Rights Watch, Open Society Foundations, Women with Disabilities Australia, International Disability Alliance and Stop Torture in Health Care, 'Sterilization of Women and Girls with Disabilities: A briefing paper', November 2011, <www.hrw.org/sites/default/files/related_material/2011_global_DR.pdf>, accessed 31 January 2013.

108 Dowse, Leanne, 'Moving Forward or Losing Ground?: The sterilisation of women and girls with disabilities in Australia', Paper prepared for Women with Disabilities Australia and presented at the Disabled Peoples' International World Summit, Winnipeg, Canada, 8–10 September 2004.

109 Information obtained from UNICEF Serbia; United Nations Children's Fund and Serbian Government Ministry of Labour and Social Policy, 'Transforming Residential Institutions for Children and Developing Sustainable Alternatives', Belgrade, 2011, pp. 4–8.

110 Convention on the Rights of the Child General Comment No. 9 (2006), p. 21.

FOCUS
Violence against children with disabilities

Jones, Lisa, et al., 'Prevalence and Risk of Violence against Children with Disabilities', pp. 899–907.

World Health Organization and the World Bank, World Report on Disability, 2011, pp. 29, 59 and 137, pp. 29, 59 and 137.

Pinheiro, Paulo Sérgio, World Report on Violence against Children, United Nations Secretary-General's Study on Violence against Children, Geneva, 2006.

Krug, Etienne G., et al., eds., World Report on Violence and Health, World Health Organization, Geneva, 2002.

Hibbard, Roberta A., et al., 'Maltreatment of Children with Disabilities', Pediatrics, vol. 119, no. 5, 1 May 2007, pp. 1018–1025.

Ammerman, Robert T., et al., 'Maltreatment in Psychiatrically Hospitalized Children and Adolescents with Developmental Disabilities: Prevalence and correlates', Journal of the American Academy of Child & Adolescent Psychiatry, vol. 33, no. 4, May 1994, pp. 567–576.

Sullivan, Patricia M., 'Violence Exposure among Children with Disabilities', Clinical Child and Family Psychology Review, vol. 12, no. 2, June 2009, pp. 196–216.

Ammerman, Robert T., and Nora J. Baladerian, Maltreatment of Children with Disabilities, National Committee to Prevent Child Abuse, Chicago, 1993.

United Nations, Convention on the Rights of Persons with Disabilities, A/RES/61/106, United Nations, New York, 2008.

Gilbert, Ruth, et al., 'Burden and Consequences of Child Maltreatment in High-Income Countries', The Lancet, vol. 373, no. 9657, 3 January 2009, pp. 68–81.

Felitti, Vincent J., et al., 'Relationship of Childhood Abuse and Household Dysfunction to Many of the Leading Causes of Death in Adults: The adverse childhood experiences (ACE) study', American Journal of Preventive Medicine, vol. 14, no. 4, May 1998, pp. 245–258.

MacMillan, Harriet L., et al., 'Interventions to Prevent Child Maltreatment and Associated Impairment', The Lancet, vol. 373, no. 9659, 17 January 2009, pp. 250–266.

Chapter 5   Humanitarian Response

111 Von der Assen, Nina, Mathijs Euwema and Huib Cornielje, 'Including Disabled Children in Psychological Programmes in Areas Affected by Armed Conflict', Intervention, vol. 8, no. 1, March 2010, pp. 29–39.

112 Bartlett, Sheridan, 'The Implications of Climate Change for Children in Lower-Income Countries', Children, Youth and Environments, vol. 18, no. 1, 2008, pp. 71–98.

113 Convention on the Rights of the Child General Comment No. 9 (2006), p. 22.

FOCUS
Risk, resilience and inclusive humanitarian action

African Child Policy Forum, 'Violence against Children in Africa: A compilation of the main findings of the various research projects conducted by the African Child Policy Forum (ACPF) since 2006', ACPF, Addis Ababa, March 2011.

Handicap International, 'Mainstreaming Disability into Disaster Risk Reduction:

A training manual', Handicap International, Kathmandu, January 2009, <www.handicap-international.fr/fileadmin/documents/publications/DisasterRiskReduc.pdf>, accessed 31 January 2013.

International Committee of the Red Cross, 'Promotion and Protection of the Rights of Children: ICRC statement to the United Nations, 2011', ICRC, Geneva, 17 October 2011, <www.icrc.org/eng/resources/documents/statement/united-nations-children-statement-2011-10-18.htm>, accessed 31 January 2013.

IRIN, 'DRC: Child disability, the forgotten crisis', IRIN, Goma, Democratic Republic of the Congo, 23 October 2009, <www.irinnews.org/Report/86710/DRC-Child-disability-the-forgotten-crisis>, accessed 2 October 2012.

Kett, Maria, and Mark van Ommeren, 'Disability, Conflict and Emergencies', The Lancet, vol. 374, no. 9704, 28 November 2009, pp. 1801–1803, <www.thelancet.com/journals/lancet/article/PIIS0140-6736%2809%2962024-9/fulltext>, accessed 31 January 2013.

Kett, Maria, and Jean-François Trani, 'Vulnerability and Disability in Darfur', Forced Migration Review, vol. 35, July 2010, pp. 12–14.

Nelson, Brett D., et al., 'Impact of Sexual Violence on Children in the Eastern Democratic Republic of Congo', Medicine, Conflict and Survival, vol. 27, no. 4, October–December 2011, pp. 211–225.

Pearn, John H., 'The Cost of War: Child injury and death', in Contemporary Issues in Childhood Diarrhoea and Malnutrition, 1st edition, edited by Zulfiqar Ahmed Bhutta, Oxford University Press, Karachi, Pakistan, pp. 334–343.

Penrose, Angela, and Mie Takaki, 'Children's Rights in Emergencies and Disasters', The Lancet, vol. 367, no. 9511, 25 February 2006, pp. 698–699.

Plan International, 'Child-Centred Disaster Risk Reduction: Building resilience through participation – Lessons from Plan International', Plan UK, London, 2010.

Handicap International and Save the Children, Out from the Shadows: Sexual Violence against Children with Disabilities, Save the Children UK, London, 2011.

Tamashiro, Tami, 'Impact of Conflict on Children's Health and Disability', Background paper prepared for the Education for All Global Monitoring Report 2011: The hidden crisis – Armed conflict and education, United Nations Educational, Scientific and Cultural Organization, Paris, June 2010, <http://unesdoc.unesco.org/images/0019/001907/190712e.pdf>, accessed 31 January 2013.

Trani, Jean-François, et al., 'Disability, Vulnerability and Citizenship: To what extent is education a protective mechanism for children with disabilities in countries affected by conflict?', International Journal of Inclusive Education, vol. 15, no. 10, 2011, pp. 1187–1203.

United Nations Children's Fund, 'Violence against Disabled Children: UN Secretary-General's Report on Violence against Children – Summary report', UNICEF, New York, 28 July 2005, pp. 4–5, <www.unicef.org/videoaudio/PDFs/UNICEF_Violence_Against_Disabled_Children_Report_Distributed_Version.pdf>, accessed 31 January 2013.

United Nations General Assembly, Report of the Special Representative of the Secretary-General for Children and Armed Conflict, A/62/228, United Nations, New York, 13 August 2007.

Women's Commission for Refugee Women and Children, Disabilities among Refugees and Conflict-Affected Populations: Resource kit for fieldworkers, Women's Commission for Refugee Women and Children, New York, June 2008, <http://womensrefugeecommission.org/resources/cat_view/68-reports/81-disabilities>, accessed 31 January 2013.

World Health Organization and the World Bank, World Report on Disability, 2011, pp. 34–37.

FOCUS
Explosive remnants of war

Under the Mine Ban Treaty, victims are defined as those who are directly impacted and therefore have been killed by a landmine blast or survived one, as well as the surviving family members of those killed and injured. Under the Convention on Cluster Munitions, victims also include affected family members and affected communities. Throughout this document, 'victims' refers to survivors, family members of those affected and affected communities; 'casualties' refers to those directly killed or injured by blasts; while 'survivors' specifically refers to those who have been directly impacted and survived landmines/Explosive Remnants of War blasts.

Landmine and Cluster Munition Monitor, Landmine Monitor 2011, Mines Action Canada, October 2011, p. 51.

'Mines' include victim-activated anti-personnel mines, anti-vehicle mines and improvised explosive devices; 2010 is the most recent year for which verified casualty totals were available for all countries at the time of publication. Please see <www.the-monitor.org>, accessed 31 January 2013, for a full definition of casualties and devices as presented here and for updated casualty data.

The Landmine Monitor identified more than 1,500 child casualties in 1999 and more than 1,600 in 2001.

This includes only the casualties for which the civilian/security status and the age were known.

Boys accounted for 1,371 of the 2,735 civilian casualties caused by explosive remnants of war (ERW) between 2008 and 2010.

Landmine and Cluster Munition Monitor, *Landmine and Cluster Munition Monitor Fact Sheet: Impact of mines/ERW on children – November 2011*, Landmine and Cluster Munition Monitor, Geneva, p. 2.

Landmine and Cluster Munition Monitor Fact Sheet: Impact of mines/ERW on children – November 2010, pp. 1–3.

Landmine and Cluster Munition Monitor Fact Sheet: Landmines and children – March 2010, pp. 2, 3.

Percentages are of civilian casualties for which the age was known. Children made up 30 per cent of casualties from all types of mines.

Landmine and Cluster Munition Monitor, 'The Issues: Landmines', Landmine and Cluster Munition Monitor, Geneva, <www.the-monitor.org/index.php/LM/The-Issues/Landmines>, accessed 31 January 2013.

Walsh, Nicolas E., and Wendy S. Walsh, 'Rehabilitation of Landmine Victims: The ultimate challenge', *Bulletin of the World Health Organization*, vol. 81, no. 9, 2003, pp. 665–670.

International Save the Children Alliance, 'Child Landmine Survivors: An inclusive approach to policy and practice', International Save the Children Alliance, London, 2000.

Watts, Hugh G., 'The Consequences for Children of Explosive Remnants of War: Land mines, unexploded ordnance, improvised explosive devices and cluster bombs', *Journal of Pediatric Rehabilitation Medicine: An Interdisciplinary Approach*, vol. 2, 2009, pp. 217–227.

Landmine and Cluster Munition Monitor Fact Sheet: Impact of mines/ERW on children – November 2010, pp. 1–3.

Watts, Hugh G., 'The Consequences for Children of Explosive Remnants of War', pp. 217–227.

Landmine and Cluster Munition Monitor Fact Sheet: Landmines and children – June 2009, pp. 1–4.

Munoz, Wanda, Ulrike Last and Teng Kimsean, *Good Practices from the Project: Towards sustainable income generating activities for mine victim and other persons with disabilities in Cambodia*, Handicap International Federation (HIC) Cambodia, Phnom Penh, Cambodia, 2010.

Child Protection in Crisis (CPC) Network, Livelihoods and Economic Strengthening Task Force, *The Impacts of Economic Strengthening Programs on Children: a review of the evidence*, CPC Network, August 2011, pp. ii, 1, 18.

Landmine and Cluster Munition Monitor Fact Sheet: Impact of mines/ERW on children – November 2010, pp. 1–3.

Handicap International, *Voices from the Ground: Landmine and explosive remnants of war survivors speak out on victim assistance*, Handicap International, Brussels, September 2009, p. 210.

Chapter 6 Measuring child disability

114 United Nations Children's Fund and the University of Wisconsin, *Monitoring Child Disability in Developing Countries: Results from the Multiple Indicator Cluster Surveys*, UNICEF, New York, 2008, p. 9.

115 Mont, Daniel, 'Measuring Disability Prevalence', Social Protection Discussion Paper No. 0706, The World Bank, Washington, D.C., March 2007, p. 35; Maulik, Pallab K., and Gary L. Darmstadt, 'Childhood Disability in Low- and Middle-Income Countries: Overview of screening, prevention, services, legislation, and epidemiology', *Pediatrics*, vol. 120, Supplement 1, July 2007, p. S21.

116 World Health Organization, *Towards a Common Language for Functioning, Disability and Health: ICF – The international classification of functioning, disability and health*, WHO, Geneva, 2002.

117 Msall, Michael E., and Dennis P. Hogan, 'Counting Children with Disability in Low-Income Countries: Enhancing prevention, promoting child development, and investing in economic well-being', *Pediatrics*, vol. 120, no. 1, July 2007, p. 183.

118 Durkin, Maureen, S., 'The Epidemiology of Developmental Disabilities in Low-Income Countries', *Mental Retardation and Developmental Disabilities Research Review*, vol. 8, no. 3, 2002, p. 211; United Nations Children's Fund and the University of Wisconsin, *Monitoring Child Disability in Developing Countries*, p. 8.

119 Lansdown, R. G., et al., 'Culturally Appropriate Measures for Monitoring Child Development at Family and Community Level: A WHO collaborative study', *Bulletin of the World Health Organization*, vol. 74, no. 3, 1996, p. 287

120 See appendix 2 of Maulik and Darmstadt, 2007.

121 Robertson, Janet, Chris Hatton and Eric Emerson, 'The Identification of Children with or at Significant Risk of Intellectual Disabilities in Low and Middle Income Countries: A review', CeDR Research Report, no. 3, Centre for Disability Research, Lancaster University, Lancaster, UK, July 2009, p. 22; United Nations Children's Fund and the University of Wisconsin, *Monitoring Child Disability in Developing Countries*, pp. 9, 58; Gladstone, M. J., et al., 'Can Western Developmental Screening Tools Be Modified for Use in a Rural Malawian Setting?', *Archives of Diseases in Childhood*, vol. 93, no. 1, January 2008, pp. 23–29.

122 Mont, Daniel, 'Measuring Disability Prevalence', p. 35; Washington Group on Disability Statistics, 'Understanding and Interpreting Disability as Measured Using the WG Short Set of Questions', 20 April 2009, p. 2.

123 United Nations Children's Fund and the University of Wisconsin, *Monitoring Child Disability in Developing Countries*, p. 8.

124 Durkin, Maureen S., 'Population-Based Studies of Childhood Disability in Developing Countries: Rationale and study design', *International Journal of Mental Health*, vol. 20, no. 2, 1991, pp. 47–60; United Nations Children's Fund and the University of Wisconsin, *Monitoring Child Disability in Developing Countries*, p. 8.

125 Durkin, Maureen S., 'Population-Based Studies of Childhood Disability in Developing Countries', pp. 47–60.

126 Ibid.; United Nations Children's Fund and the University of Wisconsin, *Monitoring Child Disability in Developing Countries*, p. 9.

127 World Health Organization and the United Nations Economic and Social Commission for Asia and the Pacific, *Training Manual on Disability Statistics*, Bangkok, 2008, pp. 107–108.

128 United Nations Children's Fund and the University of Wisconsin, *Monitoring Child Disability in Developing Countries*, pp. 8–9; Nair, M. K., et al., 'Developmental Screening Chart', *Indian Pediatrics*, vol. 28, no. 8, 1991, pp. 869–872.

129 United Nations Children's Fund and the University of Wisconsin, *Monitoring Child Disability in Developing Countries*, p. 9; Durkin, Maureen S., 'Population-Based Studies of Childhood Disability in Developing Countries', pp. 47–60.

130 Robertson, Janet, Chris Hatton and Eric Emerson, 'The Identification of Children with or at Significant Risk of Intellectual Disabilities in Low and Middle Income Countries: A review', p. 20.

FOCUS
Lessons learned

United Nations Children's Fund and the University of Wisconsin, *Monitoring Child Disability in Developing Countries: Results from the Multiple Indicator Cluster Surveys*, p. 9; Thorburn Marigold, et al., 'Identification of Childhood Disability in Jamaica: The ten question screen', *International Journal of Rehabilitation Research*, vol. 15, no. 2, June 1992, pp. 115–127.

United Nations Children's Fund and the University of Wisconsin, *Monitoring Child Disability in Developing Countries: Results from the Multiple Indicator Cluster Surveys*, p. 9.

Durkin, Maureen S., 'Population-Based Studies of Childhood Disability in Developing Countries', pp. 47–60; United Nations Children's Fund and the University of Wisconsin, *Monitoring Child Disability in Developing Countries*, pp. 9–10.

Zaman, Sultana S., et al., 'Validity of the 'Ten Questions' for Screening Serious Childhood Disability: Results from urban Bangladesh', *International Journal of Epidemiology*, vol. 19, no. 3, 1990, p. 613.

Previous UNICEF publications reported that the number of participating countries was 20. This number was correct when those publications were printed, but the final number of countries that administered the Ten Questions as part of MICS3 was 25.

United Nations Children's Fund and University of Wisconsin, *Monitoring Child Disability in Developing Countries*, p. 23.

FOCUS
From screening to assessment

Maulik, Pallab K., and Gary L. Darmstadt, 'Childhood Disability in Low- and Middle-Income Countries', July 2007, p. S6; United Nations Children's Fund and the University of Wisconsin, *Monitoring Child Disability in Developing Countries*, p. 58.

Statistical Tables

Economic and social statistics on the countries and areas of the world, with particular reference to children's well-being.

STATISTICAL TABLES

OVERVIEW

This reference guide presents the most recent key statistics on child survival, development and protection for the world's countries, areas and regions. It includes, for the first time, a table on early childhood development.

The statistical tables in this volume also support UNICEF's focus on progress and results towards internationally agreed-upon goals and compacts relating to children's rights and development. UNICEF is the lead agency responsible for monitoring the child-related goals of the Millennium Declaration as well as the Millennium Development Goals (MDGs) and indicators. UNICEF is also a key partner in the United Nations' work on monitoring these targets and indicators.

Efforts have been made to maximize the comparability of statistics across countries and time. Nevertheless, data used at the country level may differ in terms of the methods used to collect data or arrive at estimates, and in terms of the populations covered. Furthermore, data presented here are subject to evolving methodologies, revisions of time series data (e.g., immunization, maternal mortality ratios) and changing regional classifications. Also, data comparable from one year to the next are unavailable for some indicators. It is therefore not advisable to compare data from consecutive editions of *The State of the World's Children*.

The numbers presented in this reference guide are available online at <www.unicef.org/sowc2013> and via the UNICEF global statistical databases at <www.childinfo.org>. Please refer to these websites for the latest tables and for any updates or corrigenda subsequent to printing.

General note on the data

Data presented in the following statistical tables are derived from the UNICEF global databases and are accompanied by definitions, sources and, where necessary, additional footnotes. The tables draw on inter-agency estimates and nationally representative household surveys such as Multiple Indicator Cluster Surveys (MICS) and Demographic and Health Surveys (DHS). In addition, data from other United Nations organizations have been used. Data presented in this year's statistical tables generally reflect information available as of August 2012. More detailed information on methodology and data sources is available at <www.childinfo.org>.

This volume includes the latest population estimates and projections from *World Population Prospects: The 2010 revision* and *World Urbanization Prospects: The 2011 revision* (United Nations Department of Economic and Social Affairs, Population Division). Data quality is likely to be adversely affected for countries that have recently suffered disasters, especially where basic country infrastructure has been fragmented or where major population movements have occurred.

Multiple Indicator Cluster Surveys (MICS): UNICEF supports countries in collecting reliable and globally mapped data through MICS. Since 1995, around 240 surveys have been conducted in over 100 countries and areas. The fifth round of MICS, involving around 60 countries, is under way. MICS are among the largest sources of data for monitoring progress towards internationally agreed-upon development goals for children, including the MDGs. More information is available at <www.childinfo.org/mics.html>.

Child mortality estimates

Each year, in *The State of the World's Children*, UNICEF reports a series of mortality estimates for children – including the annual infant mortality rate, the under-five mortality rate and the number of under-five deaths – for at least two reference years. These figures represent the best estimates available at the time of printing and are based on the work of the United Nations Inter-agency Group for Child Mortality Estimation (IGME), which includes UNICEF, the World Health Organization (WHO), the World Bank and the United Nations Population Division. IGME mortality estimates are updated annually through a detailed review of all newly available data points, which often results in adjustments to previously reported estimates. As a result, consecutive editions of *The State of the World's Children* should not be used for analysing mortality trends over time. Comparable global and regional under-five mortality estimates for the period 1970–2011 are presented on page 95. Country-specific mortality indicators for 1970–2011, based on the most recent IGME estimates, are presented in Table 10 (for the years 1970, 1990, 2000 and 2011) and are available at <www.childinfo.org> and <www.childmortality.org>.

Under-five mortality rate (per 1,000 live births)

UNICEF Region	1970	1975	1980	1985	1990	1995	2000	2005	2010	2011
Sub-Saharan Africa	236	212	197	184	178	170	154	133	112	109
Eastern and Southern Africa	214	191	183	170	162	155	135	112	88	84
West and Central Africa	259	237	215	202	197	190	175	155	135	132
Middle East and North Africa	190	157	122	90	72	61	52	44	37	36
South Asia	195	175	154	135	119	104	89	75	64	62
East Asia and Pacific	120	92	75	62	55	49	39	29	22	20
Latin America and Caribbean	117	100	81	65	53	43	34	26	22	19
CEE/CIS	88	75	68	56	48	45	35	28	22	21
Least developed countries	238	223	206	186	171	156	136	118	102	98
World	**141**	**123**	**111**	**96**	**87**	**82**	**73**	**63**	**53**	**51**

Under-five deaths (millions)

UNICEF Region	1970	1975	1980	1985	1990	1995	2000	2005	2010	2011
Sub-Saharan Africa	3.1	3.2	3.4	3.5	3.8	4.0	4.0	3.8	3.4	3.4
Eastern and Southern Africa	1.3	1.4	1.5	1.6	1.7	1.7	1.6	1.5	1.2	1.2
West and Central Africa	1.6	1.7	1.8	1.9	2.1	2.2	2.2	2.2	2.1	2.1
Middle East and North Africa	1.2	1.1	1.0	0.8	0.7	0.5	0.4	0.4	0.4	0.4
South Asia	5.3	5.1	5.0	4.6	4.3	3.9	3.3	2.7	2.4	2.3
East Asia and Pacific	5.2	3.5	2.3	2.4	2.2	1.6	1.3	0.9	0.6	0.6
Latin America and Caribbean	1.2	1.1	0.9	0.8	0.6	0.5	0.4	0.3	0.2	0.2
CEE/CIS	0.5	0.6	0.5	0.4	0.4	0.2	0.2	0.1	0.1	0.1
Least developed countries	3.3	3.4	3.5	3.5	3.5	3.5	3.3	3.0	2.7	2.6
World	**16.9**	**14.8**	**13.1**	**12.7**	**12.0**	**10.8**	**9.6**	**8.2**	**7.1**	**6.9**

Notes on specific tables

TABLE 1. BASIC INDICATORS

Under-five mortality rate by gender: For the first time, IGME has produced gender-specific estimates of the under-five mortality rate. Details on the estimation methods are available in the annex of the latest IGME report, at <www.childmortality.org>.

Share of household income: The percentage share of household income received by the wealthiest 20 per cent and the poorest 40 per cent of households has been moved from Table 1 to Table 7, where it is now presented alongside other economic indicators.

TABLE 2. NUTRITION

Underweight, stunting, wasting and overweight: UNICEF and WHO have initiated a process to harmonize anthropometric data used for computation and estimation of regional and global averages and trend analysis. As part of this process, regional and global averages for underweight (moderate and severe), stunting, wasting and overweight prevalences are derived from a model described in M. de Onis et al., 'Methodology for Estimating Regional and Global Trends of Child Malnutrition'

(*International Journal of Epidemiology*, vol. 33, 2004, pp. 1260–1270). Owing to differences in data sources (i.e., new empirical data are incorporated as made available) and estimation methodology, these regional average prevalence estimates may not be comparable to the averages published in previous editions of *The State of the World's Children*.

Vitamin A supplementation: Emphasizing the importance for children of receiving two annual doses of vitamin A (spaced 4–6 months apart), this report presents only full coverage of vitamin A supplementation. In the absence of a direct method to measure this indicator, full coverage is reported as the lower coverage estimate from rounds 1 and 2 in a given year.

TABLE 3. HEALTH

Diarrhoea treatment: For the first time, the table includes diarrhoea treatment with oral rehydration salts (ORS). ORS is a key commodity for child survival and therefore it is crucial to monitor its coverage. This replaces the indicator used in previous years, diarrhoea treatment with oral rehydration therapy and continued feeding, which will continue to be available at <www.childinfo.org>.

Water and sanitation: The drinking water and sanitation coverage estimates in this report come from the WHO/UNICEF Joint Monitoring Programme for Water Supply and Sanitation (JMP). These are the official United Nations estimates for measuring progress towards the MDG target for drinking water and sanitation. Full details of the JMP methodology can be found at <www.childinfo.org> and <www.wssinfo.org>. As the JMP estimates use linear regression applied to data from all available household sample surveys and censuses, and additional data become available between each issue of estimates, subsequent JMP estimates should not be compared.

Immunization: This report presents WHO and UNICEF estimates of national immunization coverage. These are official United Nations estimates for measuring progress towards the MDG indicator for measles-containing vaccine coverage. Since 2000, the estimates are updated once annually in July, following a consultation process wherein countries are provided draft reports for review and comment. As the system incorporates new empirical data, each annual revision supersedes prior data releases, and coverage levels from earlier revisions are not comparable. A more detailed explanation of the process can be found at <www.childinfo.org/immunization_countryreports.html>.

Regional averages for the six reported antigens are computed as follows:
- For BCG, regional averages include only those countries where BCG is included in the national routine immunization schedule.
- For DPT, polio, measles, HepB and Hib vaccines, regional averages include all countries.
- For protection at birth (PAB) from tetanus, regional averages include only the countries where maternal and neonatal tetanus is endemic.

TABLE 4. HIV/AIDS

In 2012, the Joint United Nations Programme on HIV/AIDS (UNAIDS) released new global, regional and country level HIV and AIDS estimates for 2011 that reflect key changes in WHO HIV treatment guidelines for adults and children and for prevention of mother-to-child transmission of HIV as well as improvements in assumptions of the probability of HIV transmission from mother to child and net survival rates for infected children. In addition, there are also more reliable data available from population-based surveys, expanded national sentinel surveillance systems and programme service statistics in a number of countries. Based on the refined methodology, UNAIDS has retrospectively generated new estimates of HIV prevalence, the number of people living with HIV and those needing treatment, AIDS-related deaths, new HIV infections and the number of children whose parents have died due to all causes including AIDS for past

years. Only new estimates should be used for trend analysis. The new HIV and AIDS estimates included in this table will also be published in the forthcoming UNAIDS *Global AIDS Report, 2012*.

Overall, the global and regional figures published in *The State of the World's Children 2013* are not comparable to estimates previously published. More information on HIV and AIDS estimates, methodology and updates can be found at <www.unaids.org>.

TABLE 8. WOMEN

Maternal mortality ratio (adjusted): The table presents the 'adjusted' maternal mortality ratios for the year 2010, as produced by the Maternal Mortality Estimation Inter-agency Group (MMEIG), composed of WHO, UNICEF, the United Nations Population Fund (UNFPA) and the World Bank, together with independent technical experts. To derive these estimates, the inter-agency group used a dual approach: making adjustments to correct misclassification and underreporting in existing estimates of maternal mortality from civil registration systems, and using a model to generate estimates for countries without reliable national-level estimates of maternal mortality. These 'adjusted' estimates should not be compared to previous inter-agency estimates. The full report – with complete country and regional estimates for the years 1990, 1995, 2000, 2005 and 2010, as well as details on the methodology – can be found at <www.childinfo.org/ maternal_mortality.html>.

TABLE 9. CHILD PROTECTION

Violent discipline: Estimates used in UNICEF publications and in MICS country reports prior to 2010 were calculated using household weights that did not take into account the last-stage selection of children for the administration of the child discipline module in MICS surveys. (A random selection of one child aged 2–14 is undertaken for the administration of the child discipline module.) In January 2010, it was decided that more accurate estimates are produced by using a household weight that takes the last-stage selection into account. MICS 3 data were recalculated using this approach. All UNICEF publications produced after 2010, including *The State of the World's Children 2013*, use the revised estimates.

Child labour: New data from the fourth round of MICS (MICS4, 2009–2012) included in the table have been recalculated according to the indicator definition used in MICS3 surveys, to ensure cross-country comparability. In this definition, the activities of fetching water or collecting firewood are classified as household chores rather than as an economic activity. Under this approach, a child between the ages of 5–14 years old would have to be engaged in fetching water or collecting firewood for at least 28 hours per week to be considered as a child labourer.

TABLE 10. THE RATE OF PROGRESS

The under-five mortality rate (U5MR) is used as the principal indicator of progress in child well-being. In 1970, around 16.9 million children under 5 years old were dying every year. In 2011, by comparison, the estimated number of children who died before their fifth birthday stood at 6.9 million – highlighting a significant long-term decline in the global number of under-five deaths.

U5MR has several advantages as a gauge of child well-being:

- First, U5MR measures an end result of the development process rather than an 'input' such as school enrolment level, per capita calorie availability or number of doctors per thousand population – all of which are means to an end.

- Second, U5MR is known to be the result of a wide variety of inputs: for example, antibiotics to treat pneumonia; insecticide-treated mosquito nets to prevent malaria; the nutritional well-being and health knowledge of mothers; the level of immunization and oral rehydration therapy use; the availability of maternal and child health services, including antenatal care; income and food availability in the family; the availability of safe drinking water and basic sanitation; and the overall safety of the child's environment.

- Third, U5MR is less susceptible to the fallacy of the average than, for example, per capita gross national income (GNI). This is because the natural scale does not allow the children of the rich to be one thousand times more likely to survive, even if the human-made scale does permit them to have one thousand times as much income. In other words, it is much more difficult for a wealthy minority to affect a nation's U5MR, and this indicator therefore presents a more accurate, if far from perfect, picture of the health status of the majority of children and of society as a whole.

The speed of progress in reducing U5MR can be assessed by calculating its annual rate of reduction (ARR). Unlike the comparison of absolute changes, ARR measures relative changes that reflect differences compared to the starting value.

As lower levels of under-five mortality are reached, the same absolute reduction represents a greater percentage reduction. ARR therefore shows a higher rate of progress for a 10-point absolute reduction, for example, if that reduction happens at a lower level of under-five mortality versus a higher level over the same time period. A 10-point decrease in U5MR from 100 in 1990 to 90 in 2011 represents a reduction of 10 per cent, corresponding to an ARR of about 0.5 per cent, whereas the same 10-point decrease from 20 to 10 over the same period represents a reduction of 50 per cent or an ARR of 3.3 per cent. (A negative value for the percentage reduction indicates an increase in U5MR during the period specified.)

When used in conjunction with gross domestic product (GDP) growth rates, U5MR and its rate of reduction can therefore give a picture of the progress being made by any country, area or region, over any period of time, towards the satisfaction of some of the most essential human needs.

As Table 10 shows, there is no fixed relationship between the annual reduction rate of U5MR and the annual rate of growth in per capita GDP. Comparing these two indicators helps shed light on the relationship between economic advances and human development.

Finally, the table gives the total fertility rate for each country and area and the corresponding ARR. It is clear that many of the nations that have achieved significant reductions in their U5MR have also achieved significant reductions in fertility.

TABLES 12–13. EQUITY

Diarrhoea treatment: For the first time, these tables include diarrhoea treatment with oral rehydration salts. This replaces the indicator used in previous years, diarrhoea treatment with oral rehydration therapy and continued feeding.

Explanation of symbols

The following symbols are common across all tables:

- − Data are not available.
- x Data refer to years or periods other than those specified in the column heading. Such data are not included in the calculation of regional and global averages, with the exception of 2005–2006 data from India.
- y Data differ from the standard definition or refer to only part of a country. If they fall within the noted reference period, such data are included in the calculation of regional and global averages.
- * Data refer to the most recent year available during the period specified in the column heading.
- ** Excludes China.

Sources and years for specific data points are available at <www.childinfo.org>. Symbols that appear in specific tables are explained in the footnotes to those tables.

Regional classification

Averages presented at the end of each of the 14 statistical tables are calculated using data from countries and areas as classified below.

Sub-Saharan Africa
Eastern and Southern Africa; West and Central Africa; Djibouti; Sudan[1]

Eastern and Southern Africa
Angola; Botswana; Burundi; Comoros; Eritrea; Ethiopia; Kenya; Lesotho; Madagascar; Malawi; Mauritius; Mozambique; Namibia; Rwanda; Seychelles; Somalia; South Africa; South Sudan[1]; Swaziland; Uganda; United Republic of Tanzania; Zambia; Zimbabwe

West and Central Africa
Benin; Burkina Faso; Cameroon; Cape Verde; Central African Republic; Chad; Congo; Côte d'Ivoire; Democratic Republic of the Congo; Equatorial Guinea; Gabon; Gambia; Ghana; Guinea; Guinea-Bissau; Liberia; Mali; Mauritania; Niger; Nigeria; Sao Tome and Principe; Senegal; Sierra Leone; Togo

Middle East and North Africa
Algeria; Bahrain; Djibouti; Egypt; Iran (Islamic Republic of); Iraq; Jordan; Kuwait; Lebanon; Libya; Morocco; Oman; Qatar; Saudi Arabia; State of Palestine; Sudan[1]; Syrian Arab Republic; Tunisia; United Arab Emirates; Yemen

South Asia
Afghanistan; Bangladesh; Bhutan; India; Maldives; Nepal; Pakistan; Sri Lanka

East Asia and Pacific
Brunei Darussalam; Cambodia; China; Cook Islands; Democratic People's Republic of Korea; Fiji; Indonesia; Kiribati; Lao People's Democratic Republic; Malaysia; Marshall Islands; Micronesia (Federated States of); Mongolia; Myanmar; Nauru; Niue; Palau; Papua New Guinea; Philippines; Republic of Korea; Samoa; Singapore; Solomon Islands; Thailand; Timor-Leste; Tonga; Tuvalu; Vanuatu; Viet Nam

Latin America and Caribbean
Antigua and Barbuda; Argentina; Bahamas; Barbados; Belize; Bolivia (Plurinational State of); Brazil; Chile; Colombia; Costa Rica; Cuba; Dominica; Dominican Republic; Ecuador; El Salvador; Grenada; Guatemala; Guyana; Haiti; Honduras; Jamaica; Mexico; Nicaragua; Panama; Paraguay; Peru; Saint Kitts and Nevis; Saint Lucia; Saint Vincent and the Grenadines; Suriname; Trinidad and Tobago; Uruguay; Venezuela (Bolivarian Republic of)

CEE/CIS
Albania; Armenia; Azerbaijan; Belarus; Bosnia and Herzegovina; Bulgaria; Croatia; Georgia; Kazakhstan; Kyrgyzstan; Montenegro; Republic of Moldova; Romania; Russian Federation; Serbia; Tajikistan; the former Yugoslav Republic of Macedonia; Turkey; Turkmenistan; Ukraine; Uzbekistan

Least developed countries/areas
[Classified as such by the United Nations High Representative for the Least Developed Countries, Landlocked Developing Countries and Small Island Developing States (UN-OHRLLS)]. Afghanistan; Angola; Bangladesh; Benin; Bhutan; Burkina Faso; Burundi; Cambodia; Central African Republic; Chad; Comoros; Democratic Republic of the Congo; Djibouti; Equatorial Guinea; Eritrea; Ethiopia; Gambia; Guinea; Guinea-Bissau; Haiti; Kiribati; Lao People's Democratic Republic; Lesotho; Liberia; Madagascar; Malawi; Mali; Mauritania; Mozambique; Myanmar; Nepal; Niger; Rwanda; Samoa; Sao Tome and Principe; Senegal; Sierra Leone; Solomon Islands; Somalia; South Sudan[1]; Sudan[1]; Timor-Leste; Togo; Tuvalu; Uganda; United Republic of Tanzania; Vanuatu; Yemen; Zambia

Under-five mortality rankings

The following list ranks countries and areas in descending order of their estimated 2011 under-five mortality rate (U5MR), a critical indicator of the well-being of children. Countries and areas are listed alphabetically in the tables on the following pages.

Countries and areas	Under-5 mortality rate (2011) Value	Rank
Sierra Leone	185	1
Somalia	180	2
Mali	176	3
Chad	169	4
Democratic Republic of the Congo	168	5
Central African Republic	164	6
Guinea-Bissau	161	7
Angola	158	8
Burkina Faso	146	9
Burundi	139	10
Cameroon	127	11
Guinea	126	12
Niger	125	13
Nigeria	124	14
South Sudan[1]	121	15
Equatorial Guinea	118	16
Côte d'Ivoire	115	17
Mauritania	112	18
Togo	110	19
Benin	106	20
Swaziland	104	21
Mozambique	103	22
Afghanistan	101	23
Gambia	101	23
Congo	99	25
Djibouti	90	26
Uganda	90	26
Sao Tome and Principe	89	28
Lesotho	86	29
Sudan[1]	86	29
Malawi	83	31
Zambia	83	31
Comoros	79	33
Ghana	78	34
Liberia	78	34
Ethiopia	77	36
Yemen	77	36
Kenya	73	38
Pakistan	72	39
Haiti	70	40
Eritrea	68	41
United Republic of Tanzania	68	41
Zimbabwe	67	43
Gabon	66	44
Senegal	65	45
Tajikistan	63	46
Madagascar	62	47
Myanmar	62	47
India	61	49
Papua New Guinea	58	50
Bhutan	54	51
Rwanda	54	51
Timor-Leste	54	51
Turkmenistan	53	54
Bolivia (Plurinational State of)	51	55
Uzbekistan	49	56
Nepal	48	57
Kiribati	47	58
South Africa	47	58
Bangladesh	46	60
Azerbaijan	45	61
Cambodia	43	62
Lao People's Democratic Republic	42	63
Micronesia (Federated States of)	42	63
Namibia	42	63
Nauru	40	66
Iraq	38	67
Guyana	36	68
Democratic People's Republic of Korea	33	69
Morocco	33	69
Indonesia	32	71
Kyrgyzstan	31	72
Mongolia	31	72
Algeria	30	74
Guatemala	30	74
Suriname	30	74
Tuvalu	30	74
Kazakhstan	28	78
Trinidad and Tobago	28	78
Botswana	26	80
Marshall Islands	26	80
Nicaragua	26	80
Dominican Republic	25	83
Iran (Islamic Republic of)	25	83
Philippines	25	83
Ecuador	23	86
State of Palestine	22	87
Paraguay	22	87
Solomon Islands	22	87
Viet Nam	22	87
Cape Verde	21	91
Egypt	21	91
Georgia	21	91
Honduras	21	91
Jordan	21	91
Niue	21	91
Saint Vincent and the Grenadines	21	91
Barbados	20	98
Panama	20	98
Palau	19	100
Samoa	19	100
Armenia	18	102
Colombia	18	102
Jamaica	18	102
Peru	18	102
Belize	17	106
Bahamas	16	107
Brazil	16	107
Fiji	16	107
Libya	16	107
Mexico	16	107
Republic of Moldova	16	107
Saint Lucia	16	107
Tunisia	16	107
China	15	115
El Salvador	15	115
Mauritius	15	115
Syrian Arab Republic	15	115
Tonga	15	115
Turkey	15	115
Venezuela (Bolivarian Republic of)	15	115
Albania	14	122
Argentina	14	122
Seychelles	14	122
Grenada	13	125
Romania	13	125
Vanuatu	13	125
Bulgaria	12	128
Dominica	12	128
Russian Federation	12	128
Sri Lanka	12	128
Thailand	12	128
Kuwait	11	133
Maldives	11	133
Bahrain	10	135
Cook Islands	10	135
Costa Rica	10	135
The former Yugoslav Republic of Macedonia	10	135
Ukraine	10	135
Uruguay	10	135
Chile	9	141
Lebanon	9	141
Oman	9	141
Saudi Arabia	9	141
Antigua and Barbuda	8	145
Bosnia and Herzegovina	8	145
Latvia	8	145
Qatar	8	145
Slovakia	8	145
United States	8	145
Brunei Darussalam	7	151
Malaysia	7	151
Montenegro	7	151
Saint Kitts and Nevis	7	151
Serbia	7	151
United Arab Emirates	7	151
Belarus	6	157
Canada	6	157
Cuba	6	157
Hungary	6	157
Lithuania	6	157
Malta	6	157
New Zealand	6	157
Poland	6	157
Australia	5	165
Croatia	5	165
Republic of Korea	5	165
United Kingdom	5	165
Austria	4	169
Belgium	4	169
Czech Republic	4	169
Denmark	4	169
Estonia	4	169
France	4	169
Germany	4	169
Greece	4	169
Ireland	4	169
Israel	4	169
Italy	4	169
Monaco	4	169
Netherlands	4	169
Spain	4	169
Switzerland	4	169
Andorra	3	184
Cyprus	3	184
Finland	3	184
Iceland	3	184
Japan	3	184
Luxembourg	3	184
Norway	3	184
Portugal	3	184
Singapore	3	184
Slovenia	3	184
Sweden	3	184
San Marino	2	195
Holy See	–	–
Liechtenstein	–	–

[1] Due to the cession in July 2011 of the Republic of South Sudan by the Republic of the Sudan, and its subsequent admission to the United Nations on 14 July 2011, disaggregated data for the Sudan and South Sudan as separate States are not yet available for all indicators. Aggregated data presented are for the Sudan pre-cession, and these data are included in the averages for the Eastern and Southern Africa, Middle East and North Africa, and sub-Saharan Africa regions as well as the least developed countries/areas category. For the purposes of this report, South Sudan is designated as a least developed country.

TABLE 1: BASIC INDICATORS

Countries and areas	Under-5 mortality rank	Under-5 mortality rate (U5MR) 1990	Under-5 mortality rate (U5MR) 2011	U5MR by sex 2011 male	U5MR by sex 2011 female	Infant mortality rate (under 1) 1990	Infant mortality rate (under 1) 2011	Neonatal mortality rate 2011	Total population (thousands) 2011	Annual no. of births (thousands) 2011	Annual no. of under-5 deaths (thousands) 2011	GNI per capita (US$) 2011	Life expectancy at birth (years) 2011	Total adult literacy rate (%) 2007–2011*	Primary school net enrolment ratio (%) 2008–2011*
Afghanistan	23	192	101	103	99	129	73	36	32,358	1,408	128	410 x	49	–	–
Albania	122	41	14	15	14	36	13	7	3,216	41	1	3,980	77	96	80
Algeria	74	66	30	32	28	54	26	17	35,980	712	21	4,470	73	73	97
Andorra	184	8	3	4	3	7	3	1	86	–	0	41,750 x	–	–	79
Angola	8	243	158	165	150	144	96	43	19,618	803	120	4,060	51	70	86
Antigua and Barbuda	145	27	8	9	7	23	6	4	90	–	0	12,060	–	99	88
Argentina	122	28	14	16	13	24	13	8	40,765	693	10	9,740	76	98	–
Armenia	102	47	18	19	15	40	16	11	3,100	47	1	3,360	74	100	–
Australia	165	9	5	5	4	8	4	3	22,606	307	1	46,200 x	82	–	97
Austria	169	9	4	5	4	8	4	3	8,413	74	0	48,300	81	–	–
Azerbaijan	61	95	45	47	43	75	39	19	9,306	184	8	5,290	71	100	85
Bahamas	107	22	16	17	15	18	14	7	347	5	0	21,970 x	76	–	98
Bahrain	135	21	10	10	10	18	9	4	1,324	23	0	15,920 x	75	92	–
Bangladesh	60	139	46	48	44	97	37	26	150,494	3,016	134	770	69	57	–
Barbados	98	18	20	22	18	16	18	10	274	3	0	12,660 x	77	–	95
Belarus	157	17	6	6	5	14	4	3	9,559	107	1	5,830	70	100	92
Belgium	169	10	4	5	4	9	4	2	10,754	123	1	46,160	80	–	99
Belize	106	44	17	19	15	35	15	8	318	8	0	3,690	76	–	97
Benin	20	177	106	109	103	107	68	31	9,100	356	36	780	56	42	94
Bhutan	51	138	54	57	50	96	42	25	738	15	1	2,070	67	53 x	90
Bolivia (Plurinational State of)	55	120	51	54	48	83	39	22	10,088	264	13	2,040	67	91	–
Bosnia and Herzegovina	145	19	8	9	7	17	7	5	3,752	32	0	4,780	76	98	87
Botswana	80	53	26	28	24	41	20	11	2,031	47	1	7,480	53	84	87
Brazil	107	58	16	17	14	49	14	10	196,655	2,996	44	10,720	73	90	–
Brunei Darussalam	151	12	7	8	7	9	6	4	406	8	0	31,800 x	78	95	–
Bulgaria	128	22	12	13	11	19	11	7	7,446	75	1	6,550	73	98	100
Burkina Faso	9	208	146	151	142	105	82	34	16,968	730	101	570	55	29	58
Burundi	10	183	139	145	133	110	86	43	8,575	288	39	250	50	67	–
Cambodia	62	117	43	47	37	85	36	19	14,305	317	13	830	63	74	96
Cameroon	11	145	127	135	120	90	79	33	20,030	716	88	1,210	52	71	94
Canada	157	8	6	6	5	7	5	4	34,350	388	2	45,560	81	–	–
Cape Verde	91	58	21	23	20	45	18	10	501	10	0	3,540	74	84	93
Central African Republic	6	169	164	170	157	112	108	46	4,487	156	25	470	48	56	71
Chad	4	208	169	177	160	113	97	42	11,525	511	79	690	50	34	–
Chile	141	19	9	10	8	16	8	5	17,270	245	2	12,280	79	99	94
China	115	49	15	15	14	39	13	9	1,347,565	16,364	249	4,930	73	94	100 z
Colombia	102	34	18	20	16	28	15	11	46,927	910	16	6,110	74	93	92
Comoros	33	122	79	85	74	86	59	32	754	28	2	770	61	75	–
Congo	25	119	99	103	94	75	64	32	4,140	145	14	2,270	57	–	91
Cook Islands	135	19	10	11	8	16	8	5	20	–	0	–	–	–	98
Costa Rica	135	17	10	11	9	15	9	6	4,727	73	1	7,660	79	96	–
Côte d'Ivoire	17	151	115	125	105	104	81	41	20,153	679	75	1,100	55	56	61
Croatia	165	13	5	6	5	11	4	3	4,396	43	0	13,850	77	99	96
Cuba	157	13	6	6	5	11	5	3	11,254	110	1	5,460 x	79	100	100
Cyprus	184	11	3	3	3	10	3	1	1,117	13	0	29,450 x	80	98	99
Czech Republic	169	14	4	4	4	13	3	2	10,534	116	0	18,520	78	–	–
Democratic People's Republic of Korea	69	45	33	35	32	23	26	18	24,451	348	12	d	69	100	–
Democratic Republic of the Congo	5	181	168	178	158	117	111	47	67,758	2,912	465	190	48	67	–
Denmark	169	9	4	4	3	7	3	2	5,573	64	0	60,390	79	–	96
Djibouti	26	122	90	95	84	94	72	33	906	26	2	1,270 x	58	–	45
Dominica	128	17	12	13	11	14	11	8	68	–	0	7,090	–	–	98
Dominican Republic	83	58	25	27	23	45	21	14	10,056	216	5	5,240	73	90	93
Ecuador	86	52	23	25	21	41	20	10	14,666	298	7	4,140	76	92	98
Egypt	91	86	21	22	20	63	18	7	82,537	1,886	40	2,600	73	72	96
El Salvador	115	60	15	17	14	47	13	6	6,227	126	2	3,480	72	84	95
Equatorial Guinea	16	190	118	124	112	118	80	37	720	26	3	14,540	51	94	56
Eritrea	41	138	68	74	61	86	46	22	5,415	193	13	430	62	68	35
Estonia	169	20	4	4	3	16	3	2	1,341	16	0	15,200	75	100	96
Ethiopia	36	198	77	82	72	118	52	31	84,734	2,613	194	400	59	39	82
Fiji	107	30	16	18	15	25	14	8	868	18	0	3,680	69	–	99
Finland	184	7	3	3	3	6	2	2	5,385	61	0	48,420	80	–	98
France	169	9	4	5	4	7	3	2	63,126	792	3	42,420	82	–	99
Gabon	44	94	66	72	59	69	49	25	1,534	42	3	7,980	63	88	–

TABLE 1 | BASIC INDICATORS ▶

Countries and areas	Under-5 mortality rank	Under-5 mortality rate (U5MR) 1990	Under-5 mortality rate (U5MR) 2011	U5MR by sex 2011 male	U5MR by sex 2011 female	Infant mortality rate (under 1) 1990	Infant mortality rate (under 1) 2011	Neonatal mortality rate 2011	Total population (thousands) 2011	Annual no. of births (thousands) 2011	Annual no. of under-5 deaths (thousands) 2011	GNI per capita (US$) 2011	Life expectancy at birth (years) 2011	Total adult literacy rate (%) 2007–2011*	Primary school net enrolment ratio (%) 2008–2011*
Gambia	23	165	101	107	94	78	58	34	1,776	67	6	610	58	50	69
Georgia	91	47	21	23	18	40	18	15	4,329	51	1	2,860	74	100	100
Germany	169	9	4	4	4	7	3	2	82,163	699	3	43,980	80	–	100
Ghana	34	121	78	83	72	76	52	30	24,966	776	60	1,410	64	67	84
Greece	169	13	4	5	4	12	4	3	11,390	117	1	25,030	80	97	–
Grenada	125	21	13	13	12	17	10	7	105	2	0	7,220	76	–	97
Guatemala	74	78	30	33	28	56	24	15	14,757	473	14	2,870	71	75	99
Guinea	12	228	126	128	123	135	79	39	10,222	394	48	440	54	41	77
Guinea-Bissau	7	210	161	174	147	125	98	44	1,547	59	9	600	48	54	75
Guyana	68	63	36	40	32	48	29	20	756	13	0	2,900 x	70	–	84
Haiti	40	143	70	74	66	99	53	25	10,124	266	19	700	62	49 x	–
Holy See	–	–	–	–	–	–	–	–	0	–	–	–	–	–	–
Honduras	91	55	21	23	20	43	18	11	7,755	205	4	1,970	73	85	96
Hungary	157	19	6	7	6	17	5	4	9,966	100	1	12,730	74	99	98
Iceland	184	6	3	3	2	5	2	1	324	5	0	35,020	82	–	99
India	49	114	61	59	64	81	47	32	1,241,492	27,098	1,655	1,410	65	63	98
Indonesia	71	82	32	34	29	54	25	15	242,326	4,331	134	2,940	69	93	99
Iran (Islamic Republic of)	83	61	25	25	25	47	21	14	74,799	1,255	33	4,520 x	73	85	–
Iraq	67	46	38	41	35	37	31	20	32,665	1,144	42	2,640	69	78	–
Ireland	169	9	4	4	4	8	3	2	4,526	72	0	38,580	81	–	100
Israel	169	12	4	5	4	10	4	2	7,562	156	1	28,930	82	–	97
Italy	169	10	4	4	3	8	3	2	60,789	557	2	35,330	82	99	99
Jamaica	102	35	18	21	16	28	16	11	2,751	50	1	4,980	73	87	82
Japan	184	6	3	4	3	5	2	1	126,497	1,073	4	45,180	83	–	100
Jordan	91	37	21	22	19	31	18	12	6,330	154	3	4,380	73	93	91
Kazakhstan	78	57	28	32	24	48	25	14	16,207	345	11	8,220	67	100	100
Kenya	38	98	73	78	67	64	48	27	41,610	1,560	107	820	57	87	84
Kiribati	58	88	47	50	45	64	38	19	101	–	0	2,110	–	–	–
Kuwait	133	17	11	12	10	14	9	5	2,818	50	1	48,900 x	75	94	98
Kyrgyzstan	72	70	31	34	28	58	27	16	5,393	131	4	920	68	99	95
Lao People's Democratic Republic	63	148	42	44	39	102	34	18	6,288	140	6	1,130	67	73 x	97
Latvia	145	21	8	9	8	17	7	5	2,243	24	0	12,350	73	100	96
Lebanon	141	33	9	10	9	27	8	5	4,259	65	1	9,110	73	90	93
Lesotho	29	88	86	93	79	71	63	39	2,194	60	5	1,220	48	90	74
Liberia	34	241	78	83	74	161	58	27	4,129	157	12	240	57	61	–
Libya	107	44	16	17	16	33	13	10	6,423	144	2	12,320 x	75	89	–
Liechtenstein	–	–	–	–	–	–	–	–	36	–	–	137,070 x	–	–	99
Lithuania	157	17	6	6	5	14	5	3	3,307	35	0	12,280	72	100	96
Luxembourg	184	8	3	3	3	7	2	2	516	6	0	78,130	80	–	97
Madagascar	47	161	62	65	58	98	43	23	21,315	747	45	430	67	64	–
Malawi	31	227	83	87	79	134	53	27	15,381	686	52	340	54	75	97
Malaysia	151	17	7	7	6	15	6	3	28,859	579	4	8,420	74	93	–
Maldives	133	105	11	12	10	76	9	7	320	5	0	6,530	77	98 x	97
Mali	3	257	176	182	169	132	98	49	15,840	728	121	610	51	31	66
Malta	157	11	6	7	5	10	5	4	418	4	0	18,620 x	80	92 x	94
Marshall Islands	80	52	26	29	23	41	22	12	55	–	0	3,910	–	–	99
Mauritania	18	125	112	120	104	81	76	40	3,542	118	13	1,000	59	58	74
Mauritius	115	24	15	16	14	21	13	9	1,307	16	0	8,240	73	89	93
Mexico	107	49	16	17	14	38	13	7	114,793	2,195	34	9,240	77	93	100
Micronesia (Federated States of)	63	56	42	47	36	44	34	17	112	3	0	2,900	69	–	–
Monaco	169	8	4	4	3	6	3	2	35	–	0	183,150 x	–	–	–
Mongolia	72	107	31	35	26	76	26	12	2,800	65	2	2,320	68	97	99
Montenegro	151	18	7	8	7	16	7	5	632	8	0	7,060	75	98	83
Morocco	69	81	33	35	30	64	28	19	32,273	620	21	2,970	72	56	94
Mozambique	22	226	103	107	99	151	72	34	23,930	889	86	470	50	56	92
Myanmar	47	107	62	69	56	77	48	30	48,337	824	53	d	65	92	–
Namibia	63	73	42	45	38	49	30	18	2,324	60	2	4,700	62	89	86
Nauru	66	40	40	56	24	32	32	22	10	–	0	–	–	–	–
Nepal	57	135	48	49	47	94	39	27	30,486	722	34	540	69	60	–
Netherlands	169	8	4	4	4	7	3	3	16,665	181	1	49,730	81	–	100
New Zealand	157	11	6	7	5	9	5	3	4,415	64	0	29,350 x	81	–	99
Nicaragua	80	66	26	29	22	50	22	13	5,870	138	4	1,170	74	78 x	94
Niger	13	314	125	127	122	133	66	32	16,069	777	89	360	55	29 x	58

TABLE 1 | BASIC INDICATORS ▶

Countries and areas	Under-5 mortality rank	Under-5 mortality rate (U5MR) 1990	Under-5 mortality rate (U5MR) 2011	U5MR by sex 2011 male	U5MR by sex 2011 female	Infant mortality rate (under 1) 1990	Infant mortality rate (under 1) 2011	Neonatal mortality rate 2011	Total population (thousands) 2011	Annual no. of births (thousands) 2011	Annual no. of under-5 deaths (thousands) 2011	GNI per capita (US$) 2011	Life expectancy at birth (years) 2011	Total adult literacy rate (%) 2007–2011*	Primary school net enrolment ratio (%) 2008–2011*
Nigeria	14	214	124	129	119	127	78	39	162,471	6,458	756	1,200	52	61	58
Niue	91	14	21	21	21	12	18	10	1	–	0	–	–	–
Norway	184	8	3	3	3	7	3	2	4,925	61	0	88,890	81	–	99
Oman	141	48	9	9	8	36	7	5	2,846	50	0	19,260 x	73	87	98
Pakistan	39	122	72	76	68	95	59	36	176,745	4,764	352	1,120	65	55	74
Palau	100	32	19	23	14	27	14	9	21	–	0	7,250	–	–	–
Panama	98	33	20	21	18	26	17	9	3,571	70	1	7,910	76	94	98
Papua New Guinea	50	88	58	60	55	64	45	23	7,014	208	12	1,480	63	61	–
Paraguay	87	53	22	25	20	41	19	13	6,568	158	3	2,970	72	94	86
Peru	102	75	18	20	17	54	14	9	29,400	591	11	5,500	74	90	98
Philippines	83	57	25	29	22	40	20	12	94,852	2,358	57	2,210	69	95	89
Poland	157	17	6	6	5	15	5	4	38,299	410	2	12,480	76	100	96
Portugal	184	15	3	4	3	11	3	2	10,690	97	0	21,250	79	95	99
Qatar	145	20	8	8	7	17	6	4	1,870	21	0	80,440	78	96	96
Republic of Korea	165	8	5	5	4	6	4	2	48,391	479	3	20,870	81	–	99
Republic of Moldova	107	35	16	17	15	29	14	8	3,545	44	1	1,980	69	99	90
Romania	125	37	13	14	11	31	11	8	21,436	221	3	7,910	74	98	88
Russian Federation	128	27	12	13	10	23	10	7	142,836	1,689	20	10,400	69	100	96
Rwanda	51	156	54	57	51	95	38	21	10,943	449	23	570	55	71	99
Saint Kitts and Nevis	151	28	7	8	6	22	6	5	53	–	0	12,480	–	–	86
Saint Lucia	107	23	16	17	14	18	14	9	176	3	0	6,680	75	–	90
Saint Vincent and the Grenadines	91	27	21	23	19	21	20	13	109	2	0	6,100	72	–	98
Samoa	100	30	19	21	16	25	16	8	184	4	0	3,190	72	99	95
San Marino	195	12	2	2	2	11	2	1	32	–	0	50,400 x	–	–	92
Sao Tome and Principe	28	96	89	92	86	62	58	29	169	5	0	1,360	65	89	99
Saudi Arabia	141	43	9	10	8	34	8	5	28,083	605	6	17,820	74	87	90
Senegal	45	136	65	69	60	69	47	26	12,768	471	30	1,070	59	50	78
Serbia	151	29	7	8	6	25	6	4	9,854	110	1	5,680	75	98	95
Seychelles	122	17	14	15	13	14	12	9	87	–	0	11,130	–	92	–
Sierra Leone	1	267	185	194	176	158	119	49	5,997	227	42	340	48	42	–
Singapore	184	8	3	3	2	6	2	1	5,188	47	0	42,930	81	96	–
Slovakia	145	18	8	9	7	16	7	4	5,472	58	0	16,070	75	–	–
Slovenia	184	10	3	3	3	9	2	2	2,035	20	0	23,610	79	100	97
Solomon Islands	87	42	22	21	22	34	18	11	552	17	0	1,110	68	–	–
Somalia	2	180	180	190	170	108	108	50	9,557	416	71	d	51	–	–
South Africa	58	62	47	50	44	48	35	19	50,460	1,052	47	6,960	53	89	90
South Sudanᵉ	15	217	121	122	119	129	76	38	10,314	–	43	a	–	–	–
Spain	169	11	4	5	4	9	4	3	46,455	499	2	30,990	81	98	100
Sri Lanka	128	29	12	13	11	24	11	8	21,045	373	5	2,580	75	91	94
State of Palestine	87	43	22	23	21	36	20	13	4,152	137	3	a	73	95	89
Sudanᵉ	29	123	86	91	81	77	57	31	34,318	–	95		–	–	–
Suriname	74	52	30	33	26	44	26	16	529	10	0	7,640 x	71	95	91
Swaziland	21	83	104	113	94	61	69	35	1,203	35	4	3,300	49	87	86
Sweden	184	7	3	3	3	6	2	2	9,441	113	0	53,230	81	–	99
Switzerland	169	8	4	5	4	7	4	3	7,702	77	0	76,380	82	–	99
Syrian Arab Republic	115	36	15	16	14	30	13	9	20,766	466	7	2,750 x	76	83	99
Tajikistan	46	114	63	70	56	89	53	25	6,977	194	12	870	68	100	98
Thailand	128	35	12	13	11	29	11	8	69,519	824	10	4,420	74	94 x	90
The former Yugoslav Republic of Macedonia	135	38	10	11	9	34	9	6	2,064	22	0	4,730	75	97	98
Timor-Leste	51	180	54	57	51	135	46	24	1,154	44	2	2,730 x	62	58	86
Togo	19	147	110	118	102	85	73	36	6,155	195	21	560	57	57	94
Tonga	115	25	15	18	13	21	13	8	105	3	0	3,580	72	99 x	–
Trinidad and Tobago	78	37	28	31	24	32	25	18	1,346	20	1	15,040	70	99	97
Tunisia	107	51	16	18	15	40	14	10	10,594	179	3	4,070	75	78	99
Turkey	115	72	15	16	14	60	12	9	73,640	1,289	20	10,410	74	91	97
Turkmenistan	54	94	53	57	48	75	45	22	5,105	109	5	4,110	65	100	–
Tuvalu	74	58	30	33	27	45	25	14	10	–	0	5,010	–	–	–
Uganda	26	178	90	97	83	106	58	28	34,509	1,545	131	510	54	73	91
Ukraine	135	19	10	11	9	17	9	5	45,190	494	5	3,120	68	100	91
United Arab Emirates	151	22	7	7	6	19	6	4	7,891	94	1	40,760	77	90 x	–
United Kingdom	165	9	5	6	5	8	4	3	62,417	761	4	37,780	80	–	100
United Republic of Tanzania	41	158	68	70	65	97	45	25	46,218	1,913	122	540	58	73	98
United States	145	11	8	8	7	9	6	4	313,085	4,322	32	48,450	79	–	96

TABLE 1 | BASIC INDICATORS

Countries and areas	Under-5 mortality rank	Under-5 mortality rate (U5MR) 1990	Under-5 mortality rate (U5MR) 2011	U5MR by sex 2011 male	U5MR by sex 2011 female	Infant mortality rate (under 1) 1990	Infant mortality rate (under 1) 2011	Neonatal mortality rate 2011	Total population (thousands) 2011	Annual no. of births (thousands) 2011	Annual no. of under-5 deaths (thousands) 2011	GNI per capita (US$) 2011	Life expectancy at birth (years) 2011	Total adult literacy rate (%) 2007–2011*	Primary school net enrolment ratio (%) 2008–2011*
Uruguay	135	23	10	11	9	20	9	5	3,380	49	1	11,860	77	98	99
Uzbekistan	56	75	49	55	42	62	42	15	27,760	589	30	1,510	68	99	92
Vanuatu	125	39	13	14	12	31	11	7	246	7	0	2,870	71	83	–
Venezuela (Bolivarian Republic of)	115	31	15	17	13	26	13	8	29,437	598	9	11,920	74	96	95
Viet Nam	87	50	22	25	19	36	17	12	88,792	1,458	32	1,260	75	93	98
Yemen	36	126	77	80	73	89	57	32	24,800	940	70	1,070	65	64	78
Zambia	31	193	83	86	80	114	53	27	13,475	622	46	1,160	49	71	93
Zimbabwe	43	79	67	73	61	53	43	30	12,754	377	24	640	51	–	–

MEMORANDUM

Countries and areas	Under-5 mortality rank	U5MR 1990	U5MR 2011	U5MR male	U5MR female	IMR 1990	IMR 2011	Neonatal mortality rate 2011	Total population (thousands) 2011	Annual no. of births (thousands) 2011	Annual no. of under-5 deaths (thousands) 2011	GNI per capita (US$) 2011	Life expectancy at birth (years) 2011	Total adult literacy rate (%)	Primary school net enrolment ratio (%)
Sudan and South Sudan[σ]	–	–	–	–	–	–	–	–	1,447	–		1,300 x	61	–	–

SUMMARY INDICATORS[#]

	Under-5 mortality rank	U5MR 1990	U5MR 2011	U5MR male	U5MR female	IMR 1990	IMR 2011	Neonatal mortality rate 2011	Total population (thousands) 2011	Annual no. of births (thousands) 2011	Annual no. of under-5 deaths (thousands) 2011	GNI per capita (US$) 2011	Life expectancy at birth (years) 2011	Total adult literacy rate (%)	Primary school net enrolment ratio (%)
Sub-Saharan Africa		178	109	114	103	107	69	34	876,497	32,584	3,370	1,269	55	63	76
Eastern and Southern Africa		162	84	89	79	100	55	29	418,709	14,399	1,177	1,621	56	68	86
West and Central Africa		197	132	138	126	116	83	39	422,564	16,712	2,096	937	53	57	67
Middle East and North Africa		72	36	38	34	54	28	16	415,633	10,017	351	6,234	71	77	90
South Asia		119	62	61	63	85	48	32	1,653,679	37,402	2,309	1,319	66	62	92
East Asia and Pacific		55	20	21	19	41	17	11	2,032,532	28,448	590	4,853	73	94	96
Latin America and Caribbean		53	19	21	17	42	16	10	591,212	10,790	203	8,595	74	91	95
CEE/CIS		48	21	23	19	40	18	10	405,743	5,823	125	7,678	70	98	95
Least developed countries		171	98	102	93	107	65	33	851,103	28,334	2,649	695	59	60	80
World		87	51	53	50	61	37	22	6,934,761	135,056	6,914	9,513	69	84	91

σ Due to the cession in July 2011 of the Republic of South Sudan by the Republic of the Sudan, and its subsequent admission to the United Nations on 14 July 2011, disaggregated data for the Sudan and South Sudan as separate States are not yet available for all indicators. Aggregated data presented are for the Sudan pre-cession (see Memorandum item).

\# For a complete list of countries and areas in the regions, subregions and country categories, see page 98.

DEFINITIONS OF THE INDICATORS

Under-5 mortality rate – Probability of dying between birth and exactly 5 years of age, expressed per 1,000 live births.

Infant mortality rate – Probability of dying between birth and exactly 1 year of age, expressed per 1,000 live births.

Neonatal mortality rate – Probability of dying during the first 28 completed days of life, expressed per 1,000 live births.

GNI per capita – Gross national income (GNI) is the sum of value added by all resident producers, plus any product taxes (less subsidies) not included in the valuation of output, plus net receipts of primary income (compensation of employees and property income) from abroad. GNI per capita is GNI divided by midyear population. GNI per capita in US dollars is converted using the World Bank Atlas method.

Life expectancy at birth – Number of years newborn children would live if subject to the mortality risks prevailing for the cross section of population at the time of their birth.

Total adult literacy rate – Number of literate persons aged 15 and above, expressed as a percentage of the total population in that age group.

Primary school net enrolment ratio – Number of children enrolled in primary or secondary school who are of official primary school age, expressed as a percentage of the total number of children of official primary school age. Because of the inclusion of primary-school-aged children enrolled in secondary school, this indicator can also be referred to as a primary adjusted net enrolment ratio.

MAIN DATA SOURCES

Under-5 and infant mortality rates – United Nations Inter-agency Group for Child Mortality Estimation (UNICEF, World Health Organization, United Nations Population Division and the World Bank).

Neonatal mortality rate – World Health Organization, using civil registrations, surveillance systems and household surveys.

Total population and births – United Nations Population Division.

Under-5 deaths – United Nations Inter-agency Group for Child Mortality Estimation (UNICEF, World Health Organization, United Nations Population Division and the World Bank).

GNI per capita – The World Bank.

Life expectancy at birth – United Nations Population Division.

Total adult literacy rate and primary school net enrolment ratio – UNESCO Institute for Statistics.

NOTES

a low-income country (GNI per capita is $1,025 or less).

b lower-middle-income country (GNI per capita is $1,026 to $4,035).

c upper-middle-income country (GNI per capita is $4,036 to $12,475).

d high-income country (GNI per capita is $12,476 or more).

– Data not available.

x Data refer to years or periods other than those specified in the column heading. Such data are not included in the calculation of regional and global averages.

z Data provided by the Chinese Ministry of Education. The UNESCO Institute for Statistics dataset does not currently include net enrolment rates for China.

* Data refer to the most recent year available during the period specified in the column heading.

TABLE 2: NUTRITION

Countries and areas	Low birthweight (%) 2007–2011*	Early initiation of breastfeeding (%)	Exclusive breastfeeding <6 months (%)	Introduction of solid, semi-solid or soft foods 6–8 months (%)	Breastfeeding at age 2 (%)	Underweight (%)θ 2007–2011* moderate & severe	Underweight (%)θ severe	Stunting (%)θ 2007–2011* moderate & severe	Wasting (%)θ 2007–2011* moderate & severe	Overweight (%)θ 2007–2011* moderate & severe	Vitamin A supplementation full coverageΔ (%) 2011	Iodized salt consumption (%) 2007–2011*
Afghanistan	–	–	–	29 x	54 x	33 x	12 x	59 x	9 x	5 x	100	28 x
Albania	7 x	43	39	78	31	5	2	19	9	23	–	76 y
Algeria	6 x	50 x	7 x	39 x, y	22 x	3	1 x	15 x	4 x	13 x	–	61 x
Andorra	–	–	–	–	–	–	–	–	–	–	–	–
Angola	12 x	55	11 x	77 x	37 x	16 y	7 y	29 y	8 y	–	55	45
Antigua and Barbuda	5	–	–	–	–	–	–	–	–	–	–	–
Argentina	7	–	–	–	28	2 x	0 x	8 x	1 x	10 x	–	–
Armenia	7	36	35	48 y	23	5	1	19	4	17	–	97 x
Australia	7 x	–	–	–	–	–	–	–	–	–	–	–
Austria	7 x	–	–	–	–	–	–	–	–	–	–	–
Azerbaijan	10 x	32 x	12 x	83 x	16 x	8 x	2 x	25 x	7 x	14 x	–	54 x
Bahamas	11	–	–	–	–	–	–	–	–	–	–	–
Bahrain	–	–	–	–	–	–	–	–	–	–	–	–
Bangladesh	22 x	36 x	64	71	90	36	10	41	16	2	94	84 x
Barbados	12	–	–	–	–	–	–	–	–	–	–	–
Belarus	4 x	21 x	9 x	38 x	4 x	1	1 x	4	2	10 x	–	94 y
Belgium	–	–	–	–	–	–	–	–	–	–	–	–
Belize	14	51 x	10 x	–	27 x	4 x	1	22 x	2	14 x	–	–
Benin	15 x	32	43 x	76 y	92	18 x	5 x	43 x	8 x	11 x	98	86
Bhutan	10	59	49	67	66	13	3	34	6	8	–	96 x
Bolivia (Plurinational State of)	6	64	60	83	40	4	1	27	1	9	21	89 y
Bosnia and Herzegovina	5 x	57 x	18 x	29 x	10 x	1 x	0 x	10 x	4 x	26 x	–	62 x
Botswana	13	40	20	46 y	6	11	4	31	7	11	75	65
Brazil	8	43 x	41 y	70 x	25 x	2 x	–	7 x	2 x	7	–	96 x
Brunei Darussalam	–	–	–	–	–	–	–	–	–	–	–	–
Bulgaria	9	–	–	–	–	–	–	–	–	14 x	–	100 x
Burkina Faso	16 x	20 x	25	61	80	26	7	35	11	–	87	34 x
Burundi	11 x	–	69	70 y	79	29	8	58	6	3	83	98 x
Cambodia	11	65	74	82 y	43	28	7	40	11	2	92	83 y
Cameroon	11 x	20 x	20	63 x, y	24	15	5	33	6	6	–	49 x
Canada	6 x	–	–	–	–	–	–	–	–	–	–	–
Cape Verde	6 x	73 x	60	80 x	13 x	–	–	–	–	–	–	75
Central African Republic	14	43	34	56 x, y	32	24	8	41	7	2	0	65
Chad	20	29	3	46	59	30	13	39	16	3	–	54
Chile	6	–	–	–	–	–	–	–	–	10	–	–
China	3	41	28	43 y	–	4	–	10	3	7	–	97 y
Colombia	6 x	57	43	86	33	3	1	13	1	5	–	–
Comoros	25 x	25 x	21 x	34 x	45 x	–	–	–	–	22 x	–	82 x
Congo	13 x	39 x	19 x	78 x	21 x	11 x	3 x	30 x	8 x	9 x	–	82 x
Cook Islands	3 x	–	–	–	–	–	–	–	–	–	–	–
Costa Rica	7	–	15 x	92	40	1	–	6	1	8	–	–
Côte d'Ivoire	17 x	25 x	4 x	51 x	37 x	16 y	5 y	27 y	5 y	–	100	84 x
Croatia	5 x	–	–	–	–	–	–	–	–	–	–	–
Cuba	5	70 x	49	77	17	–	–	–	–	–	–	88 x
Cyprus	–	–	–	–	–	–	–	–	–	–	–	–
Czech Republic	7 x	–	–	–	–	–	–	–	–	4 x	–	–
Democratic People's Republic of Korea	6	18	65 x	31 x	36	19	4	32	5	–	100	25 y
Democratic Republic of the Congo	10	43	37	52	53	24	8	43	9	–	98	59
Denmark	5 x	–	–	–	–	–	–	–	–	–	–	–
Djibouti	10 x	67	1 x	35 x	18 x	23 y	5 y	31 y	10 y	10 x	95	0 x
Dominica	10	–	–	–	–	–	–	–	–	–	–	–
Dominican Republic	11	65	8	88	12	3	0	10	2	8	–	19 x
Ecuador	8	–	40 x	77 x	23 x	6 x	–	–	–	5 x	–	–
Egypt	13	56	53	70	35	6	1	29	7	21	–	79
El Salvador	9	33	31	72 y	54	6 y	1 y	19 y	1 y	6	–	62 x
Equatorial Guinea	13 x	–	24 x	–	–	11 x	–	35 x	3 x	8 x	–	33 x
Eritrea	14 x	78 x	52 x	43 x	62 x	35 x	13 x	44 x	15 x	2 x	46	68 x
Estonia	4 x	–	–	–	–	–	–	–	–	–	–	–
Ethiopia	20 x	52	52	55 x	82	29	9	44	10	2	71	15 y
Fiji	10 x	57 x	40 x	–	–	–	–	–	–	–	–	–
Finland	4 x	–	–	–	–	–	–	–	–	–	–	–
France	–	–	–	–	–	–	–	–	–	–	–	–

TABLE 2 | NUTRITION ▶

Countries and areas	Low birthweight (%) 2007–2011*	Early initiation of breastfeeding (%)	Exclusive breastfeeding <6 months (%)	Introduction of solid, semi-solid or soft foods 6–8 months (%)	Breastfeeding at age 2 (%)	Underweight (%)θ 2007–2011* moderate & severe	severe	Stunting (%)θ 2007–2011* moderate & severe	Wasting (%)θ 2007–2011* moderate & severe	Overweight (%)θ 2007–2011* moderate & severe	Vitamin A supplementation full coverageΔ (%) 2011	Iodized salt consumption (%) 2007–2011*
Gabon	14 x	71 x	6 x	62 x	9 x	8 x	2 x	25 x	4 x	6 x	–	36 x
Gambia	10	52	34	34	31	18	4	24	10	2	93	21
Georgia	5	69	55	43 y	17	1	1	11	2	20	–	100
Germany	–	–	–	–	–	–	–	–	–	4 x	–	–
Ghana	13	52	63	76	44	14	3	28	9	6	–	32 x
Greece	–	–	–	–	–	–	–	–	–	–	–	–
Grenada	9	–	–	–	–	–	–	–	–	–	–	–
Guatemala	11	56	50	71 y	46	13 y	–	48 y	1 y	5	28	76
Guinea	12 x	40 x	48	32 y	–	21	7	40	8	–	88	41
Guinea-Bissau	11	55	38	43	65	18	5	32	6	3	100	12
Guyana	14	43 x	33	81	49	11	2	18	5	6	–	11
Haiti	25 x	44 x	41 x	90 x	35 x	18 x	6 x	29 x	10 x	4 x	36	3 x
Holy See	–	–	–	–	–	–	–	–	–	–	–	–
Honduras	10 x	79 x	30 x	84 x	48 x	8 x	1 x	29 x	1 x	6 x	–	–
Hungary	9 x	–	–	–	–	–	–	–	–	–	–	–
Iceland	4 x	–	–	–	–	–	–	–	–	–	–	–
India	28 x	41 x	46 x	56 x	77 x	43 x	16 x	48 x	20 x	2 x	66	71
Indonesia	9	29	32	85	50	18	5	36	13	14	76	62 y
Iran (Islamic Republic of)	7 x	56 x	23 x	68 x	58 x	–	–	–	–	–	–	99 x
Iraq	15 x	31 x	25 x	62 x	36 x	6 x	2 x	26 x	6 x	15 x	–	28 x
Ireland	–	–	–	–	–	–	–	–	–	–	–	–
Israel	8 x	–	–	–	–	–	–	–	–	–	–	–
Italy	–	–	–	–	–	–	–	–	–	–	–	–
Jamaica	12 x	62 x	15 x	36 x	24 2	2	–	4	2	–	–	–
Japan	8 x	–	–	–	–	–	–	–	–	–	–	–
Jordan	13	39	22	84 y	11	2	0	8	2	7	–	88 x
Kazakhstan	6 x	64 x	17 x	50 x	16 x	4 x	1 x	17 x	5 x	17 x	–	92 x
Kenya	8	58	32	85	54	16	4	35	7	5	–	98
Kiribati	–	–	69	–	82	–	–	–	–	–	–	–
Kuwait	–	–	–	–	–	–	–	–	–	9	–	–
Kyrgyzstan	5 x	65 x	32 x	60 x	26 x	2 x	0 x	18 x	3 x	11 x	–	76 x
Lao People's Democratic Republic	11 x	30 x	26 x	41 x	48 x	31 x	9 x	48 x	7 x	1 x	92	84 x
Latvia	5 x	–	–	–	–	–	–	–	–	–	–	–
Lebanon	12	–	15	35 x	15	–	–	–	–	17 x	–	71
Lesotho	11	53	54	68	35	13	2	39	4	7	–	84
Liberia	14	44	34 y	51 y	41	15 y	2 y	42 y	3 y	4	96	–
Libya	–	–	–	–	–	–	–	–	–	22	–	–
Liechtenstein	–	–	–	–	–	–	–	–	–	–	–	–
Lithuania	4 x	–	–	–	–	–	–	–	–	–	–	–
Luxembourg	8 x	–	–	–	–	–	–	–	–	–	–	–
Madagascar	16	72	51	86	61	36 x	–	50	15 x	–	91	53
Malawi	13 x	58 x	72	86	77	13	3	47	4	9	96	50 x
Malaysia	11	–	–	–	–	13 x	–	17 x	–	–	–	18
Maldives	22 x	64	48	91	68	17	3	19	11	7	–	44 x
Mali	19 x	46 x	38 x	25 x	56 x	27 x	10 x	38 x	15 x	–	96	79 x
Malta	6 x	–	–	–	–	–	–	–	–	–	–	–
Marshall Islands	18	73	31	77 y	53	–	–	–	–	–	–	–
Mauritania	34	81	46	61 y	47 y	20 y	4 y	23 y	12 y	–	100	23
Mauritius	14 x	–	21 x	–	–	–	–	–	–	–	–	–
Mexico	7	18	19	27	–	3 x	–	16 x	2 x	8 x	–	91 x
Micronesia (Federated States of)	18 x	–	–	–	–	–	–	–	–	–	–	–
Monaco	–	–	–	–	–	–	–	–	–	–	–	–
Mongolia	5	71	59	78	66	5	2	16	2	14 x	85	70
Montenegro	4 x	25 x	19 x	35 x	13 x	2 x	1 x	7 x	4 x	16 x	–	71 x
Morocco	15 x	52 x	31 x	66 x	15 x	3	–	15	2	11	–	21 x
Mozambique	16	63	41	86	52	15	4	43	6	7	100	25
Myanmar	9	76	24	81 y	65	23	6	35	8	3	96	93
Namibia	16 x	71	24 x	91 x	28 x	17	4	29	8	5	–	63 x
Nauru	27	76	67	65 y	65	5	1	24	1	3	–	–
Nepal	18	45	70	66	93	29	8	41	11	1	91	80
Netherlands	–	–	–	–	–	–	–	–	–	–	–	–
New Zealand	6 x	–	–	–	–	–	–	–	–	–	–	–
Nicaragua	9	54	31	76 y	43	6	1	22	1	6	2	97 x

TABLE 2 | NUTRITION ▶

Countries and areas	Low birthweight (%) 2007–2011*	Early initiation of breastfeeding (%)	Exclusive breastfeeding <6 months (%)	Introduction of solid, semi-solid or soft foods 6–8 months (%)	Breastfeeding at age 2 (%)	Underweight (%)θ 2007–2011* moderate & severe	Underweight severe	Stunting (%)θ 2007–2011* moderate & severe	Wasting (%)θ 2007–2011* moderate & severe	Overweight (%)θ 2007–2011* moderate & severe	Vitamin A supplementation full coverageΔ (%) 2011	Iodized salt consumption (%) 2007–2011*
Niger	27 x	42	27	65 y	–	39 y	12 y	51 y	12 y	4 x	95	32
Nigeria	12	38	13	76	32	23	9	41	14	11	73	97 x
Niue	0 x	–	–	–	–	–	–	–	–	–	–	–
Norway	5 x	–	–	–	–	–	–	–	–	–	–	–
Oman	12	85 x	–	91 x	73 x	9	1	10	7	2	–	69 x
Pakistan	32	29	37	36 y	55	32	12	44	15	6	90	69
Palau	–	–	–	–	–	–	–	–	–	–	–	–
Panama	10 x	–	–	–	–	4 y	–	19 y	1 y	–	–	–
Papua New Guinea	11 x	–	56 x	76 x, y	72 x	18	5 x	43 x	5 x	3 x	12	92 x
Paraguay	6	47	24	67 y	14	3 x	–	18 x	1 x	7 x	–	93
Peru	8	51	71	82	55 y	4	1	20	0	–	–	91
Philippines	21	54	34	90	34	22 y	–	32 y	7 y	3	91	45 x
Poland	6 x	–	–	–	–	–	–	–	–	–	–	–
Portugal	8 x	–	–	–	–	–	–	–	–	–	–	–
Qatar	–	–	–	–	–	–	–	–	–	–	–	–
Republic of Korea	4 x	–	–	–	–	–	–	–	–	–	–	–
Republic of Moldova	6 x	65 x	46 x	18 x	2 x	3 x	1 x	10 x	5 x	9 x	–	60 x
Romania	8 x	–	16 x	41 x	–	4 x	1 x	13 x	4 x	8 x	–	74 x
Russian Federation	6	–	–	–	–	–	–	–	–	–	–	35 x
Rwanda	7	71	85	79	84	11	2	44	3	7	76	99
Saint Kitts and Nevis	8	–	–	–	–	–	–	–	–	–	–	100 x
Saint Lucia	11	–	–	–	–	–	–	–	–	–	–	–
Saint Vincent and the Grenadines	8	–	–	–	–	–	–	–	–	–	–	–
Samoa	10	88	51	71 y	74	–	–	–	–	–	–	–
San Marino	–	–	–	–	–	–	–	–	–	–	–	–
Sao Tome and Principe	8 x	45	51	74	20	13	3	29	11	12	44	86
Saudi Arabia	–	–	–	–	–	–	–	–	–	6 x	–	–
Senegal	19	23 x	39	61 x	51	18	5	27	10	3	–	47
Serbia	5	8	14	84	15	2	1	7	4	16	–	32
Seychelles	–	–	–	–	–	–	–	–	–	–	–	–
Sierra Leone	11	45	32	25	48	22	8	44	9	10	99	63
Singapore	8 x	–	–	–	–	3 x	0 x	4 x	4 x	3 x	–	–
Slovakia	7 x	–	–	–	–	–	–	–	–	–	–	–
Slovenia	–	–	–	–	–	–	–	–	–	–	–	–
Solomon Islands	13	75	74	81 y	67	12	2	33	4	3	–	–
Somalia	–	26 x	9 x	16 x	35 x	32 x	12 x	42 x	13 x	5 x	12	1 x
South Africa	–	61 x	8 x	49 x	31 x	9	–	24	5	–	44	–
South Sudanσ	–	–	45	21	38	28	12	31	23	–	–	54
Spain	–	–	–	–	–	–	–	–	–	–	–	–
Sri Lanka	17	80	76	87 y	84	21	4	17	15	1	–	92 y
State of Palestine	7 x	–	27 x	–	–	–	–	–	–	–	–	86 x
Sudanσ	–	–	41	51	40	32	13	35	16	–	–	10
Suriname	11 x	34 x	2 x	58 x	15 x	7 x	1 x	11 x	5 x	4 x	–	–
Swaziland	9	55	44	66	11	6	1	31	1	11	41	52
Sweden	–	–	–	–	–	–	–	–	–	–	–	–
Switzerland	–	–	–	–	–	–	–	–	–	–	–	–
Syrian Arab Republic	10	46	43	–	25	10	–	28	12	18	–	79 x
Tajikistan	10 x	57 y	25 x	15 x	34 x	15	6	39	7	–	99	62
Thailand	7	50 x	15	–	–	7 x	1 x	16 x	5 x	8 x	–	47 x
The former Yugoslav Republic of Macedonia	6	21	23	41	13	1	0	5	2	16 x	–	94 x
Timor-Leste	12 x	82	52	82	33	45	15	58	19	6	59	60
Togo	11	46	62	44	64	17	4	30	5	2	22	32
Tonga	3 x	–	–	–	–	–	–	–	–	–	–	–
Trinidad and Tobago	19 x	41 x	13 x	83 x	22 x	–	–	–	–	5 x	–	28 x
Tunisia	5 x	87 x	6 x	61 x, y	15 x	3 x	–	9 x	3 x	9 x	–	97 x
Turkey	11	39	42	68 y	22	2	0	12	1	–	–	69
Turkmenistan	4 x	60 x	11 x	54 x	37 x	8 x	2 x	19 x	7 x	–	–	87 x
Tuvalu	6	15	35	40 y	51	2	0	10	3	6	–	–
Uganda	14 x	42 x	62	75 x	46	14	3	33	5	3	60	96 x
Ukraine	4	41	18	86	6	–	–	–	–	–	–	18 x
United Arab Emirates	–	–	–	–	–	–	–	–	–	–	–	–
United Kingdom	8 x	–	–	–	–	–	–	–	–	–	–	–

TABLE 2 | NUTRITION

Countries and areas	Low birthweight (%) 2007–2011*	Early initiation of breastfeeding (%)	Exclusive breastfeeding <6 months (%)	Introduction of solid, semi-solid or soft foods 6–8 months (%)	Breastfeeding at age 2 (%)	Underweight (%)θ 2007–2011* moderate & severe	severe	Stunting (%)θ 2007–2011* moderate & severe	Wasting (%)θ 2007–2011* moderate & severe	Overweight (%)θ 2007–2011* moderate & severe	Vitamin A supplementation full coverageΔ (%) 2011	Iodized salt consumption (%) 2007–2011*
United Republic of Tanzania	8	49	50	92	51	16	4	42	5	6	97	59
United States	8 x	–	–	–	–	1 x	0 x	3 x	0 x	8 x	–	–
Uruguay	9	59	65	35 y	27	5 x	2 x	15 x	2 x	9 x	–	–
Uzbekistan	5 x	67 x	26 x	47 x	38 x	4 x	1 x	19 x	4 x	13 x	95	53 x
Vanuatu	10	72	40	68	32	–	–	–	–	5	–	23
Venezuela (Bolivarian Republic of)	8	–	–	–	–	4	–	16	5	6	–	–
Viet Nam	5	40	17	50	19	12	2	23	4	–	99 w	45
Yemen	–	30 x	12 x	76 x	–	43 x	19 x	58 x	15 x	5 x	9	30 x
Zambia	11	57	61	94	42	15	3	45	5	8	72	77 x
Zimbabwe	11	69 x	31	86	20	10	2	32	3	6	56	94 y

MEMORANDUM

Sudan and South Sudanσ	–	–	–	–	–	–	–	–	–	5 x	–	–

SUMMARY INDICATORS#

Sub-Saharan Africa	12	48	37	71	50	21	7	40	9	7	78	48
Eastern and Southern Africa	–	56	52	84	59	18	5	40	7	5	72	50
West and Central Africa	12	41	25	65	43	23	8	39	12	9	83	–
Middle East and North Africa	–	–	–	–	–	8	–	20	9	12	–	–
South Asia	28	39	47	55	75	33	14	39	16	3	73	71
East Asia and Pacific	6	41	28	57	42 **	6	4 **	12	4	5	85 **	87
Latin America and Caribbean	8	–	37	–	–	3	–	12	2	7	–	–
CEE/CIS	7	–	–	–	–	2	–	12	1	16	–	–
Least developed countries	–	52	49	68	64	23	7	38	10	4	82	50
World	15	42	39	60	58 **	16	10 **	26	8	7	75 **	76

σ Due to the cession in July 2011 of the Republic of South Sudan by the Republic of the Sudan, and its subsequent admission to the United Nations on 14 July 2011, disaggregated data for the Sudan and South Sudan as separate States are not yet available for all indicators. Aggregated data presented are for the Sudan pre-cession (see Memorandum item).

For a complete list of countries and areas in the regions, subregions and country categories, see page 98.

DEFINITIONS OF THE INDICATORS

Low birthweight – Percentage of infants weighing less than 2,500 grams at birth.

Early initiation of breastfeeding – Percentage of infants who are put to the breast within one hour of birth.

Exclusive breastfeeding <6 months – Percentage of children aged 0–5 months who are fed exclusively with breast milk in the 24 hours prior to the survey.

Introduction of solid, semi-solid or soft foods [6–8 months] – Percentage of children aged 6–8 months who received solid, semi-solid or soft foods in the 24 hours prior to the survey.

Breastfeeding at age 2 – Percentage of children aged 20–23 months who received breast milk in the 24 hours prior to the survey.

Underweight – Moderate and severe: Percentage of children aged 0–59 months who are below minus two standard deviations from median weight-for-age of the World Health Organization (WHO) Child Growth Standards; severe: Percentage of children aged 0–59 months who are below minus three standard deviations from median weight-for-age of the WHO Child Growth Standards.

Stunting – Moderate and severe: Percentage of children aged 0–59 months who are below minus two standard deviations from median height-for-age of the WHO Child Growth Standards.

Wasting – Moderate and severe: Percentage of children aged 0–59 months who are below minus two standard deviations from median weight-for-height of the WHO Child Growth Standards.

Overweight – Moderate and severe: Percentage of children aged 0–59 months who are above two standard deviations from median weight-for-height of the WHO Child Growth Standards.

Vitamin A supplementation full coverage – The estimated percentage of children aged 6–59 months reached with 2 doses of vitamin A supplements.

Iodized salt consumption – Percentage of households consuming adequately iodized salt (15 parts per million or more).

MAIN DATA SOURCES

Low birthweight – Demographic and Health Surveys (DHS), Multiple Indicator Cluster Surveys (MICS), other national household surveys, data from routine reporting systems, UNICEF and WHO.

Breastfeeding – DHS, MICS, other national household surveys and UNICEF.

Underweight, stunting, wasting and overweight – DHS, MICS, other national household surveys, WHO and UNICEF.

Vitamin A supplementation – UNICEF.

Iodized salt consumption – DHS, MICS, other national household surveys and UNICEF.

NOTES

– Data not available.

w Identifies countries with national vitamin A supplementation programmes targeted towards a reduced age range. Coverage figure is reported as targeted.

x Data refer to years or periods other than those specified in the column heading. Such data are not included in the calculation of regional and global averages, with the exception of 2005–2006 data from India. Estimates from data years prior to 2000 are not displayed.

y Data differ from the standard definition or refer to only part of a country. If they fall within the noted reference period, such data are included in the calculation of regional and global averages.

Δ Full coverage with vitamin A supplements is reported as the lower percentage of 2 annual coverage points (i.e., lower point between round 1 [January–June] and round 2 [July–December] of 2011).

* Data refer to the most recent year available during the period specified in the column heading.

** Excludes China.

θ Regional averages for underweight (moderate and severe), stunting (moderate and severe), wasting (moderate and severe) and overweight (including obesity) are estimated using statistical modeling of data from the UNICEF and WHO Joint Global Nutrition Database, 2011 revision (completed July 2012). The severe underweight indicator was not included in this exercise; regional averages for this indicator are based on a population-weighted average calculated by UNICEF.

TABLE 3: HEALTH

Countries and areas	Use of improved drinking water sources (%) 2010			Use of improved sanitation facilities (%) 2010			Routine EPI vaccines financed by govt. (%) 2011	Immunization coverage (%) 2011							Newborns protected against tetanus^	Pneumonia (%) 2007–2012*		Diarrhoea (%) 2007–2012*	Malaria (%) 2007–2012*		
	total	urban	rural	total	urban	rural		BCG	DPT1β	DPT3β	Polio3	MCV	HepB3	Hib3		Care-seeking for suspected pneumonia	Antibiotic treatment for suspected pneumonia	Treatment with oral rehydration salts (ORS)	Antimalarial treatment among febrile children	Children sleeping under ITNs	Households with at least one ITN
Afghanistan	50	78	42	37	60	30	–	68	86	66	66	62	66	66	60	61	64	53	–	–	–
Albania	95	96	94	94	95	93	–	99	99	99	99	99	99	99	87	70	60	54	–	–	–
Algeria	83	85	79	95	98	88	–	99	99	95	95	95	95	95	90	53 x	59 x	19 x	–	–	–
Andorra	100	100	100	100	100	100	–	–	99	99	99	99	99	99	–	–	–	–	–	–	–
Angola	51	60	38	58	85	19	–	88	99	86	85	88	86	86	70	–	–	–	28	26	35
Antigua and Barbuda	–	95	–	–	98	–	–	99	99	99	99	99	99	99	–	–	–	–	–	–	–
Argentina	–	98	–	–	–	–	–	99	98	93	95	93	93	93	–	–	–	–	–	–	–
Armenia	98	99	97	90	95	80	–	96	98	95	96	97	95	95	–	57	36	33	–	–	–
Australia	100	100	100	100	100	100	–	–	92	92	92	94	92	92	–	–	–	–	–	–	–
Austria	100	100	100	100	100	100	–	–	93	83	83	76	83	83	–	–	–	–	–	–	–
Azerbaijan	80	88	71	82	86	78	78	82	79	74	80	67	48	38	–	36 x	–	21 x	1 x	1 x	–
Bahamas	–	98	–	100	100	100	–	–	99	98	97	90	95	98	92	–	–	–	–	–	–
Bahrain	–	100	–	–	100	–	100	–	99	99	99	99	99	99	94	–	–	–	–	–	–
Bangladesh	81	85	80	56	57	55	30	95	99	96	96	96	96	96	94	35	71	78	–	–	–
Barbados	100	100	100	100	100	100	–	–	93	91	91	93	91	91	–	–	–	–	–	–	–
Belarus	100	100	99	93	91	97	–	99	99	98	98	99	98	21	–	90 x	67 x	36 x	–	–	–
Belgium	100	100	100	100	100	100	–	–	99	98	98	95	97	98	–	–	–	–	–	–	–
Belize	98	98	99	90	93	87	–	98	98	95	95	98	95	95	88	71 x	44 x	27 x	–	–	–
Benin	75	84	68	13	25	5	17	97	94	85	85	72	85	85	92	31	–	50	38	71	80
Bhutan	96	99	94	44	73	29	4	95	98	95	95	95	95	–	89	74	49	61	–	–	–
Bolivia (Plurinational State of)	88	96	71	27	35	10	–	90	90	82	82	84	82	82	74	51	64	35	–	–	–
Bosnia and Herzegovina	99	100	98	95	99	92	–	94	94	88	89	89	88	85	–	91 x	73 x	35 x	–	–	–
Botswana	96	99	92	62	75	41	100	99	98	96	96	94	93	96	92	14 x	–	49 x	–	–	–
Brazil	98	100	85	79	85	44	–	99	99	96	97	97	96	97	92	50	–	–	–	–	–
Brunei Darussalam	–	–	–	–	–	–	–	96	99	97	99	91	93	96	95	–	–	–	–	–	–
Bulgaria	100	100	100	100	100	100	–	98	96	95	95	95	96	95	–	–	–	–	–	–	–
Burkina Faso	79	95	73	17	50	6	32	99	93	91	90	63	91	91	88	56	47	21	35	47	57
Burundi	72	83	71	46	49	46	3	90	99	96	94	92	96	96	80	55	43	38	17	45	52
Cambodia	64	87	58	31	73	20	23	94	96	94	94	93	94	94	91	64	39	34	–	4 x	5 x
Cameroon	77	95	52	49	58	36	9	80	90	66	67	76	66	66	75	30	–	17	21	21	36
Canada	100	100	99	100	100	99	–	–	98	95	99	98	70	95	–	–	–	–	–	–	–
Cape Verde	88	90	85	61	73	43	100	99	99	90	90	96	90	90	92	–	–	–	–	–	–
Central African Republic	67	92	51	34	43	28	–	74	64	54	47	62	54	54	80	30	31	16	32	36	47
Chad	51	70	44	13	30	6	11	53	45	22	31	28	22	22	60	26	31	13	36	10	42
Chile	96	99	75	96	98	83	–	91	98	94	93	91	94	94	–	–	–	–	–	–	–
China	91	98	85	64	74	56	100	99	99	99	99	99	99	–	–	–	–	–	–	–	–
Colombia	92	99	72	77	82	63	–	83	95	85	85	88	85	85	79	64	–	54	–	–	3 x
Comoros	95	91	97	36	50	30	–	76	94	83	86	72	83	83	85	56 x	–	19 x	63 x	9 x	–
Congo	71	95	32	18	20	15	9	95	90	90	90	90	90	90	83	52	–	35	25	26	27
Cook Islands	–	98	–	100	100	100	–	98	98	93	93	89	93	93	–	–	–	–	–	–	–
Costa Rica	97	100	91	95	95	96	–	78	DPT1β	85	82	83	84	81	–	–	–	–	–	–	–
Côte d'Ivoire	80	91	68	24	36	11	30	74	75	62	58	49	62	62	82	38	–	17	18	39	68
Croatia	99	100	97	99	99	98	–	99	97	96	96	96	97	96	–	–	–	–	–	–	–
Cuba	94	96	89	91	94	81	–	99	96	96	99	99	96	96	–	97	70	51	–	–	–
Cyprus	100	100	100	100	100	100	–	–	99	99	99	87	96	96	–	–	–	–	–	–	–
Czech Republic	100	100	100	98	99	97	–	–	99	99	99	98	99	99	–	–	–	–	–	–	–
Democratic People's Republic of Korea	98	99	97	80	86	71	–	98	95	94	99	99	94	–	93	80	88	74	–	–	–
Democratic Republic of the Congo	45	79	27	24	24	24	0	67	79	70	78	71	70	70	70	40	42	27	39	38	51
Denmark	100	100	100	100	100	100	–	–	94	91	91	87	–	91	–	–	–	–	–	–	–
Djibouti	88	99	54	50	63	10	0	89	89	87	87	84	87	87	79	62 x	43 x	62 x	1	20	30
Dominica	–	96	–	–	–	–	–	99	99	98	99	99	98	98	–	–	–	–	–	–	–
Dominican Republic	86	87	84	83	87	75	–	98	91	84	84	79	80	71	90	70	57	41	–	–	–
Ecuador	94	96	89	92	96	84	–	99	99	99	99	98	98	99	85	–	–	–	–	–	–
Egypt	99	100	99	95	97	93	100	98	97	96	96	96	96	–	86	73	58	28	–	–	–
El Salvador	88	94	76	87	89	83	–	91	90	89	89	89	90	90	88	67	51	58	–	–	–
Equatorial Guinea	–	–	–	–	–	–	100	73	65	33	39	51	–	–	75	–	–	29 x	49 x	1 x	–
Eritrea	–	–	–	–	–	4	3	99	99	99	99	99	99	99	93	44 x	–	45 x	13	49	71
Estonia	98	99	97	95	96	94	100	99	96	93	93	94	94	93	–	–	–	–	–	–	–
Ethiopia	44	97	34	21	29	19	–	69	61	51	62	57	51	51	88	27	7	26	10	33	53
Fiji	98	100	95	83	94	71	–	99	99	99	99	94	99	99	94	–	–	–	–	–	–
Finland	100	100	100	100	100	100	100	–	99	99	99	97	–	99	–	–	–	–	–	–	–

TABLE 3 | HEALTH ▶

Countries and areas	Use of improved drinking water sources (%) 2010 total	urban	rural	Use of improved sanitation facilities (%) 2010 total	urban	rural	Routine EPI vaccines financed by govt. (%) 2011	Immunization coverage (%) 2011 BCG	DPT1β	DPT3β	Polio3	MCV	HepB3	Hib3	Newborns protected against tetanusᴧ	Pneumonia (%) 2007-2012 Care-seeking for suspected pneumonia	Antibiotic treatment for suspected pneumonia	Diarrhoea (%) 2007-2012 Treatment with oral rehydration salts (ORS)	Malaria (%) 2007-2012 Antimalarial treatment among febrile children	Children sleeping under ITNs	Households with at least one ITN
France	100	100	100	100	100	100	–	–	99	99	99	89	65	97	–	–	–	–	–	–	–
Gabon	87	95	41	33	33	30	100	89	69	45	44	55	45	45	75	48 x	–	25 x	–	55	70
Gambia	89	92	85	68	70	65	100	90	99	96	95	91	96	96	91	69	70	39	30	33	51
Georgia	98	100	96	95	96	93	78	96	95	94	90	94	92	92	–	74 x	56 x	40 x	–	–	–
Germany	100	100	100	100	100	100	–	–	99	99	95	94	93	93	–	–	–	–	–	–	–
Ghana	86	91	80	14	19	8	–	98	94	91	91	91	91	91	88	41	56	35	53	39	48
Greece	100	100	99	98	99	97	–	91	99	99	99	99	95	83	–	–	–	–	–	–	–
Grenada	–	97	–	97	96	97	–	–	98	99	99	95	94	94	–	–	–	–	–	–	–
Guatemala	92	98	87	78	87	70	–	89	91	85	86	87	85	85	85	64 x	–	37	–	–	–
Guinea	74	90	65	18	32	11	24	93	86	59	57	58	59	59	80	42 x	–	33 x	74	5	8
Guinea-Bissau	64	91	53	20	44	9	–	93	92	76	73	61	76	76	80	52	35	19	51	36	53
Guyana	94	98	93	84	88	82	–	97	97	93	93	98	93	93	90	65	18	50	6	24	26
Haiti	69	85	51	17	24	10	–	75	83	59	59	59	–	–	70	31 x	3 x	40 x	5 x	–	–
Holy See	–	–	–	–	–	–	–	–	–	–	–	–	–	–	–	–	–	–	–	–	–
Honduras	87	95	79	77	85	69	–	99	99	98	98	99	98	98	94	56 x	54 x	56 x	1 x	–	–
Hungary	100	100	100	100	100	100	100	99	99	99	99	99	–	99	–	–	–	–	–	–	–
Iceland	100	100	100	100	100	100	–	–	98	96	96	93	–	96	–	–	–	–	–	–	–
India	92	97	90	34	58	23	100	87	83	72	70	74	47	–	87	69 x	13 x	26 x	8 x	–	–
Indonesia	82	92	74	54	73	39	100	82	86	63	70	89	63	–	85	66	–	35	1	3	3
Iran (Islamic Republic of)	96	97	92	100	100	100	100	99	99	99	99	99	99	–	95	93 x	–	–	–	–	–
Iraq	79	91	56	73	76	67	–	92	90	77	78	76	76	–	85	82 x	82 x	31 x	1 x	0 x	–
Ireland	100	100	100	99	100	98	–	41	98	95	95	92	95	95	–	–	–	–	–	–	–
Israel	100	100	100	100	100	100	–	–	96	94	94	98	99	93	–	–	–	–	–	–	–
Italy	100	100	100	–	–	–	–	–	98	96	96	90	96	96	–	–	–	–	–	–	–
Jamaica	93	98	88	80	78	82	–	99	99	99	99	88	99	99	80	75 x	52 x	40 x	–	–	–
Japan	100	100	100	100	100	100	–	94	99	98	96	94	–	–	–	–	–	–	–	–	–
Jordan	97	98	92	98	98	98	100	95	98	98	98	98	98	98	90	75	79	20	–	–	–
Kazakhstan	95	99	90	97	97	98	–	96	99	99	99	99	99	95	–	71 x	32 x	74 x	–	–	–
Kenya	59	82	52	32	32	32	57	92	95	88	88	87	88	88	73	56	50	39	23	47	56
Kiribati	–	–	–	–	–	–	–	86	99	99	95	90	95	95	–	81	51	62	–	–	–
Kuwait	99	99	99	100	100	100	–	99	99	99	99	99	99	99	95	–	–	–	–	–	–
Kyrgyzstan	90	99	85	93	94	93	–	98	97	96	94	97	96	96	–	62 x	45 x	20 x	–	–	–
Lao People's Democratic Republic	67	77	62	63	89	50	6	77	83	78	79	69	78	78	80	32 x	52 x	46 x	8 x	41 x	45 x
Latvia	99	100	96	–	–	–	100	95	97	94	94	99	91	93	–	–	–	–	–	–	–
Lebanon	100	100	100	–	100	–	–	–	84	81	75	79	81	81	–	74 x	–	44 x	–	–	–
Lesotho	78	91	73	26	32	24	42	95	93	83	91	85	83	83	83	66	–	51	–	–	–
Liberia	73	88	60	18	29	7	91	73	61	49	56	40	49	49	91	62	–	53	57	37	50
Libya	–	–	–	97	97	96	–	99	98	98	98	98	98	98	–	–	–	–	–	–	–
Liechtenstein	–	–	–	–	95	–	–	–	–	–	–	–	–	–	–	–	–	–	–	–	–
Lithuania	–	98	–	–	95	–	100	98	95	92	92	94	95	92	–	–	–	–	–	–	–
Luxembourg	100	100	100	100	100	100	–	–	99	99	99	96	89	89	–	–	–	–	–	–	–
Madagascar	46	74	34	15	21	12	21	82	96	89	88	70	89	89	78	42	–	17	20	46	57
Malawi	83	95	80	51	49	51	–	99	99	97	86	96	97	97	87	70	–	69	43	39	57
Malaysia	100	100	99	96	96	95	–	99	99	99	99	95	97	99	90	–	–	–	–	–	–
Maldives	98	100	97	97	98	97	100	98	97	96	96	96	96	–	95	22 x	–	57	–	–	–
Mali	64	87	51	22	35	14	–	89	85	72	71	56	72	72	89	38 x	–	14 x	35	70	85
Malta	100	100	100	100	100	100	–	–	99	96	96	84	82	96	–	–	–	–	–	–	–
Marshall Islands	94	92	99	75	83	53	2	99	99	94	95	97	97	92	–	–	–	–	–	–	–
Mauritania	50	52	48	26	51	9	21	86	91	75	73	67	75	75	80	45	24	20	21	–	12
Mauritius	99	100	99	89	91	88	100	99	99	98	98	99	98	98	95	–	–	–	–	–	–
Mexico	96	97	91	85	87	79	–	99	99	97	97	98	98	97	88	–	–	–	–	–	–
Micronesia (Federated States of)	–	–	–	–	–	–	–	75	96	84	83	92	83	72	–	–	–	–	–	–	–
Monaco	100	100	–	100	100	–	–	89	99	99	99	99	99	99	–	–	–	–	–	–	–
Mongolia	82	100	53	51	64	29	69	99	99	99	99	98	99	99	–	87	72	38 x	–	–	–
Montenegro	98	99	96	90	92	87	100	97	98	95	95	91	91	90	–	89 x	57 x	16 x	–	–	–
Morocco	83	98	61	70	83	52	–	99	99	99	98	95	98	99	89	70	–	23 x	–	–	–
Mozambique	47	77	29	18	38	5	20	91	90	76	73	82	76	76	83	65	22	55	30	18	28
Myanmar	83	93	78	76	83	73	–	93	99	99	99	99	52	–	93	69	34	61	–	11	–
Namibia	93	99	90	32	57	17	–	89	88	82	85	74	82	82	83	53 x	–	63	20	34	54
Nauru	88	88	–	65	65	–	100	99	99	99	99	99	99	99	–	69	47	–	–	–	–
Nepal	89	93	88	31	48	27	20	97	96	92	92	88	92	92	82	50	7	39	1	–	–
Netherlands	100	100	100	100	100	100	100	–	99	97	97	96	–	97	–	–	–	–	–	–	–

TABLE 3 | HEALTH ▶

Countries and areas	Use of improved drinking water sources (%) 2010			Use of improved sanitation facilities (%) 2010			Routine EPI vaccines financed by govt. (%) 2011	Immunization coverage (%) 2011							Newborns protected against tetanus^	Pneumonia (%) 2007-2012*		Diarrhoea (%) 2007-2012*	Malaria (%) 2007-2012*		
	total	urban	rural	total	urban	rural		BCG	DPT1β	DPT3β	Polio3	MCV	HepB3	Hib3		Care-seeking for suspected pneumonia	Antibiotic treatment for suspected pneumonia	Treatment with oral rehydration salts (ORS)	Antimalarial treatment among febrile children	Children sleeping under ITNs	House-holds with at least one ITN
New Zealand	100	100	100	–	–	–	100	–	95	95	95	93	95	94	–	–	–	–	–	–	–
Nicaragua	85	98	68	52	63	37	–	98	99	98	99	99	98	98	81	58 x	–	59	2 x	–	–
Niger	49	100	39	9	34	4	14	61	80	75	44	76	75	75	84	51	–	34	–	64	76
Nigeria	58	74	43	31	35	27	–	64	53	47	73	71	50	–	60	45	23	26	49	29	42
Niue	100	100	100	100	100	100	5	99	99	98	98	99	98	99	–	–	–	–	–	–	–
Norway	100	100	100	100	100	100	100	–	99	94	94	93	–	95	–	–	–	–	–	–	–
Oman	89	93	78	99	100	95	–	99	99	99	99	99	99	99	91	–	–	–	–	–	–
Pakistan	92	96	89	48	72	34	–	85	88	80	75	80	80	80	75	69	50	41	3	–	0
Palau	85	83	96	100	100	100	0	–	99	84	98	85	91	85	–	–	–	–	–	–	–
Panama	–	97	–	–	–	–	–	97	95	87	91	97	87	87	–	–	–	–	–	–	–
Papua New Guinea	40	87	33	45	71	41	45	83	83	61	58	60	62	61	61	63 x	–	–	–	–	–
Paraguay	86	99	66	71	90	40	–	94	97	90	87	93	90	90	85	–	–	–	–	–	–
Peru	85	91	65	71	81	37	–	91	94	91	91	96	91	91	85	68	51	32	–	–	–
Philippines	92	93	92	74	79	69	–	84	85	80	80	79	76	14	76	50	42	47	0 x	–	–
Poland	–	100	–	–	96	–	–	93	99	99	99	98	98	99	–	–	–	–	–	–	–
Portugal	99	99	100	100	100	100	100	96	98	97	97	96	97	97	–	–	–	–	–	–	–
Qatar	100	100	100	100	100	100	–	97	94	93	93	99	93	93	–	–	–	–	–	–	–
Republic of Korea	98	100	88	100	100	100	–	99	99	99	98	99	99	–	–	–	–	–	–	–	–
Republic of Moldova	96	99	93	85	89	82	–	98	96	93	96	91	96	78	–	60 x	–	33 x	–	–	–
Romania	–	99	–	–	–	–	100	99	96	89	89	93	96	89	–	–	–	–	–	–	–
Russian Federation	97	99	92	70	74	59	–	95	97	97	97	98	97	–	–	–	–	–	–	–	–
Rwanda	65	76	63	55	52	56	11	99	98	97	93	95	97	97	85	50	–	29	11	70	82
Saint Kitts and Nevis	99	99	99	96	96	96	–	99	99	97	98	99	98	98	–	–	–	–	–	–	–
Saint Lucia	96	98	95	65	71	63	–	97	98	97	97	95	97	97	–	–	–	–	–	–	–
Saint Vincent and the Grenadines	–	–	–	–	–	96	–	99	98	95	95	99	96	96	–	–	–	–	–	–	–
Samoa	96	96	96	98	98	98	100	99	99	91	91	67	91	91	–	–	–	68	–	–	–
San Marino	–	–	–	–	–	–	–	–	90	86	86	83	86	85	–	–	–	–	–	–	–
Sao Tome and Principe	89	89	88	26	30	19	15	99	98	96	96	91	96	96	–	75	–	49	8	56	61
Saudi Arabia	–	97	–	–	100	–	–	98	99	98	98	98	98	98	–	–	–	–	–	–	–
Senegal	72	93	56	52	70	39	32	95	94	83	73	82	83	83	88	50	–	22	8	35	63
Serbia	99	99	98	92	96	88	–	99	91	91	91	95	89	91	–	90	82	36	–	–	–
Seychelles	–	100	–	–	98	–	100	99	99	99	99	99	99	99	–	–	–	–	–	–	–
Sierra Leone	55	87	35	13	23	6	2	96	94	84	81	80	84	84	85	74	58	73	62	30	36
Singapore	100	100	–	100	100	–	–	99	98	96	96	95	96	–	–	–	–	–	–	–	–
Slovakia	100	100	100	100	100	99	100	97	99	99	99	98	99	99	–	–	–	–	–	–	–
Slovenia	99	100	99	100	100	100	–	–	98	96	96	95	–	96	–	–	–	–	–	–	–
Solomon Islands	–	–	–	–	98	–	47	89	94	88	93	73	88	88	85	73	23	–	19	40	49
Somalia	29	66	7	23	52	6	0	41	52	41	49	46	–	–	64	13 x	32 x	13 x	8 x	11 x	12 x
South Africa	91	99	79	79	86	67	100	78	77	72	73	78	76	72	77	65 x	–	40 x	–	–	–
South Sudan^σ	–	–	–	–	–	–	0	57	58	46	64	64	–	–	44	48	33	39	36	25	53
Spain	100	100	100	100	100	100	–	–	99	97	97	95	97	97	–	–	–	–	–	–	–
Sri Lanka	91	99	90	92	88	93	39	99	99	99	99	99	99	99	95	58	–	50	0	3	5
State of Palestine	85	86	81	92	92	92	–	98	99	99	99	99	98	–	–	65 x	–	–	–	–	–
Sudan^σ	–	–	–	–	–	–	2	92	98	93	93	87	93	93	74	56	66	22	65	–	25
Suriname	92	97	81	83	90	66	–	–	90	86	86	85	86	86	93	74 x	37 x	44 x	–	3 x	–
Swaziland	71	91	65	57	64	55	–	98	98	91	85	98	91	91	86	58	61	57	2	2	10
Sweden	100	100	100	100	100	100	–	23	99	98	98	96	–	98	–	–	–	–	–	–	–
Switzerland	100	100	100	100	100	100	0	–	95	95	95	92	–	95	–	–	–	–	–	–	–
Syrian Arab Republic	90	93	86	95	96	93	–	90	86	72	75	80	66	72	94	77 x	71 x	50 x	–	–	–
Tajikistan	64	92	54	94	95	94	18	97	98	96	98	98	96	96	–	64 x	41 x	73	2 x	1 x	2 x
Thailand	96	97	95	96	95	96	100	99	99	99	99	98	99	98	–	84 x	65 x	57 x	–	–	–
The former Yugoslav Republic of Macedonia	100	100	99	88	92	82	–	98	95	95	95	95	89	89	–	93 x	74 x	62	–	–	–
Timor-Leste	69	91	60	47	73	37	100	68	69	67	66	62	67	–	81	71	45	71	6	42	42
Togo	61	89	40	13	26	3	25	90	95	81	81	67	81	81	81	32	41	11	34	57	57
Tonga	100	100	100	96	98	96	100	99	99	99	99	99	99	99	–	–	–	–	–	–	–
Trinidad and Tobago	94	98	93	92	92	92	–	–	96	90	91	92	90	90	–	74 x	34 x	–	–	–	–
Tunisia	–	99	–	–	96	–	–	98	98	98	98	96	98	43	96	59 x	–	55 x	–	–	–
Turkey	100	100	99	90	97	75	–	97	98	97	97	97	96	97	90	41 x	–	–	–	–	–
Turkmenistan	–	97	–	98	99	97	–	98	98	97	99	99	97	71	–	83 x	50 x	40 x	–	–	–
Tuvalu	98	98	97	85	88	81	–	99	99	96	96	96	96	96	–	–	–	–	–	–	–
Uganda	72	95	68	34	34	34	19	86	91	82	82	75	82	82	85	79	47	44	65	43	60
Ukraine	98	98	98	94	96	89	–	90	73	50	58	67	21	26	–	–	–	–	–	–	–
United Arab Emirates	100	100	100	98	98	95	–	98	94	94	94	94	94	94	–	–	–	–	–	–	–

TABLE 3 | HEALTH

Countries and areas	Use of improved drinking water sources (%) 2010			Use of improved sanitation facilities (%) 2010			Routine EPI vaccines financed by govt. (%) 2011	Immunization coverage (%) 2011								Pneumonia (%) 2007-2012*		Diarrhoea (%) 2007-2012*	Malaria (%) 2007-2012*		
	total	urban	rural	total	urban	rural	2011	BCG	DPT1β	DPT3β	Polio3	MCV	HepB3	Hib3	Newborns protected against tetanusλ	Care-seeking for suspected pneumonia	Antibiotic treatment for suspected pneumonia	Treatment with oral rehydration salts (ORS)	Antimalarial treatment among febrile children	Children sleeping under ITNs	House-holds with at least one ITN
United Kingdom	100	100	100	100	100	100	–	–	98	95	95	90	–	95	–	–	–	–	–	–	–
United Republic of Tanzania	53	79	44	10	20	7	23	99	96	90	88	93	90	90	88	71	–	44	59	64	64
United States	99	100	94	100	100	99	–	–	98	94	94	90	91	88	–	–	–	–	–	–	–
Uruguay	100	100	100	100	100	99	–	99	99	95	95	95	95	95	–	–	–	–	–	–	–
Uzbekistan	87	98	81	100	100	100	–	99	99	99	99	99	99	99	–	68 x	56 x	28 x	–	–	–
Vanuatu	90	98	87	57	64	54	16	81	78	68	67	52	59	–	75	–	–	23	53	56	68
Venezuela (Bolivarian Republic of)	–	–	–	–	–	–	–	95	90	78	78	86	78	78	50	72 x	–	38 x	–	–	–
Viet Nam	95	99	93	76	94	68	30	98	97	95	96	96	95	95	87	73	68	47	1	9	10
Yemen	55	72	47	53	93	34	13	59	89	81	81	71	81	81	66	44 x	38 x	33 x	–	–	–
Zambia	61	87	46	48	57	43	19	88	87	81	83	83	81	81	81	68	47	60	34	50	64
Zimbabwe	80	98	69	40	52	32	–	98	99	99	99	92	93	93	66	48	31	21	2	10	29
MEMORANDUM																					
Sudan and South Sudanσ	58 †	67 †	52 †	26 †	44 †	14 †	–	–	–	–	–	–	–	–	–	–	–	–	–	–	–
SUMMARY INDICATORS#																					
Sub-Saharan Africa	61	83	49	30	43	23	27	79	79	71	76	74	70	60	76	49	34	32	38	38	50
Eastern and Southern Africa	61	87	50	35	54	27	39	85	85	79	79	79	76	76	81	55	30	39	31	41	54
West and Central Africa	62	82	47	26	35	20	17	73	71	62	72	69	63	44	72	44	33	27	42	36	49
Middle East and North Africa	86	93	76	82	91	70	75	93	96	92	92	90	91	48	85	–	–	–	–	–	–
South Asia	90	96	88	38	60	28	90	87	85	75	73	77	57	23	85	65	24	34	7	–	–
East Asia and Pacific	90	97	84	67	77	58	95	95	95	91	92	95	89	10	85**	64**	–	43**	–	6**	–
Latin America and Caribbean	94	98	81	79	84	60	–	95	96	92	92	93	90	90	85	–	–	–	–	–	–
CEE/CIS	96	99	91	85	87	80	–	96	95	92	93	94	89	58	–	–	–	–	–	–	–
Least developed countries	63	82	56	35	48	30	19	82	87	78	79	76	75	74	81	50	43	42	36	41	53
World	89	96	81	63	79	47	84	88	89	83	84	84	75	43	82**	60**	31**	35**	19**	–	–

σ Due to the cession in July 2011 of the Republic of South Sudan by the Republic of the Sudan, and its subsequent admission to the United Nations on 14 July 2011, disaggregated data for the Sudan and South Sudan as separate States are not yet available for all indicators. Aggregated data presented are for the Sudan pre-cession (see Memorandum item).

For a complete list of countries and areas in the regions, subregions and country categories, see page 98.

DEFINITIONS OF THE INDICATORS

Use of improved drinking water sources – Percentage of the population using any of the following as the main drinking water source: drinking water supply piped into dwelling, plot, yard or neighbour's yard; public tap or standpipe; tube well or borehole; protected dug well; protected spring; rainwater; bottled water plus one of the previous sources as a secondary source.
Use of improved sanitation facilities – Percentage of the population using any of the following sanitation facilities, not shared with other households: flush or pour-flush latrine connected to a piped sewerage system, septic tank or pit latrine; ventilated improved pit latrine; pit latrine with a slab; covered pit; composting toilet.
Routine EPI vaccines financed by government – Percentage of EPI vaccines that are routinely administered in a country to protect children and are financed by the national government (including loans).
EPI – Expanded programme on immunization: The immunizations in this programme include those against tuberculosis (TB); diphtheria, pertussis (whooping cough) and tetanus (DPT); polio; and measles, as well as vaccination of pregnant women to protect babies against neonatal tetanus. Other vaccines, e.g., against hepatitis B (HepB), *Haemophilus influenzae* type b (Hib) or yellow fever, may be included in the programme in some countries.
BCG – Percentage of live births who received bacille Calmette-Guérin (vaccine against tuberculosis).
DPT1 – Percentage of surviving infants who received their first dose of diphtheria, pertussis and tetanus vaccine.
DPT3 – Percentage of surviving infants who received three doses of diphtheria, pertussis and tetanus vaccine.
Polio3 – Percentage of surviving infants who received three doses of the polio vaccine.
MCV – Percentage of surviving infants who received the first dose of the measles-containing vaccine.
HepB3 – Percentage of surviving infants who received three doses of hepatitis B vaccine.
Hib3 – Percentage of surviving infants who received three doses of *Haemophilus influenzae* type b vaccine.
Newborns protected against tetanus – Percentage of newborns protected at birth against tetanus.
Care-seeking for suspected pneumonia – Percentage of children under age 5 with suspected pneumonia (cough and fast or difficult breathing due to a problem in the chest) in the two weeks preceding the survey and who were taken to an appropriate health-care provider.
Antibiotic treatment for suspected pneumonia – Percentage of children under age 5 with suspected pneumonia (cough and fast or difficult breathing due to a problem in the chest) in the two weeks preceding the survey who received antibiotics.
Diarrhoea treatment with oral rehydration salts (ORS) – Percentage of children under age 5 who had diarrhoea in the two weeks preceding the survey and who received oral rehydration salts (ORS packets or pre-packaged ORS fluids).
Antimalarial treatment among febrile children – Percentage of children under age 5 who were ill with fever in the two weeks preceding the survey and received any antimalarial medicine. NB: This indicator refers to antimalarial treatment among all febrile children, rather than among confirmed malaria cases, and thus should be interpreted with caution. For more information, please refer to http://www.childinfo.org/malaria_maltreatment.php.
Children sleeping under ITNs – Percentage of children under age 5 who slept under an insecticide-treated mosquito net the night prior to the survey.
Households with at least one ITN – Percentage of households with at least one insecticide-treated mosquito net.

MAIN DATA SOURCES

Use of improved drinking water sources and improved sanitation facilities – UNICEF and World Health Organization (WHO), Joint Monitoring Programme.
Routine EPI vaccines financed by government – As reported by governments on UNICEF and WHO Joint Reporting Form.
Immunization – UNICEF and WHO.
Suspected pneumonia care-seeking and treatment – Demographic and Health Surveys (DHS), Multiple Indicator Cluster Surveys (MICS) and other national household surveys.
Diarrhoea treatment – DHS, MICS and other national household surveys.
Malaria prevention and treatment – DHS, MICS, Malaria Indicator Surveys (MIS) and other national household surveys.

NOTES

– Data not available.

x Data refer to years or periods other than those specified in the column heading. Such data are not included in the calculation of regional and global averages, with the exception of 2005–2006 data from India. Estimates from data years prior to 2000 are not displayed.

β Coverage for DPT1 should be at least as high as DPT3. Discrepancies where DPT1 coverage is less than DPT3 reflect deficiencies in the data collection and reporting process. UNICEF and WHO are working with national and territorial systems to eliminate these discrepancies.

λ WHO and UNICEF have employed a model to calculate the percentage of births that can be considered as protected against tetanus because pregnant women were given two doses or more of tetanus toxoid (TT) vaccine. The model aims to improve the accuracy of this indicator by capturing or including other potential scenarios where women might be protected (e.g., women who receive doses of TT in supplemental immunization activities). A fuller explanation of the methodology can be found at <www.childinfo.org>.

† The WHO/UNICEF Joint Monitoring Programme for Water Supply and Sanitation (JMP) closed its databases for these estimates before the cession of the Republic of South Sudan by the Republic of the Sudan. Aggregated data presented are for the Sudan pre-cession. Disaggregated data for the Sudan and South Sudan as separate States will be published by the JMP in 2013.

* Data refer to the most recent year available during the period specified in the column heading.

** Excludes China.

TABLE 4: HIV/AIDS

Countries and areas	Adult HIV prevalence (%) 2011	People of all ages living with HIV (thousands) 2011 estimate	low	high	Women living with HIV (thousands) 2011	Children living with HIV (thousands) 2011	HIV prevalence among young people (%) 2011 total	male	female	Comprehensive knowledge of HIV (%) 2007–2011* male	female	Condom use among young people with multiple partners (%) 2007–2011* male	female	Children orphaned by AIDS (thousands) 2011	Children orphaned due to all causes (thousands) 2011	Orphan school attendance ratio (%) 2007–2011*
Afghanistan	<0.1	6	3	17	1	–	<0.1	<0.1	<0.1	–	–	–	–	–	–	–
Albania	–	–	–	–	–	–	–	–	–	22	36	55	–	–	–	–
Algeria	–	–	13	28	–	–	–	–	–	–	13 x	–	–	–	–	–
Andorra	–	–	–	–	–	–	–	–	–	–	–	–	–	–	–	–
Angola	2.1	230	160	340	120	34	1.1	0.6	1.6	32	25	–	–	140	1,300	85
Antigua and Barbuda	–	–	–	–	–	–	–	–	–	53	46	–	–	–	–	–
Argentina	0.4	95	79	120	35	–	0.2	0.2	0.2	–	–	–	–	–	–	–
Armenia	0.2	4	2	7	<1	–	0.1	0.1	0.1	9	16	86	–	–	–	–
Australia	0.2	22	18	27	7	–	0.1	0.1	0.1	–	–	–	–	–	–	–
Austria	0.4	18	13	24	5	–	0.3	0.3	0.2	–	–	–	–	–	–	–
Azerbaijan	0.1	7	5	9	1	–	<0.1	<0.1	<0.1	5 x	5 x	29 x	–	–	–	–
Bahamas	2.8	7	6	7	3	–	0.4	0.3	0.5	–	–	–	–	–	–	–
Bahrain	–	–	–	–	–	–	–	–	–	–	–	–	–	–	–	–
Bangladesh	<0.1	8	5	16	<1	–	<0.1	<0.1	<0.1	18	8	–	–	–	–	84 x
Barbados	0.9	1	1	2	<0.5	–	0.3	0.3	0.2	–	–	–	–	–	–	–
Belarus	0.4	20	15	30	6	–	0.3	0.4	0.2	–	–	–	–	–	–	–
Belgium	0.3	20	16	26	6	–	0.2	0.2	0.2	–	–	–	–	–	–	–
Belize	2.3	5	4	5	2	–	1.0	1.0	1.0	–	40 x	–	–	–	–	66 x
Benin	1.2	64	56	73	33	9	0.6	0.3	0.8	35 x	16 x	44	35	47	380	90
Bhutan	0.3	1	<1	3	<0.5	–	0.2	0.3	0.2	–	21	–	–	–	–	70
Bolivia (Plurinational State of)	0.3	17	9	30	1	–	0.1	0.2	<0.1	28	24	41	–	–	–	–
Bosnia and Herzegovina	–	–	–	–	–	–	–	–	–	–	44 x	–	–	–	–	–
Botswana	23.4	300	280	310	160	15	6.6	4.1	9.0	–	–	–	–	100	140	–
Brazil	0.3	490	430	570	200	–	0.1	0.1	0.1	–	–	–	–	–	–	–
Brunei Darussalam	–	–	–	–	–	–	–	–	–	–	–	–	–	–	–	–
Bulgaria	0.1	4	3	6	1	–	0.1	0.1	0.1	–	–	–	–	–	–	–
Burkina Faso	1.1	120	100	150	56	23	0.5	0.3	0.6	36	31	75	65	130	880	101
Burundi	1.3	80	72	93	38	19	0.4	0.3	0.6	47	45	–	–	120	610	82
Cambodia	0.6	64	52	96	31	–	0.1	0.1	0.1	44	44	–	–	–	–	86
Cameroon	4.6	550	510	600	280	60	2.1	1.2	2.9	34 x	32 x	67	47	340	1,300	91 x
Canada	0.3	71	63	89	13	–	0.1	0.1	0.1	–	–	–	–	–	–	–
Cape Verde	1.0	3	2	5	3	–	0.6	0.1	1.1	–	–	–	–	–	–	–
Central African Republic	4.6	130	100	130	62	20	1.9	1.2	2.6	26 x	17 x	73 x	59 x	140	350	89 x
Chad	3.1	210	180	280	100	34	1.5	0.9	2.1	–	10	–	57 p	180	880	117
Chile	0.5	51	34	73	5	–	0.2	0.3	<0.1	–	–	–	–	–	–	–
China	<0.1	780	620	940	231	–	–	–	–	–	–	–	–	–	–	–
Colombia	0.5	150	90	240	29	–	0.3	0.4	0.1	–	24	–	39	–	–	–
Comoros	0.1	<0.5	<0.5	<0.5	<0.1	–	<0.1	0.1	<0.1	–	–	–	–	–	–	–
Congo	3.3	83	74	92	40	13	1.8	1.2	2.5	22	8	40	26	51	230	–
Cook Islands	–	–	–	–	–	–	–	–	–	–	–	–	–	–	–	–
Costa Rica	0.3	9	7	10	4	–	0.1	0.1	0.2	–	–	–	–	–	–	–
Côte d'Ivoire	3.0	360	320	400	170	61	1.0	0.6	1.4	–	–	57	34	410	1,200	83 x
Croatia	<0.1	1	<1	2	<0.5	–	<0.1	<0.1	<0.1	–	–	–	–	–	–	–
Cuba	0.2	14	12	16	3	–	<0.1	<0.1	<0.1	–	54	–	66	–	–	–
Cyprus	–	–	–	–	–	–	–	–	–	–	–	–	–	–	–	–
Czech Republic	<0.1	2	2	2	<1	–	<0.1	<0.1	<0.1	–	–	–	–	–	–	–
Democratic People's Republic of Korea	–	–	–	–	–	–	–	–	–	–	8	–	–	–	–	–
Democratic Republic of the Congo	–	–	–	–	–	–	–	–	–	–	15	–	16	–	–	74
Denmark	0.2	6	5	7	2	–	0.1	0.1	0.1	–	–	–	–	–	–	–
Djibouti	1.4	9	7	12	5	1	0.2	0.1	0.3	–	18 x	–	–	9	46	–
Dominica	–	–	–	–	–	–	–	–	–	48	56	–	–	–	–	–
Dominican Republic	0.7	44	37	50	24	–	0.2	0.1	0.4	34	41	62	34	–	–	98
Ecuador	0.4	35	19	84	8	–	0.2	0.2	0.1	–	–	–	–	–	–	–
Egypt	<0.1	10	6	18	2	–	<0.1	<0.1	<0.1	18	5	–	–	–	–	–
El Salvador	0.6	24	12	59	10	–	0.3	0.3	0.3	–	27	–	–	–	–	–
Equatorial Guinea	4.7	20	17	29	10	3	2.8	1.6	4.1	–	–	–	–	6	46	–
Eritrea	0.6	23	13	52	12	4	0.2	0.1	0.3	–	–	–	–	19	280	–
Estonia	1.3	10	8	12	3	–	0.2	0.2	0.2	–	–	–	–	–	–	–
Ethiopia	1.4	790	720	870	390	180	0.3	0.2	0.4	34	24	47	–	950	4,600	90
Fiji	0.1	<0.5	<0.2	<0.5	<0.2	–	<0.1	<0.1	<0.1	–	–	–	–	–	–	–
Finland	0.1	3	3	4	<1	–	<0.1	<0.1	<0.1	–	–	–	–	–	–	–

TABLE 4 | HIV/AIDS ▶

Countries and areas	Adult HIV prevalence (%) 2011	People of all ages living with HIV (thousands) 2011 estimate	low	high	Women living with HIV (thousands) 2011	Children living with HIV (thousands) 2011	HIV prevalence among young people (%) 2011 total	male	female	Comprehensive knowledge of HIV (%) 2007–2011* male	female	Condom use among young people with multiple partners (%) 2007–2011* male	female	Children orphaned by AIDS (thousands) 2011	Children orphaned due to all causes (thousands) 2011	Orphan school attendance ratio (%) 2007–2011*
France	0.4	160	130	200	46	–	0.1	0.2	0.1	–	–	–	–	–	–	–
Gabon	5.0	46	34	67	24	3	2.1	1.2	3.0	–	–	–	–	21	64	–
Gambia	1.5	14	7	28	8	–	0.8	0.4	1.2	–	33	–	49 p	–	–	103
Georgia	0.2	5	2	8	1	–	0.2	0.2	0.2	–	–	–	–	–	–	–
Germany	0.1	73	66	82	11	–	0.1	0.1	<0.1	–	–	–	–	–	–	–
Ghana	1.5	230	200	260	110	31	0.6	0.4	0.9	34	28	42	–	180	970	76
Greece	0.2	11	10	13	3	–	0.1	0.1	0.1	–	–	–	–	–	–	–
Grenada	–	–	–	–	–	–	–	–	–	60	65	–	–	–	–	–
Guatemala	0.8	65	19	280	26	–	0.4	0.4	0.5	24	22	74	27 p	–	–	–
Guinea	1.4	85	68	100	41	11	0.6	0.4	0.9	–	–	–	–	52	570	–
Guinea-Bissau	2.5	24	20	28	12	3	1.5	0.9	2.0	–	15	–	50	8	110	109
Guyana	1.1	6	6	7	3	–	0.3	0.2	0.3	47	54	76	–	–	–	–
Haiti	1.8	120	96	130	61	13	0.8	0.4	1.1	40 x	34 x	51 x	23 x	87	420	86 x
Holy See	–	–	–	–	–	–	–	–	–	–	–	–	–	–	–	–
Honduras	–	33	25	45	10	–	–	–	–	–	30 x	–	27 x	–	–	108 x
Hungary	0.1	4	3	5	1	–	<0.1	0.1	<0.1	–	–	–	–	–	–	–
Iceland	0.3	<1	<0.5	<1	<0.2	–	0.1	0.1	0.1	–	–	–	–	–	–	–
India	–	–	–	–	–	–	–	–	–	36 x	20 x	32 x	17 x,p	–	–	72 x
Indonesia	0.3	380	240	570	110	–	0.2	0.2	0.2	15 y	10 y	–	–	–	–	–
Iran (Islamic Republic of)	0.2	96	80	120	13	–	<0.1	<0.1	<0.1	–	–	–	–	–	–	–
Iraq	–	–	–	–	–	–	–	–	–	–	3 x	–	–	–	–	84 x
Ireland	0.3	8	6	10	2	–	0.1	0.1	0.1	–	–	–	–	–	–	–
Israel	0.2	9	7	11	3	–	0.1	0.1	<0.1	–	–	–	–	–	–	–
Italy	0.4	150	120	200	49	–	0.1	0.1	0.1	–	–	–	–	–	–	–
Jamaica	1.8	30	24	39	10	–	0.7	0.9	0.6	54	63	77	57	–	–	–
Japan	<0.1	8	6	10	2	–	<0.1	<0.1	<0.1	–	–	–	–	–	–	–
Jordan	–	–	–	–	–	–	–	–	–	–	13 y	–	–	–	–	–
Kazakhstan	0.2	19	17	23	8	–	<0.1	<0.1	0.1	–	22 x	–	–	–	–	–
Kenya	6.2	1,600	1,500	1,700	800	220	2.6	1.6	3.5	55	48	67	37	1,100	2,600	–
Kiribati	–	–	–	–	–	–	–	–	–	49	44	33	–	–	–	–
Kuwait	–	–	–	–	–	–	–	–	–	–	–	–	–	–	–	–
Kyrgyzstan	0.4	12	9	19	4	–	0.3	0.3	0.3	–	20 x	–	–	–	–	–
Lao People's Democratic Republic	0.3	10	8	15	5	–	0.1	0.1	0.2	–	–	–	–	–	–	–
Latvia	0.7	9	7	13	3	–	0.1	0.2	0.1	–	–	–	–	–	–	–
Lebanon	0.1	3	2	4	1	–	0.1	0.1	0.1	–	–	–	–	–	–	–
Lesotho	23.3	320	300	340	170	41	10.9	6.4	15.4	29	39	60	45	140	200	98
Liberia	1.0	25	21	32	12	5	0.2	0.1	0.3	27	21	28	16	33	230	85
Libya	–	–	–	–	–	–	–	–	–	–	–	–	–	–	–	–
Liechtenstein	–	–	–	–	–	–	–	–	–	–	–	–	–	–	–	–
Lithuania	0.1	2	1	2	<0.5	–	<0.1	<0.1	<0.1	–	–	–	–	–	–	–
Luxembourg	0.3	<1	<1	1	<0.5	–	0.1	0.1	0.1	–	–	–	–	–	–	–
Madagascar	0.3	34	26	47	10	–	0.1	0.2	0.1	26	23	9	7	–	–	74
Malawi	10.0	910	850	970	430	170	3.5	2.1	4.9	45	42	41	31	610	1,000	97
Malaysia	0.4	81	72	89	8	–	0.1	0.1	<0.1	–	–	–	–	–	–	–
Maldives	<0.1	<0.1	<0.1	<0.1	<0.1	–	<0.1	<0.1	<0.1	–	35 y	–	–	–	–	–
Mali	1.1	110	83	140	55	–	0.2	0.1	0.3	–	15	–	27 p	–	–	92
Malta	0.1	<0.5	<0.5	<0.5	<0.1	–	<0.1	<0.1	<0.1	–	–	–	–	–	–	–
Marshall Islands	–	–	–	–	–	–	–	–	–	39	27	23 p	9 p	–	–	–
Mauritania	1.1	24	13	41	13	–	0.3	0.2	0.4	14	5	–	–	–	–	66
Mauritius	1.0	7	5	10	2	–	0.5	0.6	0.4	–	–	–	–	–	–	–
Mexico	0.2	180	160	200	32	–	0.1	0.1	<0.1	–	–	–	–	–	–	–
Micronesia (Federated States of)	–	–	–	–	–	–	–	–	–	–	–	–	–	–	–	–
Monaco	–	–	–	–	–	–	–	–	–	–	–	–	–	–	–	–
Mongolia	<0.1	<1	<1	<1	<0.5	–	<0.1	<0.1	0.1	29	32	69	65 p	–	–	102
Montenegro	–	–	–	–	–	–	–	–	–	–	–	–	–	–	–	–
Morocco	0.2	32	21	46	15	–	0.1	0.1	0.1	–	–	–	–	–	–	–
Mozambique	11.3	1,400	1,200	1,600	750	200	5.5	2.8	8.2	34	36	37	33	800	2,000	83
Myanmar	0.6	220	180	260	77	–	0.3	0.2	0.3	–	32	–	–	–	–	–
Namibia	13.4	190	160	230	100	20	4.6	2.7	6.5	62	65	82	74	75	120	100
Nauru	–	–	–	–	–	–	–	–	–	10	13	17 p	8 p	–	–	–
Nepal	0.3	49	32	100	10	–	0.1	0.1	0.1	34	26	45	–	–	–	–
Netherlands	0.2	25	20	36	8	–	0.1	0.1	0.1	–	–	–	–	–	–	–

TABLE 4 | HIV/AIDS ▶

Countries and areas	Adult HIV prevalence (%) 2011	People of all ages living with HIV (thousands) 2011 estimate	low	high	Women living with HIV (thousands) 2011	Children living with HIV (thousands) 2011	HIV prevalence among young people (%) 2011 total	male	female	Comprehensive knowledge of HIV (%) 2007–2011* male	female	Condom use among young people with multiple partners (%) 2007–2011* male	female	Children orphaned by AIDS (thousands) 2011	Children orphaned due to all causes (thousands) 2011	Orphan school attendance ratio (%) 2007–2011*
New Zealand	0.1	3	2	3	<1	–	<0.1	<0.1	<0.1	–	–	–	–	–	–	–
Nicaragua	0.2	8	3	19	5	–	0.1	0.1	0.2	–	–	–	–	–	–	–
Niger	0.8	65	57	70	33	–	0.4	0.2	0.5	16 x	13 x	42 x,p	–	–	–	67 x
Nigeria	3.7	3,400	3,000	3,800	1,700	440	2.0	1.1	2.9	33	22	56	29	2,200	10,800	117
Niue	–	–	–	–	–	–	–	–	–	–	–	–	–	–	–	–
Norway	0.1	5	4	6	1	–	<0.1	0.1	<0.1	–	–	–	–	–	–	–
Oman	–	–	–	–	–	–	–	–	–	–	–	–	–	–	–	–
Pakistan	0.1	130	76	260	28	–	0.1	0.1	0.1	–	3	–	–	–	–	–
Palau	–	–	–	–	–	–	–	–	–	–	–	–	–	–	–	–
Panama	0.8	18	12	29	4	–	0.3	0.4	0.1	–	–	–	–	–	–	–
Papua New Guinea	0.7	28	24	33	12	4	0.3	0.2	0.4	–	–	–	–	12	250	–
Paraguay	0.3	13	6	32	4	–	0.2	0.2	0.2	–	–	–	51	–	–	–
Peru	0.4	74	38	200	20	–	0.2	0.2	0.1	–	19	–	38 p	–	–	–
Philippines	<0.1	19	16	24	4	–	<0.1	<0.1	<0.1	–	21	–	–	–	–	–
Poland	0.1	35	28	46	10	–	0.1	0.1	<0.1	–	–	–	–	–	–	–
Portugal	0.7	48	37	62	14	–	0.2	0.3	0.2	–	–	–	–	–	–	–
Qatar	–	–	–	–	–	–	–	–	–	–	–	–	–	–	–	–
Republic of Korea	<0.1	15	12	19	4	–	<0.1	<0.1	<0.1	–	–	–	–	–	–	–
Republic of Moldova	0.5	15	12	17	6	–	0.1	0.1	0.1	39 y	42 y	–	–	–	–	–
Romania	0.1	16	13	20	5	–	<0.1	<0.1	<0.1	–	–	–	–	–	–	–
Russian Federation	–	–	730	1,300	–	–	–	–	–	–	–	–	–	–	–	–
Rwanda	2.9	210	180	250	110	27	1.3	0.8	1.7	47	53	58 p	29 p	170	660	91
Saint Kitts and Nevis	–	–	–	–	–	–	–	–	–	50	53	–	–	–	–	–
Saint Lucia	–	–	–	–	–	–	–	–	–	–	–	–	–	–	–	–
Saint Vincent and the Grenadines	–	–	–	–	–	–	–	–	–	–	–	–	–	–	–	–
Samoa	–	–	–	–	–	–	–	–	–	6	3	–	–	–	–	–
San Marino	–	–	–	–	–	–	–	–	–	–	–	–	–	–	–	–
Sao Tome and Principe	1.0	<1	<1	1	<0.5	–	0.4	0.4	0.3	43	43	59	–	–	–	–
Saudi Arabia	–	–	–	–	–	–	–	–	–	–	–	–	–	–	–	–
Senegal	0.7	53	43	65	28	–	0.4	0.3	0.5	31	29	49	–	–	–	97
Serbia	0.1	4	2	5	<1	–	<0.1	<0.1	<0.1	48	54	63	65 p	–	–	–
Seychelles	–	–	–	–	–	–	–	–	–	–	–	–	–	–	–	–
Sierra Leone	1.6	49	39	69	27	4	0.9	0.5	1.3	–	23	–	12	18	310	88
Singapore	0.1	3	3	5	1	–	<0.1	<0.1	<0.1	–	–	–	–	–	–	–
Slovakia	<0.1	<0.5	<0.5	<1	<0.2	–	<0.1	<0.1	<0.1	–	–	–	–	–	–	–
Slovenia	0.1	<1	<0.5	<1	<0.2	–	<0.1	0.1	<0.1	–	–	–	–	–	–	–
Solomon Islands	–	–	–	–	–	–	–	–	–	35	29	39	18	–	–	–
Somalia	0.7	35	23	52	15	–	0.3	0.3	0.4	–	4 x	–	–	–	–	78 x
South Africa	17.3	5,600	5,300	5,900	2,900	460	8.6	5.3	11.9	–	–	–	–	2,100	3,500	101
South Sudanσ	3.1	150	100	200	77	16	1.7	1.0	2.5	–	10	–	7	75	410	78
Spain	0.4	150	130	160	35	–	0.1	0.2	0.1	–	–	–	–	–	–	–
Sri Lanka	<0.1	4	3	11	1	–	<0.1	<0.1	<0.1	–	–	–	–	–	–	–
State of Palestine	–	–	–	–	–	–	–	–	–	–	–	–	–	–	–	–
Sudanσ	0.4	69	56	84	22	–	0.2	0.2	0.2	11	5	–	–	–	–	96
Suriname	1.0	3	2	5	2	–	0.2	0.2	0.2	–	41 x	–	80 x	–	–	–
Swaziland	26.0	190	180	200	100	17	10.8	6.3	15.3	54	58	85	69	75	110	99
Sweden	0.2	9	7	13	3	–	<0.1	<0.1	<0.1	–	–	–	–	–	–	–
Switzerland	0.4	20	16	27	6	–	0.2	0.2	0.1	–	–	–	–	–	–	–
Syrian Arab Republic	–	–	–	–	–	–	–	–	–	–	7 x	–	–	–	–	–
Tajikistan	0.3	11	8	15	4	–	0.1	0.1	0.1	13	14	78	–	–	–	–
Thailand	1.2	490	450	550	200	–	0.2	0.3	0.2	–	46 x	–	–	–	–	93 x
The former Yugoslav Republic of Macedonia	–	–	–	–	–	–	–	–	–	–	27 x	–	36 x,p	–	–	–
Timor-Leste	–	–	–	–	–	–	–	–	–	20	12	–	–	–	–	75
Togo	3.4	150	120	190	73	19	1.5	0.9	2.1	42	33	54	39	89	250	86
Tonga	–	–	–	–	–	–	–	–	–	–	–	–	–	–	–	–
Trinidad and Tobago	1.5	13	12	15	7	–	0.8	0.6	1.0	–	54 x	–	67 x	–	–	–
Tunisia	<0.1	2	2	2	<0.5	–	<0.1	<0.1	<0.1	–	–	–	–	–	–	–
Turkey	<0.1	6	4	8	2	–	<0.1	<0.1	<0.1	–	–	–	–	–	–	–
Turkmenistan	–	–	–	–	–	–	–	–	–	–	5 x	–	–	–	–	–
Tuvalu	–	–	–	–	–	–	–	–	–	61	39	–	–	–	–	–
Uganda	7.2	1,400	1,300	1,500	670	190	3.8	2.4	5.3	39	39	31	24	1,100	2,600	88

TABLE 4 | HIV/AIDS

Countries and areas	Adult HIV prevalence (%) 2011	People of all ages living with HIV (thousands) 2011			Women living with HIV (thousands) 2011	Children living with HIV (thousands) 2011	HIV prevalence among young people (%) 2011			Comprehensive knowledge of HIV (%) 2007–2011*		Condom use among young people with multiple partners (%) 2007–2011*		Children orphaned by AIDS (thousands) 2011	Children orphaned due to all causes (thousands) 2011	Orphan school attendance ratio (%) 2007–2011*
		estimate	low	high			total	male	female	male	female	male	female			
Ukraine	0.8	230	180	310	94	–	0.1	0.1	0.1	43	45	64	63	–	–	–
United Arab Emirates	–	–	–	–	–	–	–	–	–	–	–	–	–	–	–	–
United Kingdom	0.3	94	74	120	29	–	0.1	0.1	0.1	–	–	–	–	–	–	–
United Republic of Tanzania	5.8	1,600	1,500	1,700	760	230	2.9	1.8	4.0	43	48	36	32	1,300	3,000	90
United States	0.6	1,300	1,000	2,000	300	–	0.2	0.3	0.2	–	–	–	–	–	–	–
Uruguay	0.6	12	6	33	4	–	0.3	0.4	0.2	–	–	–	–	–	–	–
Uzbekistan	–	–	–	–	–	–	–	–	–	–	31 x	–	–	–	–	–
Vanuatu	–	–	–	–	–	–	–	–	–	–	15	–	–	–	–	92
Venezuela (Bolivarian Republic of)	0.5	99	51	230	25	–	0.2	0.4	0.1	–	–	–	–	–	–	–
Viet Nam	0.5	250	200	330	48	–	0.2	0.3	0.2	–	51	–	–	–	–	–
Yemen	0.2	22	19	25	9	–	0.1	0.1	0.1	–	2 x,y	–	–	–	–	–
Zambia	12.5	970	900	1,100	460	170	5.0	3.1	7.0	41	38	43	42 p	680	1,200	92
Zimbabwe	14.9	1,200	1,200	1,300	600	200	5.6	3.6	7.6	47	52	51	39 p	1,000	1,300	95

MEMORANDUM

Sudan and South Sudan σ	–	–	–	–	–	–	–	–	–	–	–	–	–	–	–	–

SUMMARY INDICATORS #

Sub-Saharan Africa	4.8	23,500	22,100	24,900	11,800	3,100	2.2	1.3	3.0	36	28	49	30	15,200	53,600	95
Eastern and Southern Africa	7.0	17,200	16,300	17,800	8,700	2,200	3.1	1.9	4.3	40	36	44	30	10,700	27,200	89
West and Central Africa	2.6	6,300	5,700	6,800	3,200	850	1.3	0.7	1.8	33	21	56	30	4,500	26,300	100
Middle East and North Africa	0.1	260	220	320	74	32	0.1	0.1	0.1	–	–	–	–	160	6,000	–
South Asia	0.2	2,500	1,600	3,400	890	110	0.1	0.1	0.1	34	17	33	17	600	42,900	72
East Asia and Pacific	0.2	2,400	2,100	2,700	720	64	0.1	0.1	0.1	–	23 **	–	–	510	28,700	–
Latin America and Caribbean	0.4	1,600	1,300	1,900	540	58	0.2	0.2	0.2	–	–	–	–	600	9,500	–
CEE/CIS	0.6	1,500	1,100	1,800	410	18	0.1	0.1	0.1	–	–	–	–	170	6,500	–
Least developed countries	1.9	10,300	9,600	10,900	5,000	1,600	0.9	0.6	1.3	30	24	–	–	7,800	43,200	88
World	0.8	34,000	31,400	35,900	15,000	3,400	0.4	0.3	0.5	–	21 **	–	–	17,300	151,000	–

σ Due to the cession in July 2011 of the Republic of South Sudan by the Republic of the Sudan, and its subsequent admission to the United Nations on 14 July 2011, disaggregated data for the Sudan and South Sudan as separate States are not yet available for all indicators. Aggregated data presented are for the Sudan pre-cession (see Memorandum item).

For a complete list of countries and areas in the regions, subregions and country categories, see page 98.

DEFINITIONS OF THE INDICATORS

Adult HIV prevalence – Estimated percentage of adults (aged 15–49) living with HIV as of 2011.

People living with HIV – Estimated number of people (all ages) living with HIV as of 2011.

Women living with HIV – Estimated number of women (aged 15+) living with HIV as of 2011.

Children living with HIV – Estimated number of children (aged 0–14) living with HIV as of 2011.

HIV prevalence among young people – Estimated percentage of young men and women (aged 15–24) living with HIV as of 2011.

Comprehensive knowledge of HIV – Percentage of young men and women (aged 15–24) who correctly identify the two major ways of preventing the sexual transmission of HIV (using condoms and limiting sex to one faithful, uninfected partner), who reject the two most common local misconceptions about HIV transmission and who know that a healthy-looking person can be HIV-positive.

Condom use among young people with multiple partners – Among young people (aged 15–24) who reported having had more than one sexual partner in the past 12 months, the percentage who reported using a condom the last time they had sex with any partner.

Children orphaned by AIDS – Estimated number of children (aged 0–17) who have lost one or both parents to AIDS as of 2011.

Children orphaned due to all causes – Estimated number of children (aged 0–17) who have lost one or both parents to any cause as of 2011.

Orphan school attendance ratio – Percentage of children (aged 10–14) who have lost both biological parents and who are currently attending school as a percentage of non-orphaned children of the same age who live with at least one parent and who are attending school.

MAIN DATA SOURCES

Estimated adult HIV prevalence – UNAIDS, *Report on the Global AIDS Epidemic*, 2012.

Estimated number of people living with HIV – UNAIDS, *Report on the Global AIDS Epidemic*, 2012.

Estimated number of women living with HIV – UNAIDS, *Report on the Global AIDS Epidemic*, 2012.

Estimated number of children living with HIV – UNAIDS, *Report on the Global AIDS Epidemic*, 2012.

HIV prevalence among young people – UNAIDS, *Report on the Global AIDS Epidemic*, 2012.

Comprehensive knowledge of HIV – AIDS Indicator Surveys (AIS), Demographic and Health Surveys (DHS), Multiple Indicator Cluster Surveys (MICS) and other national household surveys; HIV/AIDS Survey Indicators Database, <www.measuredhs.com/hivdata>.

Condom use among young people with multiple partners – AIS, DHS, MICS and other national household surveys; HIV/AIDS Survey Indicators Database, <www.measuredhs.com/hivdata>.

Children orphaned by AIDS – UNAIDS, *Report on the Global AIDS Epidemic*, 2012.

Children orphaned by all causes – UNAIDS, *Report on the Global AIDS Epidemic*, 2012.

Orphan school attendance ratio – AIS, DHS, MICS and other national household surveys; HIV/AIDS Survey Indicators Database, <www.measuredhs.com/hivdata>.

NOTES

– Data not available.

x Data refer to years or periods other than those specified in the column heading. Such data are not included in the calculation of regional and global averages, with the exception of 2005–2006 data from India. Estimates from data years prior to 2000 are not displayed.

y Data differ from the standard definition or refer to only part of a country. If they fall within the noted reference period, such data are included in the calculation of regional and global averages.

p Based on small denominators (typically 25–49 unweighted cases).

* Data refer to the most recent year available during the period specified in the column heading.

** Excludes China.

TABLE 5: EDUCATION

Countries and areas	Youth (15–24 years) literacy rate (%) 2007–2011*		Number per 100 population 2011		Pre-primary school participation — Gross enrolment ratio (%) 2008–2011*		Primary school participation — Gross enrolment ratio (%) 2008–2011*		Net enrolment ratio (%) 2008–2011*		Net attendance ratio (%) 2007–2011*		Survival rate to last primary grade (%) 2008–2011* / 2007–2011*		Secondary school participation — Net enrolment ratio (%) 2008–2011*		Net attendance ratio (%) 2007–2011*	
	male	female	mobile phones	Internet users	male	female	male	female	male	female	male	female	admin. data	survey data	male	female	male	female
Afghanistan	–	–	54	5	–	–	114	79	–	–	66 x	40 x	–	90 x	–	–	18 x	6 x
Albania	99	99	96	49	56	55	87	87	80	80	90	91	95	100	–	–	84	82
Algeria	94 x	89 x	99	14	79	76	113	107	98	96	97 x	96 x	95	93 x	–	–	57 x	65 x
Andorra	–	–	75	81	104	99	84	85	78	79	–	–	–	–	74	75	–	–
Angola	80	66	48	15	103	105	137	112	93	78	77	75	32	83 x	12	11	21	17
Antigua and Barbuda	–	–	182	82	76	76	106	97	91	84	–	–	–	–	85	85	–	–
Argentina	99	99	135	48	73	75	118	117	–	–	–	–	94	–	78	87	–	–
Armenia	100	100	104	–	29	34	101	104	–	–	99 x	98 x	–	100 x	85	88	93 x	95 x
Australia	–	–	108	79	79	78	105	105	97	98	–	–	–	–	85	86	–	–
Austria	–	–	155	80	100	100	100	99	100	99	–	–	97	–	–	–	–	–
Azerbaijan	100	100	109	50	26	25	94	93	85	84	74 x	72 x	96	100 x	–	–	83	82
Bahamas	–	–	86	65	–	–	113	115	–	–	–	–	89	–	82	88	–	–
Bahrain	100	100	128	77	–	–	–	–	–	–	86 x	87 x	–	99 x	–	–	77 x	85 x
Bangladesh	75	78	56	5	14	13	–	–	–	–	85 y	88 y	66	94 x	45	50	–	–
Barbados	–	–	127	72	108	108	119	122	–	–	–	–	–	–	81	88	–	–
Belarus	100	100	112	40	100	98	100	100	–	–	93 x	94 x	100	100 x	–	–	95 x	97 x
Belgium	–	–	117	78	118	118	105	104	99	99	–	–	93	–	–	–	–	–
Belize	–	–	64	–	45	47	127	116	–	–	95 x	95 x	90	98 x	–	–	58 x	60 x
Benin	66	45	85	4	18	19	135	117	–	–	65 x	58 x	–	89 x	–	–	34 x	23 x
Bhutan	80 x	68 x	66	21	2	2	110	112	88	91	91	93	91	94	50	54	54	56
Bolivia (Plurinational State of)	100	99	83	30	45	45	105	104	–	–	97	97	–	96	68	69	78	75
Bosnia and Herzegovina	100	100	85	60	17	17	111	113	86	88	97 x	98 x	99	100 x	–	–	89 x	89 x
Botswana	94	97	143	7	19	19	112	108	87	88	86	88	93	–	57	65	36 x	44 x
Brazil	97	99	123	45	–	–	–	–	–	–	95 x	95 x	–	88 x	–	–	74 x	80 x
Brunei Darussalam	100	100	109	56	88	88	107	109	–	–	–	–	96	–	95	99	–	–
Bulgaria	98	98	141	51	80	79	103	102	99	100	–	–	97	–	84	82	–	–
Burkina Faso	47	33	45	3	3	3	79	72	61	56	49 x	44 x	64	89 x	18	14	17 x	15 x
Burundi	78	78	14	1	9	9	157	155	–	–	73	74	56	82 x	18	15	7	7
Cambodia	88	86	70	3	13	13	130	124	96	95	85 y	85 y	–	92 x	–	–	45 y	44 y
Cameroon	89	77	52	5	28	29	129	111	–	–	82 x	77 x	66	87 x	–	–	39 x	37 x
Canada	–	–	75	83	71	71	99	98	–	–	–	–	–	–	–	–	–	–
Cape Verde	97	99	79	32	70	70	114	105	95	92	–	–	–	–	61	71	–	–
Central African Republic	72	58	25	2	6	6	109	78	81	61	56 x	47 x	46	62 x	18	10	12 x	9 x
Chad	53	41	32	2	2	2	107	78	–	–	56	48	28	94 x	–	–	20	12
Chile	99	99	130	54	55	58	108	103	94	94	–	–	–	–	81	84	–	–
China	99	99	73	38	54	54	110	113	100 z	100 z	–	–	99 z	–	–	–	–	–
Colombia	98	99	98	40	49	49	116	114	92	91	90	92	85	95	72	77	73	79
Comoros	86	85	29	6	22	21	109	100	–	–	31 x	31 x	–	19 x	–	–	10 x	11 x
Congo	87 x	78 x	94	6	12	13	118	112	92	89	86 x	87 x	–	93 x	–	–	39 x	40 x
Cook Islands	–	–	–	–	166	149	107	110	98	99	–	–	–	–	76	82	–	–
Costa Rica	98	99	92	42	71	72	110	109	–	–	96	96	89	–	–	–	59 x	65 x
Côte d'Ivoire	72	62	86	2	4	4	96	80	67	56	59 x	51 x	61	90 x	–	–	32 x	22 x
Croatia	100	100	116	71	62	61	93	93	95	97	–	–	99	–	88	94	–	–
Cuba	100	100	12	23	100	100	104	102	100	100	–	–	95	–	86	85	–	–
Cyprus	100	100	98	58	81	81	106	105	99	99	–	–	–	–	96	96	–	–
Czech Republic	–	–	122	73	107	105	106	106	–	–	–	–	100	–	–	–	–	–
Democratic People's Republic of Korea	100	100	4	–	–	–	–	–	–	–	99	99	–	–	–	–	98	98
Democratic Republic of the Congo	68	62	23	1	3	3	100	87	–	–	78	72	55	75	–	–	35	28
Denmark	–	–	126	90	97	96	99	99	95	97	–	–	99	–	88	91	–	–
Djibouti	–	–	21	7	4	4	62	56	47	42	67 x	66 x	64	92 x	28	20	45 x	37 x
Dominica	–	–	164	51	111	114	113	111	–	–	–	–	88	–	–	–	–	–
Dominican Republic	96	98	87	36	38	38	115	102	96	90	95	96	–	78	58	67	56	68
Ecuador	98	99	105	31	109	115	114	115	–	–	92 y	93 y	–	–	–	–	71 y	73 y
Egypt	91	84	101	36	24	23	103	98	–	–	90	87	–	99	71	69	70	70
El Salvador	96	96	126	18	63	65	117	111	95	95	–	–	86	–	57	59	–	–
Equatorial Guinea	98	98	59	–	47	63	88	85	57	56	61 x	60 x	62	–	–	–	23 x	22 x
Eritrea	92	87	4	6	14	13	48	41	37	33	69 x	64 x	69	–	32	25	23 x	21 x
Estonia	100	100	139	77	96	96	100	98	96	96	–	–	98	–	91	93	–	–
Ethiopia	63	47	17	1	5	5	106	97	85	80	64	65	47	84 x	–	–	16	16
Fiji	–	–	84	28	17	19	106	104	99	99	–	–	91	–	–	–	–	–
Finland	–	–	166	89	68	68	99	99	98	98	–	–	100	–	94	94	–	–

TABLE 5 | EDUCATION ▶

Countries and areas	Youth (15–24 years) literacy rate (%) 2007–2011* male	female	Number per 100 population 2011 mobile phones	Internet users	Pre-primary gross enrolment ratio (%) 2008–2011* male	female	Primary gross enrolment ratio (%) 2008–2011* male	female	Primary net enrolment ratio (%) 2008–2011* male	female	Primary net attendance ratio (%) 2007–2011* male	female	Survival rate to last primary grade (%) admin. data 2008–2011*	survey data 2007–2011*	Secondary net enrolment ratio (%) 2008–2011* male	female	Secondary net attendance ratio (%) 2007–2011* male	female
France	–	–	105	80	109	108	111	109	99	99	–	–	–	–	98	99	–	–
Gabon	99	97	117	8	41	43	184	179	–	–	94 x	94 x	–	–	–	–	34 x	36 x
Gambia	72	62	89	11	30	31	82	84	68	70	40	45	61	93	–	–	34	34
Georgia	100	100	102	37	52	64	107	111	–	–	95	96	96	98 x	–	–	85 x	88 x
Germany	–	–	132	83	114	113	103	102	–	–	–	–	96	–	–	–	–	–
Ghana	82	80	85	14	68	70	107	107	84	85	72	74	72	81	51	47	40	44
Greece	99	99	106	53	–	–	–	–	–	–	–	–	–	–	–	–	–	–
Grenada	–	–	–	–	95	102	103	103	96	99	–	–	–	–	95	86	–	–
Guatemala	89	85	140	12	70	72	119	114	100	98	–	–	–	–	43	40	23 x	24 x
Guinea	70	57	44	1	14	14	103	86	83	70	55 x	48 x	66	96 x	36	22	27 x	17 x
Guinea-Bissau	79	65	26	3	7	7	127	119	77	73	69	65	–	79	–	–	27	20
Guyana	–	–	69	32	74	78	83	86	82	86	94	96	83	100	78	83	70	79
Haiti	74	70	41	–	–	–	–	–	–	–	48 x	52 x	–	85 x	–	–	18 x	21 x
Holy See	–	–	–	–	a	a	a	a	–	–	–	–	–	–	a	a	–	–
Honduras	94	96	104	16	43	44	116	116	95	97	87 x	90 x	–	–	–	–	35 x	43 x
Hungary	99	99	117	59	85	84	102	101	98	98	–	–	98	–	91	91	–	–
Iceland	–	–	106	95	97	97	99	100	99	100	–	–	–	–	87	89	–	–
India	88	74	72	10	54	56	116	116	99	98	85 x	81 x	–	95 x	–	–	59 x	49 x
Indonesia	100	99	98	18	43	44	117	119	–	–	98	98	–	–	68	67	57 y	59 y
Iran (Islamic Republic of)	99	99	75	21	41	44	114	115	–	–	94 x	91 x	94	–	92	80	–	–
Iraq	85	81	78	5	–	–	–	–	–	–	91 x	80 y	–	93 x	–	–	46 x	34 x
Ireland	–	–	108	77	99	97	108	108	99	100	–	–	–	–	98	100	–	–
Israel	–	–	122	70	103	109	103	103	97	97	–	–	99	–	97	100	–	–
Italy	100	100	152	57	100	96	102	101	100	99	–	–	100	–	94	94	–	–
Jamaica	93	98	108	32	113	113	91	87	83	81	97 x	98 x	95	99 x	80	87	89 x	93 x
Japan	–	–	103	80	–	–	103	103	–	–	–	–	100	–	99	100	–	–
Jordan	99	99	118	35	33	31	92	92	91	91	99	99	–	–	83	88	85	89
Kazakhstan	100	100	143	45	48	47	111	111	–	–	99 x	98 x	100	100 x	89	88	95 x	95 x
Kenya	92	94	65	28	52	52	115	112	84	85	72	75	–	96	52	48	40	42
Kiribati	–	–	14	10	–	–	111	115	–	–	–	–	–	–	–	–	55 y	63 y
Kuwait	99	99	–	74	81	83	104	107	97	100	–	–	96	–	86	93	–	–
Kyrgyzstan	100	100	105	20	19	19	100	99	95	95	91 x	93 x	98	99 x	79	79	88 x	91 x
Lao People's Democratic Republic	89 x	79 x	87	9	22	22	131	122	98	95	81 x	77 x	–	65 x	42	38	39 x	32 x
Latvia	100	100	103	72	85	82	101	100	95	97	–	–	95	–	83	84	–	–
Lebanon	98	99	79	52	82	81	106	103	94	93	98	98	92	93 x	71	79	77	85
Lesotho	86	98	48	4	–	–	104	102	72	75	87	91	69	84 x	23	37	26	40
Liberia	71	82	49	3	–	–	101	91	–	–	32	28	–	–	–	–	14	14
Libya	100	100	156	17	–	–	–	–	–	–	–	–	–	–	–	–	–	–
Liechtenstein	–	–	102	85	102	105	109	102	100	98	–	–	–	79	64	64	–	–
Lithuania	100	100	151	65	75	73	96	95	96	96	–	–	98	–	91	91	–	–
Luxembourg	–	–	148	91	87	86	99	100	96	98	–	–	–	–	84	86	–	–
Madagascar	66	64	38	2	9	9	150	147	–	–	78	80	35	89	23	24	27	28
Malawi	87	87	25	3	–	–	133	138	–	–	76 x	79 x	53	81 x	28	27	19	20
Malaysia	98	98	127	61	64	69	–	–	–	–	–	–	98	–	65	71	52	63
Maldives	99	99	166	34	113	115	111	107	97	97	82	84	–	99	35	24	38	24
Mali	56	34	68	2	3	3	86	75	71	61	62	55	75	96 x	38	24	–	–
Malta	97	99	125	69	119	115	101	101	93	94	–	–	80	–	82	80	–	–
Marshall Islands	–	–	–	–	45	47	102	101	–	–	–	–	83	–	–	–	–	–
Mauritania	71	65	93	5	–	–	99	105	73	76	56	59	71	77	–	–	21	17
Mauritius	96	98	99	35	97	96	99	100	92	94	–	–	98	–	–	–	–	–
Mexico	98	98	82	36	101	102	115	113	99	100	97 x	97 x	94	–	70	73	–	–
Micronesia (Federated States of)	–	–	–	–	–	–	–	–	–	–	–	–	–	–	–	–	–	–
Monaco	–	–	86	–	–	–	–	–	–	–	–	–	–	–	–	–	–	–
Mongolia	94	97	105	20	76	79	123	121	100	99	95	97	94	99	–	–	91	95
Montenegro	99	99	–	40	32	30	107	106	–	–	97 x	98 x	–	97 x	–	–	90 x	92 x
Morocco	87	72	113	51	65	50	115	108	95	93	91 x	88 x	91	–	–	–	39 x	36 x
Mozambique	79	65	33	4	–	–	121	109	95	89	82	80	27	60	17	15	21	20
Myanmar	96	96	3	1	10	10	126	126	–	–	90	91	75	93	49	52	52 y	53 y
Namibia	91	95	105	12	–	–	108	107	84	89	91	93	83	89 x	–	–	47	62
Nauru	–	–	65	–	96	93	90	96	–	–	–	–	–	–	–	–	52 y	69 y
Nepal	88	78	44	9	–	–	–	–	–	–	67 y	70 y	–	95 x	–	–	46 x	38 x
Netherlands	–	–	–	92	93	93	108	107	–	–	–	–	–	–	87	88	–	–

TABLE 5 | EDUCATION ▶

Countries and areas	Youth (15–24 years) literacy rate (%) 2007–2011* male	female	Number per 100 population 2011 mobile phones	Internet users	Pre-primary school participation Gross enrolment ratio (%) 2008–2011* male	female	Primary school participation Gross enrolment ratio (%) 2008–2011* male	female	Net enrolment ratio (%) 2008–2011* male	female	Net attendance ratio (%) 2007–2011* male	female	Survival rate to last primary grade (%) 2008–2011* admin. data	2007–2011* survey data	Secondary school participation Net enrolment ratio (%) 2008–2011* male	female	Net attendance ratio (%) 2007–2011* male	female
New Zealand	–	–	109	86	91	95	101	101	99	100	–	–	–	–	94	95	–	–
Nicaragua	85 x	89 x	82	11	55	56	119	116	93	95	71 y	70 y	–	56 x	43	49	35 x	47 x
Niger	52 x	23 x	27	1	4	4	73	60	64	52	44 x	31 x	69	88 x	13	8	13 x	8 x
Nigeria	78	66	59	28	14	14	87	79	60	55	65	60	80	98	–	–	45	43
Niue	–	–	–	–	–	–	–	–	–	–	–	–	–	–	–	–	–	–
Norway	–	–	117	94	100	98	99	99	99	99	–	–	–	99	94	94	–	–
Oman	98	98	169	68	45	45	107	104	100	97	–	–	–	–	89	90	–	–
Pakistan	79	61	62	9	–	–	104	85	81	67	70	62	62	–	38	29	35	29
Palau	–	–	75	–	–	–	–	–	–	–	–	–	–	–	–	–	–	–
Panama	98	97	204	43	67	67	109	106	99	98	–	–	94	–	66	72	–	–
Papua New Guinea	65	72	34	2	101	99	63	57	–	–	–	–	–	–	–	–	–	–
Paraguay	99	99	99	24	35	35	101	98	86	86	87	89	78	–	58	62	81 x	80 x
Peru	98	97	110	37	79	79	108	108	98	98	96	96	90	95	77	78	81 y	82 y
Philippines	97	98	92	29	51	52	107	105	88	90	88 x	89 x	76	90 x	56	67	55 x	70 x
Poland	100	100	128	65	65	66	98	97	96	96	–	–	98	–	90	92	–	–
Portugal	100	100	115	55	82	82	116	112	99	100	–	–	–	–	–	–	–	–
Qatar	96	98	123	86	57	54	103	103	96	97	–	–	–	–	76	93	–	–
Republic of Korea	–	–	109	84	118	119	106	105	99	98	–	–	99	–	96	95	–	–
Republic of Moldova	99	100	105	38	76	75	94	93	90	90	84 x	85 x	95	100 x	78	79	82 x	85 x
Romania	97	97	109	44	79	79	96	95	88	87	–	–	97	–	82	83	–	–
Russian Federation	100	100	179	49	91	89	99	99	95	96	–	–	96	–	–	–	–	–
Rwanda	77	78	41	7	10	11	141	144	–	–	86	89	–	76 x	–	–	15	16
Saint Kitts and Nevis	–	–	–	–	92	88	93	94	86	86	–	–	74	–	89	88	–	–
Saint Lucia	–	–	123	42	62	59	96	92	90	89	–	–	92	–	85	85	–	–
Saint Vincent and the Grenadines	–	–	121	43	79	80	109	101	–	–	–	–	–	–	85	96	–	–
Samoa	99	100	–	–	35	41	107	109	93	97	88 y	89 y	–	–	73	83	51 y	70 y
San Marino	–	–	112	50	96	89	89	101	91	93	–	–	–	–	–	–	–	–
Sao Tome and Principe	95	96	68	20	44	48	131	130	–	–	86	85	68	84	44	52	30	31
Saudi Arabia	99	97	191	48	–	–	106	106	90	89	–	–	–	–	78	83	–	–
Senegal	74	56	73	18	12	14	84	89	76	80	60	63	60	93 x	–	–	35	32
Serbia	99	99	125	42	53	53	96	96	95	94	98	99	99	99	89	91	88	90
Seychelles	99	99	146	43	106	97	117	117	–	–	–	–	–	–	–	–	–	–
Sierra Leone	69	50	36	–	7	7	129	120	–	–	73	76	–	93	–	–	40	33
Singapore	100	100	149	75	–	–	–	–	–	–	–	–	99	–	–	–	–	–
Slovakia	–	–	109	74	92	89	102	102	–	–	–	–	98	–	–	–	–	–
Slovenia	100	100	107	72	87	85	98	97	97	97	–	–	100	–	91	92	–	–
Solomon Islands	–	–	50	6	49	50	–	–	–	–	63 y	69 y	–	–	–	–	29 y	30 y
Somalia	–	–	7	1	–	–	–	–	–	–	18 x	15 x	–	85 x	–	–	12 x	8 x
South Africa	97	98	127	21	65	65	104	100	90	91	80 x	83 x	–	–	–	–	41 x	48 x
South Sudanᵍ	–	–	–	–	–	–	–	–	–	–	32	25	–	65	–	–	8	4
Spain	100	100	114	68	126	127	106	105	100	100	–	–	99	–	94	96	–	–
Sri Lanka	98	99	87	15	–	–	99	99	94	94	–	–	–	–	–	–	–	–
State of Palestine	99	99	–	55	40	39	92	90	90	88	91 x	92 x	–	–	81	87	–	–
Sudanᵍ	–	–	–	–	–	–	–	–	–	–	78	72	–	82	–	–	33	30
Suriname	98	99	179	32	85	86	116	111	91	91	95 x	94 x	90	92 x	46	55	56 x	67 x
Swaziland	92	95	64	18	22	23	121	111	86	85	96	97	84	93	29	37	42	52
Sweden	–	–	119	91	95	95	102	101	100	99	–	–	99	–	94	94	–	–
Switzerland	–	–	130	85	99	100	103	102	99	99	–	–	–	–	84	82	–	–
Syrian Arab Republic	96	94	63	23	10	9	119	116	100	98	87 x	86 x	95	100 x	67	67	63 x	63 x
Tajikistan	100	100	91	13	9	8	104	100	99	96	99 y	96 y	99	100 x	90	80	89 x	74 x
Thailand	98 x	98 x	113	24	98	101	91	90	90	89	98 x	98 x	–	99 x	68	76	77 x	83 x
The former Yugoslav Republic of Macedonia	99	99	109	57	25	26	89	91	97	99	99	98	–	99	–	–	84	81
Timor-Leste	80	79	53	1	–	–	119	115	86	86	71	73	67	91	34	39	43	48
Togo	88	75	50	4	9	9	147	132	–	–	91	87	59	90	–	–	51	40
Tonga	99 x	100 x	53	25	–	–	–	–	–	–	–	–	–	–	–	–	–	–
Trinidad and Tobago	100	100	136	55	–	–	107	103	98	97	98 x	98 x	89	98 x	–	–	84 x	90 x
Tunisia	98	96	117	39	–	–	111	107	–	–	95 x	93 x	95	–	–	–	–	–
Turkey	99	97	89	42	22	21	103	101	98	97	94 y	92 y	92	95 x	77	71	–	–
Turkmenistan	100	100	69	5	–	–	–	–	–	–	99 x	99 x	–	100 x	–	–	84 x	84 x
Tuvalu	–	–	22	30	–	–	–	–	–	–	–	–	–	–	–	–	35 y	47 y
Uganda	90	85	48	13	14	14	120	122	90	92	82 y	80 y	32	72 x	–	–	17 y	17 y
Ukraine	100	100	123	31	99	96	99	100	91	91	70	76	98	100	86	86	85	85

TABLE 5 | EDUCATION

Countries and areas	Youth (15–24 years) literacy rate (%) 2007–2011* male	female	Number per 100 population 2011 mobile phones	Internet users	Pre-primary school participation Gross enrolment ratio (%) 2008–2011* male	female	Primary school participation Gross enrolment ratio (%) 2008–2011* male	female	Net enrolment ratio (%) 2008–2011* male	female	Net attendance ratio (%) 2007–2011* male	female	Survival rate to last primary grade (%) admin data 2008–2011*	survey data 2007–2011*	Secondary school participation Net enrolment ratio (%) 2008–2011* male	female	Net attendance ratio (%) 2007–2011* male	female
United Arab Emirates	94 x	97 x	149	70	–	–	–	–	–	–	–	–	–	–	–	–	–	–
United Kingdom	–	–	131	82	81	82	106	106	100	100	–	–	–	–	95	97	–	–
United Republic of Tanzania	78	76	56	12	33	34	101	103	98	98	79	82	81	91 x	–	–	26	24
United States	–	–	106	78	68	70	102	101	95	96	–	–	93	–	89	90	–	–
Uruguay	98	99	141	51	89	89	115	111	100	99	–	–	95	–	66	73	–	–
Uzbekistan	100	100	92	30	26	26	95	93	93	91	96 x	96 x	98	100 x	93	91	91 x	90 x
Vanuatu	94	94	–	–	58	59	120	114	–	–	80	82	71	88	46	49	38	36
Venezuela (Bolivarian Republic of)	98	99	98	40	71	76	104	101	95	95	91 x	93 x	92	82 x	68	76	30 x	43 x
Viet Nam	97	96	143	35	84	79	109	103	–	–	98	98	–	99	–	–	78	84
Yemen	96	74	47	15	1	1	96	78	86	70	75 x	64 x	–	73 x	49	31	49 x	27 x
Zambia	82	67	61	12	–	–	115	116	91	94	81	82	53	87	–	–	38	36
Zimbabwe	–	–	72	16	–	–	–	–	–	–	87	89	–	79 x	–	–	48	49

MEMORANDUM

Sudan and South Sudan[σ]	–	–	56	19	–	–	–	–	–	–	–	–	–	–	–	–	–	–

SUMMARY INDICATORS[#]

Sub-Saharan Africa	76	67	53	13	18	18	103	96	78	74	72	70	60	–	–	–	31	29
Eastern and Southern Africa	80	72	51	11	21	22	113	108	88	85	75	75	49	–	33	30	23	23
West and Central Africa	73	61	54	14	14	14	96	86	69	64	68	64	68	90	–	–	40	36
Middle East and North Africa	94	89	94	29	25	23	103	97	92	87	–	–	–	–	68	63	–	–
South Asia	86	73	69	9	48	49	107	105	93	91	83	79	–	95	54	46	55	46
East Asia and Pacific	99	99	81	35	56	56	110	112	96	96	96 **	97 **	95	–	70	74	61 **	63 **
Latin America and Caribbean	97	97	107	39	70	70	116	112	96	95	–	–	91	–	71	76	–	–
CEE/CIS	99	99	132	42	57	56	100	99	95	95	–	–	96	–	83	82	–	–
Least developed countries	76	68	42	6	13	13	106	100	82	78	76	75	56	–	35	29	27	24
World	92	87	85	33	48	48	107	105	92	90	82 **	79 **	81	–	64	61	49 **	45 **

σ Due to the cession in July 2011 of the Republic of South Sudan by the Republic of the Sudan, and its subsequent admission to the United Nations on 14 July 2011, disaggregated data for the Sudan and South Sudan as separate States are not yet available for all indicators. Aggregated data presented are for the Sudan pre-cession (see Memorandum item).

\# For a complete list of countries and areas in the regions, subregions and country categories, see page 98.

DEFINITIONS OF THE INDICATORS

Youth literacy rate – Number of literate persons aged 15–24 years, expressed as a percentage of the total population in that group.

Mobile phones – The number of active subscriptions to a public mobile telephone service, including the number of prepaid SIM cards active during the past three months.

Internet users – The estimated number of Internet users, including those using the Internet from any device (including mobile phones) in the last 12 months.

Pre-primary school gross enrolment ratio – Number of children enrolled in pre-primary school, regardless of age, expressed as a percentage of the total number of children of official pre-primary school age.

Primary school gross enrolment ratio – Number of children enrolled in primary school, regardless of age, expressed as a percentage of the total number of children of official primary school age.

Primary school net enrolment ratio – Number of children enrolled in primary or secondary school who are of official primary school age, expressed as a percentage of the total number of children of official primary school age. Because of the inclusion of primary-school-aged children enrolled in secondary school, this indicator can also be referred to as a primary adjusted net enrolment ratio.

Primary school net attendance ratio – Number of children attending primary or secondary school who are of official primary school age, expressed as a percentage of the total number of children of official primary school age. Because of the inclusion of primary-school-aged children attending secondary school, this indicator can also be referred to as a primary adjusted net attendance ratio.

Survival rate to last primary grade – Percentage of children entering the first grade of primary school who eventually reach the last grade of primary school.

Secondary school net enrolment ratio – Number of children enrolled in secondary school who are of official secondary school age, expressed as a percentage of the total number of children of official secondary school age. Secondary net enrolment ratio does not include secondary-school-aged children enrolled in tertiary education owing to challenges in age reporting and recording at that level.

Secondary school net attendance ratio – Number of children attending secondary or tertiary school who are of official secondary school age, expressed as a percentage of the total number of children of official secondary school age. Because of the inclusion of secondary-school-aged children attending tertiary school, this indicator can also be referred to as a secondary adjusted net attendance ratio.

All data refer to official International Standard Classifications of Education (ISCED) for the primary and secondary education levels and thus may not directly correspond to a country-specific school system.

MAIN DATA SOURCES

Youth literacy – UNESCO Institute for Statistics (UIS).

Phone and Internet use – International Telecommunications Union, Geneva.

Pre-primary, primary and secondary enrolment – UIS. Estimates based on administrative data from International Education Management Information Systems (EMIS) with United Nations population estimates.

Primary and secondary school attendance – Demographic and Health Surveys (DHS), Multiple Indicator Cluster Surveys (MICS) and other national household surveys.

Survival rate to last primary grade – Administrative data: UIS; survey data: DHS and MICS. Regional and global averages calculated by UNICEF.

NOTES

– Data not available.

x Data refer to years or periods other than those specified in the column heading. Such data are not included in the calculation of regional and global averages, with the exception of 2005–2006 data from India. Estimates from data years prior to 2000 are not displayed.

y Data differ from the standard definition or refer to only part of a country. If they fall within the noted reference period, such data are included in the calculation of regional and global averages.

z Data provided by the Chinese Ministry of Education. The UNESCO Institute for Statistics dataset does not currently include net enrolment rates or primary school survival for China.

* Data refer to the most recent year available during the period specified in the column heading.

** Excludes China.

TABLE 6: DEMOGRAPHIC INDICATORS

Countries and areas	Population (thousands) 2011			Population annual growth rate (%)		Crude death rate			Crude birth rate			Life expectancy			Total fertility rate 2011	Urbanized population (%) 2011	Average annual growth rate of urban population (%)	
	total	under 18	under 5	1990–2011	2011–2030x	1970	1990	2011	1970	1990	2011	1970	1990	2011			1990–2011	2011–2030x
Afghanistan	32,358	17,219	5,686	4.3	2.6	29	22	16	52	52	43	35	42	49	6.2	24	5.6	4.1
Albania	3,216	877	203	-0.1	0.1	8	6	6	33	25	13	67	72	77	1.5	53	1.7	1.5
Algeria	35,980	11,641	3,464	1.7	1.0	16	6	5	49	32	20	53	67	73	2.2	73	3.3	1.7
Andorra	86	16	4	2.3	1.4	–	–	–	–	–	–	–	–	–	–	87	1.9	1.0
Angola	19,618	10,399	3,393	3.1	2.4	27	23	14	52	53	41	37	41	51	5.3	59	5.3	3.3
Antigua and Barbuda	90	28	8	1.7	0.8	–	–	–	–	–	–	–	–	–	–	30	0.9	1.5
Argentina	40,765	12,105	3,423	1.1	0.7	9	8	8	23	22	17	66	72	76	2.2	93	1.4	0.8
Armenia	3,100	763	225	-0.6	0.0	5	8	9	23	21	15	70	68	74	1.7	64	-0.9	0.3
Australia	22,606	5,190	1,504	1.3	1.1	9	7	7	20	15	14	71	77	82	2.0	89	1.5	1.2
Austria	8,413	1,512	381	0.4	0.1	13	11	9	15	11	9	70	75	81	1.4	68	0.6	0.5
Azerbaijan	9,306	2,430	846	1.2	0.8	7	7	7	29	27	20	65	65	71	2.2	54	1.2	1.4
Bahamas	347	95	27	1.4	0.9	6	6	5	26	24	15	66	69	76	1.9	84	1.7	1.1
Bahrain	1,324	311	102	4.7	1.2	7	3	3	38	29	19	64	72	75	2.5	89	4.7	1.3
Bangladesh	150,494	55,515	14,421	1.7	1.0	23	10	6	47	36	20	42	59	69	2.2	28	3.4	2.7
Barbados	274	59	15	0.3	0.1	9	8	9	22	16	11	69	75	77	1.6	44	1.7	1.1
Belarus	9,559	1,766	527	-0.3	-0.4	7	11	14	16	14	11	71	71	70	1.5	75	0.3	0.0
Belgium	10,754	2,182	619	0.4	0.2	12	11	10	15	12	11	71	76	80	1.8	97	0.4	0.3
Belize	318	131	37	2.4	1.7	8	5	4	42	37	24	66	72	76	2.7	45	2.2	1.8
Benin	9,100	4,568	1,546	3.1	2.5	26	17	12	48	47	39	40	49	56	5.2	45	4.3	3.7
Bhutan	738	258	70	1.3	1.0	23	14	7	47	38	20	41	53	67	2.3	36	5.0	2.6
Bolivia (Plurinational State of)	10,088	4,254	1,230	2.0	1.5	20	11	7	46	36	26	46	59	67	3.3	67	2.9	2.0
Bosnia and Herzegovina	3,752	686	167	-0.7	-0.4	7	9	10	23	15	8	66	67	76	1.1	48	0.3	0.6
Botswana	2,031	788	229	1.8	0.8	13	7	13	46	35	23	55	64	53	2.7	62	3.7	1.5
Brazil	196,655	59,010	14,662	1.3	0.6	10	7	6	35	24	15	59	66	73	1.8	85	1.9	0.8
Brunei Darussalam	406	124	37	2.3	1.3	7	4	3	36	29	19	67	73	78	2.0	76	3.0	1.7
Bulgaria	7,446	1,249	378	-0.8	-0.8	9	12	15	16	12	10	71	71	73	1.5	73	-0.3	-0.2
Burkina Faso	16,968	8,824	3,047	2.9	2.8	23	17	12	48	47	43	41	49	55	5.8	27	6.0	5.2
Burundi	8,575	3,813	1,221	2.0	1.5	20	19	14	44	46	34	44	46	50	4.2	11	4.7	4.0
Cambodia	14,305	5,480	1,505	1.9	1.0	20	12	8	42	44	22	44	56	63	2.5	20	3.1	2.4
Cameroon	20,030	9,420	3,102	2.4	1.9	19	14	14	45	42	36	46	53	52	4.4	52	3.7	2.8
Canada	34,350	6,926	1,936	1.0	0.8	7	7	8	17	14	11	73	77	81	1.7	81	1.3	0.9
Cape Verde	501	190	50	1.7	0.8	15	9	5	41	39	20	53	65	74	2.3	63	3.4	1.7
Central African Republic	4,487	2,098	658	2.0	1.8	23	17	16	43	41	35	42	49	48	4.5	39	2.3	2.8
Chad	11,525	5,992	2,047	3.1	2.5	22	17	16	46	47	44	44	51	50	5.9	22	3.3	3.5
Chile	17,270	4,615	1,222	1.3	0.6	10	6	6	29	23	14	62	74	79	1.8	89	1.6	0.8
China	1,347,565	317,892	82,205	0.8	0.2	9	7	7	36	21	12	63	69	73	1.6	51	3.9	1.8
Colombia	46,927	15,951	4,509	1.6	1.0	9	6	5	38	27	19	61	68	74	2.3	75	2.1	1.3
Comoros	754	366	124	2.6	2.3	18	11	9	47	37	37	48	56	61	4.9	28	2.6	3.0
Congo	4,140	1,940	637	2.6	2.1	14	12	11	43	38	35	53	56	57	4.5	64	3.4	2.7
Cook Islands	20	8	2	0.7	0.4	–	–	–	–	–	–	–	–	–	–	74	1.9	0.8
Costa Rica	4,727	1,405	359	2.1	1.0	7	4	4	33	27	16	67	76	79	1.8	65	3.2	1.6
Côte d'Ivoire	20,153	9,539	2,992	2.3	2.1	21	13	12	52	41	34	44	53	55	4.3	51	3.5	3.2
Croatia	4,396	806	215	-0.1	-0.3	10	11	12	15	12	10	69	72	77	1.5	58	0.2	0.3
Cuba	11,254	2,343	543	0.3	-0.1	7	7	7	29	17	10	70	74	79	1.5	75	0.4	0.0
Cyprus	1,117	244	65	1.8	0.8	7	7	7	19	19	12	73	77	80	1.5	70	2.0	1.1
Czech Republic	10,534	1,836	567	0.1	0.1	12	12	10	16	12	11	70	72	78	1.5	73	0.0	0.2
Democratic People's Republic of Korea	24,451	6,757	1,706	0.9	0.4	7	5	10	35	21	14	62	71	69	2.0	60	1.1	0.7
Democratic Republic of the Congo	67,758	35,852	12,037	3.0	2.4	21	19	16	48	50	43	44	47	48	5.7	34	4.0	3.8
Denmark	5,573	1,212	327	0.4	0.3	10	12	10	15	12	11	73	75	79	1.9	87	0.5	0.4
Djibouti	906	382	115	2.3	1.8	20	14	10	49	42	29	43	51	58	3.7	77	2.4	1.9
Dominica	68	21	6	-0.2	0.1	–	–	–	–	–	–	–	–	–	–	67	-0.3	0.4
Dominican Republic	10,056	3,672	1,051	1.6	1.0	11	6	6	42	30	21	58	68	73	2.5	70	2.7	1.5
Ecuador	14,666	5,234	1,469	1.7	1.0	12	6	5	42	29	20	58	69	76	2.4	67	2.7	1.7
Egypt	82,537	30,537	9,092	1.8	1.3	16	9	5	41	32	23	50	62	73	2.7	43	1.8	2.0
El Salvador	6,227	2,394	631	0.7	0.7	13	8	7	43	32	20	57	66	72	2.2	65	2.0	1.3
Equatorial Guinea	720	327	111	3.1	2.2	25	20	14	39	47	36	40	47	51	5.1	39	3.7	3.0
Eritrea	5,415	2,588	879	2.6	2.3	21	16	8	47	41	36	43	48	62	4.4	21	4.0	4.4
Estonia	1,341	250	80	-0.7	-0.2	11	13	13	15	14	12	71	69	75	1.7	69	-0.9	0.0
Ethiopia	84,734	40,698	11,915	2.7	1.8	21	18	9	47	48	31	43	47	59	4.0	17	4.1	3.6
Fiji	868	300	91	0.8	0.5	8	6	7	34	29	21	60	66	69	2.6	52	1.9	1.2
Finland	5,385	1,084	303	0.4	0.2	10	10	10	14	13	11	70	75	80	1.9	84	0.6	0.4
France	63,126	13,837	3,985	0.5	0.4	11	9	9	17	13	13	72	77	82	2.0	86	1.2	0.8
Gabon	1,534	642	188	2.4	1.8	20	11	9	34	38	27	47	61	63	3.2	86	3.4	2.0

TABLE 6 | DEMOGRAPHIC INDICATORS ▶

Countries and areas	Population (thousands) 2011			Population annual growth rate (%)		Crude death rate			Crude birth rate			Life expectancy			Total fertility rate 2011	Urbanized population (%) 2011	Average annual growth rate of urban population (%)	
	total	under 18	under 5	1990–2011	2011–2030x	1970	1990	2011	1970	1990	2011	1970	1990	2011			1990–2011	2011–2030x
Gambia	1,776	897	292	2.9	2.4	26	13	9	51	47	38	38	53	58	4.8	57	4.8	3.2
Georgia	4,329	892	258	-1.1	-0.7	9	9	11	19	17	12	67	71	74	1.5	53	-1.3	-0.3
Germany	82,163	13,437	3,504	0.2	-0.2	12	11	11	14	11	9	71	75	80	1.4	74	0.2	0.1
Ghana	24,966	11,174	3,591	2.5	2.0	17	11	8	47	39	31	49	57	64	4.1	52	4.2	3.0
Greece	11,390	2,001	600	0.5	0.1	8	9	10	17	10	10	72	77	80	1.5	61	0.7	0.6
Grenada	105	35	10	0.4	0.1	9	8	6	28	28	19	64	69	76	2.2	39	1.2	1.0
Guatemala	14,757	7,072	2,192	2.4	2.3	15	9	5	44	39	32	52	62	71	3.9	50	3.3	3.2
Guinea	10,222	5,045	1,691	2.7	2.3	30	21	13	49	46	38	34	44	54	5.2	35	3.8	3.7
Guinea-Bissau	1,547	739	244	2.0	2.0	26	22	16	46	46	38	37	43	48	5.0	44	4.1	3.2
Guyana	756	297	60	0.2	0.8	12	10	6	37	25	18	56	61	70	2.2	28	0.0	1.0
Haiti	10,124	4,271	1,245	1.7	1.1	18	13	9	39	37	26	47	55	62	3.3	53	4.7	2.6
Holy See	0	0	0	-2.5	-0.1	–	–	–	–	–	–	–	–	–	–	100	-2.5	-0.1
Honduras	7,755	3,338	975	2.2	1.7	15	7	5	47	38	26	52	66	73	3.1	52	3.4	2.6
Hungary	9,966	1,800	493	-0.2	-0.2	11	14	13	15	12	10	69	69	74	1.4	69	0.1	0.4
Iceland	324	81	24	1.1	1.0	7	7	6	21	17	15	74	78	82	2.1	94	1.3	1.1
India	1,241,492	448,336	128,542	1.7	1.1	16	11	8	38	31	22	49	58	65	2.6	31	2.6	2.3
Indonesia	242,326	77,471	21,210	1.3	0.8	15	8	7	40	26	18	52	62	69	2.1	51	3.7	1.9
Iran (Islamic Republic of)	74,799	20,819	6,269	1.5	0.6	16	8	5	42	34	17	51	62	73	1.6	69	2.4	0.9
Iraq	32,665	16,146	5,294	3.0	2.8	12	7	6	45	38	35	58	67	69	4.6	66	2.8	2.9
Ireland	4,526	1,137	370	1.2	0.9	11	9	6	22	14	16	71	75	81	2.1	62	1.6	1.4
Israel	7,562	2,417	754	2.5	1.4	7	6	5	26	22	21	72	76	82	2.9	92	2.6	1.4
Italy	60,789	10,308	2,910	0.3	0.0	10	10	10	17	10	9	71	77	82	1.4	68	0.4	0.4
Jamaica	2,751	956	254	0.7	0.2	8	7	7	36	26	18	68	71	73	2.3	52	1.0	0.6
Japan	126,497	20,375	5,418	0.2	-0.3	7	7	9	19	10	8	72	79	83	1.4	91	1.0	0.0
Jordan	6,330	2,747	817	2.9	1.5	11	5	4	51	36	25	61	70	73	3.0	83	3.6	1.7
Kazakhstan	16,207	4,800	1,726	-0.1	0.8	9	9	10	26	23	21	62	67	67	2.5	54	-0.3	1.0
Kenya	41,610	20,317	6,805	2.7	2.4	15	10	10	51	42	37	52	59	57	4.7	24	4.4	4.1
Kiribati	101	36	10	1.6	1.4	–	–	–	–	–	–	–	–	–	–	44	2.7	2.0
Kuwait	2,818	863	282	1.4	1.9	6	3	3	49	21	18	67	72	75	2.3	98	1.4	1.9
Kyrgyzstan	5,393	1,957	624	1.0	1.1	11	8	7	31	31	24	60	66	68	2.7	35	0.7	1.8
Lao People's Democratic Republic	6,288	2,581	682	1.9	1.1	18	13	6	42	42	22	46	54	67	2.7	34	5.7	3.3
Latvia	2,243	382	117	-0.8	-0.4	11	13	14	14	14	11	70	69	73	1.5	68	-0.9	-0.2
Lebanon	4,259	1,271	328	1.8	0.5	9	7	7	33	26	15	65	69	73	1.8	87	2.0	0.6
Lesotho	2,194	970	276	1.4	0.8	17	10	15	43	36	28	49	59	48	3.1	28	4.6	2.9
Liberia	4,129	2,057	700	3.2	2.4	23	21	11	49	46	39	41	42	57	5.2	48	2.2	3.2
Libya	6,423	2,293	717	1.9	1.0	16	4	4	49	26	23	52	68	75	2.5	78	2.0	1.3
Liechtenstein	36	7	2	1.1	0.7	–	–	–	–	–	–	–	–	–	–	14	0.3	1.1
Lithuania	3,307	616	173	-0.5	-0.4	9	11	14	17	15	11	71	71	72	1.5	67	-0.6	-0.1
Luxembourg	516	110	29	1.4	1.1	12	10	8	13	13	12	70	75	80	1.7	85	1.7	1.3
Madagascar	21,315	10,570	3,378	3.0	2.7	21	16	6	48	45	35	44	51	67	4.6	33	4.6	4.3
Malawi	15,381	8,116	2,829	2.4	3.2	24	18	12	52	48	44	41	47	54	6.0	16	3.8	4.7
Malaysia	28,859	10,244	2,796	2.2	1.3	7	5	5	33	28	20	64	70	74	2.6	73	4.0	1.9
Maldives	320	104	26	1.8	0.9	21	9	4	50	41	17	44	61	77	1.7	41	4.0	2.6
Mali	15,840	8,525	2,995	2.9	2.8	30	21	14	49	49	46	34	44	51	6.2	35	4.8	4.3
Malta	418	77	20	0.6	0.2	9	8	8	16	16	9	70	75	80	1.3	95	0.8	0.3
Marshall Islands	55	20	5	0.7	1.1	–	–	–	–	–	–	–	–	–	–	72	1.2	1.5
Mauritania	3,542	1,635	522	2.7	2.0	18	11	9	47	41	33	47	56	59	4.5	41	2.9	3.0
Mauritius	1,307	344	81	1.0	0.3	7	6	7	29	22	13	63	69	73	1.6	42	0.8	0.8
Mexico	114,793	39,440	10,943	1.5	0.9	10	5	5	43	28	19	61	71	77	2.3	78	1.9	1.2
Micronesia (Federated States of)	112	48	13	0.7	0.8	9	7	6	41	34	24	62	66	69	3.4	23	0.1	1.6
Monaco	35	7	2	0.7	0.0	–	–	–	–	–	–	–	–	–	–	100	0.7	0.0
Mongolia	2,800	934	317	1.2	1.2	15	10	6	44	32	23	56	61	68	2.5	69	2.0	2.0
Montenegro	632	145	39	0.2	0.0	3	5	10	10	11	12	69	76	75	1.6	63	1.5	0.4
Morocco	32,273	10,790	3,048	1.3	0.8	17	8	6	47	30	19	52	64	72	2.2	57	2.0	1.4
Mozambique	23,930	12,086	3,877	2.7	2.1	25	21	14	48	43	37	39	43	50	4.8	31	4.6	3.3
Myanmar	48,337	14,832	3,981	1.0	0.6	16	11	8	40	27	17	50	57	65	2.0	33	2.3	2.2
Namibia	2,324	994	288	2.4	1.4	15	9	8	43	38	26	53	61	62	3.2	38	3.9	2.8
Nauru	10	4	1	0.6	0.4	–	–	–	–	–	–	–	–	–	–	100	0.6	0.4
Nepal	30,486	12,883	3,453	2.2	1.4	21	13	6	44	39	24	43	54	69	2.7	17	5.3	3.4
Netherlands	16,665	3,526	907	0.5	0.2	8	9	8	17	13	11	74	77	81	1.8	83	1.4	0.5
New Zealand	4,415	1,091	320	1.2	0.9	9	8	7	22	17	14	71	75	81	2.2	86	1.3	1.0
Nicaragua	5,870	2,390	684	1.7	1.1	14	7	5	46	37	23	54	64	74	2.6	58	2.1	1.7
Niger	16,069	8,922	3,196	3.4	3.4	26	24	13	56	56	48	38	41	55	7.0	18	4.2	5.3
Nigeria	162,471	79,931	27,195	2.4	2.4	22	19	14	46	44	40	42	46	52	5.5	50	4.1	3.5

TABLE 6 | DEMOGRAPHIC INDICATORS ▶

Countries and areas	Population (thousands) 2011 total	under 18	under 5	Population annual growth rate (%) 1990–2011	2011–2030x	Crude death rate 1970	1990	2011	Crude birth rate 1970	1990	2011	Life expectancy 1970	1990	2011	Total fertility rate 2011	Urbanized population (%) 2011	Average annual growth rate of urban population (%) 1990–2011	2011–2030x
Niue	1	1	0	-2.3	-1.5	–	–	–	–	–	–	–	–	–	–	38	-1.4	-0.5
Norway	4,925	1,117	309	0.7	0.7	10	11	8	17	14	12	74	77	81	1.9	79	1.2	0.9
Oman	2,846	910	290	2.0	1.2	16	5	4	49	38	18	51	71	73	2.2	73	2.5	1.6
Pakistan	176,745	73,756	22,064	2.2	1.5	15	10	7	43	40	27	53	61	65	3.3	36	3.0	2.6
Palau	21	7	2	1.5	1.0	–	–	–	–	–	–	–	–	–	–	84	2.4	1.4
Panama	3,571	1,213	345	1.9	1.2	8	5	5	37	26	20	65	72	76	2.5	75	3.5	1.7
Papua New Guinea	7,014	3,168	975	2.5	2.0	17	10	7	44	35	30	46	56	63	3.9	12	1.6	3.6
Paraguay	6,568	2,587	744	2.1	1.5	7	6	5	37	33	24	65	68	72	2.9	62	3.2	2.1
Peru	29,400	10,421	2,902	1.4	1.0	14	7	5	42	30	20	53	66	74	2.5	77	2.0	1.3
Philippines	94,852	39,205	11,161	2.1	1.5	9	7	6	39	33	25	61	65	69	3.1	49	2.1	2.3
Poland	38,299	7,023	2,008	0.0	-0.1	8	10	10	17	15	11	70	71	76	1.4	61	0.0	0.1
Portugal	10,690	1,930	501	0.4	-0.2	11	10	10	21	11	9	67	74	79	1.3	61	1.5	0.5
Qatar	1,870	302	97	6.5	1.2	6	2	2	36	24	12	66	74	78	2.2	99	6.8	1.3
Republic of Korea	48,391	9,842	2,488	0.6	0.2	9	6	6	32	16	10	61	72	81	1.4	83	1.1	0.4
Republic of Moldova	3,545	740	223	-1.0	-0.6	10	10	13	18	19	12	65	68	69	1.5	48	-0.9	0.6
Romania	21,436	3,928	1,093	-0.4	-0.3	9	11	12	21	14	10	68	69	74	1.4	53	-0.4	0.0
Russian Federation	142,836	26,115	8,264	-0.2	-0.2	9	12	14	14	14	12	69	68	69	1.5	74	-0.1	0.0
Rwanda	10,943	5,352	1,909	2.1	2.5	20	32	12	51	45	41	44	33	55	5.3	19	8.1	4.3
Saint Kitts and Nevis	53	17	5	1.3	0.9	–	–	–	–	–	–	–	–	–	–	32	0.9	1.7
Saint Lucia	176	55	15	1.2	0.7	9	6	6	39	28	17	64	71	75	2.0	18	-1.3	-1.4
Saint Vincent and the Grenadines	109	35	9	0.1	0.1	11	7	7	40	25	17	61	69	72	2.0	49	0.9	0.8
Samoa	184	81	22	0.6	0.5	10	7	5	39	32	24	55	65	72	3.8	20	0.3	0.3
San Marino	32	6	2	1.3	0.3	–	–	–	–	–	–	–	–	–	–	94	1.5	0.4
Sao Tome and Principe	169	79	24	1.8	1.7	13	10	8	41	38	31	55	61	65	3.6	63	3.5	2.5
Saudi Arabia	28,083	9,923	3,186	2.6	1.7	15	5	4	47	36	22	52	69	74	2.7	82	3.0	1.9
Senegal	12,768	6,425	2,125	2.7	2.4	24	13	9	51	44	37	41	53	59	4.7	43	3.1	3.3
Serbia	9,854	2,089	551	0.1	-0.2	9	10	12	18	15	11	68	72	75	1.6	56	0.7	0.4
Seychelles	87	43	14	1.0	0.3	–	–	–	–	–	–	–	–	–	–	54	1.4	1.0
Sierra Leone	5,997	2,965	984	2.0	1.9	29	25	15	47	44	38	35	39	48	4.9	39	2.8	2.9
Singapore	5,188	1,104	238	2.6	0.7	5	5	5	23	19	9	68	76	81	1.3	100	2.6	0.7
Slovakia	5,472	1,024	281	0.2	0.1	9	10	10	18	15	11	70	71	75	1.3	55	0.0	0.3
Slovenia	2,035	344	102	0.3	0.1	10	10	10	17	11	10	69	73	79	1.5	50	0.2	0.4
Solomon Islands	552	254	81	2.8	2.2	13	11	6	45	40	31	54	57	68	4.2	20	4.7	4.0
Somalia	9,557	4,896	1,701	1.8	2.8	24	20	15	51	45	43	40	45	51	6.3	38	2.9	4.1
South Africa	50,460	18,045	4,989	1.5	0.4	14	8	15	38	29	21	53	62	53	2.4	62	2.3	1.1
South Sudanσ	10,314	–	–	2.6	2.3	–	–	–	–	–	–	–	–	–	–	18	4.0	3.9
Spain	46,455	8,306	2,546	0.8	0.4	9	9	9	20	10	11	72	77	81	1.5	77	1.0	0.6
Sri Lanka	21,045	6,183	1,886	0.9	0.5	9	7	7	31	20	18	63	70	75	2.3	15	0.3	2.0
State of Palestine	4,152	2,051	635	3.3	2.6	13	5	4	50	45	33	56	68	73	4.4	74	3.7	2.9
Sudanσ	34,318	–	–	2.5	2.1	–	–	–	–	–	–	–	–	–	–	33	3.2	2.9
Suriname	529	176	47	1.3	0.7	9	7	7	37	23	18	63	67	71	2.3	70	2.0	1.1
Swaziland	1,203	548	158	1.6	1.0	18	10	14	49	43	29	48	59	49	3.3	21	1.2	1.5
Sweden	9,441	1,916	562	0.5	0.5	10	11	10	14	14	12	74	78	81	1.9	85	0.6	0.7
Switzerland	7,702	1,435	382	0.7	0.3	9	9	8	16	12	10	73	78	82	1.5	74	0.7	0.5
Syrian Arab Republic	20,766	8,923	2,446	2.5	1.5	11	5	4	47	36	22	60	71	76	2.9	56	3.1	2.2
Tajikistan	6,977	3,052	883	1.3	1.3	10	8	6	40	39	28	60	63	68	3.2	27	0.5	2.1
Thailand	69,519	17,111	4,270	0.9	0.3	10	5	7	38	19	12	60	73	74	1.6	34	1.6	1.6
The former Yugoslav Republic of Macedonia	2,064	445	112	0.4	-0.1	8	8	9	24	17	11	66	71	75	1.4	59	0.5	0.4
Timor-Leste	1,154	616	201	2.1	2.9	23	18	8	42	43	38	40	46	62	6.1	28	3.6	4.1
Togo	6,155	2,831	870	2.5	1.8	20	14	11	49	42	32	45	53	57	4.0	38	3.8	3.0
Tonga	105	46	14	0.4	0.8	7	6	6	36	31	27	65	70	72	3.9	23	0.6	1.5
Trinidad and Tobago	1,346	334	96	0.5	0.0	7	7	8	27	21	15	65	69	70	1.6	14	2.7	1.7
Tunisia	10,594	3,001	885	1.2	0.7	14	6	6	39	27	17	54	69	75	2.0	66	1.9	1.1
Turkey	73,640	23,107	6,489	1.5	0.9	16	8	5	39	26	18	50	63	74	2.1	72	2.4	1.6
Turkmenistan	5,105	1,785	499	1.6	1.0	11	8	8	37	35	21	58	63	65	2.4	49	1.9	1.8
Tuvalu	10	4	1	0.4	0.6	–	–	–	–	–	–	–	–	–	–	51	1.5	1.3
Uganda	34,509	19,042	6,638	3.2	2.9	16	17	12	49	50	45	50	47	54	6.1	16	4.8	5.3
Ukraine	45,190	7,977	2,465	-0.6	-0.6	9	13	16	15	13	11	71	70	68	1.5	69	-0.5	-0.2
United Arab Emirates	7,891	1,590	451	7.0	1.5	7	3	1	37	26	13	62	72	77	1.7	84	7.3	1.7
United Kingdom	62,417	13,153	3,858	0.4	0.6	12	11	9	15	14	12	72	76	80	1.9	80	0.5	0.8
United Republic of Tanzania	46,218	23,690	8,267	2.8	3.0	18	15	10	48	44	41	47	51	58	5.5	27	4.5	4.7
United States	313,085	75,491	21,629	1.0	0.8	9	9	8	16	16	14	71	75	79	2.1	82	1.4	1.0
Uruguay	3,380	912	245	0.4	0.3	10	10	9	21	18	15	69	73	77	2.1	93	0.6	0.4

TABLE 6 | DEMOGRAPHIC INDICATORS

Countries and areas	Population (thousands) 2011			Population annual growth rate (%)		Crude death rate			Crude birth rate			Life expectancy			Total fertility rate 2011	Urbanized population (%) 2011	Average annual growth rate of urban population (%)	
	total	under 18	under 5	1990–2011	2011–2030ᵅ	1970	1990	2011	1970	1990	2011	1970	1990	2011			1990–2011	2011–2030ᵅ
Uzbekistan	27,760	9,849	2,802	1.4	1.0	10	7	7	36	35	21	63	67	68	2.3	36	0.9	1.7
Vanuatu	246	109	34	2.5	2.2	14	8	5	42	36	29	52	63	71	3.8	25	3.8	3.4
Venezuela (Bolivarian Republic of)	29,437	10,215	2,935	1.9	1.2	7	5	5	37	29	20	64	71	74	2.4	94	2.4	1.3
Viet Nam	88,792	25,532	7,202	1.3	0.7	18	8	5	41	30	16	48	66	75	1.8	31	3.4	2.5
Yemen	24,800	12,697	4,179	3.5	2.7	24	12	6	51	52	38	40	56	65	5.1	32	5.5	4.3
Zambia	13,475	7,169	2,509	2.6	3.1	17	17	15	49	44	46	49	47	49	6.3	39	2.5	4.3
Zimbabwe	12,754	5,841	1,706	0.9	1.7	13	9	13	48	37	29	55	61	51	3.2	39	2.3	3.0
MEMORANDUM																		
Sudan and South Sudanᵟ	–	20,660	6,472	–	–	19	14	9	46	41	32	45	53	61	4.3	–	–	–
SUMMARY INDICATORS#																		
Sub-Saharan Africa	876,497	428,333	140,617	2.5	2.3	20	16	12	47	44	37	44	50	55	4.9	37	3.8	3.4
Eastern and Southern Africa	418,709	196,675	63,188	2.5	2.2	19	15	12	47	43	35	47	51	56	4.5	30	3.6	3.4
West and Central Africa	422,564	210,616	70,843	2.6	2.4	22	18	13	47	45	39	42	48	53	5.3	43	3.9	3.5
Middle East and North Africa	415,633	157,845	48,169	2.1	1.5	16	8	5	44	34	24	52	63	71	2.8	60	2.7	1.9
South Asia	1,653,679	614,255	176,150	1.8	1.1	17	11	8	40	33	23	49	59	66	2.7	31	2.8	2.4
East Asia and Pacific	2,032,532	533,810	141,248	1.0	0.4	10	7	7	36	23	14	61	68	73	1.8	50	3.4	1.8
Latin America and Caribbean	591,212	195,081	52,898	1.4	0.9	10	7	6	36	27	18	60	68	74	2.2	79	2.0	1.1
CEE/CIS	405,743	95,460	28,590	0.2	0.1	10	11	11	20	18	14	66	68	70	1.8	65	0.3	0.6
Least developed countries	851,103	395,405	124,162	2.4	2.1	22	15	10	47	43	33	43	51	59	4.2	29	3.9	3.6
World	6,934,761	2,207,145	638,681	1.3	0.9	12	9	8	33	26	19	59	65	69	2.4	52	2.2	1.7

σ Due to the cession in July 2011 of the Republic of South Sudan by the Republic of the Sudan, and its subsequent admission to the United Nations on 14 July 2011, disaggregated data for the Sudan and South Sudan as separate States are not yet available for all indicators. Aggregated data presented are for the Sudan pre-cession (see Memorandum item).

\# For a complete list of countries and areas in the regions, subregions and country categories, see page 98.

DEFINITIONS OF THE INDICATORS

Crude death rate – Annual number of deaths per 1,000 population.

Crude birth rate – Annual number of births per 1,000 population.

Life expectancy – Number of years newborn children would live if subject to the mortality risks prevailing for the cross section of population at the time of their birth.

Total fertility rate – Number of children who would be born per woman if she lived to the end of her childbearing years and bore children at each age in accordance with prevailing age-specific fertility rates.

Urbanized population – Percentage of population living in urban areas as defined according to the national definition used in the most recent population census.

MAIN DATA SOURCES

Population – United Nations Population Division. Growth rates calculated by UNICEF based on data from United Nations Population Division.

Crude death and birth rates – United Nations Population Division.

Life expectancy – United Nations Population Division.

Total fertility rate – United Nations Population Division.

NOTES

– Data not available.

ᵅ Based on medium-fertility variant projections.

TABLE 7: ECONOMIC INDICATORS

Countries and areas	GNI per capita 2011 US$	GNI per capita 2011 PPP US$	GDP per capita average annual growth rate (%) 1970–1990	GDP per capita average annual growth rate (%) 1990–2011	Average annual rate of inflation (%) 1990–2011	Population below international poverty line of US$1.25 per day (%) 2006–2011*	Public spending as a % of GDP (2007–2010*) allocated to: health	education	military	ODA inflow in millions US$ 2010	ODA inflow as a % of recipient GNI 2010	Debt service as a % of exports of goods and services 2010	Share of household income (%, 2005–2011*) poorest 40%	richest 20%
Afghanistan	410 x	910 x, e	–	–	–	–	2	–	2	6,374	–	–	23	37
Albania	3,980	8,900	-0.7 x	5.3	13	1	3	–	2	338	3	9	20	43
Algeria	4,470	8,370 e	1.6	1.5	12	–	5	4	3	199	0	1	–	–
Andorra	41,750 x	–	-1.4	2.5 x	3 x	–	5	4	–	–	–	–	–	–
Angola	4,060	5,290	–	4.1	205	54 x	–	3	5	239	0	4	8 x	62 x
Antigua and Barbuda	12,060	15,670 e	7.8 x	0.6	4	–	4	2	–	19	2	–	–	–
Argentina	9,740	17,250	-0.8	2.3	8	1	6	6	1	155	0	16	14	49
Armenia	3,360	6,140	–	6.1	47	1	2	4	4	340	4	31	22	40
Australia	46,200 x	36,910 x	1.6	2.2	3	–	6	5	2	–	–	–	–	–
Austria	48,300	41,970	2.5	1.8	1	–	8	5	1	–	–	–	22 x	38 x
Azerbaijan	5,290	9,020	–	5.9	50	0	1	3	3	156	0	1	20	42
Bahamas	21,970 x	29,850 x, e	1.9	0.7	4	–	3	–	–	–	–	–	–	–
Bahrain	15,920 x	21,240 x	-1.0 x	1.3 x	3 x	–	3	3	3	–	–	–	–	–
Bangladesh	770	1,940	0.6	3.6	4	43	1	2	1	1,417	1	3	21	41
Barbados	12,660 x	18,850 x, e	1.7	1.1 x	3 x	–	4	7	–	16	–	–	–	–
Belarus	5,830	14,560	–	4.7	113	0	4	5	1	137	0	4	23	36
Belgium	46,160	39,300	2.2	1.6	2	–	7	6	1	–	–	–	21 x	41 x
Belize	3,690	6,070 e	2.9	1.8	1	–	4	6	1	25	2	11	–	–
Benin	780	1,630	0.5	1.3	5	47 x	2	5	1	691	10	–	18 x	46 x
Bhutan	2,070	5,480	–	5.3	7	10	5	5	–	131	9	–	17	45
Bolivia (Plurinational State of)	2,040	4,920	-1.1	1.6	7	16	3	–	2	676	4	8	9	59
Bosnia and Herzegovina	4,780	9,200	–	8.3 x	5 x	0	7	–	1	492	3	16	18	43
Botswana	7,480	14,560	8.1	3.4	9	–	8	8	3	157	1	1	–	–
Brazil	10,720	11,500	2.3	1.6	49	6	4	6	2	664	0	19	10	59
Brunei Darussalam	31,800 x	49,790 x	-2.2 x	-0.4 x	5 x	–	–	2	3	–	–	–	–	–
Bulgaria	6,550	13,980	3.4 x	3.3	37	0	4	4	2	–	–	14	22	37
Burkina Faso	570	1,310	1.3	2.8	3	45	4	5	1	1,065	12	–	17	47
Burundi	250	610	1.2	-1.4	14	81	5	7	3	632	40	1	21	43
Cambodia	830	2,260	–	6.5 x	4 x	23	2	2	1	737	7	1	19	46
Cameroon	1,210	2,360	3.4	0.8	4	10	2	4	2	538	2	4	17	46
Canada	45,560	39,830	2.0	1.8	2	–	7	5	1	–	–	–	20 x	40 x
Cape Verde	3,540	4,000	–	5.0	2	21 x	3	6	1	329	21	4	12 x	56 x
Central African Republic	470	810	-1.3	-0.5	3	63	2	1	2	264	13	–	10	61
Chad	690	1,370	-0.9	3.1	6	62 x	4	3	6	490	7	–	17 x	47 x
Chile	12,280	16,160	1.5	3.4	6	1	4	5	3	198	0	15	12	58
China	4,930	8,430	6.6	9.3	5	13	2	–	2	648	0	2	15	48
Colombia	6,110	9,640	1.9	1.6	13	8	5	5	4	910	0	19	10	60
Comoros	770	1,120	-0.1 x	-0.8	4	46 x	2	8	–	68	13	–	8 x	68 x
Congo	2,270	3,280	3.3	0.4	8	54 x	–	6	1	1,314	15	–	13	53
Cook Islands	–	–	–	–	–	–	–	–	–	13	–	–	–	–
Costa Rica	7,660	11,950 e	0.7	2.6	12	3	7	6	–	96	0	7	12	56
Côte d'Ivoire	1,100	1,730	-1.7	-0.6	5	24	1	5	2	848	4	–	16	48
Croatia	13,850	19,330	–	2.8	24	0	7	4	2	149	0	–	20	42
Cuba	5,460 x	–	3.9	3.0 x	4 x	–	11	14	3	129	–	–	–	–
Cyprus	29,450 x	30,910 x	5.9 x	2.0	3	–	2	8	2	–	–	–	–	–
Czech Republic	18,520	24,190	–	2.7	5	–	6	5	1	–	–	–	–	–
Democratic People's Republic of Korea	a	–	–	–	–	–	–	–	–	79	–	–	–	–
Democratic Republic of the Congo	190	350	-2.2	-2.6	211	88	–	3	1	3,413	28	–	15	51
Denmark	60,390	42,330	2.0	1.4	2	–	9	9	1	–	–	–	–	–
Djibouti	1,270 x	2,450 x	–	-1.4 x	3 x	19 x	5	8	4	133	–	7	17 x	46 x
Dominica	7,090	12,460 e	5.2 x	2.2	3	–	4	4	–	32	9	7	–	–
Dominican Republic	5,240	9,490 e	2.1	3.9	11	2	2	2	1	177	0	7	13	53
Ecuador	4,140	8,310	1.3	1.5	5	5	3	–	4	153	0	8	13	54
Egypt	2,600	6,160	4.3	2.8	7	2	2	4	2	594	0	5	22	40
El Salvador	3,480	6,690 e	-1.9	2.4	4	9	4	4	1	284	1	12	13	53
Equatorial Guinea	14,540	24,110	–	18.2	11	–	3	–	–	85	1	–	–	–
Eritrea	430	580 e	–	-0.8 x	13 x	–	1	–	–	161	8	–	–	–
Estonia	15,200	21,270	–	5.5 x	6 x	1 x	5	6	2	–	–	–	18 x	43 x
Ethiopia	400	1,110	–	3.3	7	39 x	2	5	1	3,529	12	4	22	39
Fiji	3,680	4,590	0.6	1.3	4	6	3	4	2	76	3	1	16	50
Finland	48,420	37,990	2.9	2.5	2	–	7	7	2	–	–	–	24 x	37 x

TABLE 7 | ECONOMIC INDICATORS ▶

Countries and areas	GNI per capita 2011 US$	GNI per capita 2011 PPP US$	GDP per capita average annual growth rate (%) 1970–1990	GDP per capita average annual growth rate (%) 1990–2011	Average annual rate of inflation (%) 1990–2011	Population below international poverty line of US$1.25 per day (%) 2006–2011*	Public spending as a % of GDP (2007–2010*) health	Public spending as a % of GDP (2007–2010*) education	Public spending as a % of GDP (2007–2010*) military	ODA inflow in millions US$ 2010	ODA inflow as a % of recipient GNI 2010	Debt service as a % of exports of goods and services 2010	Share of household income (%, 2005–2011*) poorest 40%	Share of household income (%, 2005–2011*) richest 20%
France	42,420	35,860	2.1	1.2	2	–	9	6	3	–	–	–	–	–
Gabon	7,980	13,650	0.2	-0.7	6	5 x	1	–	1	104	1	–	16	48
Gambia	610	2,060	0.6	0.9	6	34 x	3	4	–	121	16	5	13 x	53 x
Georgia	2,860	5,390	3.1	2.7	67	15	3	3	6	626	5	15	16	47
Germany	43,980	40,170	2.3	1.3	1	–	8	5	1	–	–	–	22 x	37 x
Ghana	1,410	1,820	-2.0	2.5	26	29	3	5	0	1,694	6	3	15	49
Greece	25,030	26,040	1.3	2.2	5	–	7	–	3	–	–	–	19 x	41 x
Grenada	7,220	10,530 e	4.2 x	2.9	4	–	4	–	–	34	6	12	–	–
Guatemala	2,870	4,800 e	0.2	1.3	7	14	2	3	0	398	1	10	10	60
Guinea	440	1,050	–	2.9	8	43	1	2	–	214	5	5	17	46
Guinea-Bissau	600	1,250	0.0	-1.2	17	49 x	2	–	–	141	16	–	19 x	43 x
Guyana	2,900 x	3,460 x, e	-1.3	2.8 x	11 x	–	7	3	–	153	6	2	–	–
Haiti	700	1,190 e	–	-1.0 x	15 x	62 x	1	–	–	3,076	46	6	9 x	63 x
Holy See	–	–	–	–	–	–	–	–	–	–	–	–	–	–
Honduras	1,970	3,840 e	0.8	1.6	13	18	3	–	2	576	4	5	8	60
Hungary	12,730	20,380	3.0	2.5	11	0	5	5	1	–	–	–	21	40
Iceland	35,020	31,640	3.2	2.1	5	–	7	8	0	–	–	–	–	–
India	1,410	3,620	2.0	4.9	6	33	1	–	3	2,807	0	5	21	42
Indonesia	2,940	4,530	4.6	2.7	14	18	1	4	1	1,393	0	16	20	43
Iran (Islamic Republic of)	4,520 x	11,400 x	-2.3	2.7 x	22 x	2 x	2	5	2	122	–	–	17	45
Iraq	2,640	3,770	–	-1.9 x	13 x	3	3	–	6	2,192	3	–	21	40
Ireland	38,580	33,310	–	0.6 x	1 x	–	7	6	1	–	–	–	20 x	42 x
Israel	28,930	27,290	1.9	1.8	5	–	4	6	6	–	–	–	16 x	45 x
Italy	35,330	32,350	2.8	0.8	3	–	7	5	2	–	–	–	18 x	42 x
Jamaica	4,980	7,770 e	-1.3	0.5	15	0 x	3	6	1	141	1	19	14 x	52 x
Japan	45,180	35,510	3.4	0.7	-1	–	7	3	1	–	–	–	–	–
Jordan	4,380	5,970	2.5 x	2.6	4	0	6	–	6	955	3	4	19	44
Kazakhstan	8,220	11,310	–	4.1	54	0	3	4	1	222	0	70	22	38
Kenya	820	1,720	1.2	0.4	9	43 x	–	7	2	1,631	5	4	14	53
Kiribati	2,110	3,480 e	-5.3	1.1	3	–	10	–	–	23	11	–	–	–
Kuwait	48,900 x	53,820 x	-6.7 x	1.4 x	6 x	–	3	–	4	–	–	–	–	–
Kyrgyzstan	920	2,290	–	0.7	35	6	3	6	3	373	8	14	18	43
Lao People's Democratic Republic	1,130	2,600	–	4.7	21	34	1	2	0	416	6	13	19	45
Latvia	12,350	17,820	3.4	4.4	17	0	4	6	1	–	–	74	18	44
Lebanon	9,110	14,000	–	2.5	7	–	4	2	4	449	1	14	–	–
Lesotho	1,220	2,070	2.4	2.3	8	43 x	5	13	2	257	10	2	10 x	56 x
Liberia	240	520	-4.0	5.5	30	84	4	3	0	1,423	177	1	18	45
Libya	12,320 x	16,750 x, e	–	–	–	–	2	–	1	9	–	–	–	–
Liechtenstein	137,070 x	–	2.2	3.0 x	1 x	–	–	2	–	–	–	–	–	–
Lithuania	12,280	19,690	–	3.6	20	0	5	6	2	–	–	32	18	44
Luxembourg	78,130	63,540	2.6	2.7	3	–	5	–	1	–	–	–	21 x	39 x
Madagascar	430	950	-2.3	-0.3	13	81	3	3	1	473	5	–	15	50
Malawi	340	870	0.0	1.3	25	74 x	4	–	1	1,027	21	–	18 x	47 x
Malaysia	8,420	15,190	4.0	3.1	4	0	2	6	2	2	0	5	13	51
Maldives	6,530	8,540	–	5.8 x	5 x	–	5	9	–	111	8	20	17 x	44 x
Mali	610	1,050	0.1	2.1	5	50	3	4	2	1,093	12	–	20	41
Malta	18,620 x	24,170 x	6.0	2.4	3	–	6	6	1	–	–	–	–	–
Marshall Islands	3,910	–	–	0.5	2	–	16	–	–	91	49	–	–	–
Mauritania	1,000	2,410	-1.1	1.3	8	23	2	4	3	373	10	–	16	47
Mauritius	8,240	14,760	3.2 x	3.5	6	–	2	3	0	125	1	2	–	–
Mexico	9,240	15,120	1.7	1.3	12	1	3	5	1	473	0	8	13	54
Micronesia (Federated States of)	2,900	3,610 e	–	0.4	2	31 x	13	–	–	125	41	–	7 x	64 x
Monaco	183,150 x	–	1.4	2.1 x	1 x	–	3	1	–	–	–	–	–	–
Mongolia	2,320	4,360	–	3.3	24	–	4	5	1	304	5	4	18	44
Montenegro	7,060	13,720	–	3.4 x	7 x	0	7	–	1	77	2	–	22	39
Morocco	2,970	4,910	1.9	2.5	3	3	2	5	3	994	1	9	17	48
Mozambique	470	980	-1.0 x	4.3	17	60	4	–	1	1,959	21	3	15	51
Myanmar	a	–	1.6	7.4 x	24 x	–	0	–	–	358	–	8	–	–
Namibia	4,700	6,600	-2.1 x	1.9	9	32 x	4	6	3	259	2	–	8 x	69 x
Nauru	–	–	–	–	–	–	–	–	–	28	–	–	–	–
Nepal	540	1,260	1.1	1.9	7	25	2	5	2	821	5	4	20	41
Netherlands	49,730	43,770	1.6	1.9	2	–	8	6	2	–	–	–	–	–

TABLE 7 | ECONOMIC INDICATORS ▶

Countries and areas	GNI per capita 2011 US$	GNI per capita 2011 PPP US$	GDP per capita average annual growth rate (%) 1970–1990	GDP per capita average annual growth rate (%) 1990–2011	Average annual rate of inflation (%) 1990–2011	Population below international poverty line of US$1.25 per day (%) 2006–2011*	Public spending as a % of GDP (2007–2010*) allocated to: health	Public spending as a % of GDP (2007–2010*) allocated to: education	Public spending as a % of GDP (2007–2010*) allocated to: military	ODA inflow in millions US$ 2010	ODA inflow as a % of recipient GNI 2010	Debt service as a % of exports of goods and services 2010	Share of household income (%, 2005–2011*) poorest 40%	Share of household income (%, 2005–2011*) richest 20%
New Zealand	29,350 x	29,140 x	1.1 x	1.8 x	2 x	–	8	6	1	–	–	–	–	–
Nicaragua	1,170	2,840 e	-3.7	1.9	17	12 x	5	–	1	628	10	11	16	47
Niger	360	720	-2.0	-0.2	4	44	3	4	1	749	14	–	20	43
Nigeria	1,200	2,300	-1.3	2.1	20	68	2	–	1	2,069	1	0	13	54
Niue	–	–	–	–	–	–	–	–	–	15	–	–	–	–
Norway	88,890	58,090	3.2	2.0	4	–	8	7	2	–	–	–	24 x	37 x
Oman	19,260 x	25,770 x	3.1	2.7	5	–	2	4	10	-40	–	–	–	–
Pakistan	1,120	2,880	2.6	1.9	10	21	1	3	3	3,021	2	10	23	40
Palau	7,250	12,330 e	–	-0.1 x	3 x	–	9	–	–	26	20	–	–	–
Panama	7,910	14,740 e	0.3	3.4	2	7	5	4	–	129	1	5	11	56
Papua New Guinea	1,480	2,590 e	-1.0	0.1	8	–	2	–	0	513	6	13	–	–
Paraguay	2,970	5,310	3.1	0.3	10	7	3	4	1	105	1	4	11	56
Peru	5,500	10,160	-0.6	3.2	10	5	3	3	1	-254	0	15	12	53
Philippines	2,210	4,160	0.5	1.9	7	18	1	3	1	535	0	15	15	50
Poland	12,480	20,450	–	4.4	10	0	5	6	2	–	–	–	20	42
Portugal	21,250	24,530	2.5	1.5	4	–	8	6	2	–	–	–	–	–
Qatar	80,440	87,030	–	0.8 x	11 x	–	2	2	2	–	–	–	–	–
Republic of Korea	20,870	30,290	6.2	4.1	4	–	4	5	3	–	–	–	–	–
Republic of Moldova	1,980	3,670	1.8 x	-0.1	38	0	6	10	0	468	7	9	20	41
Romania	7,910	15,140	0.9 x	2.8	44	0	4	4	2	–	–	29	21	38
Russian Federation	10,400	20,050	–	2.3	52	0	3	4	4	–	–	13	17	47
Rwanda	570	1,240	1.2	2.3	9	63	5	4	1	1,034	19	2	13	57
Saint Kitts and Nevis	12,480	14,490 e	6.3 x	1.6	5	–	4	4	–	11	2	17	–	–
Saint Lucia	6,680	9,080 e	5.3 x	0.7	3	–	5	4	–	41	5	6	–	–
Saint Vincent and the Grenadines	6,100	10,560 e	3.3	3.2	4	–	3	5	–	17	3	14	–	–
Samoa	3,190	4,430 e	–	2.8	6	–	5	5	–	147	27	3	–	–
San Marino	50,400 x	–	1.7	3.2 x	3 x	–	6	–	–	–	–	–	–	–
Sao Tome and Principe	1,360	2,080	–	–	–	28 x	3	–	–	–	–	5	14 x	56 x
Saudi Arabia	17,820	24,870	-1.4	0.2	5	–	2	6	8	–	–	–	–	–
Senegal	1,070	1,960	-0.5	1.1	4	34 x	3	6	2	931	7	–	17	46
Serbia	5,680	11,640	–	1.4	23 x	0	6	5	2	651	2	24	23	37
Seychelles	11,130	25,320 e	2.9	2.0	6	0	3	–	1	56	7	4	9	70
Sierra Leone	340	850	-0.5	1.1	16	53 x	1	4	2	475	25	2	16 x	49 x
Singapore	42,930	59,790	5.9	3.5	1	–	2	4	5	–	–	–	–	–
Slovakia	16,070	22,610	–	3.7	6	0	6	5	1	–	–	–	24	36
Slovenia	23,610	27,110	–	3.2	12	0 x	6	6	2	–	–	–	21 x	39 x
Solomon Islands	1,110	2,360 e	–	-0.9	7	–	5	7	–	340	61	6	–	–
Somalia	a	–	-0.8	–	–	–	–	–	–	499	–	–	–	–
South Africa	6,960	10,790	0.1	1.3	8	14	3	5	1	1,032	0	5	7	68
South Sudanᵍ	b	–	–	–	–	–	–	–	–	–	–	–	–	–
Spain	30,990	31,930	1.9	1.9	4	–	7	5	1	–	–	–	19 x	42 x
Sri Lanka	2,580	5,560	3.0	4.1	10	7	2	3	4	581	1	9	17	48
State of Palestine	b	–	–	-2.4 x	4 x	0	–	–	–	2,519	–	–	19	43
Sudanᵍ	–	–	–	–	–	–	–	–	–	–	–	–	–	–
Suriname	7,640 x	7,710 x, e	-2.2 x	1.7 x	46 x	–	4	–	–	104	–	–	–	–
Swaziland	3,300	5,970	3.1	1.8	9	41	4	8	3	92	3	2	11	57
Sweden	53,230	42,350	1.8	2.2	2	–	8	7	1	–	–	–	23 x	37 x
Switzerland	76,380	50,900	1.7 x	0.9	1	–	6	5	1	–	–	–	20 x	41 x
Syrian Arab Republic	2,750 x	5,090 x	2.2	1.8 x	7 x	2 x	1	5	4	137	0	3	19 x	44 x
Tajikistan	870	2,310	–	0.2	73	7	2	5	–	430	8	18	21	39
Thailand	4,420	8,390	4.7	2.8	3	0	3	4	2	-11	0	5	17	47
The former Yugoslav Republic of Macedonia	4,730	11,490	–	1.2	22	0	5	–	2	178	2	12	15	49
Timor-Leste	2,730 x	5,210 x, e	–	1.9 x	7 x	37	9	16	5	292	11	–	21	41
Togo	560	1,030	-0.3	-0.1	4	39	1	3	2	421	15	–	19	42
Tonga	3,580	4,690 e	–	1.5	6	–	5	–	–	70	19	–	–	–
Trinidad and Tobago	15,040	24,940 e	0.5	4.8	5	–	3	–	–	4	0	–	–	–
Tunisia	4,070	9,090	2.5	3.3	4	1 x	3	6	1	551	1	9	16	48
Turkey	10,410	16,730	2.0	2.4	44	0	5	–	3	1,049	0	33	17	45
Turkmenistan	4,110	8,350 e	–	5.8	86	–	1	–	–	43	0	–	–	–
Tuvalu	5,010	–	–	2.1	3	–	10	–	–	13	35	–	–	–
Uganda	510	1,320	–	3.7	7	38	2	3	2	1,730	10	1	15	51

TABLE 7 | ECONOMIC INDICATORS

Countries and areas	GNI per capita 2011		GDP per capita average annual growth rate (%)		Average annual rate of inflation (%)	Population below international poverty line of US$1.25 per day (%)	Public spending as a % of GDP (2007–2010*) allocated to:			ODA inflow in millions US$ 2010	ODA inflow as a % of recipient GNI 2010	Debt service as a % of exports of goods and services 2010	Share of household income (%, 2005–2011*)	
	US$	PPP US$	1970–1990	1990–2011	1990–2011	2006–2011*	health	education	military	2010	2010	2010	poorest 40%	richest 20%
Ukraine	3,120	7,080	–	0.6	67	0	4	5	3	624	0	39	24	36
United Arab Emirates	40,760	48,220 e	-4.3 x	-1.9	5	–	2	1	6	–	–	–	–	–
United Kingdom	37,780	36,970	2.1	2.4	2	–	8	6	3	–	–	–	–	–
United Republic of Tanzania	540	1,510	–	2.5	13	68	3	7	1	2,961	13	3	18	45
United States	48,450	48,890	2.1	1.7	2	–	8	5	5	–	–	–	16 x	46 x
Uruguay	11,860	14,740	0.9	2.1	15	0	5	–	2	49	0	12	14	51
Uzbekistan	1,510	3,440 e	–	2.5	78	–	2	–	–	229	1	–	19 x	44 x
Vanuatu	2,870	4,500 e	1.2 x	0.6	3	–	3	5	–	108	15	–	–	–
Venezuela (Bolivarian Republic of)	11,920	12,620	-1.7	0.4	32	7	3	4	1	53	0	8	14	49
Viet Nam	1,260	3,260	–	6.0	10	17	3	5	2	2,945	3	2	19	43
Yemen	1,070	2,180	–	1.1	15	18 x	2	5	4	666	–	2	18	45
Zambia	1,160	1,490	-2.3	0.8	28	69	4	1	2	913	6	1	10	59
Zimbabwe	640	–	-0.4	-3.0	1	–	–	2	1	738	11	–	–	–

MEMORANDUM

Sudan and South Sudan^σ	1,300 x	2,020 x	0.1	3.4	26	20	2	–	–	2,055	4	4	18	42

SUMMARY INDICATORS#

Sub-Saharan Africa	1,269	2,269	0.0	2.0	29	53	3	5	1	40,604	4	3	15	50
Eastern and Southern Africa	1,621	2,868	0.3	1.9	34	51	3	5	1	19,572	3	4	16	50
West and Central Africa	937	1,721	-0.5	2.0	21	59	–	5	1	18,844	5	1	15	50
Middle East and North Africa	6,234	9,655	-0.1	0.8	7	–	2	4	5	11,535	1	5	19	43
South Asia	1,319	3,366	2.0	4.5	6	32	–	–	–	15,263	1	5	21	42
East Asia and Pacific	4,853	8,185	5.6	7.5	5	14	2 **	4 **	2 **	9,289	0	4	16	47
Latin America and Caribbean	8,595	11,759	1.4	1.7	28	5	4	5	1	9,272	0	13	12	56
CEE/CIS	7,678	14,216	–	2.5	51	0	3	4	3	6,582	0	23	19	43
Least developed countries	695	1,484	-0.1	3.1	45	51	2	4	2	44,538	8	4	19	45
World	9,513	11,580	2.4	2.6	8	22	6 **	5 **	3 **	90,358	0	9	17	46

σ Due to the cession in July 2011 of the Republic of South Sudan by the Republic of the Sudan, and its subsequent admission to the United Nations on 14 July 2011, disaggregated data for the Sudan and South Sudan as separate States are not yet available for all indicators. Aggregated data presented are for the Sudan pre-cession (see Memorandum item).

\# For a complete list of countries and areas in the regions, subregions and country categories, see page 98.

DEFINITIONS OF THE INDICATORS

GNI per capita – Gross national income (GNI) is the sum of value added by all resident producers, plus any product taxes (less subsidies) not included in the valuation of output, plus net receipts of primary income (compensation of employees and property income) from abroad. GNI per capita is GNI divided by midyear population. GNI per capita in US dollars is converted using the World Bank Atlas method.

GNI per capita (PPP US$) – GNI per capita converted to international dollars, taking into account differences in price levels (purchasing power) between countries. Based on data from the International Comparison Programme (ICP).

GDP per capita – Gross domestic product (GDP) is the sum of value added by all resident producers; plus any product taxes (less subsidies) not included in the valuation of output. GDP per capita is GDP divided by midyear population. Growth is calculated from constant price GDP data in local currency.

Population below international poverty line of US$1.25 per day – Percentage of the population living on less than US$1.25 per day at 2005 prices, adjusted for purchasing power parity (PPP). The new poverty threshold reflects revisions to PPP exchange rates based on the results of the 2005 ICP. The revisions reveal that the cost of living is higher across the developing world than previously estimated. As a result of these revisions, poverty rates for individual countries cannot be compared with poverty rates reported in previous editions. More detailed information on the definition, methodology and sources of the data presented is available at <www.worldbank.org>.

ODA – Net official development assistance.

Debt service – Sum of interest payments and repayments of principal on external public and publicly guaranteed long-term debts.

Share of household income – Percentage of income received by the 20 per cent of households with the highest income and by the 40 per cent of households with the lowest income.

MAIN DATA SOURCES

GNI per capita – The World Bank.
GDP per capita – The World Bank.
Rate of inflation – The World Bank.
Population below international poverty line of US$1.25 per day – The World Bank.
Spending on health, education and military – The World Bank.
ODA – Organisation for Economic Co-operation and Development.
Debt service – The World Bank.
Share of household income – The World Bank.

NOTES

a low-income country (GNI per capita is $1,025 or less).

b lower-middle-income country (GNI per capita is $1,026 to $4,035).

c upper-middle-income country (GNI per capita is $4,036 to $12,475).

d high-income country (GNI per capita is $12,476 or more).

– Data not available.

x Data refer to years or periods other than those specified in the column heading. Such data are not included in the calculation of regional and global averages.

e Estimate is based on regression; other PPP figures are extrapolated from the 2005 ICP benchmark estimates.

* Data refer to the most recent year available during the period specified in the column heading.

** Excludes China.

TABLE 8: WOMEN

Countries and areas	Life expectancy: females as a % of males 2011	Adult literacy rate: females as a % of males 2007–2011*	Enrolment ratios: females as a % of males 2008–2011* Primary GER	Secondary GER	Survival rate to last grade of primary: females as a % of males 2008–2011*	Contraceptive prevalence (%) 2007–2012*	Antenatal care (%) 2007–2012* At least one visit	At least four visits	Delivery care (%) 2007–2012* Skilled attendant at birth	Institutional delivery	C-section	Maternal mortality ratio† 2007–2011* Reported	2010 Adjusted	Lifetime risk of maternal death (1 in:)
Afghanistan	101	–	69	51	–	21	48	15	39	33	4	330	460	32
Albania	108	97	99	98	100	69	97	67	99	97	19	21	27	2,200
Algeria	104	79 x	94	102	104	61 x	89 x	–	95 x	95 x	–	–	97	430
Andorra	–	–	101	105	–	–	–	–	–	–	–	–	–	–
Angola	106	70	81	69	73	6 x	80	–	47	46	–	–	450	39
Antigua and Barbuda	–	101	92	101	–	–	100	–	100	–	–	0	–	–
Argentina	110	100	99	112	101	78 x	99 x	89 x	95	99	–	44	77	560
Armenia	109	100	102	102	–	55	99	93	100	99	13	9	30	1,700
Australia	106	–	99	95	–	71 x	98	92	–	99	31	–	7	8,100
Austria	107	–	99	96	103	–	–	–	–	–	24	–	4	18,200
Azerbaijan	109	100	99	98	102	51 x	77 x	45 x	88 x	78 x	5 x	24	43	1,000
Bahamas	109	–	102	105	96	45 x	98	–	99	–	–	0	47	1,100
Bahrain	102	97	–	–	–	–	100	–	97	–	–	–	20	1,800
Bangladesh	102	85	–	113	114	61	55	26	32	29	17	220	240	170
Barbados	109	–	98	109	–	–	100	–	100	–	–	0 x	51	1,300
Belarus	118	100	100	–	–	73 x	99 x	–	100	100 x	22	1	4	16,300
Belgium	107	–	100	97	103	75 x	–	–	–	–	18	–	8	7,500
Belize	104	–	91	–	103	34 x	94 x	–	94	89	–	55	53	610
Benin	107	55	87	–	–	13	86	61 x	84	87	4 x	400 x	350	53
Bhutan	106	59 x	102	101	105	66	97	77	65	63	12	260 x	180	210
Bolivia (Plurinational State of)	107	91	99	99	–	61	86	72	71	68	19	310	190	140
Bosnia and Herzegovina	107	97	102	103	99	36 x	99 x	–	100 x	100 x	–	3	8	11,400
Botswana	96	101	96	106	104	53	94	73	95	99	–	160	160	220
Brazil	110	100	–	–	–	81 x	98	91	97 x	98	50	75	56	910
Brunei Darussalam	106	97	101	103	100	–	99	–	100	100	–	–	24	1,900
Bulgaria	110	99	100	95	99	–	–	–	100	93	31	8	11	5,900
Burkina Faso	104	59	91	76	109	16	94	34	66	66	2	340	300	55
Burundi	106	85	99	72	118	22	99	33	60	60	4	500	800	31
Cambodia	105	80	95	90	–	51	89	59	71	54	3	210	250	150
Cameroon	104	80	86	83	98	23	85	–	64	61	2 x	670 x	690	31
Canada	106	–	100	98	–	74 x	100	99	100	99	26	–	12	5,200
Cape Verde	111	89	92	120	–	61 x	98 x	72 x	78 x	76	11 x	54	79	480
Central African Republic	107	62	71	58	90	15	68	38	54	53	5	540 x	890	26
Chad	106	54	73	42	96	5	53	23	23	16	2	1,100 x	1,100	15
Chile	108	100	95	103	–	58 x	–	–	100	100	–	20	25	2,200
China	105	94	103	104	–	85 x	94	–	100	98	27	30	37	1,700
Colombia	110	100	98	110	101	79	97	89	99	99	43	63	92	430
Comoros	105	87	92	–	–	26 x	75 x	–	62 x	–	–	380 x	280	67
Congo	105	–	95	–	–	45	93	–	94	92	3 x	780 x	560	39
Cook Islands	–	–	102	110	–	29	100	–	100	100	–	0	–	–
Costa Rica	106	100	99	106	103	82	90	86	99	99	21 y	23	40	1,300
Côte d'Ivoire	104	72	83	–	96	18	91	–	59	57	6 x	540 x	400	53
Croatia	110	99	100	107	101	–	–	–	100	–	19	9	17	4,100
Cuba	105	100	98	99	102	74	100	100	100	100	–	41	73	1,000
Cyprus	106	98	99	100	–	–	99	–	–	100	–	–	10	6,300
Czech Republic	108	–	99	101	100	–	–	–	100	–	20	2	5	12,100
Democratic People's Republic of Korea	110	100	–	–	–	69 x	100	94	100	95	13	77	81	670
Democratic Republic of the Congo	107	74	87	58	88	17	89	45	80	75	7	550	540	30
Denmark	106	–	100	102	100	–	–	–	–	–	21	–	12	4,500
Djibouti	105	–	90	80	101	23	92 x	–	93 x	87 x	12	550 x	200	140
Dominica	–	–	98	109	105	–	100	–	100	–	–	0	–	–
Dominican Republic	108	100	88	112	–	73	99	95	98	98	42	160	150	240
Ecuador	108	97	101	103	–	73 x	84 x	58 x, y	98 x	85 x	26 x	61	110	350
Egypt	105	79	96	96	–	60	74	66	79	72	28	55	66	490
El Salvador	114	94	95	101	101	73	94	78 y	96	85	25	56	81	490
Equatorial Guinea	105	93	97	–	108	10 x	86 x	–	65 x	–	–	–	240	88
Eritrea	108	73	84	76	94	8 x	70 x	41 x	28 x	26 x	3 x	–	240	86
Estonia	115	100	99	102	100	–	–	–	100 x	–	–	7 x	2	25,100
Ethiopia	106	59	91	82	100	29	43	19	10	10	2	680	350	67
Fiji	108	–	98	109	95	32	100	–	100	–	–	23	26	1,400
Finland	108	–	99	105	100	–	100 x	–	–	100	16	–	5	12,200

TABLE 8 | WOMEN ▶

Countries and areas	Life expectancy: females as a % of males 2011	Adult literacy rate: females as a % of males 2007–2011*	Enrolment ratios: females as a % of males 2008–2011* Primary GER	Enrolment ratios: females as a % of males 2008–2011* Secondary GER	Survival rate to last grade of primary: females as a % of males 2008–2011*	Contraceptive prevalence (%) 2007–2012*	Antenatal care (%) 2007–2012* At least one visit	Antenatal care (%) 2007–2012* At least four visits	Delivery care (%) 2007–2012* Skilled attendant at birth	Delivery care (%) 2007–2012* Institutional delivery	Delivery care (%) 2007–2012* C-section	Maternal mortality ratio[1] Reported 2007–2011*	Maternal mortality ratio[1] Adjusted 2010	Maternal mortality ratio[1] Lifetime risk of maternal death (1 in:) 2010
France	108	–	99	101	–	71 x	100 x	–	–	–	21	–	8	6,200
Gabon	103	92	97	–	–	33 x	94 x	63 x	86 x	85 x	6 x	520 x	230	130
Gambia	104	67	102	95	94	13	98	72	57	56	3	730 x	360	56
Georgia	110	100	103	–	105	53	98	90	100	98	24	19	67	960
Germany	106	–	100	95	101	–	100 x	–	–	–	29	–	7	10,600
Ghana	103	84	100	91	91	34	96	87	68	67	11	450	350	68
Greece	106	98	–	–	–	76 x	–	–	–	–	–	–	3	25,500
Grenada	104	–	100	103	–	54 x	100	–	99	–	–	0	24	1,700
Guatemala	111	87	96	93	–	54	93	–	52	51	16	140	120	190
Guinea	106	58	84	59	76	9 x	88	50	46	39	2	980 x	610	30
Guinea-Bissau	107	60	94	–	–	14	93	70	44	42	–	410 x	790	25
Guyana	109	–	104	111	96	43	92	79	92	89	13	86	280	150
Haiti	104	84 x	–	–	–	32 x	85 x	54 x	26 x	25 x	3 x	630 x	350	83
Holy See	–	–	–	–	–	–	–	–	–	–	–	–	–	–
Honduras	107	100	100	123	–	65 x	92 x	81 x	67 x	67 x	13 x	–	100	270
Hungary	111	100	99	99	100	–	–	–	100	–	31	19	21	3,300
Iceland	104	–	100	103	–	–	–	–	–	–	17	–	5	8,900
India	105	68 x	100	92	–	55	74 x	37 x	52	47	9 x	210	200	170
Indonesia	105	94	102	100	–	61	93	82	79	55	15	230	220	210
Iran (Islamic Republic of)	105	90	101	86	100	79 x	98 x	94 x	97 x	96 x	40 x	25 x	21	2,400
Iraq	110	82	–	–	–	50 x	84 x	–	80	65	21 x	84 x	63	310
Ireland	106	–	100	105	–	65 x	100 x	–	100 x	100	25	–	6	8,100
Israel	106	–	101	102	98	–	–	–	–	–	–	–	7	5,100
Italy	107	99	99	99	100	–	99 x	68 x	–	99 x	40	–	4	20,300
Jamaica	107	112	95	103	102	72	99	87	98	97	15	95 x	110	370
Japan	109	–	100	100	100	54 x	–	–	–	100 x	–	–	5	13,100
Jordan	104	93	100	106	–	59	99	94	99	99	19	19	63	470
Kazakhstan	118	100	100	97	100	51 x	100 x	–	100	100 x	–	17	51	770
Kenya	104	93	98	90	–	46	92	47	44	43	6	490	360	55
Kiribati	–	–	104	111	–	22	88	71	80	66	10	0	–	–
Kuwait	102	97	103	107	100	–	100	–	100	–	–	–	14	2,900
Kyrgyzstan	113	99	99	99	99	48 x	97 x	–	99	97 x	–	64	71	480
Lao People's Democratic Republic	104	77 x	93	83	–	38 x	35 x	–	20 x	17 x	2	410 x	470	74
Latvia	115	100	99	98	100	–	92 x	–	100 x	–	–	32	34	2,000
Lebanon	106	92	97	112	103	54	96 x	–	98 x	–	–	–	25	2,100
Lesotho	97	115	98	138	124	47	92	70	62	59	7	1,200	620	53
Liberia	104	88	91	–	–	11	79	66	46	37	4	990	770	24
Libya	107	86	–	–	–	–	93	–	100	–	–	–	58	620
Liechtenstein	–	–	94	103	96	–	–	–	–	–	–	–	–	–
Lithuania	117	100	99	98	100	–	100 x	–	100 x	–	–	9	8	9,400
Luxembourg	107	–	101	102	–	–	–	–	100 x	100 x	29	–	20	3,200
Madagascar	105	91	98	94	105	40	86	49	44	35	2	500	240	81
Malawi	100	84	104	91	103	46	95	46	71	73	5	680	460	36
Malaysia	106	95	–	107	100	–	91	–	99	99	–	30	29	1,300
Maldives	103	100 x	96	–	–	35	99	85	95	95	32	140 x	60	870
Mali	104	47	87	70	95	8 x	70 x	35 x	49 x	45 x	2 x	460 x	540	28
Malta	106	103 x	101	89	91	–	100 x	–	–	100	–	–	8	8,900
Marshall Islands	–	–	99	103	91	45	81	77	99	85	9	140	–	–
Mauritania	106	79	105	85	99	9	75	16 x	61	48	3 x	690	510	44
Mauritius	109	95	101	100	99	76 x	–	–	98 x	98 x	–	22 x	60	1,000
Mexico	106	97	99	107	102	73	96	86	95	80	43	52	50	790
Micronesia (Federated States of)	103	–	–	–	–	55	80	–	100	–	–	0	100	290
Monaco	–	–	–	–	–	–	–	–	–	–	–	–	–	–
Mongolia	112	101	98	107	102	55	99	–	99	99	21	47	63	600
Montenegro	107	98	98	101	–	39 x	97 x	–	100	100	–	13	8	7,400
Morocco	107	64	94	–	100	67	77	–	74	73	16	130	100	400
Mozambique	104	61	90	82	94	12	92	–	55	58	2 x	500	490	43
Myanmar	105	95	100	106	107	46	83	–	71	36	–	320 x	200	250
Namibia	102	99	99	–	107	55	95	70	81	81	13	450	200	160
Nauru	–	–	106	120	–	36	95	40	97	99	8	300 x	–	–
Nepal	103	66	–	–	–	50	58	50	36	35	5	280 x	170	190
Netherlands	105	–	99	99	–	69	–	–	–	100	14	–	6	10,500

TABLE 8 | WOMEN ▶

Countries and areas	Life expectancy: females as a % of males 2011	Adult literacy rate: females as a % of males 2007–2011*	Enrolment ratios: females as a % of males 2008–2011* Primary GER	Secondary GER	Survival rate to last grade of primary: females as a % of males 2008–2011*	Contraceptive prevalence (%) 2007–2012*	Antenatal care (%) 2007–2012* At least one visit	At least four visits	Delivery care (%) 2007–2012* Skilled attendant at birth	Institutional delivery	C-section	Maternal mortality ratio† Reported 2007–2011*	Adjusted 2010	Lifetime risk of maternal death (1 in:) 2010
New Zealand	105	–	100	105	–	–	–	–	–	–	23	–	15	3,300
Nicaragua	109	100 x	98	110	–	72	90	78	74	74	20	63	95	350
Niger	102	35 x	82	66	94	18	46 x	15 x	18 x	17 x	1 x	650 x	590	23
Nigeria	103	70	91	88	107	15	58	45	39	35	2	550	630	29
Niue	–	–	–	–	–	23 x	100	–	100	–	–	0 x	–	–
Norway	106	–	100	98	100	88 x	–	–	–	–	16	–	7	7,900
Oman	107	90	97	99	–	24	99	96	99	99	14	26	32	1,200
Pakistan	103	59	82	76	92	27	61	28	43	41	7	280	260	110
Palau	–	–	–	–	–	22	90	81	100	100	–	0	–	–
Panama	107	99	97	107	100	52	96	–	89	88	–	60	92	410
Papua New Guinea	107	90	89	–	–	32 x	79 x	55 x	53 x	52 x	–	730 x	230	110
Paraguay	106	98	97	105	106	79	96	91	82	–	33	100	99	310
Peru	107	89	100	98	101	75	95	94	85	85	23	93	67	570
Philippines	110	101	98	108	111	51	91	78	62	44	10	160 x	99	300
Poland	112	100	99	99	100	–	–	–	100 x	–	21	2	5	14,400
Portugal	108	97	97	104	–	67 x	100 x	–	100 x	–	31	–	8	9,200
Qatar	99	99	100	121	–	–	100	–	100	–	–	–	7	5,400
Republic of Korea	109	–	99	99	100	80	–	–	–	–	32	–	16	4,800
Republic of Moldova	111	99	100	102	104	68 x	98 x	89 x	100	99	9 x	15	41	1,500
Romania	110	99	99	99	100	70 x	94 x	76 x	99	98 x	19 x	21	27	2,600
Russian Federation	119	100	100	98	–	80	–	–	100	–	–	17	34	2,000
Rwanda	105	90	102	102	–	52	98	35	69	69	7	480	340	54
Saint Kitts and Nevis	–	–	100	99	90	54	100	–	100	–	–	0	–	–
Saint Lucia	108	–	96	99	97	–	99	–	100	–	–	0 x	35	1,400
Saint Vincent and the Grenadines	106	–	93	102	–	48 x	100	–	99	–	–	0 x	48	940
Samoa	109	100	102	114	–	29	93	58	81	81	13	29 x	100	260
San Marino	–	–	113	102	–	–	–	–	–	–	–	–	–	–
Sao Tome and Principe	105	90	100	103	121	38	98	72	82	79	5	160	70	330
Saudi Arabia	103	90	99	95	–	24	97	–	97	–	–	–	24	1,400
Senegal	104	63	106	88	105	13	93	50	65	73	6	390	370	54
Serbia	106	97	99	102	100	61	99	94	100	100	25	9	12	4,900
Seychelles	–	101	100	109	–	–	–	–	–	–	–	57 x	–	–
Sierra Leone	103	59	93	–	–	11	93	75	63	50	5	860	890	23
Singapore	106	96	–	–	100	–	–	–	–	100 x	–	–	3	25,300
Slovakia	111	–	99	101	100	–	97 x	–	100	–	24	10	6	12,200
Slovenia	109	100	99	100	100	–	100 x	–	100	–	–	10	12	5,900
Solomon Islands	104	–	–	–	–	35	74	65	86	85	6	150	93	240
Somalia	106	–	–	–	–	15 x	26 x	6 x	33 x	9 x	–	1,000 x	1,000	16
South Africa	102	96	96	105	–	60 x	97	87	91 x	89 x	21 x	400 x	300	140
South Sudanᵍ	–	–	–	–	4	–	40	17	19	12	1	2,100 x	–	–
Spain	108	98	99	102	101	66 x	–	–	–	–	26	–	6	12,000
Sri Lanka	109	97	100	–	–	68	99	93	99	98	24	39 x	35	1,200
State of Palestine	105	94	98	108	–	50 x	99 x	–	99 x	97 x	15 x	–	64	330
Sudanᵍ	–	–	–	–	–	9	56	47	23	21	7	94 x	–	–
Suriname	110	99	95	123	122	46 x	90 x	–	90 x	88 x	–	180	130	320
Swaziland	98	99	92	100	107	65	97	77	82	80	12	590 x	320	95
Sweden	105	–	99	99	100	–	100 x	–	–	–	–	–	4	14,100
Switzerland	106	–	100	97	–	–	–	–	–	–	30	–	8	9,500
Syrian Arab Republic	104	86	98	100	101	54	88	64	96	78	26	65 x	70	460
Tajikistan	110	100	96	87	101	37	89	49	88	88	–	45	65	430
Thailand	109	96 x	99	108	–	80	99	80	100	99	24	12 x	48	1,400
The former Yugoslav Republic of Macedonia	106	97	101	99	–	40	99	94	98	98	25	4	10	6,300
Timor-Leste	103	83	96	101	111	22	84	55	29	22	2	560	300	55
Togo	106	61	90	–	123	15	72	55	59	67	9	–	300	80
Tonga	108	100 x	–	–	–	32	98	–	98	98	–	36	110	230
Trinidad and Tobago	110	99	97	107	106	43 x	96 x	–	98 x	97 x	–	–	46	1,300
Tunisia	106	82	96	106	102	60 x	96 x	68 x	95 x	89 x	21 x	–	56	860
Turkey	106	89	98	91	103	73	92	74	91	90	37	29 x	20	2,200
Turkmenistan	114	100	–	–	–	48 x	99 x	83 x	100 x	98 x	3 x	12	67	590
Tuvalu	–	–	–	–	–	31	97	67	98	93	7	0 x	–	–
Uganda	103	78	101	85	101	30	93	48	57	57	5	440	310	49
Ukraine	118	100	101	98	101	67	99	75	99	99	10	16	32	2,200

TABLE 8 | WOMEN

Countries and areas	Life expectancy: females as a % of males 2011	Adult literacy rate: females as a % of males 2007–2011*	Enrolment ratios: females as a % of males 2008–2011*		Survival rate to last grade of primary: females as a % of males 2008–2011*	Contraceptive prevalence (%) 2007–2012*	Antenatal care (%) 2007–2012*		Delivery care (%) 2007–2012*			Maternal mortality ratio†		
			Primary GER	Secondary GER			At least one visit	At least four visits	Skilled attendant at birth	Institutional delivery	C-section	2007–2011* Reported	2010 Adjusted	2010 Lifetime risk of maternal death (1 in:)
United Arab Emirates	103	102 x	–	–	–	–	100	–	100	100	–	0	12	4,000
United Kingdom	105	–	100	102	–	84	–	–	–	–	26	–	12	4,600
United Republic of Tanzania	103	85	102	–	113	34	88	43	49	50	5	450	460	38
United States	107	–	99	101	89	79	–	–	–	–	31	13	21	2,400
Uruguay	110	101	97	–	104	78 x	96	90	100	–	34	34	29	1,600
Uzbekistan	110	100	97	99	101	65 x	99 x	–	100 x	97 x	–	21	28	1,400
Vanuatu	106	96	95	102	94	38	84	–	74	80	–	86	110	230
Venezuela (Bolivarian Republic of)	108	100	97	110	105	–	94 x	–	95 x	95 x	–	63	92	410
Viet Nam	105	96	94	109	–	78	94	60	93	92	20	69	59	870
Yemen	105	58	82	62	–	28 x	47 x	14 x	36 x	24 x	9 x	370 x	200	90
Zambia	102	77	101	–	95	41	94	60	47	48	3	590	440	37
Zimbabwe	97	–	–	–	–	59	90	65	66	65	5	960	570	52

MEMORANDUM

Sudan and South Sudanσ	106	–	–	–	–	–	–	–	–	–	–	–	730	31

SUMMARY INDICATORS#

Sub-Saharan Africa	104	76	93	82	101	24	77	46	49	47	4	–	500	39
Eastern and Southern Africa	104	82	96	89	103	34	81	44	44	43	4	–	410	52
West and Central Africa	104	70	89	76	100	17	74	47	55	52	4	–	570	32
Middle East and North Africa	105	82	94	92	–	48	77	–	73	62	–	–	170	190
South Asia	104	69	98	91	–	52	70	35	49	44	9	–	220	150
East Asia and Pacific	105	94	102	104	–	64 **	93	77 **	92	84	23	–	82	680
Latin America and Caribbean	109	98	97	108	102	–	96	89	90	89	40	–	81	520
CEE/CIS	113	98	99	97	101	73	–	–	97	–	–	–	32	1,700
Least developed countries	104	76	94	84	102	35	74	38	48	44	6	–	430	52
World	106	90	97	97	100 **	55 **	81	50 **	66	61	16	–	210	180

σ Due to the cession in July 2011 of the Republic of South Sudan by the Republic of the Sudan, and its subsequent admission to the United Nations on 14 July 2011, disaggregated data for the Sudan and South Sudan as separate States are not yet available for all indicators. Aggregated data presented are for the Sudan pre-cession (see Memorandum item).

For a complete list of countries and areas in the regions, subregions and country categories, see page 98.

DEFINITIONS OF THE INDICATORS

Life expectancy – Number of years newborn children would live if subject to the mortality risks prevailing for the cross section of population at the time of their birth.

Adult literacy rate – The number of persons aged 15 years and over who can both read and write with understanding a short, simple statement about everyday life, expressed as a percentage of the total population in that age group.

Primary gross enrolment ratio (GER) – Total enrolment in primary school, regardless of age, expressed as a percentage of the official primary-school-aged population.

Secondary gross enrolment ratio (GER) – Total enrolment in secondary school, regardless of age, expressed as a percentage of the official secondary-school-aged population.

Survival rate to last grade of primary – Percentage of children entering the first grade of primary school who eventually reach the last grade (administrative data).

Contraceptive prevalence – Percentage of women (aged 15–49) in union currently using any contraceptive method.

Antenatal care – Percentage of women (aged 15–49) attended at least once during pregnancy by skilled health personnel (doctor, nurse or midwife) and the percentage attended by any provider at least four times.

Skilled attendant at birth – Percentage of births attended by skilled heath personnel (doctor, nurse or midwife).

Institutional delivery – Percentage of women (aged 15–49) who gave birth in a health facility.

C-section – Percentage of births delivered by Caesarian section. (C-section rates between 5 and 15 per cent are expected given adequate levels of emergency obstetric care.)

Maternal mortality ratio – Number of deaths of women from pregnancy-related causes per 100,000 live births during the same time period. The 'reported' column shows country-reported figures that are not adjusted for under-reporting or misclassification. For the 'adjusted' column, see note at right (†). Maternal mortality ratio values have been rounded according to the following scheme: <100, no rounding; 100–999, rounded to nearest 10; and >1,000, rounded to nearest 100.

Lifetime risk of maternal death – Lifetime risk of maternal death takes into account both the probability of becoming pregnant and the probability of dying as a result of pregnancy, accumulated across a woman's reproductive years.

MAIN DATA SOURCES

Life expectancy – United Nations Population Division.

Adult literacy – UNESCO Institute for Statistics (UIS).

Primary and secondary school enrolment – UIS.

Survival rate to last primary grade – UIS. Regional and global averages calculated by UNICEF.

Contraceptive prevalence rate – Demographic and Health Surveys (DHS), Multiple Indicator Cluster Surveys (MICS) and other nationally representative sources; United Nations Population Division.

Antenatal care – DHS, MICS and other nationally representative sources.

Skilled attendant at birth – DHS, MICS and other nationally representative sources.

Institutional delivery – DHS, MICS and other nationally representative sources.

C-section – DHS, MICS and other nationally representative sources.

Maternal mortality ratio (reported) – Nationally representative sources, including household surveys and vital registration.

Maternal mortality ratio (adjusted) – United Nations Maternal Mortality Estimation Inter-agency Group (WHO, UNICEF, UNFPA and the World Bank).

Lifetime risk of maternal death – United Nations Maternal Mortality Estimation Inter-agency Group (WHO, UNICEF, UNFPA and the World Bank).

NOTES

– Data not available.

x Data refer to years or periods other than those specified in the column heading. Such data are not included in the calculation of regional and global averages, with the exception of 2005–2006 data from India. Estimates from data years prior to 2000 are not displayed.

* Data refer to the most recent year available during the period specified in the column heading.

** Excludes China.

† The maternal mortality data in the column headed 'reported' refer to data reported by national authorities. The data in the column headed 'adjusted' refer to the 2010 United Nations inter-agency maternal mortality estimates that were released in May 2012. Periodically, the United Nations Maternal Mortality Estimation Inter-agency Group (WHO, UNICEF, UNFPA and the World Bank) produces internationally comparable sets of maternal mortality data that account for the well-documented problems of under-reporting and misclassification of maternal deaths, and that also include estimates for countries with no data. Please note that these values are not comparable with previously reported maternal mortality ratio 'adjusted' values, mainly due to an increase in the number of countries and data sources included in the latest round of estimation. Comparable time series on maternal mortality ratios for the years 1990, 1995, 2000, 2005 and 2010 are available at <www.childinfo.org>.

TABLE 9: CHILD PROTECTION

| Countries and areas | Child labour (%)+ 2002–2011* | | | Child marriage (%) 2002–2011* | | Birth registration (%) 2005–2011* | Female genital mutilation/cutting (%) 2002–2011* | | | Justification of wife beating (%) 2002–2011* | | Violent discipline (%)+ 2005–2011* | | |
| | | | | | | | prevalence | | attitudes | | | | | |
	total	male	female	married by 15	married by 18	total	women[a]	daughters[b]	support for the practice[c]	male	female	total	male	female
Afghanistan	10	11	10	15	40	37	–	–	–	–	90	74	75	74
Albania	12	14	9	0	10	99	–	–	–	36	30	75	78	71
Algeria	5 y	6 y	4 y	0	2	99	–	–	–	–	68	88	89	87
Andorra	–	–	–	–	–	–	–	–	–	–	–	–	–	–
Angola	24 x	22 x	25 x	–	–	29 x	–	–	–	–	–	–	–	–
Antigua and Barbuda	–	–	–	–	–	–	–	–	–	–	–	–	–	–
Argentina	7 y	8 y	5 y	–	–	91 x, y	–	–	–	–	–	–	–	–
Armenia	4 y	5 y	3 y	0	7	100	–	–	–	20	9	70	72	67
Australia	–	–	–	–	–	–	–	–	–	–	–	–	–	–
Austria	–	–	–	–	–	–	–	–	–	–	–	–	–	–
Azerbaijan	7 y	8 y	5 y	1	12	94	–	–	–	58	49	75	79	71
Bahamas	–	–	–	–	–	–	–	–	–	–	–	–	–	–
Bahrain	5 x	6 x	3 x	–	–	–	–	–	–	–	–	–	–	–
Bangladesh	13	18	8	32	66	10	–	–	–	36	36	–	–	–
Barbados	–	–	–	–	–	–	–	–	–	–	–	–	–	–
Belarus	5	6	4	0	7	–	–	–	–	–	–	84	87	80
Belgium	–	–	–	–	–	–	–	–	–	–	–	–	–	–
Belize	6	7	5	3	26	95	–	–	–	–	9	71	71	70
Benin	46	47	45	8	34	60	13	2	1	14	47	–	–	–
Bhutan	3	3	3	6	26	100	–	–	–	–	68	–	–	–
Bolivia (Plurinational State of)	26 y	28 y	24 y	3	22	76 y	–	–	–	–	16	–	–	–
Bosnia and Herzegovina	5	7	4	0	6	100	–	–	–	–	5	38	40	36
Botswana	9 y	11 y	7 y	–	–	72	–	–	–	–	–	–	–	–
Brazil	3 y	4 y	2 y	11	36	93 y	–	–	–	–	–	–	–	–
Brunei Darussalam	–	–	–	–	–	–	–	–	–	–	–	–	–	–
Bulgaria	–	–	–	–	–	–	–	–	–	–	–	–	–	–
Burkina Faso	39	42	36	10	52	77	76	13 y	9	34	44	83	84	82
Burundi	26	26	27	3	20	75	–	–	–	44	73	–	–	–
Cambodia	37 y	–	–	2	18	62	–	–	–	22 y	46 y	–	–	–
Cameroon	31	31	30	11	36	70	1	1	7	–	56	93	93	93
Canada	–	–	–	–	–	–	–	–	–	–	–	–	–	–
Cape Verde	3 x, y	4 x, y	3 x, y	3	18	91	–	–	–	16 y	17	–	–	–
Central African Republic	29	27	30	29	68	61	24	1 y	11	80 y	80	92	92	92
Chad	26	25	28	29	68	16	44	18	38	–	62	84	85	84
Chile	3	3	2	–	–	100 y	–	–	–	–	–	–	–	–
China	–	–	–	–	–	–	–	–	–	–	–	–	–	–
Colombia	9 y	12 y	6 y	6	23	97	–	–	–	–	–	–	–	–
Comoros	27 x	26 x	28 x	–	–	83 x	–	–	–	–	–	–	–	–
Congo	25	24	25	7	33	81 y	–	–	–	–	76	–	–	–
Cook Islands	–	–	–	–	–	–	–	–	–	–	–	–	–	–
Costa Rica	5	6	3	–	–	–	–	–	–	–	–	–	–	–
Côte d'Ivoire	35	36	34	8	35	55	36	9	20	–	65	91	91	91
Croatia	–	–	–	–	–	–	–	–	–	–	–	–	–	–
Cuba	–	–	–	9	40	100 y	–	–	–	–	–	–	–	–
Cyprus	–	–	–	–	–	–	–	–	–	–	–	–	–	–
Czech Republic	–	–	–	–	–	–	–	–	–	–	–	–	–	–
Democratic People's Republic of Korea	–	–	–	–	–	100	–	–	–	–	–	–	–	–
Democratic Republic of the Congo	15	13	17	9	39	28	–	–	–	–	76	92	92	91
Denmark	–	–	–	–	–	–	–	–	–	–	–	–	–	–
Djibouti	8	8	8	2	5	89	93	49	37	–	–	72	73	71
Dominica	–	–	–	–	–	–	–	–	–	–	–	–	–	–
Dominican Republic	13	18	8	12	41	79	–	–	–	–	4	67	69	65
Ecuador	8	7	8	4	22	90	–	–	–	–	–	–	–	–
Egypt	7	8	5	2	17	99	91	24 y	54	–	39 y	92 y	–	–
El Salvador	5 y	7 y	3 y	5	25	99	–	–	–	–	–	–	–	–
Equatorial Guinea	28 x	28 x	28 x	–	–	32 x	–	–	–	–	–	–	–	–
Eritrea	–	–	–	20	47	–	89	63	49	–	71	–	–	–
Estonia	–	–	–	–	–	–	–	–	–	–	–	–	–	–
Ethiopia	27 y	31 y	24 y	16	41	7	74	38	–	45	68	–	–	–
Fiji	–	–	–	–	–	–	–	–	–	–	–	72 y	–	–
Finland	–	–	–	–	–	–	–	–	–	–	–	–	–	–
France	–	–	–	–	–	–	–	–	–	–	–	–	–	–
Gabon	–	–	–	11 x	34 x	89 x	–	–	–	–	–	–	–	–

TABLE 9 | CHILD PROTECTION ▶

Countries and areas	Child labour (%)[+] 2002–2011*			Child marriage (%) 2002–2011*		Birth registration (%) 2005–2011*	Female genital mutilation/cutting (%) 2002–2011*			Justification of wife beating (%) 2002–2011*		Violent discipline (%)[+] 2005–2011*		
							prevalence		attitudes					
	total	male	female	married by 15	married by 18	total	women[a]	daughters[b]	support for the practice[c]	male	female	total	male	female
Gambia	19	21	18	7	36	53	76	42 y	64	–	75	90	90	91
Georgia	18	20	17	1	14	99	–	–	–	–	7	67	70	63
Germany	–	–	–	–	–	–	–	–	–	–	–	–	–	–
Ghana	34	34	34	5	21	63	4	0 y	2	26 y	44	94	94	94
Greece	–	–	–	–	–	–	–	–	–	–	–	–	–	–
Grenada	–	–	–	–	–	–	–	–	–	–	–	–	–	–
Guatemala	21 y	–	–	7	30	97	–	–	–	–	–	–	–	–
Guinea	25	26	24	20	63	43	96	57	69	–	86	–	–	–
Guinea-Bissau	38	40	36	7	22	24	50	39	34	–	40 y	82	82	81
Guyana	16	17	16	6	23	88	–	–	–	19	16	76	79	74
Haiti	21	22	19	6	30	81	–	–	–	–	29	–	–	–
Holy See	–	–	–	–	–	–	–	–	–	–	–	–	–	–
Honduras	16	16	15	11	39	94	–	–	–	–	16	–	–	–
Hungary	–	–	–	–	–	–	–	–	–	–	–	–	–	–
Iceland	–	–	–	–	–	–	–	–	–	–	–	–	–	–
India	12	12	12	18	47	41	–	–	–	51	54	–	–	–
Indonesia	7 y	8 y	6 y	4	22	53	–	–	–	16 y	31 y	–	–	–
Iran (Islamic Republic of)	–	–	–	–	–	–	–	–	–	–	–	–	–	–
Iraq	11	12	9	3	17	95	–	–	–	–	59	86	87	84
Ireland	–	–	–	–	–	–	–	–	–	–	–	–	–	–
Israel	–	–	–	–	–	–	–	–	–	–	–	–	–	–
Italy	–	–	–	–	–	–	–	–	–	–	–	–	–	–
Jamaica	6	7	5	1	9	98	–	–	–	22 y	3 y	89	90	87
Japan	–	–	–	–	–	–	–	–	–	–	–	–	–	–
Jordan	2 y	3 y	0 y	1	10	–	–	–	–	–	90 y	–	–	–
Kazakhstan	2	2	2	0	6	100	–	–	–	17	12	49	54	45
Kenya	26 x	27 x	25 x	6	26	60	27	–	9	44	53	–	–	–
Kiribati	–	–	–	3	20	94	–	–	–	60	76	81 y	–	–
Kuwait	–	–	–	–	–	–	–	–	–	–	–	–	–	–
Kyrgyzstan	4	4	3	1	10	94	–	–	–	–	38	54 y	58 y	49 y
Lao People's Democratic Republic	11	10	13	–	–	72	–	–	–	–	81	74	75	72
Latvia	–	–	–	–	–	–	–	–	–	–	–	–	–	–
Lebanon	2	3	1	1	6	100	–	–	–	–	10 y	82	82	82
Lesotho	23 x	25 x	21 x	2	19	45	–	–	–	48	37	–	–	–
Liberia	21	21	21	11	38	4 y	58	–	–	30	59	94	94	94
Libya	–	–	–	–	–	–	–	–	–	–	–	–	–	–
Liechtenstein	–	–	–	–	–	–	–	–	–	–	–	–	–	–
Lithuania	–	–	–	–	–	–	–	–	–	–	–	–	–	–
Luxembourg	–	–	–	–	–	–	–	–	–	–	–	–	–	–
Madagascar	28 y	29 y	27 y	14	48	80	–	–	–	30	32	–	–	–
Malawi	26	25	26	12	50	–	–	–	–	13	13	–	–	–
Malaysia	–	–	–	–	–	–	–	–	–	–	–	–	–	–
Maldives	–	–	–	0	4	93	–	–	–	14 y	31 y	–	–	–
Mali	21	22	21	15	55	81	89	75	73	–	87	–	–	–
Malta	–	–	–	–	–	–	–	–	–	–	–	–	–	–
Marshall Islands	–	–	–	6	26	96	–	–	–	58	56	–	–	–
Mauritania	16	18	15	15	35	56	72	66	53	–	–	–	–	–
Mauritius	–	–	–	–	–	–	–	–	–	–	–	–	–	–
Mexico	5	6	5	5	23	–	–	–	–	–	–	–	–	–
Micronesia (Federated States of)	–	–	–	–	–	–	–	–	–	–	–	–	–	–
Monaco	–	–	–	–	–	–	–	–	–	–	–	–	–	–
Mongolia	10	10	11	0	5	99	–	–	–	9 y	10	46	48	43
Montenegro	10	12	8	0	5	98	–	–	–	–	11	63	64	61
Morocco	8	9	8	3	16	85 x, y	–	–	–	–	64	91	92	90
Mozambique	22	21	24	21	56	31	–	–	–	–	36	–	–	–
Myanmar	–	–	–	–	–	72	–	–	–	–	–	–	–	–
Namibia	–	–	–	2	9	67	–	–	–	41	35	–	–	–
Nauru	–	–	–	2	27	83	–	–	–	–	–	–	–	–
Nepal	34 y	30 y	38 y	10	41	42	–	–	–	22	23	–	–	–
Netherlands	–	–	–	–	–	–	–	–	–	–	–	–	–	–
New Zealand	–	–	–	–	–	–	–	–	–	–	–	–	–	–
Nicaragua	15 x	18 x	11 x	10	41	81 y	–	–	–	–	14	–	–	–
Niger	43	43	43	36	75	32 y	2	1	3	–	70	–	–	–

TABLE 9 | CHILD PROTECTION ▶

Countries and areas	Child labour (%)+ 2002–2011*			Child marriage (%) 2002–2011*		Birth registration (%) 2005–2011*	Female genital mutilation/cutting (%) 2002–2011*			Justification of wife beating (%) 2002–2011*		Violent discipline (%)+ 2005–2011*		
							prevalence		attitudes					
	total	male	female	married by 15	married by 18	total	women[a]	daughters[b]	support for the practice[c]	male	female	total	male	female
Nigeria	29	29	29	16	39	30	30 y	30 y	22	30	43	–	–	–
Niue	–	–	–	–	–	–	–	–	–	–	–	–	–	–
Norway	–	–	–	–	–	–	–	–	–	–	–	–	–	–
Oman	–	–	–	–	–	–	–	–	–	–	–	–	–	–
Pakistan	–	–	–	7	24	27	–	–	–	–	–	–	–	–
Palau	–	–	–	–	–	–	–	–	–	–	–	–	–	–
Panama	7 y	10 y	4 y	–	–	–	–	–	–	–	–	–	–	–
Papua New Guinea	–	–	–	2	21	–	–	–	–	–	–	–	–	–
Paraguay	15	17	12	–	18	–	–	–	–	–	–	–	–	–
Peru	34 y	31 y	36 y	3	19	93	–	–	–	–	–	–	–	–
Philippines	–	–	–	2	14	83 x	–	–	–	–	14	–	–	–
Poland	–	–	–	–	–	–	–	–	–	–	–	–	–	–
Portugal	3 x, y	4 x, y	3 x, y	–	–	–	–	–	–	–	–	–	–	–
Qatar	–	–	–	–	–	–	–	–	–	–	–	–	–	–
Republic of Korea	–	–	–	–	–	–	–	–	–	–	–	–	–	–
Republic of Moldova	16	20	12	1	19	98 x	–	–	–	22 y	21	–	–	–
Romania	1 x	1 x	1 x	–	–	–	–	–	–	–	–	–	–	–
Russian Federation	–	–	–	–	–	–	–	–	–	–	–	–	–	–
Rwanda	29	27	30	1	8	63	–	–	–	25	56	–	–	–
Saint Kitts and Nevis	–	–	–	–	–	–	–	–	–	–	–	–	–	–
Saint Lucia	–	–	–	–	–	–	–	–	–	–	–	–	–	–
Saint Vincent and the Grenadines	–	–	–	–	–	–	–	–	–	–	–	–	–	–
Samoa	–	–	–	–	–	48	–	–	–	46	61	–	–	–
San Marino	–	–	–	–	–	–	–	–	–	–	–	–	–	–
Sao Tome and Principe	8	8	7	5	34	75	–	–	–	22	20	–	–	–
Saudi Arabia	–	–	–	–	–	–	–	–	–	–	–	–	–	–
Senegal	17 y	18 y	16 y	12	33	75	26	13 y	17	25	60	–	–	–
Serbia	4	5	4	1	5	99	–	–	–	7 y	3	67	70	64
Seychelles	–	–	–	–	–	–	–	–	–	–	–	–	–	–
Sierra Leone	26	27	25	18	44	78	88	10 y	72	–	73	82	81	82
Singapore	–	–	–	–	–	–	–	–	–	–	–	–	–	–
Slovakia	–	–	–	–	–	–	–	–	–	–	–	–	–	–
Slovenia	–	–	–	–	–	–	–	–	–	–	–	–	–	–
Solomon Islands	–	–	–	3	22	–	–	–	–	65	69	72 y	–	–
Somalia	49	45	54	8	45	3	98	46	65	–	76 y	–	–	–
South Africa	–	–	–	1	6	92 y	–	–	–	–	–	–	–	–
South Sudanσ	–	–	–	9	52	35	–	–	–	–	79	–	–	–
Spain	–	–	–	–	–	–	–	–	–	–	–	–	–	–
Sri Lanka	–	–	–	2	12	97	–	–	–	–	53 y	–	–	–
State of Palestine	–	–	–	7	19	96 y	–	–	–	–	–	95	–	–
Sudanσ	–	–	–	7	33	59	88	37 y	42	–	47	–	–	–
Suriname	6	7	5	3	19	97	–	–	–	–	13	86	87	85
Swaziland	7	8	7	1	7	50	–	–	–	23 y	28	89	90	88
Sweden	–	–	–	–	–	–	–	–	–	–	–	–	–	–
Switzerland	–	–	–	–	–	–	–	–	–	–	–	–	–	–
Syrian Arab Republic	4	5	3	3	13	95	–	–	–	–	–	89	90	88
Tajikistan	10	9	11	1	13	88	–	–	–	–	74 y	78	80	75
Thailand	8	8	8	3	20	99	–	–	–	–	–	–	–	–
The former Yugoslav Republic of Macedonia	13	12	13	1	7	100	–	–	–	–	15	69	71	67
Timor-Leste	4	4	4	3	19	55	–	–	–	81	86	–	–	–
Togo	28	28	29	6	25	78	4	0 y	2	–	43	93	94	93
Tonga	–	–	–	–	–	–	–	–	–	–	–	–	–	–
Trinidad and Tobago	1	1	1	2	8	96	–	–	–	–	8	77	78	77
Tunisia	–	–	–	–	–	–	–	–	–	–	–	–	–	–
Turkey	3 y	3 y	2 y	3	14	94	–	–	–	–	25	–	–	–
Turkmenistan	–	–	–	1	7	96	–	–	–	–	38 y	–	–	–
Tuvalu	–	–	–	0	10	50	–	–	–	73	70	–	–	–
Uganda	25 y	27 y	24 y	10	40	30	1	1 y	9	44	58	–	–	–
Ukraine	7	8	7	0	10	100	–	–	–	11	4	70	76	65
United Arab Emirates	–	–	–	–	–	–	–	–	–	–	–	–	–	–
United Kingdom	–	–	–	–	–	–	–	–	–	–	–	–	–	–
United Republic of Tanzania	21 y	23 y	19 y	7	37	16	15	3	6	38	54	–	–	–
United States	–	–	–	–	–	–	–	–	–	–	–	–	–	–

TABLE 9 | CHILD PROTECTION

Countries and areas	Child labour (%) 2002–2011*			Child marriage (%) 2002–2011*		Birth registration (%) 2005–2011*	Female genital mutilation/cutting (%) 2002–2011*			Justification of wife beating (%) 2002–2011*		Violent discipline (%) 2005–2011*		
							prevalence		attitudes					
	total	male	female	married by 15	married by 18	total	women[a]	daughters[b]	support for the practice[c]	male	female	total	male	female
Uruguay	8 y	8 y	8 y	–	–	–	–	–	–	–	–	–	–	–
Uzbekistan	–	–	–	0	7	100	–	–	–	59 y	70	–	–	–
Vanuatu	–	–	–	9	27	26	–	–	–	–	–	78 y	–	–
Venezuela (Bolivarian Republic of)	8 x	9 x	6 x	–	–	92 x	–	–	–	–	–	–	–	–
Viet Nam	7	7	7	1	9	95	–	–	–	–	36	74	76	71
Yemen	23	21	24	11	32	22	23 x, y	20 x, y	41 x, y	–	–	95	95	95
Zambia	41 y	42 y	40 y	9	42	14	1	–	–	49	62	–	–	–
Zimbabwe	–	–	–	4	31	49	1	–	–	34	40	–	–	–
MEMORANDUM														
Sudan and South Sudan[σ]	13 x	14 x	12 x	–	–	–	–	–	–	–	–	–	–	–
SUMMARY INDICATORS[#]														
Sub-Saharan Africa	27	28	26	12	37	41	40	24	21	35	55	–	–	–
Eastern and Southern Africa	27	28	25	9	34	37	42	–	–	40	55	–	–	–
West and Central Africa	27	28	27	14	41	42	34	23	22	30	56	–	–	–
Middle East and North Africa	9	10	8	3	17	81	–	–	–	–	52	90	–	–
South Asia	12	13	12	18	46	37	–	–	–	49	52	–	–	–
East Asia and Pacific	8 **	8 **	7 **	3 **	18 **	70 **	–	–	–	–	30 **	–	–	–
Latin America and Caribbean	9	9	7	7	29	93	–	–	–	–	–	–	–	–
CEE/CIS	5	6	4	1	10	96	–	–	–	–	27	–	–	–
Least developed countries	23	24	22	16	46	35	–	–	–	36	54	–	–	–
World	15 **	15 **	14 **	11 **	34 **	51 **	–	–	–	–	47 **	–	–	–

σ Due to the cession in July 2011 of the Republic of South Sudan by the Republic of the Sudan, and its subsequent admission to the United Nations on 14 July 2011, disaggregated data for the Sudan and South Sudan as separate States are not yet available for all indicators. Aggregated data presented are for the Sudan pre-cession (see Memorandum item).

For a complete list of countries and areas in the regions, subregions and country categories, see page 98.

DEFINITIONS OF THE INDICATORS

Child labour – Percentage of children 5–14 years old involved in child labour at the moment of the survey. A child is considered to be involved in child labour under the following conditions: children 5–11 years old who, during the reference week, did at least one hour of economic activity or at least 28 hours of household chores, or children 12–14 years old who, during the reference week, did at least 14 hours of economic activity or at least 28 hours of household chores.

Child marriage – Percentage of women 20–24 years old who were first married or in union before they were 15 years old and percentage of women 20–24 years old who were first married or in union before they were 18 years old.

Birth registration – Percentage of children less than 5 years old who were registered at the moment of the survey. The numerator of this indicator includes children whose birth certificate was seen by the interviewer or whose mother or caretaker says the birth has been registered.

Female genital mutilation/cutting – (a) Women: percentage of women 15–49 years old who have been mutilated/cut; (b) daughters: percentage of women 15–49 years old with at least one mutilated/cut daughter; (c) support for the practice: percentage of women 15–49 years old who believe that the practice of female genital mutilation/cutting should continue.

Justification of wife beating – Percentage of women and men 15–49 years old who consider a husband to be justified in hitting or beating his wife for at least one of the specified reasons, i.e., if his wife burns the food, argues with him, goes out without telling him, neglects the children or refuses sexual relations.

Violent discipline – Percentage of children 2–14 years old who experience any violent discipline (psychological aggression and/or physical punishment).

MAIN DATA SOURCES

Child labour – Multiple Indicator Cluster Surveys (MICS), Demographic and Health Surveys (DHS) and other national surveys.

Child marriage – MICS, DHS and other national surveys.

Birth registration – MICS, DHS, other national surveys and vital registration systems.

Female genital mutilation/cutting – MICS, DHS and other national surveys.

Justification of wife beating – MICS, DHS and other national surveys.

Violent discipline – MICS, DHS and other national surveys.

NOTES

– Data not available.

x Data refer to years or periods other than those specified in the column heading. Such data are not included in the calculation of regional and global averages.

y Data differ from the standard definition or refer to only part of a country. If they fall within the noted reference period, such data are included in the calculation of regional and global averages.

+ A more detailed explanation of the methodology and the changes in calculating these estimates can be found in the General Note on the Data, page 94.

* Data refer to the most recent year available during the period specified in the column heading.

** Excludes China.

TABLE 10: THE RATE OF PROGRESS

Countries and areas	Under-5 mortality rank	Under-5 mortality rate				Annual rate of reduction (%)θ Under-5 mortality rate				Reduction since 1990 (%)θ	Reduction since 2000 (%)θ	GDP per capita average annual growth rate (%)		Total fertility rate			Average annual rate of reduction (%) Total fertility rate	
		1970	1990	2000	2011	1970–1990	1990–2000	2000–2011	1990–2011			1970–1990	1990–2011	1970	1990	2011	1970–1990	1990–2011
Afghanistan	23	309	192	136	101	2.4	3.4	2.7	3.1	47	26	–	–	7.7	8.0	6.2	-0.2	1.2
Albania	122	–	41	26	14	–	4.5	5.5	5.0	65	46	-0.7 x	5.3	4.9	3.2	1.5	2.1	3.6
Algeria	74	199	66	46	30	5.5	3.6	3.9	3.8	55	35	1.6	1.5	7.4	4.7	2.2	2.3	3.6
Andorra	184	–	8	5	3	–	5.1	3.8	4.4	60	34	-1.4	2.5 x	–	–	–	–	–
Angola	8	–	243	199	158	–	2.0	2.1	2.1	35	21	–	4.1	7.3	7.2	5.3	0.1	1.4
Antigua and Barbuda	145	–	27	15	8	–	5.9	6.1	6.0	72	49	7.8 x	0.6	–	–	–	–	–
Argentina	122	58	28	20	14	3.7	3.1	3.3	3.2	49	31	-0.8	2.1	3.1	3.0	2.2	0.1	1.5
Armenia	102	–	47	30	18	–	4.6	4.8	4.7	63	41	–	6.1	3.2	2.5	1.7	1.2	1.8
Australia	165	21	9	6	5	4.2	3.8	2.9	3.4	51	27	1.6	2.2	2.7	1.9	2.0	1.9	-0.2
Austria	169	29	9	6	4	5.6	5.2	2.6	3.8	55	25	2.5	1.8	2.3	1.5	1.4	2.4	0.3
Azerbaijan	61	–	95	69	45	–	3.2	3.9	3.6	53	35	–	5.9	4.6	3.0	2.2	2.2	1.5
Bahamas	107	31	22	17	16	1.8	2.6	0.4	1.4	26	4	1.9	0.7	3.5	2.6	1.9	1.5	1.6
Bahrain	135	81	21	12	10	6.9	5.0	2.0	3.4	51	19	-1.0 x	1.3 x	6.5	3.7	2.5	2.8	1.9
Bangladesh	60	226	139	84	46	2.4	5.0	5.5	5.3	67	45	0.6	3.6	6.9	4.5	2.2	2.1	3.4
Barbados	98	47	18	17	20	4.8	0.4	-1.2	-0.5	-10	-15	1.7	1.1 x	3.1	1.7	1.6	2.9	0.5
Belarus	157	–	17	14	6	–	2.3	8.1	5.3	67	59	–	4.7	2.3	1.9	1.5	1.0	1.2
Belgium	169	24	10	6	4	4.3	5.4	2.7	4.0	57	26	2.2	1.6	2.2	1.6	1.8	1.7	-0.7
Belize	106	–	44	26	17	–	5.1	4.0	4.5	62	36	2.9	1.8	6.3	4.5	2.7	1.7	2.4
Benin	20	261	177	140	106	1.9	2.4	2.5	2.4	40	24	0.5	1.3	6.7	6.7	5.2	0.0	1.2
Bhutan	51	286	138	89	54	3.6	4.4	4.6	4.5	61	40	–	5.3	6.7	5.8	2.3	0.7	4.3
Bolivia (Plurinational State of)	55	226	120	81	51	3.2	3.9	4.3	4.1	58	37	-1.1	1.6	6.6	4.9	3.3	1.5	1.9
Bosnia and Herzegovina	145	–	19	10	8	–	6.7	2.0	4.3	59	20	–	8.3 x	2.9	1.7	1.1	2.6	1.9
Botswana	80	131	53	81	26	4.5	-4.3	10.4	3.4	51	68	8.1	3.4	6.6	4.7	2.7	1.7	2.6
Brazil	107	129	58	36	16	4.0	4.9	7.5	6.3	73	56	2.3	1.6	5.0	2.8	1.8	2.9	2.1
Brunei Darussalam	151	–	12	10	7	–	2.5	2.6	2.6	41	25	-2.2 x	-0.4 x	5.8	3.5	2.0	2.4	2.7
Bulgaria	128	39	22	21	12	2.9	0.7	4.9	2.9	45	42	3.4 x	3.3	2.2	1.7	1.5	1.1	0.6
Burkina Faso	9	291	208	182	146	1.7	1.4	2.0	1.7	30	19	1.3	2.8	6.6	6.8	5.8	-0.2	0.8
Burundi	10	229	183	165	139	1.1	1.0	1.5	1.3	24	15	1.2	-1.4	6.8	6.5	4.2	0.2	2.1
Cambodia	62	–	117	102	43	–	1.4	7.9	4.8	64	58	–	6.5 x	5.9	5.7	2.5	0.2	3.9
Cameroon	11	206	145	140	127	1.8	0.4	0.8	0.6	12	9	3.4	0.8	6.2	5.9	4.4	0.2	1.4
Canada	157	22	8	6	6	4.9	2.9	0.9	1.9	33	10	2.0	1.8	2.2	1.7	1.7	1.5	-0.1
Cape Verde	91	160	58	39	21	5.1	4.0	5.5	4.8	63	45	–	5.0	6.9	5.3	2.3	1.3	3.9
Central African Republic	6	226	169	172	164	1.5	-0.2	0.5	0.2	3	5	-1.3	-0.5	6.0	5.8	4.5	0.1	1.1
Chad	4	257	208	189	169	1.1	1.0	1.0	1.0	19	10	-0.9	3.1	6.5	6.7	5.9	-0.1	0.6
Chile	141	82	19	11	9	7.4	5.5	2.0	3.6	53	19	1.5	3.4	4.0	2.6	1.8	2.1	1.7
China	115	117	49	35	15	4.3	3.3	7.9	5.8	70	58	6.6	9.3	5.5	2.3	1.6	4.3	1.9
Colombia	102	105	34	25	18	5.6	3.2	3.1	3.2	48	29	1.9	1.6	5.6	3.1	2.3	2.9	1.3
Comoros	33	219	122	100	79	2.9	2.0	2.1	2.0	35	20	-0.1 x	-0.8	7.1	5.6	4.9	1.2	0.7
Congo	25	152	119	109	99	1.2	0.9	0.9	0.9	17	9	3.3	0.4	6.3	5.4	4.5	0.8	0.8
Cook Islands	135	61	19	17	10	5.8	1.1	5.3	3.3	50	44	–	–	–	–	–	–	–
Costa Rica	135	71	17	13	10	7.1	2.9	2.2	2.5	41	22	0.7	2.6	5.0	3.2	1.8	2.3	2.6
Côte d'Ivoire	17	233	151	139	115	2.2	0.9	1.7	1.3	24	17	-1.7	-0.6	7.9	6.3	4.3	1.2	1.7
Croatia	165	–	13	8	5	–	4.3	4.5	4.4	60	39	–	2.8	2.0	1.7	1.5	0.9	0.6
Cuba	157	41	13	9	6	5.6	4.5	3.5	4.0	56	32	3.9	3.0 x	4.0	1.8	1.5	4.2	0.9
Cyprus	184	–	11	7	3	–	5.3	6.7	6.0	72	52	5.9 x	2.0	2.6	2.4	1.5	0.4	2.4
Czech Republic	169	–	14	7	4	–	7.6	4.9	6.2	73	42	–	2.7	2.0	1.8	1.5	0.6	1.0
Democratic People's Republic of Korea	69	–	45	58	33	–	-2.5	5.0	1.4	26	42	–	–	4.0	2.4	2.0	2.6	0.9
Democratic Republic of the Congo	5	244	181	181	168	1.5	0.0	0.7	0.4	8	8	-2.2	-2.6	6.2	7.1	5.7	-0.7	1.1
Denmark	169	16	9	6	4	3.2	4.4	3.8	4.1	57	34	2.0	1.4	2.1	1.7	1.9	1.2	-0.6
Djibouti	26	–	122	106	90	–	1.4	1.5	1.5	26	15	–	-1.4 x	7.4	6.2	3.7	0.9	2.5
Dominica	128	54	17	15	12	5.7	1.6	2.1	1.8	32	21	5.2 x	2.2	–	–	–	–	–
Dominican Republic	83	122	58	39	25	3.7	4.1	4.0	4.1	58	36	2.1	3.9	6.2	3.5	2.5	2.9	1.5
Ecuador	86	138	52	34	23	4.8	4.3	3.7	4.0	56	33	1.3	1.5	6.3	3.7	2.4	2.7	1.9
Egypt	91	237	86	44	21	5.1	6.6	6.8	6.7	75	52	4.3	2.8	5.9	4.4	2.7	1.6	2.3
El Salvador	115	158	60	34	15	4.8	5.7	7.3	6.6	75	55	-1.9	2.4	6.2	4.0	2.2	2.3	2.8
Equatorial Guinea	16	–	190	152	118	–	2.2	2.3	2.3	38	22	–	18.2	5.7	5.9	5.1	-0.2	0.7
Eritrea	41	247	138	98	68	2.9	3.4	3.4	3.4	51	31	–	-0.8 x	6.6	6.2	4.4	0.3	1.7
Estonia	169	–	20	11	4	–	6.2	9.7	8.1	82	66	–	5.5 x	2.1	1.9	1.7	0.4	0.6
Ethiopia	36	230	198	139	77	0.7	3.6	5.3	4.5	61	44	–	3.3	6.8	7.1	4.0	-0.2	2.7
Fiji	107	53	30	22	16	2.9	2.8	2.8	2.8	45	26	0.6	1.3	4.5	3.4	2.6	1.5	1.2
Finland	184	16	7	4	3	4.4	4.4	3.6	4.0	57	33	2.9	2.5	1.9	1.7	1.9	0.3	-0.3
France	169	18	9	5	4	3.6	4.9	2.5	3.6	53	24	2.1	1.2	2.5	1.8	2.0	1.8	-0.6
Gabon	44	–	94	82	66	–	1.4	2.1	1.7	31	20	0.2	-0.7	4.7	5.2	3.2	-0.5	2.3

TABLE 10 | THE RATE OF PROGRESS ▶

Countries and areas	Under-5 mortality rank	Under-5 mortality rate				Annual rate of reduction (%)[θ] Under-5 mortality rate				Reduction since 1990 (%)[θ]	Reduction since 2000 (%)[θ]	GDP per capita average annual growth rate (%)		Total fertility rate			Average annual rate of reduction (%) Total fertility rate	
		1970	1990	2000	2011	1970–1990	1990–2000	2000–2011	1990–2011			1970–1990	1990–2011	1970	1990	2011	1970–1990	1990–2011
Gambia	23	286	165	130	101	2.8	2.3	2.4	2.3	39	23	0.6	0.9	6.1	6.1	4.8	0.0	1.1
Georgia	91	–	47	33	21	–	3.6	4.2	3.9	56	37	3.1	2.7	2.6	2.2	1.5	0.9	1.6
Germany	169	26	9	5	4	5.6	4.5	2.7	3.6	53	26	2.3	1.3	2.0	1.4	1.4	1.9	-0.2
Ghana	34	183	121	99	78	2.1	2.0	2.2	2.1	36	21	-2.0	2.5	7.0	5.6	4.1	1.1	1.5
Greece	169	38	13	8	4	5.5	5.0	5.1	5.0	65	43	1.3	2.2	2.4	1.4	1.5	2.5	-0.3
Grenada	125	–	21	16	13	–	2.9	1.9	2.4	39	18	4.2 x	2.9	4.6	3.8	2.2	0.9	2.6
Guatemala	74	172	78	48	30	4.0	4.8	4.2	4.5	61	37	0.2	1.3	6.2	5.6	3.9	0.6	1.7
Guinea	12	316	228	175	126	1.6	2.7	3.0	2.8	45	28	–	2.9	6.8	6.7	5.2	0.1	1.3
Guinea-Bissau	7	242	210	186	161	0.7	1.2	1.3	1.3	24	14	0.0	-1.2	6.1	6.6	5.0	-0.5	1.4
Guyana	68	78	63	49	36	1.0	2.5	2.8	2.7	43	27	-1.3	2.8 x	5.6	2.6	2.2	3.8	0.7
Haiti	40	229	143	102	70	2.3	3.4	3.4	3.4	51	31	–	-1.0 x	5.8	5.4	3.3	0.3	2.4
Holy See	–	–	–	–	–	–	–	–	–	–	–	–	–	–	–	–	–	–
Honduras	91	156	55	35	21	5.2	4.5	4.5	4.5	61	39	0.8	1.6	7.3	5.1	3.1	1.7	2.4
Hungary	157	43	19	11	6	4.2	5.3	5.1	5.2	66	43	3.0	2.5	2.0	1.8	1.4	0.6	1.2
Iceland	184	16	6	4	3	4.6	4.8	4.0	4.4	60	36	3.2	2.1	3.0	2.2	2.1	1.6	0.1
India	49	189	114	88	61	2.5	2.6	3.3	3.0	46	30	2.0	4.9	5.5	3.9	2.6	1.7	2.0
Indonesia	71	164	82	53	32	3.5	4.4	4.6	4.5	61	39	4.6	2.7	5.5	3.1	2.1	2.8	1.9
Iran (Islamic Republic of)	83	203	61	44	25	6.0	3.3	5.1	4.3	59	43	-2.3	2.7 x	6.5	4.8	1.6	1.5	5.1
Iraq	67	115	46	43	38	4.6	0.7	1.1	0.9	18	11	–	-1.9 x	7.4	6.0	4.6	1.0	1.2
Ireland	169	23	9	7	4	4.6	2.5	5.1	3.9	56	43	–	0.6 x	3.8	2.0	2.1	3.2	-0.3
Israel	169	–	12	7	4	–	5.1	4.3	4.7	63	38	1.9	1.8	3.8	3.0	2.9	1.2	0.1
Italy	169	33	10	6	4	6.1	5.5	3.8	4.6	62	34	2.8	0.8	2.5	1.3	1.4	3.2	-0.5
Jamaica	102	63	35	26	18	3.0	3.0	3.0	3.0	47	28	-1.3	0.5	5.5	2.9	2.3	3.1	1.2
Japan	184	18	6	5	3	5.1	3.5	2.5	3.0	47	24	3.4	0.7	2.1	1.6	1.4	1.5	0.6
Jordan	91	97	37	28	21	4.8	2.7	2.7	2.7	44	26	2.5 x	2.6	7.9	5.8	3.0	1.6	3.1
Kazakhstan	78	79	57	42	28	1.7	3.0	3.7	3.3	50	33	–	4.1	3.5	2.8	2.5	1.1	0.5
Kenya	38	153	98	113	73	2.2	-1.5	4.0	1.4	26	36	1.2	0.4	8.1	6.0	4.7	1.5	1.2
Kiribati	58	154	88	65	47	2.8	2.9	2.9	2.9	46	27	-5.3	1.1	–	–	–	–	–
Kuwait	133	60	17	13	11	6.4	2.9	1.4	2.1	36	14	-6.7 x	1.4 x	7.2	2.6	2.3	5.1	0.6
Kyrgyzstan	72	143	70	47	31	3.6	3.9	4.0	4.0	56	35	–	0.7	4.9	3.9	2.7	1.2	1.8
Lao People's Democratic Republic	63	–	148	81	42	–	6.0	6.0	6.0	72	48	–	4.7	6.0	6.2	2.7	-0.1	4.0
Latvia	145	–	21	17	8	–	1.7	6.7	4.3	60	52	3.4	4.4	1.9	1.9	1.5	0.0	1.2
Lebanon	141	57	33	19	9	2.7	5.6	6.5	6.0	72	51	–	2.5	5.1	3.1	1.8	2.4	2.7
Lesotho	29	177	88	117	86	3.5	-2.9	2.8	0.1	2	27	2.4	2.3	5.8	4.9	3.1	0.8	2.1
Liberia	34	280	241	164	78	0.7	3.9	6.7	5.4	68	52	-4.0	5.5	6.7	6.5	5.2	0.1	1.1
Libya	107	139	44	27	16	5.7	4.9	4.7	4.8	63	40	–	–	7.6	4.8	2.5	2.3	3.1
Liechtenstein	–	–	–	–	–	–	–	–	–	–	–	2.2	3.0 x	–	–	–	–	–
Lithuania	157	26	17	12	6	2.0	3.9	6.6	5.3	67	52	–	3.6	2.3	2.0	1.5	0.7	1.4
Luxembourg	184	22	8	5	3	4.7	5.4	3.9	4.6	62	35	2.6	2.7	2.0	1.6	1.7	1.1	-0.3
Madagascar	47	176	161	104	62	0.4	4.4	4.8	4.6	62	41	-2.3	-0.3	7.3	6.3	4.6	0.8	1.5
Malawi	31	334	227	164	83	1.9	3.2	6.2	4.8	64	50	0.0	1.3	7.3	6.8	6.0	0.4	0.6
Malaysia	151	54	17	11	7	5.8	4.8	4.4	4.6	62	39	4.0	3.1	4.9	3.5	2.6	1.6	1.4
Maldives	133	266	105	53	11	4.6	6.9	14.5	10.9	90	80	–	5.8 x	7.2	6.1	1.7	0.8	6.1
Mali	3	373	257	214	176	1.9	1.8	1.8	1.8	32	18	0.1	2.1	6.9	7.1	6.2	-0.1	0.6
Malta	157	27	11	8	6	4.4	3.7	2.5	3.1	48	24	6.0	2.4	2.0	2.1	1.3	-0.2	2.2
Marshall Islands	80	98	52	38	26	3.2	3.2	3.3	3.3	50	30	–	0.5	–	–	–	–	–
Mauritania	18	197	125	118	112	2.3	0.6	0.5	0.5	10	5	-1.1	1.3	6.8	5.9	4.5	0.7	1.4
Mauritius	115	85	24	19	15	6.3	2.5	1.9	2.2	37	19	3.2 x	3.5	4.0	2.3	1.6	2.7	1.7
Mexico	107	108	49	29	16	4.0	5.2	5.6	5.4	68	46	1.7	1.3	6.7	3.4	2.3	3.4	1.9
Micronesia (Federated States of)	63	–	56	49	42	–	1.5	1.4	1.5	26	15	–	0.4	6.9	5.0	3.4	1.7	1.8
Monaco	169	–	8	5	4	–	4.2	2.4	3.3	50	24	1.4	2.1 x	–	–	–	–	–
Mongolia	72	–	107	63	31	–	5.2	6.6	5.9	71	52	–	3.3	7.6	4.1	2.5	3.1	2.4
Montenegro	151	–	18	13	7	–	3.3	5.1	4.3	59	43	–	3.4 x	2.4	1.9	1.6	1.2	0.6
Morocco	69	177	81	53	33	3.9	4.3	4.3	4.3	60	38	1.9	2.5	7.1	4.0	2.2	2.8	2.8
Mozambique	22	275	226	172	103	1.0	2.7	4.7	3.7	54	40	-1.0 x	4.3	6.6	6.2	4.8	0.3	1.2
Myanmar	47	172	107	84	62	2.4	2.5	2.6	2.6	42	25	1.6	7.4 x	6.1	3.4	2.0	2.8	2.6
Namibia	63	113	73	74	42	2.2	-0.1	5.2	2.7	43	44	-2.1 x	1.9	6.5	5.2	3.2	1.1	2.4
Nauru	66	–	40	40	40	–	0.0	0.0	0.0	0	0	–	–	–	–	–	–	–
Nepal	57	249	135	83	48	3.1	4.8	5.0	4.9	64	42	1.1	1.9	6.1	5.2	2.7	0.8	3.2
Netherlands	169	16	8	6	4	3.2	2.9	4.0	3.5	52	35	1.6	1.8	2.4	1.6	1.8	2.2	-0.6
New Zealand	157	21	11	7	6	3.1	4.1	2.1	3.0	47	20	1.1 x	1.9	3.1	2.1	2.2	2.0	-0.2
Nicaragua	80	161	66	42	26	4.5	4.5	4.6	4.5	61	39	-2.0	-0.2	7.4	4.8	2.6	1.9	2.9
Niger	13	324	314	216	125	0.2	3.8	5.0	4.2	60	42	-2.0	2.1	7.4	7.8	7.0	-0.3	0.5
Nigeria	14	259	214	188	124	1.0	1.3	3.8	2.6	42	34	-1.3	2.1	6.5	6.4	5.5	0.1	0.7

TABLE 10 | THE RATE OF PROGRESS ▶

Countries and areas	Under-5 mortality rank	Under-5 mortality rate				Annual rate of reduction (%)θ Under-5 mortality rate				Reduction since 1990 (%)θ	Reduction since 2000 (%)θ	GDP per capita average annual growth rate (%)		Total fertility rate			Average annual rate of reduction (%) Total fertility rate	
		1970	1990	2000	2011	1970–1990	1990–2000	2000–2011	1990–2011			1970–1990	1990–2011	1970	1990	2011	1970–1990	1990–2011
Niue	91	–	14	29	21	–	-7.3	3.0	-1.9	-49	28	–	–	–	–	–	–	–
Norway	184	16	8	5	3	3.3	5.4	4.2	4.7	63	37	3.2	2.0	2.5	1.9	1.9	1.5	-0.2
Oman	141	195	48	22	9	7.1	7.8	8.3	8.1	82	60	3.1	2.7	7.3	7.2	2.2	0.1	5.5
Pakistan	39	182	122	95	72	2.0	2.5	2.5	2.5	41	24	2.6	1.9	6.6	6.0	3.3	0.5	2.8
Palau	100	–	32	25	19	–	2.6	2.6	2.6	42	25	–	-0.1 x	–	–	–	–	–
Panama	98	62	33	26	20	3.1	2.6	2.5	2.5	41	24	0.3	3.4	5.3	3.0	2.5	2.8	1.0
Papua New Guinea	50	151	88	72	58	2.7	2.0	2.0	2.0	34	19	-1.0	0.1	6.2	4.8	3.9	1.2	1.0
Paraguay	87	75	53	35	22	1.7	4.0	4.1	4.1	57	37	3.1	0.3	5.7	4.5	2.9	1.2	2.1
Peru	102	158	75	39	18	3.7	6.6	7.0	6.8	76	53	-0.6	3.2	6.3	3.8	2.5	2.5	2.1
Philippines	83	88	57	39	25	2.2	3.8	3.9	3.8	55	35	0.5	1.9	6.3	4.3	3.1	1.9	1.6
Poland	157	36	17	10	6	3.6	5.9	4.6	5.2	66	40	–	4.4	2.2	2.0	1.4	0.4	1.8
Portugal	184	66	15	7	3	7.5	7.1	6.8	6.9	77	53	2.5	1.5	3.0	1.5	1.3	3.3	0.7
Qatar	145	57	20	13	8	5.2	4.7	4.5	4.6	62	39	–	0.8 x	6.9	4.2	2.2	2.5	3.0
Republic of Korea	165	49	8	6	5	9.4	2.7	1.6	2.1	36	16	6.2	4.1	4.5	1.6	1.4	5.2	0.8
Republic of Moldova	107	70	35	24	16	3.5	3.8	3.6	3.7	54	33	1.8 x	-0.1	2.6	2.4	1.5	0.3	2.4
Romania	125	64	37	27	13	2.7	3.3	6.9	5.2	67	53	0.9 x	2.8	2.9	1.9	1.4	2.1	1.5
Russian Federation	128	40	27	21	12	2.0	2.5	5.3	4.0	56	44	–	2.3	2.0	1.9	1.5	0.3	1.0
Rwanda	51	223	156	183	54	1.8	-1.6	11.1	5.1	65	70	1.2	2.3	8.1	7.0	5.3	0.7	1.3
Saint Kitts and Nevis	151	71	28	16	7	4.6	5.5	7.2	6.4	74	55	6.3 x	1.6	–	–	–	–	–
Saint Lucia	107	63	23	18	16	5.2	2.2	1.4	1.7	31	14	5.3 x	0.7	6.1	3.4	2.0	2.9	2.6
Saint Vincent and the Grenadines	91	96	27	22	21	6.5	1.9	0.4	1.1	21	5	3.3	3.2	6.0	3.0	2.0	3.6	1.8
Samoa	100	–	30	23	19	–	2.6	1.8	2.2	37	18	–	2.8	6.1	4.8	3.8	1.2	1.1
San Marino	195	–	12	5	2	–	8.1	9.8	9.0	85	66	1.7	3.2 x	–	–	–	–	–
Sao Tome and Principe	28	96	96	93	89	-0.0	0.4	0.4	0.4	8	4	–	–	6.5	5.4	3.6	0.9	1.9
Saudi Arabia	141	–	43	21	9	–	7.3	7.3	7.3	78	55	-1.4	0.2	7.3	5.8	2.7	1.1	3.6
Senegal	45	295	136	130	65	3.9	0.4	6.4	3.5	52	50	-0.5	1.1	7.4	6.6	4.7	0.5	1.6
Serbia	151	–	29	13	7	–	8.1	5.3	6.6	75	44	–	1.4	2.4	2.1	1.6	0.6	1.4
Seychelles	122	66	17	14	14	6.9	1.8	0.0	0.9	17	0	2.9	2.0	–	–	–	–	–
Sierra Leone	1	342	267	241	185	1.2	1.0	2.4	1.7	31	23	-0.5	1.1	5.9	5.7	4.9	0.1	0.7
Singapore	184	27	8	4	3	6.4	6.5	3.7	5.0	65	33	5.9	3.5	3.2	1.8	1.3	2.9	1.5
Slovakia	145	–	18	12	8	–	4.2	3.7	3.9	56	34	–	3.7	2.5	2.0	1.3	1.0	2.0
Slovenia	184	–	10	5	3	–	6.6	6.0	6.2	73	48	–	3.2	2.3	1.5	1.5	2.0	0.2
Solomon Islands	87	102	42	31	22	4.5	3.2	3.1	3.1	48	29	–	-0.9	6.9	5.9	4.2	0.8	1.6
Somalia	2	–	180	180	180	–	0.0	0.0	0.0	0	0	-0.8	–	7.2	6.6	6.3	0.4	0.2
South Africa	58	–	62	74	47	–	-1.7	4.2	1.4	25	37	0.1	1.3	5.6	3.7	2.4	2.1	2.0
South Sudanσ	15	302	217	165	121	1.6	2.8	2.8	2.8	45	27	–	–	–	–	–	–	–
Spain	169	29	11	7	4	4.9	5.0	4.1	4.5	61	36	1.9	1.9	2.9	1.3	1.5	3.8	-0.5
Sri Lanka	128	76	29	19	12	4.8	4.1	4.1	4.1	58	36	3.0	4.1	4.3	2.5	2.3	2.8	0.4
State of Palestine	87	–	43	30	22	–	3.6	2.8	3.2	49	27	–	-2.4 x	7.9	6.5	4.4	0.9	1.9
Sudanσ	29	148	123	104	86	0.9	1.7	1.7	1.7	30	17	–	–	–	–	–	–	–
Suriname	74	–	52	40	30	–	2.6	2.7	2.7	43	26	-2.2 x	1.7 x	5.7	2.7	2.3	3.6	0.8
Swaziland	21	181	83	114	104	3.9	-3.2	0.9	-1.0	-24	9	3.1	1.8	6.9	5.7	3.3	0.9	2.7
Sweden	184	13	7	4	3	3.4	4.9	3.5	4.2	58	32	1.8	2.2	2.0	2.0	1.9	0.1	0.2
Switzerland	169	18	8	6	4	4.1	3.5	2.4	2.9	46	23	1.7 x	0.9	2.1	1.5	1.5	1.6	0.1
Syrian Arab Republic	115	113	36	23	15	5.7	4.6	3.6	4.1	58	33	2.2	1.8 x	7.6	5.3	2.9	1.8	3.0
Tajikistan	46	–	114	95	63	–	1.9	3.7	2.8	45	33	–	0.2	6.9	5.2	3.2	1.4	2.2
Thailand	128	102	35	19	12	5.3	6.4	3.7	5.0	65	34	4.7	2.8	5.6	2.1	1.6	4.9	1.4
The former Yugoslav Republic of Macedonia	135	–	38	16	10	–	8.4	4.8	6.5	74	41	–	1.2	3.1	2.1	1.4	1.9	1.9
Timor-Leste	51	–	180	109	54	–	5.0	6.4	5.7	70	51	–	1.9 x	5.9	5.3	6.1	0.5	-0.6
Togo	19	220	147	128	110	2.0	1.4	1.4	1.4	25	14	-0.3	-0.1	7.1	6.3	4.0	0.6	2.2
Tonga	115	43	25	20	15	2.9	2.2	2.2	2.2	37	21	–	1.5	5.9	4.6	3.9	1.2	0.9
Trinidad and Tobago	78	52	37	32	28	1.7	1.4	1.3	1.4	25	14	0.5	4.8	3.5	2.4	1.6	1.8	1.9
Tunisia	107	181	51	30	16	6.3	5.5	5.5	5.5	68	45	2.5	3.3	6.6	3.6	2.0	3.0	2.9
Turkey	115	194	72	35	15	5.0	7.1	7.7	7.4	79	57	2.0	2.4	5.5	3.0	2.1	3.0	1.9
Turkmenistan	54	–	94	71	53	–	2.8	2.8	2.8	44	26	–	5.8	6.3	4.3	2.4	1.9	2.9
Tuvalu	74	–	58	43	30	–	2.9	3.3	3.1	48	30	–	2.1	–	–	–	–	–
Uganda	26	190	178	141	90	0.3	2.4	4.1	3.3	49	36	–	3.7	7.1	7.1	6.1	0.0	0.8
Ukraine	135	34	19	19	10	2.8	0.4	5.6	3.1	48	46	–	0.6	2.1	1.9	1.5	0.6	1.2
United Arab Emirates	151	92	22	12	7	7.1	5.9	5.7	5.8	70	46	-4.3 x	-1.9	6.6	4.4	1.7	2.0	4.5
United Kingdom	165	21	9	7	5	4.1	3.3	2.3	2.8	45	23	2.1	2.4	2.3	1.8	1.9	1.2	-0.1
United Republic of Tanzania	41	208	158	126	68	1.4	2.2	5.7	4.0	57	47	–	2.5	6.8	6.2	5.5	0.4	0.6
United States	145	23	11	9	8	3.6	2.8	1.1	2.0	34	12	2.1	1.7	2.2	1.9	2.1	0.7	-0.3

TABLE 10 | THE RATE OF PROGRESS

Countries and areas	Under-5 mortality rank	Under-5 mortality rate				Annual rate of reduction (%)θ Under-5 mortality rate				Reduction since 1990 (%)θ	Reduction since 2000 (%)θ	GDP per capita average annual growth rate (%)		Total fertility rate			Average annual rate of reduction (%) Total fertility rate	
		1970	1990	2000	2011	1970–1990	1990–2000	2000–2011	1990–2011			1970–1990	1990–2011	1970	1990	2011	1970–1990	1990–2011
Uruguay	135	55	23	17	10	4.3	3.0	4.6	3.8	55	40	0.9	2.1	2.9	2.5	2.1	0.7	0.9
Uzbekistan	56	–	75	61	49	–	2.1	2.1	2.1	35	20	–	2.5	6.5	4.2	2.3	2.2	2.8
Vanuatu	125	102	39	23	13	4.9	5.2	5.0	5.1	66	43	1.2 x	0.6	6.3	4.9	3.8	1.2	1.2
Venezuela (Bolivarian Republic of)	115	61	31	22	15	3.4	3.3	3.6	3.4	51	33	-1.7	0.4	5.4	3.4	2.4	2.2	1.7
Viet Nam	87	–	50	34	22	–	3.9	4.1	4.0	57	36	–	6.0	7.4	3.6	1.8	3.6	3.3
Yemen	36	293	126	99	77	4.2	2.4	2.4	2.4	39	23	–	1.1	7.5	8.7	5.1	-0.7	2.5
Zambia	31	179	193	154	83	-0.4	2.3	5.6	4.0	57	46	-2.3	0.8	7.4	6.5	6.3	0.7	0.1
Zimbabwe	43	119	79	106	67	2.0	-2.9	4.1	0.8	15	37	-0.4	-3.0	7.4	5.2	3.2	1.8	2.3

MEMORANDUM

Sudan and South Sudanσ	–	–	–	–	–	–	–	–	–	–	–	0.1	3.4	6.6	6.0	4.3	0.5	1.5

SUMMARY INDICATORS#

Sub-Saharan Africa		236	178	154	109	1.4	1.5	3.1	2.3	39	29	0.0	2.0	6.7	6.2	4.9	0.3	1.2
Eastern and Southern Africa		214	162	135	84	1.4	1.8	4.3	3.1	48	38	0.3	1.9	6.8	6.0	4.5	0.6	1.4
West and Central Africa		259	197	175	132	1.4	1.2	2.6	1.9	33	24	-0.5	2.0	6.6	6.5	5.3	0.1	1.0
Middle East and North Africa		190	72	52	36	4.8	3.4	3.3	3.3	50	30	-0.1	0.8	6.7	5.0	2.8	1.5	2.8
South Asia		195	119	89	62	2.5	2.9	3.3	3.1	48	30	2.0	4.5	5.7	4.2	2.7	1.6	2.1
East Asia and Pacific		120	55	39	20	3.9	3.4	5.9	4.7	63	48	5.6	7.5	5.6	2.6	1.8	3.8	1.8
Latin America and Caribbean		117	53	34	19	4.0	4.4	5.2	4.8	64	44	1.4	1.7	5.3	3.2	2.2	2.5	1.8
CEE/CIS		88	48	35	21	3.1	3.2	4.6	3.9	56	40	–	2.5	2.8	2.3	1.8	0.9	1.3
Least developed countries		238	171	136	98	1.7	2.3	3.0	2.7	43	28	-0.1	3.1	6.7	5.9	4.2	0.6	1.7
World		141	87	73	51	2.4	1.8	3.2	2.5	41	29	2.4	2.6	4.7	3.2	2.4	1.9	1.3

σ Due to the cession in July 2011 of the Republic of South Sudan by the Republic of the Sudan, and its subsequent admission to the United Nations on 14 July 2011, disaggregated data for the Sudan and South Sudan as separate States are not yet available for all indicators. Aggregated data presented are for the Sudan pre-cession (see Memorandum item).

For a complete list of countries and areas in the regions, subregions and country categories, see page 98.

DEFINITIONS OF THE INDICATORS

Under-5 mortality rate – Probability of dying between birth and exactly 5 years of age, expressed per 1,000 live births.

Reduction since 1990 – Percentage reduction in the under-five mortality rate (U5MR) from 1990 to 2011. The United Nations Millennium Declaration in 2000 established a goal of a two-thirds (67 per cent) reduction in U5MR from 1990 to 2015. This indicator provides a current assessment of progress towards this goal.

GDP per capita – Gross domestic product (GDP) is the sum of value added by all resident producers plus any product taxes (less subsidies) not included in the valuation of output. GDP per capita is GDP divided by midyear population. Growth is calculated from constant price GDP data in local currency.

Total fertility rate – Number of children who would be born per woman if she lived to the end of her childbearing years and bore children at each age in accordance with prevailing age-specific fertility rates.

MAIN DATA SOURCES

Under-5 mortality rate – United Nations Inter-agency Group for Child Mortality Estimation (UNICEF, World Health Organization, United Nations Population Division and the World Bank).

GDP per capita – The World Bank.

Total fertility rate – United Nations Population Division.

NOTES

– Data not available.

θ A negative value indicates an increase in the under-five mortality rate.

x Data refer to years or periods other than those specified in the column heading. Such data are not included in the calculation of regional and global averages.

TABLE 11: ADOLESCENTS

Countries and areas	Population aged 10–19 Total (thousands) 2011	Proportion of total population (%) 2011	Adolescents currently married/in union (%) 2002–2011* male	female	Births by age 18 (%) 2007–2011*	Adolescent birth rate 2006–2010*	Justification of wife beating among adolescents (%) 2002–2011* male	female	Use of mass media among adolescents (%) 2002–2011* male	female	Lower secondary school gross enrolment ratio 2008–2011*	Upper secondary school gross enrolment ratio 2008–2011*	Comprehensive knowledge of HIV among adolescents (%) 2007–2011* male	female
Afghanistan	8,015	25	–	20	26	90	–	84	–	–	62	27	–	–
Albania	551	17	1	8	3	11	37	24	97	99	95	81	21	36
Algeria	6,425	18	–	2	–	4	–	66	–	–	133	50	–	12 x
Andorra	–	–	–	–	–	5	–	–	–	–	88	84	–	–
Angola	4,720	24	–	–	–	165 x	–	–	–	–	39	22	–	–
Antigua and Barbuda	–	–	–	–	–	67 x	–	–	–	–	122	80	55	40
Argentina	6,769	17	–	–	–	68	–	–	–	–	109	68	–	–
Armenia	435	14	1	8	2	28	21	8	94	92	96	85	4	10
Australia	2,917	13	–	–	–	16	–	–	–	–	113	167	–	–
Austria	929	11	–	–	–	10	–	–	–	–	102	96	–	–
Azerbaijan	1,378	15	0	10	4 x	41	63	39	97	95	92	75	2 x	3 x
Bahamas	58	17	–	–	–	41	–	–	–	–	101	90	–	–
Bahrain	153	11	–	–	–	12	–	–	–	–	–	–	–	–
Bangladesh	31,601	21	–	46	40	133 x	–	41	–	63 y	66	40	–	7
Barbados	38	14	–	–	–	50	–	–	–	–	99	103	–	–
Belarus	1,025	11	–	4	3 x	21	–	–	–	–	–	–	–	–
Belgium	1,207	11	–	–	–	11	–	–	–	–	114	109	–	–
Belize	73	23	–	15	19 x	90 x	–	11	–	–	–	–	–	39 x
Benin	2,094	23	2	22	23 x	114 x	12	41	83	64	–	–	31 x	17 x
Bhutan	148	20	–	15	15	59	–	70	–	–	78	42	–	22
Bolivia (Plurinational State of)	2,232	22	4	13	20	89 x	–	17	100	97	94	73	24	22
Bosnia and Herzegovina	434	12	–	7	–	17	–	4	–	–	99	84	–	45 x
Botswana	434	21	–	–	–	51	–	–	–	–	91	68	–	–
Brazil	33,906	17	–	25	–	71	–	–	–	–	–	–	–	–
Brunei Darussalam	65	16	–	–	–	18	–	–	–	–	–	–	–	–
Bulgaria	696	9	–	–	–	48	–	–	–	–	83	94	–	–
Burkina Faso	3,978	23	2	32	28	130	40	39	61	55	28	9	31	29
Burundi	1,946	23	1	9	11	65	56	74	83	69	34	13	45	43
Cambodia	3,222	23	2	10	7	48	25 y	42 y	73	76	60	–	41	43
Cameroon	4,481	22	–	22	33 x	127	–	58	77	61	–	–	–	32 x
Canada	4,137	12	–	–	–	14	–	–	–	–	99	102	–	–
Cape Verde	113	23	2	8	22 x	92 x	24	23	88	88	109	67	–	–
Central African Republic	1,030	23	11	55	45	133 x	87 y	79	–	–	–	–	26 x	16 x
Chad	2,690	23	–	48	47	193 x	–	59	55	24	29	18	–	10
Chile	2,769	16	–	–	–	54	–	–	–	–	100	82	–	–
China	195,432	15	–	–	–	6	–	–	–	–	92	71	–	–
Colombia	8,759	19	–	14	20	85	–	–	–	–	105	80	–	21
Comoros	161	21	–	–	–	95 x	–	–	–	–	–	–	–	–
Congo	909	22	2	19	29 x	132 x	–	76	75	63	–	–	18	8
Cook Islands	–	–	–	–	–	47 x	–	–	–	–	97	67	–	–
Costa Rica	832	18	3	11	9	67	–	–	–	–	116	75	–	–
Côte d'Ivoire	4,653	23	2	20	29 x	111	–	63	86	75	–	–	–	–
Croatia	490	11	–	–	–	13	–	–	–	–	105	87	–	–
Cuba	1,454	13	–	20	9	51	–	–	–	–	94	85	–	54
Cyprus	153	14	–	–	–	4	–	–	–	–	102	96	–	–
Czech Republic	1,069	10	–	–	–	11	–	–	–	–	93	88	–	–
Democratic People's Republic of Korea	4,103	17	–	–	–	1	–	–	–	–	–	–	–	7
Democratic Republic of the Congo	16,323	24	–	25	25	135	–	72	55	43	48	32	–	13
Denmark	701	13	–	–	–	6	–	–	–	–	116	119	–	–
Djibouti	202	22	–	4	–	27 x	–	–	–	–	44	25	–	16 x
Dominica	–	–	–	–	–	48	–	–	–	–	108	84	–	–
Dominican Republic	1,967	20	–	17	25	98 x	–	7	98	98	90	70	33	39
Ecuador	2,843	19	–	16	–	100 x	–	–	–	–	85	65	–	–
Egypt	15,964	19	–	13	7	50 x	–	50 y	–	97 y	94	51	16	3
El Salvador	1,440	23	–	21	–	65	–	–	–	–	86	44	–	–
Equatorial Guinea	154	21	–	–	–	128 x	–	–	–	–	–	–	–	–
Eritrea	1,171	22	–	29	25 x	–	–	70	–	85	44	22	–	–
Estonia	133	10	–	–	–	21	–	–	–	–	105	103	–	–
Ethiopia	20,948	25	2	19	22	79	51	64	42	38	45	16	32	24
Fiji	159	18	–	–	–	31 x	–	–	–	–	100	69	–	–
Finland	627	12	–	–	–	8	–	–	–	–	99	115	–	–
France	7,482	12	–	–	–	12	–	–	–	–	110	117	–	–

TABLE 11 | ADOLESCENTS ▶

Countries and areas	Population aged 10–19 Total (thousands) 2011	Proportion of total population (%) 2011	Adolescents currently married/in union (%) 2002–2011* male	female	Births by age 18 (%) 2007–2011*	Adolescent birth rate 2006–2010*	Justification of wife beating among adolescents (%) 2002–2011* male	female	Use of mass media among adolescents (%) 2002–2011* male	female	Lower secondary school gross enrolment ratio 2008–2011*	Upper secondary school gross enrolment ratio 2008–2011*	Comprehensive knowledge of HIV among adolescents (%) 2007–2011* male	female
Gabon	346	23	2 x	18 x	35 x	–	–	–	89 x	83 x	–	–	–	–
Gambia	421	24	–	24	23	104 x	–	74	–	–	63	45	–	33
Georgia	541	13	–	11	6	44	–	5	–	–	93	81	–	–
Germany	8,059	10	–	–	–	9	–	–	–	–	101	107	–	–
Ghana	5,412	22	1	7	16	70	37	53	90	85	83	39	30	28
Greece	1,087	10	–	–	–	12	–	–	–	–	–	–	–	–
Grenada	20	20	–	–	–	53 x	–	–	–	–	121	89	–	–
Guatemala	3,467	23	–	20	22	92	–	–	–	–	65	48	24	20
Guinea	2,334	23	3	36	44 x	153 x	–	79	66	55	46	26	–	–
Guinea–Bissau	349	23	–	19	31 x	137	–	39 y	–	–	–	–	–	12
Guyana	181	24	1	16	16	97	25	18	94	94	99	78	45	53
Haiti	2,270	22	2	17	15 x	69 x	–	29	88	83	–	–	34 x	31 x
Holy See	–	–	–	–	–	–	–	–	–	–	–	–	–	–
Honduras	1,777	23	–	20	26 x	108 x	–	18	–	98	75	71	–	28 x
Hungary	1,072	11	–	–	–	19	–	–	–	–	99	98	–	–
Iceland	45	14	–	–	–	15	–	–	–	–	97	115	–	–
India	243,492	20	5	30	22 x	39	57	53	88	72	81	50	35 x	19 x
Indonesia	42,771	18	–	14	10	52 x	–	41 y	–	79 y	92	63	2 y	6
Iran (Islamic Republic of)	12,015	16	–	16	–	31	–	–	–	–	98	87	–	–
Iraq	7,490	23	–	19	–	68	–	57	–	–	–	–	–	3 x
Ireland	567	13	–	–	–	16	–	–	–	–	110	138	–	–
Israel	1,206	16	–	–	–	14	–	–	–	–	94	110	–	–
Italy	5,742	9	–	–	–	7	–	–	–	–	107	97	–	–
Jamaica	562	21	–	5	16	72	28 y	4 y	–	–	91	95	52 y	61 y
Japan	11,799	9	–	–	–	5	–	–	–	–	103	102	–	–
Jordan	1,418	23	–	7	4	32	–	91 y	–	97 y	94	73	–	12
Kazakhstan	2,402	15	1	5	3 x	31	14	9	99	99	105	80	–	22 x
Kenya	9,322	22	0	12	26	106	54	57	91	81	91	44	52	42
Kiribati	–	–	5	16	9	39 x	65	77	58	57	99	72	46	41
Kuwait	394	14	–	–	–	14	–	–	–	–	110	89	–	–
Kyrgyzstan	1,082	20	–	8	2 x	31	–	28	–	–	94	62	–	19 x
Lao People's Democratic Republic	1,509	24	–	–	55 x	110 x	–	79	–	–	55	32	–	–
Latvia	216	10	–	–	–	15	–	–	–	–	95	96	–	–
Lebanon	772	18	–	3	–	18 x	–	22 y	–	–	90	73	–	–
Lesotho	531	24	1	16	13	92	54	48	64	69	58	29	28	35
Liberia	921	22	3	19	38	177	37	48	73	63	–	–	21	18
Libya	1,117	17	–	–	–	4 x	–	–	–	–	–	–	–	–
Liechtenstein	–	–	–	–	–	4	–	–	–	–	103	23	–	–
Lithuania	391	12	–	–	–	17	–	–	–	–	96	105	–	–
Luxembourg	63	12	–	–	–	7	–	–	–	–	110	88	–	–
Madagascar	5,060	24	11	34	36	147	33	35	61	60	42	15	26	23
Malawi	3,673	24	2	23	35	157	21	16	82	65	40	15	45	40
Malaysia	5,537	19	5	6	–	14	–	–	–	–	91	50	–	–
Maldives	66	21	–	5	1	19	–	41 y	–	100	–	–	–	22 y
Mali	3,723	24	–	40	46 x	190 x	–	83	81	79	48	26	–	14
Malta	50	12	–	–	–	20	–	–	–	–	103	97	–	–
Marshall Islands	–	–	5	21	21	105	71	47	86	85	110	92	35	27
Mauritania	791	22	–	25	19	88 x	–	–	55 x	44 x	26	22	10	4
Mauritius	211	16	–	–	–	31	–	–	–	–	96	85	–	–
Mexico	21,658	19	–	15	39	87	–	–	–	–	117	61	–	–
Micronesia (Federated States of)	27	24	–	–	–	52 x	–	–	–	–	–	–	–	–
Monaco	–	–	–	–	–	–	–	–	–	–	–	–	–	–
Mongolia	500	18	1	5	2	20	9	14	–	–	89	90	24	28
Montenegro	83	13	–	2	–	24	–	6	–	–	114	94	–	–
Morocco	6,094	19	–	11	8 x	18 x	–	64	–	90	–	–	–	–
Mozambique	5,577	23	5	43	42 x	193	–	37	95	88	34	11	31	37
Myanmar	8,665	18	–	7	–	17 x	–	–	–	–	62	38	–	31
Namibia	530	23	0	5	17	74 x	44	38	86	88	–	–	59	62
Nauru	–	–	9	18	22	84 x	–	–	89	86	–	–	8	8
Nepal	7,043	23	7	29	19	81	27	24	86	76	–	–	33	25
Netherlands	2,019	12	–	–	–	5	–	–	–	–	127	116	–	–
New Zealand	612	14	–	–	–	29	–	–	–	–	104	137	–	–

TABLE 11 | ADOLESCENTS ▶

Countries and areas	Population aged 10–19 Total (thousands) 2011	Population aged 10–19 Proportion of total population (%) 2011	Adolescents currently married/in union (%) 2002–2011* male	Adolescents currently married/in union (%) 2002–2011* female	Births by age 18 (%) 2007–2011*	Adolescent birth rate 2006–2010*	Justification of wife beating among adolescents (%) 2002–2011* male	Justification of wife beating among adolescents (%) 2002–2011* female	Use of mass media among adolescents (%) 2002–2011* male	Use of mass media among adolescents (%) 2002–2011* female	Lower secondary school gross enrolment ratio 2008–2011*	Upper secondary school gross enrolment ratio 2008–2011*	Comprehensive knowledge of HIV among adolescents (%) 2007–2011* male	Comprehensive knowledge of HIV among adolescents (%) 2007–2011* female
Nicaragua	1,319	22	–	24	28 x	109 x	–	19	–	95 x	80	54	–	–
Niger	3,776	24	3	59	51 x	199 x	–	68	66	48	19	4	14 x	12 x
Nigeria	36,205	22	1	29	28	123	35	40	82	64	47	41	28	20
Niue	–	–	–	–	–	16	–	–	–	–	–	–	–	–
Norway	646	13	–	–	–	10	–	–	–	–	98	124	–	–
Oman	462	16	–	–	–	12	–	–	–	–	108	93	–	–
Pakistan	39,894	23	–	16	10	16	–	–	–	–	44	26	–	2
Palau	–	–	–	–	–	27 x	–	–	–	–	–	–	–	–
Panama	646	18	–	–	–	88	–	–	–	–	93	54	–	–
Papua New Guinea	1,561	22	3	15	14 x	70 x	–	–	–	–	–	–	–	–
Paraguay	1,385	21	–	11	–	63	–	–	–	–	78	56	–	–
Peru	5,769	20	–	11	13	72	–	–	–	91	101	77	–	17
Philippines	20,508	22	–	10	7	53	–	15	–	94	88	76	–	19
Poland	4,300	11	–	–	–	16	–	–	–	–	97	97	–	–
Portugal	1,100	10	–	–	–	16	–	–	–	–	116	98	–	–
Qatar	151	8	–	–	–	15	–	–	–	–	101	86	–	–
Republic of Korea	6,458	13	–	–	–	2	–	–	–	–	100	94	–	–
Republic of Moldova	459	13	1	10	5 x	26	25	24	99	98	89	86	–	–
Romania	2,252	11	–	–	–	41	–	–	–	–	96	98	–	–
Russian Federation	14,023	10	–	–	–	30	–	–	–	–	90	86	–	–
Rwanda	2,356	22	0	3	5	41	35	56	88	73	43	20	44	49
Saint Kitts and Nevis	–	–	–	–	–	67 x	–	–	–	–	100	93	–	–
Saint Lucia	32	18	–	–	–	49 x	–	–	–	–	98	93	–	–
Saint Vincent and the Grenadines	21	19	–	–	–	70	–	–	–	–	119	91	–	–
Samoa	44	24	1	7	5	29	50	58	97	97	105	76	5	2
San Marino	–	–	–	–	–	1 x	–	–	–	–	99	96	–	–
Sao Tome and Principe	40	24	1	20	25	110	25	23	96	95	71	19	39	39
Saudi Arabia	4,926	18	–	–	–	7	–	–	–	–	106	95	–	–
Senegal	3,004	24	1	24	22	93	31	61	86	81	–	–	28	26
Serbia	1,207	12	1	5	3	22	6	2	99	100	99	85	43	53
Seychelles	–	–	–	–	–	62	–	–	–	–	131	104	–	–
Sierra Leone	1,366	23	–	23	38	98 x	–	63	66	51	–	–	26	16
Singapore	747	14	–	–	–	6	–	–	–	–	–	–	–	–
Slovakia	635	12	–	–	–	21	–	–	–	–	91	88	–	–
Slovenia	193	9	–	–	–	5	–	–	–	–	96	98	–	–
Solomon Islands	121	22	0	13	15	70 x	73	72	71	54	–	–	26	29
Somalia	2,140	22	–	25	–	123 x	–	75 y	–	–	–	–	–	3 x
South Africa	9,940	20	2	4	15 x	54	–	–	–	–	96	92	–	–
South Sudan⁹	–	–	–	40	28	–	–	72	–	–	–	–	–	8
Spain	4,299	9	–	–	–	13	–	–	–	–	120	133	–	–
Sri Lanka	3,165	15	–	9	4	24	–	54 y	–	88 y	–	–	–	–
State of Palestine	1,040	25	1	13	–	60	–	–	–	–	88	78	–	–
Sudan⁹	–	–	–	24	14	–	–	52	–	–	–	–	–	4
Suriname	96	18	–	11	–	66	–	19	–	–	89	56	–	41 x
Swaziland	301	25	0	4	22	111 x	34	42	94	89	67	45	52	56
Sweden	1,097	12	–	–	–	6	–	–	–	–	97	101	–	–
Switzerland	867	11	–	–	–	4	–	–	–	–	108	86	–	–
Syrian Arab Republic	4,786	23	–	10	9 x	75 x	–	–	–	–	92	37	–	6 x
Tajikistan	1,670	24	–	6	4 x	27 x	–	85 y	–	–	98	61	9	11
Thailand	10,192	15	–	15	8 x	47	–	–	–	–	91	64	–	46 x
The former Yugoslav Republic of Macedonia	280	14	–	4	2	20	–	14	–	–	90	78	–	23 x
Timor-Leste	301	26	0	8	9	54	72	81	61	62	63	49	15	11
Togo	1,416	23	0	12	17	–	–	41	–	–	–	–	–	33
Tonga	23	22	–	–	–	16	–	–	–	–	–	–	–	–
Trinidad and Tobago	189	14	–	6	–	33	–	10	–	–	92	87	–	49 x
Tunisia	1,709	16	–	–	–	6	–	–	–	–	116	73	–	–
Turkey	13,004	18	–	10	8 x	38	–	30	–	–	96	64	–	–
Turkmenistan	1,013	20	–	5	2 x	21	–	37 y	–	96 x	–	–	–	4 x
Tuvalu	–	–	2	8	3	28 x	83	69	89	95	–	–	57	31
Uganda	8,326	24	2	20	33	159 x	52	62	88	82	35	13	36	36
Ukraine	4,638	10	3	6	3	30	8	3	99	99	104	78	33	39
United Arab Emirates	898	12	–	–	–	34	–	–	–	–	–	–	–	–

TABLE 11 | ADOLESCENTS

Countries and areas	Population aged 10–19 Total (thousands) 2011	Proportion of total population (%) 2011	Adolescents currently married/in union (%) 2002–2011* male	female	Births by age 18 (%) 2007–2011*	Adolescent birth rate 2006–2010*	Justification of wife beating among adolescents (%) 2002–2011* male	female	Use of mass media among adolescents (%) 2002–2011* male	female	Lower secondary school gross enrolment ratio 2008–2011*	Upper secondary school gross enrolment ratio 2008–2011*	Comprehensive knowledge of HIV among adolescents (%) 2007–2011* male	female
United Kingdom	7,442	12	–	–	–	25	–	–	–	–	109	96	–	–
United Republic of Tanzania	10,475	23	4	18	28	128	39	52	79	70	–	–	41	46
United States	41,478	13	–	–	–	39	–	–	–	–	103	90	–	–
Uruguay	524	15	–	–	–	60	–	–	–	–	113	68	–	–
Uzbekistan	5,798	21	–	5	2 x	26	63	63	–	–	96	124	–	27 x
Vanuatu	54	22	–	13	–	–	–	–	–	–	65	41	–	14
Venezuela (Bolivarian Republic of)	5,499	19	–	16 x	–	101	–	–	–	–	90	71	–	–
Viet Nam	15,251	17	–	8	3	35	–	35	97	94	88	65	–	51
Yemen	6,073	25	–	19	–	80 x	–	–	–	–	54	34	–	2 x,y
Zambia	3,176	24	1	18	34	151 x	55	61	80	71	–	–	38	36
Zimbabwe	3,196	25	1	23	21	115	48	48	59	53	–	–	42	46

MEMORANDUM

Sudan and South Sudan[σ]	10,044	23	–	–	–	70	–	–	–	–	–	–	–	–

SUMMARY INDICATORS[#]

Sub–Saharan Africa	200,971	23	2	23	26	109	42	55	73	62	47	30	34	26
Eastern and Southern Africa	94,195	22	3	19	26	102	46	55	71	64	49	30	38	35
West and Central Africa	96,530	23	1	28	27	121	35	55	75	60	46	31	28	19
Middle East and North Africa	82,134	20	–	14	–	37	–	57	–	–	89	57	–	–
South Asia	333,425	20	5	29	22	38	56	52	88	71	75	45	34	15
East Asia and Pacific	317,250	16	–	11 **	8 **	14	–	34 **	–	85 **	89	68	–	20 **
Latin America and Caribbean	108,552	18	–	18	–	77	–	–	–	–	102	75	–	–
CEE/CIS	53,462	13	–	7	–	31	–	31	–	–	95	80	–	–
Least developed countries	193,984	23	–	27	28	106	–	55	68	61	50	26	–	22
World	1,199,890	17	–	22 **	20 **	43	–	49 **	–	73 **	82	59	–	19 **

σ Due to the cession in July 2011 of the Republic of South Sudan by the Republic of the Sudan, and its subsequent admission to the United Nations on 14 July 2011, disaggregated data for the Sudan and South Sudan as separate States are not yet available for all indicators. Aggregated data presented are for the Sudan pre-cession (see Memorandum item).

For a complete list of countries and areas in the regions, subregions and country categories, see page 98.

DEFINITIONS OF THE INDICATORS

Adolescents currently married/in union – Percentage of boys and girls aged 15–19 who are currently married or in union. This indicator is meant to provide a snapshot of the current marital status of boys and girls in this age group. However, it is worth noting that those not married at the time of the survey are still exposed to the risk of marrying before they exit adolescence.

Births by age 18 – Percentage of women aged 20–24 who gave birth before age 18. This standardized indicator from population-based surveys captures levels of fertility among adolescents up to the age of 18. Note that the data are based on the answers from women aged 20–24, whose risk of giving birth before the age of 18 is behind them.

Adolescent birth rate – Number of births per 1,000 adolescent girls aged 15–19.

Justification of wife beating among adolescents – The percentage of boys and girls aged 15–19 who consider a husband to be justified in hitting or beating his wife for at least one of the specified reasons: if his wife burns the food, argues with him, goes out without telling him, neglects the children or refuses sexual relations.

Use of mass media among adolescents – The percentage of boys and girls aged 15–19 who use at least one of the following types of information media, at least once a week: newspaper, magazine, television or radio.

Lower secondary school gross enrolment ratio – Number of children enrolled in lower secondary school, regardless of age, expressed as a percentage of the total number of children of official lower secondary school age.

Upper secondary school gross enrolment ratio – Number of children enrolled in upper secondary school, regardless of age, expressed as a percentage of the total number of children of official upper secondary school age.

Comprehensive knowledge of HIV among adolescents – Percentage of young men and women aged 15–19 who correctly identify the two major ways of preventing the sexual transmission of HIV (using condoms and limiting sex to one faithful, uninfected partner), who reject the two most common local misconceptions about HIV transmission and who know that a healthy-looking person can be HIV-positive.

MAIN DATA SOURCES

Adolescent population – United Nations Population Division.

Adolescents currently married/in union – Demographic and Health Surveys (DHS), Multiple Indicator Cluster Surveys (MICS) and other national surveys.

Births by age 18 – DHS and MICS.

Adolescent birth rate – United Nations Population Division.

Justification of wife beating among adolescents – DHS, MICS and other national surveys.

Use of mass media among adolescents – AIDS Indicator Surveys (AIS), DHS, MICS and other national surveys.

Gross enrolment ratio – UNESCO Institute for Statistics (UIS).

Comprehensive knowledge of HIV among adolescents – AIDS Indicator Surveys (AIS), DHS, MICS, Reproductive Health Surveys (RHS) and other national household surveys; HIV/AIDS Survey Indicators Database, <www.measuredhs.com/hivdata>.

NOTES

– Data not available.

x Data refer to years or periods other than those specified in the column heading. Such data are not included in the calculation of regional and global averages, with the exception of 2005–2006 data from India. Estimates from data years prior to 2000 are not displayed.

y Data differ from the standard definition or refer to only part of a country. If they fall within the noted reference period, such data are included in the calculation of regional and global averages.

* Data refer to the most recent year available during the period specified in the column heading.

** Excludes China.

TABLE 12: DISPARITIES BY RESIDENCE

Countries and areas	Birth registration (%) 2005–2011* urban	rural	ratio of urban to rural	Skilled attendant at birth (%) 2007–2012* urban	rural	ratio of urban to rural	Underweight prevalence in children under 5 (%) 2007–2011* urban	rural	ratio of rural to urban	Diarrhoea treatment with oral rehydration salts (ORS) (%) 2007–2012* urban	rural	ratio of urban to rural	Primary school net attendance ratio 2007–2011* urban	rural	ratio of urban to rural	Comprehensive knowledge of HIV (%) Females 15–24 2007–2011* urban	rural	ratio of urban to rural	Use of improved sanitation facilities (%) 2010 urban	rural	ratio of urban to rural
Afghanistan	60	33	1.8	74	31	2.4	–	–	–	48	54	0.9	73 x	47 x	1.6 x	–	–	–	60	30	2.0
Albania	99	98	1.0	100	99	1.0	5	6	1.2	33 x	36 x	0.9 x	90	91	1.0	51	26	2.0	95	93	1.0
Algeria	99	99	1.0	98 x	92 x	1.1 x	3 x	4 x	1.4 x	18 x	19 x	1.0 x	98 x	95 x	1.0 x	16 x	10 x	1.7 x	98	88	1.1
Andorra	–	–	–	–	–	–	–	–	–	–	–	–	–	–	–	–	–	–	100	100	1.0
Angola	34 x	19 x	1.7 x	71	26	2.8	–	–	–	–	–	–	85	67	1.3	–	–	–	85	19	4.5
Antigua and Barbuda	–	–	–	–	–	–	–	–	–	–	–	–	–	–	–	–	–	–	98		
Argentina	–	–	–	–	–	–	–	–	–	–	–	–	–	–	–	–	–	–	–	–	–
Armenia	99	100	1.0	100	99	1.0	3	7	2.6	22 x	28 x	0.8 x	–	–	–	16	16	1.0	95	80	1.2
Australia	–	–	–	–	–	–	–	–	–	–	–	–	–	–	–	–	–	–	100	100	1.0
Austria	–	–	–	–	–	–	–	–	–	–	–	–	–	–	–	–	–	–	100	100	1.0
Azerbaijan	96	92	1.0	97 x	80 x	1.2 x	4 x	12 x	3.1 x	19 x	5 x	3.6 x	74 x	72 x	1.0 x	7 x	2 x	3.3 x	86	78	1.1
Bahamas	–	–	–	–	–	–	–	–	–	–	–	–	–	–	–	–	–	–	100	100	1.0
Bahrain	–	–	–	–	–	–	–	–	–	–	–	–	–	–	–	–	–	–	100		
Bangladesh	13	9	1.5	54	25	2.1	28	39	1.4	84	76	1.1	86 y	86 y	1.0 y	–	–	–	57	55	1.0
Barbados	–	–	–	–	–	–	–	–	–	–	–	–	–	–	–	–	–	–	100	100	1.0
Belarus	–	–	–	100 x	100 x	1.0 x	1 x	2 x	1.7 x	38 x	33 x	1.1 x	92 x	95 x	1.0 x	–	–	–	91	97	0.9
Belgium	–	–	–	–	–	–	–	–	–	–	–	–	–	–	–	–	–	–	100	100	1.0
Belize	95	96	1.0	99 x	93 x	1.1 x	2 x	6 x	2.9 x	–	–	–	97 x	94 x	1.0 x	49 x	29 x	1.7 x	93	87	1.1
Benin	68	56	1.2	92	79	1.2	15 x	21 x	1.4 x	58	47	1.2	74 x	55 x	1.3 x	22 x	11 x	1.9 x	25	5	5.0
Bhutan	100	100	1.0	90	54	1.6	11	14	1.3	64	60	1.1	96	90	1.1	32	15	2.1	73	29	2.5
Bolivia (Plurinational State of)	79 y	72 y	1.1 y	88	51	1.7	3	6	2.3	38	32	1.2	98	96	1.0	32	9	3.5	35	10	3.5
Bosnia and Herzegovina	99	100	1.0	100 x	100 x	1.0 x	2 x	1 x	0.7 x	34 x	35 x	1.0 x	98 x	98 x	1.0 x	46 x	42 x	1.1 x	99	92	1.1
Botswana	78	67	1.2	99	90	1.1	–	–	–	47 x	51 x	0.9 x	89	85	1.0	–	–	–	75	41	1.8
Brazil	–	–	–	98 x	94 x	1.0 x	2 x	2 x	0.8 x	–	–	–	–	–	–	–	–	–	85	44	1.9
Brunei Darussalam	–	–	–	–	–	–	–	–	–	–	–	–	–	–	–	–	–	–	–	–	–
Bulgaria	–	–	–	–	–	–	–	–	–	–	–	–	–	–	–	–	–	–	100	100	1.0
Burkina Faso	93	74	1.3	93	61	1.5	–	–	–	31	19	1.6	79 x	38 x	2.1 x	46	24	1.9	50	6	8.3
Burundi	87	74	1.2	88	58	1.5	18	30	1.7	33	38	0.9	87	73	1.2	59	43	1.4	49	46	1.1
Cambodia	74	60	1.2	95	67	1.4	19	30	1.6	33	34	1.0	85 y	85 y	1.0 y	55	41	1.3	73	20	3.7
Cameroon	86	58	1.5	87	47	1.9	7	20	2.8	27	12	2.2	90 x	71 x	1.3 x	42 x	18 x	2.4 x	58	36	1.6
Canada	–	–	–	–	–	–	–	–	–	–	–	–	–	–	–	–	–	–	100	99	1.0
Cape Verde	–	–	–	91 x	64 x	1.4 x	–	–	–	–	–	–	–	–	–	–	–	–	73	43	1.7
Central African Republic	78	52	1.5	83	38	2.2	23	24	1.0	23	12	2.0	66 x	42 x	1.6 x	21 x	13 x	1.6 x	43	28	1.5
Chad	42	9	4.9	60	12	5.1	22	33	1.5	27	10	2.8	–	–	–	18	7	2.6	30	6	5.0
Chile	–	–	–	100 x	99 x	1.0 x	–	–	–	–	–	–	–	–	–	–	–	–	98	83	1.2
China	–	–	–	100	99	1.0	1	4	3.3	–	–	–	–	–	–	–	–	–	74	56	1.3
Colombia	97	95	1.0	98	86	1.1	3	5	1.6	57	49	1.2	91	91	1.0	30	21	1.4	82	63	1.3
Comoros	87 x	83 x	1.1 x	79 x	57 x	1.4 x	–	–	–	25 x	17 x	1.5 x	41 x	29 x	1.4 x	–	–	–	50	30	1.7
Congo	88 y	75 y	1.2 y	98	86	1.1	8 x	15 x	2.0 x	38	27	1.4	–	–	–	9	6	1.5	20	15	1.3
Cook Islands	–	–	–	–	–	–	–	–	–	–	–	–	–	–	–	–	–	–	100	100	1.0
Costa Rica	–	–	–	100	99	1.0	–	–	–	–	–	–	96	96	1.0	–	–	–	95	96	1.0
Côte d'Ivoire	79	41	2.0	84	45	1.9	9 x,y	20 x,y	2.2 x,y	22	14	1.5	67 x	48 x	1.4 x	–	–	–	36	11	3.3
Croatia	–	–	–	–	–	–	–	–	–	–	–	–	–	–	–	–	–	–	99	98	1.0
Cuba	100 y	100 y	1.0 y	–	–	–	–	–	–	54	37	1.4	–	–	–	55	49	1.1	94	81	1.2
Cyprus	–	–	–	–	–	–	–	–	–	–	–	–	–	–	–	–	–	–	100	100	1.0
Czech Republic	–	–	–	–	–	–	–	–	–	–	–	–	–	–	–	–	–	–	99	97	1.0
Democratic People's Republic of Korea	100	100	1.0	100	100	1.0	13	27	2.0	75	73	1.0	100	99	1.0	11	4	2.8	86	71	1.2
Democratic Republic of the Congo	24	29	0.8	96	75	1.3	17	27	1.6	26	27	1.0	86	70	1.2	21	12	1.7	24	24	1.0
Denmark	–	–	–	–	–	–	–	–	–	–	–	–	–	–	–	–	–	–	100	100	1.0
Djibouti	90	82	1.1	95 x	40 x	2.3 x	18 y	27 y	1.5 y	–	–	–	67 x	49 x	1.4 x	18 x	9 x	2.0 x	63	10	6.3
Dominica	–	–	–	–	–	–	–	–	–	–	–	–	–	–	–	–	–	–	–	–	–
Dominican Republic	83	73	1.1	98	97	1.0	3	4	1.2	42	39	1.1	95	95	1.0	42	37	1.2	87	75	1.2
Ecuador	89	92	1.0	98 x	99 x	1.0 x	–	–	–	–	–	–	–	–	–	–	–	–	96	84	1.1
Egypt	99	99	1.0	90	72	1.2	6	6	1.0	28	29	1.0	91	87	1.0	7	3	2.3	97	93	1.0
El Salvador	99	99	1.0	97	94	1.0	4 y	7 y	2.0 y	60	56	1.1	–	–	–	–	–	–	89	83	1.1
Equatorial Guinea	43 x	24 x	1.8 x	87 x	49 x	1.8 x	–	–	–	43 x	19 x	2.2 x	–	–	–	–	–	–	–	–	–
Eritrea	–	–	–	65 x	10 x	6.2 x	23 x	40 x	1.7 x	59 x	39 x	1.5 x	–	–	–	–	–	–	–	4	–
Estonia	–	–	–	–	–	–	–	–	–	–	–	–	–	–	–	–	–	–	96	94	1.0
Ethiopia	29	5	5.9	51	4	12.7	16	30	1.9	45	24	1.9	86	61	1.4	38	19	2.0	29	19	1.5
Fiji	–	–	–	–	–	–	–	–	–	–	–	–	–	–	–	–	–	–	94	71	1.3
Finland	–	–	–	–	–	–	–	–	–	–	–	–	–	–	–	–	–	–	100	100	1.0

TABLE 12 | DISPARITIES BY RESIDENCE ▶

Countries and areas	Birth registration (%) 2005–2011*			Skilled attendant at birth (%) 2007–2012*			Underweight prevalence in children under 5 (%) 2007–2011*			Diarrhoea treatment with oral rehydration salts (ORS) (%) 2007–2012*			Primary school net attendance ratio 2007–2011*			Comprehensive knowledge of HIV (%) Females 15–24 2007–2011*			Use of improved sanitation facilities (%) 2010		
	urban	rural	ratio of urban to rural	urban	rural	ratio of urban to rural	urban	rural	ratio of rural to urban	urban	rural	ratio of urban to rural	urban	rural	ratio of urban to rural	urban	rural	ratio of urban to rural	urban	rural	ratio of urban to rural
France	–	–	–	–	–	–	–	–	–	23 x	29 x	0.8 x	–	–	–	–	–	–	100	100	1.0
Gabon	90 x	87 x	1.0 x	92 x	67 x	1.4 x	–	–	–	–	–	–	–	–	–	–	–	–	33	30	1.1
Gambia	54	52	1.0	77	41	1.9	12	22	1.9	39	39	1.0	53	35	1.5	41	24	1.7	70	65	1.1
Georgia	99	98	1.0	99 x	98 x	1.0 x	1	1	1.6	44 x	36 x	1.2 x	97	95	1.0	–	–	–	96	93	1.0
Germany	–	–	–	–	–	–	–	–	–	–	–	–	–	–	–	–	–	–	100	100	1.0
Ghana	72	55	1.3	88	54	1.6	11	16	1.5	37	34	1.1	80	68	1.2	34	22	1.5	19	8	2.4
Greece	–	–	–	–	–	–	–	–	–	–	–	–	–	–	–	–	–	–	99	97	1.0
Grenada	–	–	–	–	–	–	–	–	–	–	–	–	–	–	–	–	–	–	96	97	1.0
Guatemala	96	97	1.0	77	37	2.1	8 y	16 y	1.9 y	38	37	1.0	–	–	–	32	14	2.2	87	70	1.2
Guinea	78	33	2.4	84	31	2.7	15	23	1.5	52 x	28 x	1.9 x	–	–	–	22	8	2.8	32	11	2.9
Guinea-Bissau	30	21	1.4	69 x	27 x	2.6 x	13	21	1.6	28	13	2.1	84	57	1.5	22	8	2.8	44	9	4.9
Guyana	91	87	1.0	98	90	1.1	7	12	1.7	42 x	38 x	1.1 x	96	94	1.0	72	47	1.5	88	82	1.1
Haiti	87	78	1.1	47 x	15 x	3.0 x	12 x	20 x	1.7 x	51 x	35 x	1.4 x	–	–	–	38 x	26 x	1.4 x	24	10	2.4
Holy See	–	–	–	–	–	–	–	–	–	–	–	–	–	–	–	–	–	–	–	–	–
Honduras	95	93	1.0	90 x	50 x	1.8 x	4 x	11 x	2.4 x	55 x	56 x	1.0 x	92 x	86 x	1.1 x	37 x	21 x	1.8 x	85	69	1.2
Hungary	–	–	–	–	–	–	–	–	–	–	–	–	–	–	–	–	–	–	100	100	1.0
Iceland	–	–	–	–	–	–	–	–	–	–	–	–	–	–	–	–	–	–	100	100	1.0
India	59	35	1.7	76	43	1.7	33 x	46 x	1.4 x	33 x	24 x	1.4 x	–	–	–	33 x	14 x	2.4 x	58	23	2.5
Indonesia	71	41	1.7	84	76	1.1	15	21	1.4	33	35	0.9	99	97	1.0	16 y	6 y	2.5 y	73	39	1.9
Iran (Islamic Republic of)	–	–	–	–	–	–	–	–	–	–	–	–	–	–	–	–	–	–	100	100	1.0
Iraq	95	96	1.0	86	71	1.2	6 x	7 x	1.1 x	30 x	32 x	0.9 x	92 x	78 x	1.2 x	4 x	1 x	4.4 x	76	67	1.1
Ireland	–	–	–	–	–	–	–	–	–	–	–	–	–	–	–	–	–	–	100	98	1.0
Israel	–	–	–	–	–	–	–	–	–	–	–	–	–	–	–	–	–	–	100	100	1.0
Italy	–	–	–	–	–	–	–	–	–	–	–	–	–	–	–	–	–	–	–	–	–
Jamaica	–	–	–	99	98	1.0	–	–	–	–	–	–	97 x	98 x	1.0 x	66	60	1.1	78	82	1.0
Japan	–	–	–	–	–	–	–	–	–	–	–	–	–	–	–	–	–	–	100	100	1.0
Jordan	–	–	–	99	99	1.0	2	2	1.3	20	20	1.0	–	–	–	–	–	–	98	98	1.0
Kazakhstan	100	100	1.0	100 x	100 x	1.0 x	3 x	5 x	1.7 x	–	–	–	98	98	1.0	24 x	21 x	1.1 x	97	98	1.0
Kenya	76	57	1.3	75	37	2.0	10	17	1.7	40	39	1.0	81	72	1.1	57	45	1.3	32	32	1.0
Kiribati	95	93	1.0	84	77	1.1	–	–	–	–	–	–	–	–	–	45	43	1.1	–	–	–
Kuwait	–	–	–	–	–	–	–	–	–	–	–	–	–	–	–	–	–	–	100	100	1.0
Kyrgyzstan	96	93	1.0	100 x	96 x	1.0 x	2 x	2 x	0.9 x	–	–	–	93	92	1.0	23 x	18 x	1.3 x	94	93	1.0
Lao People's Democratic Republic	84	68	1.2	68 x	11 x	6.2 x	20 x	34 x	1.7 x	79 x	43 x	1.9 x	93 x	75 x	1.2 x	–	–	–	89	50	1.8
Latvia	–	–	–	–	–	–	–	–	–	–	–	–	–	–	–	–	–	–	–	–	–
Lebanon	–	–	–	–	–	–	–	–	–	–	–	–	–	–	–	–	–	–	100	–	–
Lesotho	43	46	1.0	88	54	1.6	12	13	1.1	57	50	1.1	93	88	1.0	44	36	1.2	32	24	1.3
Liberia	5 y	3 y	1.9 y	79	32	2.4	17 y	20 y	1.2 y	57	52	1.1	46	21	2.2	26	15	1.8	29	7	4.1
Libya	–	–	–	–	–	–	–	–	–	–	–	–	–	–	–	–	–	–	97	96	1.0
Liechtenstein	–	–	–	–	–	–	–	–	–	–	–	–	–	–	–	–	–	–	–	–	–
Lithuania	–	–	–	–	–	–	–	–	–	–	–	–	–	–	–	–	–	–	95	–	–
Luxembourg	–	–	–	–	–	–	–	–	–	–	–	–	–	–	–	–	–	–	100	100	1.0
Madagascar	92	78	1.2	82	39	2.1	31 x	37 x	1.2 x	32	14	2.2	93	77	1.2	40	19	2.1	21	12	1.8
Malawi	–	–	–	84	69	1.2	10	13	1.3	72	69	1.0	88 x	88 x	1.0 x	56	38	1.5	49	51	1.0
Malaysia	–	–	–	–	–	–	–	–	–	–	–	–	–	–	–	–	–	–	96	95	1.0
Maldives	93	92	1.0	99	93	1.1	11	20	1.8	–	–	–	83	83	1.0	43	32	1.4	98	97	1.0
Mali	92	77	1.2	80 x	38 x	2.1 x	20 x	29 x	1.5 x	26 x	11 x	2.3 x	79	52	1.5	19	12	1.5	35	14	2.5
Malta	–	–	–	–	–	–	–	–	–	–	–	–	–	–	–	–	–	–	100	100	1.0
Marshall Islands	96	96	1.0	97	68	1.4	–	–	–	–	–	–	–	–	–	33	12	2.7	83	53	1.6
Mauritania	75	42	1.8	90	39	2.3	–	–	–	16 y	11 y	1.5 y	72	49	1.5	8	2	4.7	51	9	5.7
Mauritius	–	–	–	–	–	–	–	–	–	–	–	–	–	–	–	–	–	–	91	88	1.0
Mexico	–	–	–	98	87	1.1	–	–	–	–	–	–	–	–	–	–	–	–	87	79	1.1
Micronesia (Federated States of)	–	–	–	–	–	–	–	–	–	–	–	–	–	–	–	–	–	–	–	–	–
Monaco	–	–	–	–	–	–	–	–	–	–	–	–	–	–	–	–	–	–	100	–	–
Mongolia	99	99	1.0	99	98	1.0	4	5	1.2	41 x	36 x	1.1 x	97	94	1.0	36	21	1.7	64	29	2.2
Montenegro	98	99	1.0	100 x	98 x	1.0 x	2 x	1 x	0.7 x	–	–	–	97 x	98 x	1.0 x	–	–	–	92	87	1.1
Morocco	92 x,y	80 x,y	1.1 x,y	92	55	1.7	2	4	2.5	28 x	18 x	1.5 x	96 x	83 x	1.2 x	–	–	–	83	52	1.6
Mozambique	39	28	1.4	78	46	1.7	10	17	1.7	65	50	1.3	89	78	1.1	43	32	1.4	38	5	7.6
Myanmar	94	64	1.5	90	63	1.4	19	24	1.3	72	56	1.3	93	89	1.0	–	–	83	73	–	1.1
Namibia	83	59	1.4	94	73	1.3	12	19	1.7	67	60	1.1	94	91	1.0	65	65	1.0	57	17	3.4
Nauru	–	–	–	–	–	–	–	–	–	–	–	–	–	–	–	–	–	–	65	–	–
Nepal	44	42	1.0	73	32	2.3	17	30	1.8	44	39	1.1	70 y	69 y	1.0 y	40	24	1.7	48	27	1.8
Netherlands	–	–	–	–	–	–	–	–	–	–	–	–	–	–	–	–	–	–	100	100	1.0

TABLE 12 | DISPARITIES BY RESIDENCE ▶

Countries and areas	Birth registration (%) 2005–2011*			Skilled attendant at birth (%) 2007–2012*			Underweight prevalence in children under 5 (%) 2007–2011*			Diarrhoea treatment with oral rehydration salts (ORS) (%) 2007–2012*			Primary school net attendance ratio 2007–2011*			Comprehensive knowledge of HIV (%) Females 15–24 2007–2011*			Use of improved sanitation facilities (%) 2010		
	urban	rural	ratio of urban to rural	urban	rural	ratio of urban to rural	urban	rural	ratio of rural to urban	urban	rural	ratio of urban to rural	urban	rural	ratio of urban to rural	urban	rural	ratio of urban to rural	urban	rural	ratio of urban to rural
New Zealand	–	–	–	–	–	–	–	–	–	–	–	–	–	–	–	–	–	–	–	–	–
Nicaragua	87 y	77 y	1.1 y	92	56	1.7	4	7	1.7	64	55	1.2	76 y	64 y	1.2 y	–	–	–	63	37	1.7
Niger	71 y	25 y	2.9 y	71 x	8 x	8.5 x	44 y	39 y	0.9 y	31 x	16 x	2.0 x	71 x	32 x	2.2 x	31 x	8 x	3.8 x	34	4	8.5
Nigeria	49	22	2.2	65	28	2.4	16	27	1.7	41	21	1.9	78	56	1.4	30	18	1.7	35	27	1.3
Niue	–	–	–	–	–	–	–	–	–	–	–	–	–	–	–	–	–	–	100	100	1.0
Norway	–	–	–	–	–	–	–	–	–	–	–	–	–	–	–	–	–	–	100	100	1.0
Oman	–	–	–	–	–	–	–	–	–	–	–	–	–	–	–	–	–	–	100	95	1.1
Pakistan	32	24	1.3	66	33	2.0	27	33	1.3	44	40	1.1	78	62	1.3	–	–	–	72	34	2.1
Palau	–	–	–	–	–	–	–	–	–	–	–	–	–	–	–	–	–	–	100	100	1.0
Panama	–	–	–	99	84	1.2	–	–	–	–	–	–	–	–	–	–	–	–	71	41	1.7
Papua New Guinea	–	–	–	88 x	47 x	1.9 x	12 x	20 x	1.6 x	–	–	–	–	–	–	–	–	–	71	41	1.7
Paraguay	–	–	–	–	–	–	–	–	–	–	–	–	89	87	1.0	–	–	–	90	40	2.3
Peru	–	–	–	96	64	1.5	2	8	3.8	37	24	1.6	97	94	1.0	–	–	–	81	37	2.2
Philippines	87 x	78 x	1.1 x	78	48	1.6	–	–	–	58	36	1.6	–	–	–	23	17	1.4	79	69	1.1
Poland	–	–	–	–	–	–	–	–	–	–	–	–	–	–	–	–	–	–	96	–	–
Portugal	–	–	–	–	–	–	–	–	–	–	–	–	–	–	–	–	–	–	100	100	1.0
Qatar	–	–	–	–	–	–	–	–	–	–	–	–	–	–	–	–	–	–	100	100	1.0
Republic of Korea	–	–	–	–	–	–	–	–	–	–	–	–	–	–	–	–	–	–	100	100	1.0
Republic of Moldova	98 x	98 x	1.0 x	100 x	99 x	1.0 x	2 x	4 x	2.0 x	9 x	6 x	1.5 x	–	–	–	–	–	–	89	82	1.1
Romania	–	–	–	100 x	98 x	1.0 x	3 x	4 x	1.3 x	–	–	–	–	–	–	–	–	–	–	–	–
Russian Federation	–	–	–	–	–	–	–	–	–	–	–	–	–	–	–	–	–	–	74	59	1.3
Rwanda	60	64	0.9	82	67	1.2	6	12	1.9	26	30	0.9	92	87	1.1	66	50	1.3	52	56	0.9
Saint Kitts and Nevis	–	–	–	–	–	–	–	–	–	–	–	–	–	–	–	–	–	–	96	96	1.0
Saint Lucia	–	–	–	–	–	–	–	–	–	–	–	–	–	–	–	–	–	–	71	63	1.1
Saint Vincent and the Grenadines	–	–	–	–	–	–	–	–	–	–	–	–	–	–	–	–	–	–	–	96	–
Samoa	62	44	1.4	94	78	1.2	–	–	–	–	–	–	89 y	88 y	1.0 y	5	2	2.4	98	98	1.0
San Marino	–	–	–	–	–	–	–	–	–	–	–	–	–	–	–	–	–	–	–	–	–
Sao Tome and Principe	76	74	1.0	89	75	1.2	12	14	1.1	45	52	0.9	86	85	1.0	47	38	1.3	30	19	1.6
Saudi Arabia	–	–	–	–	–	–	–	–	–	–	–	–	–	–	–	–	–	–	100	–	–
Senegal	89	66	1.4	91	49	1.8	12	21	1.8	24	21	1.2	81	50	1.6	41	18	2.2	70	39	1.8
Serbia	99	99	1.0	100	100	1.0	2	1	0.7	50	22	2.3	99	98	1.0	63	41	1.5	96	88	1.1
Seychelles	–	–	–	–	–	–	–	–	–	–	–	–	–	–	–	–	–	–	98	–	–
Sierra Leone	78	78	1.0	72	59	1.2	20	22	1.1	66	75	0.9	80	72	1.1	30	19	1.6	23	6	3.8
Singapore	–	–	–	–	–	–	–	–	–	–	–	–	–	–	–	–	–	–	100	–	–
Slovakia	–	–	–	–	–	–	–	–	–	–	–	–	–	–	–	–	–	–	100	99	1.0
Slovenia	–	–	–	–	–	–	–	–	–	–	–	–	–	–	–	–	–	–	100	100	1.0
Solomon Islands	–	–	–	95	84	1.1	8	12	1.5	–	–	–	72 y	65 y	1.1 y	34	28	1.2	98	–	–
Somalia	6	2	3.7	65 x	15 x	4.5 x	20 x	38 x	1.9 x	25 x	9 x	2.9 x	30 x	9 x	3.3 x	7 x	2 x	4.1 x	52	6	8.7
South Africa	–	–	–	94 x	85 x	1.1 x	10 x	9 x	0.9 x	41 x	32 x	1.3 x	–	–	–	–	–	–	86	67	1.3
South Sudanσ	45	32	1.4	31	15	2.0	23	29	1.3	44	37	1.2	47	23	2.0	16	7	2.3	–	–	–
Spain	–	–	–	–	–	–	–	–	–	–	–	–	–	–	–	–	–	–	100	100	1.0
Sri Lanka	97	98	1.0	99	99	1.0	–	–	–	57	50	1.1	–	–	–	–	–	–	88	93	0.9
State of Palestine	97 y	96 y	1.0 y	99	98	1.0	–	–	–	–	–	–	–	–	–	–	–	–	92	92	1.0
Sudanσ	85	50	1.7	41	16	2.5	24	35	1.5	23	22	1.1	89	69	1.3	10	3	3.4	–	–	–
Suriname	98	95	1.0	95 x	82 x	1.2 x	7 x	8 x	1.1 x	24 x	60 x	0.4 x	96 x	91 x	1.1 x	45 x	32 x	1.4 x	90	66	1.4
Swaziland	62	47	1.3	89	80	1.1	4	6	1.5	65	56	1.2	97	96	1.0	70	55	1.3	64	55	1.2
Sweden	–	–	–	–	–	–	–	–	–	–	–	–	–	–	–	–	–	–	100	100	1.0
Switzerland	–	–	–	–	–	–	–	–	–	–	–	–	–	–	–	–	–	–	100	100	1.0
Syrian Arab Republic	96	95	1.0	99	93	1.1	9 x	9 x	1.0 x	56 x	44 x	1.3 x	89 x	85 x	1.0 x	7 x	7 x	1.0 x	96	93	1.0
Tajikistan	85	90	0.9	95	86	1.1	12	16	1.3	70	78	0.9	97 y	97 y	1.0 y	–	–	–	95	94	1.0
Thailand	100	99	1.0	100	100	1.0	5 x	8 x	1.7 x	50 x	59 x	0.9 x	98 x	98 x	1.0 x	43 x	47 x	0.9 x	95	96	1.0
The former Yugoslav Republic of Macedonia	100	100	1.0	98	98	1.0	1	2	2.3	19 x	30 x	0.6 x	99	98	1.0	33 x	18 x	1.8 x	92	82	1.1
Timor-Leste	50	57	0.9	59	20	2.9	35	47	1.4	65	74	0.9	79	70	1.1	14	12	1.2	73	37	2.0
Togo	93	71	1.3	91	43	2.1	10	20	1.9	15	10	1.5	94	86	1.1	39	27	1.4	26	3	8.7
Tonga	–	–	–	–	–	–	–	–	–	–	–	–	–	–	–	–	–	–	98	96	1.0
Trinidad and Tobago	–	–	–	–	–	–	–	–	–	–	–	–	–	–	–	–	–	–	92	92	1.0
Tunisia	–	–	–	98 x	89 x	1.1 x	–	–	–	58 x	50 x	1.1 x	–	–	–	–	–	–	96	–	–
Turkey	95	92	1.0	96	80	1.2	1	3	2.1	–	–	–	94 y	91 y	1.0 y	–	–	–	97	75	1.3
Turkmenistan	96	95	1.0	100 x	99 x	1.0 x	7 x	9 x	1.2 x	32 x	45 x	0.7 x	–	–	–	7 x	4 x	2.0 x	99	97	1.0
Tuvalu	60	38	1.6	–	–	–	–	–	–	–	–	–	–	–	–	38	41	0.9	88	81	1.1
Uganda	38	29	1.3	89	52	1.7	7	15	2.3	46	43	1.1	85 y	81 y	1.1 y	48	35	1.4	34	34	1.0
Ukraine	100	100	1.0	99	98	1.0	–	–	–	–	–	–	71	76	0.9	48	37	1.3	96	89	1.1

TABLE 12 | DISPARITIES BY RESIDENCE

Countries and areas	Birth registration (%) 2005–2011*			Skilled attendant at birth (%) 2007–2012*			Underweight prevalence in children under 5 (%) 2007–2011*			Diarrhoea treatment with oral rehydration salts (ORS) (%) 2007–2012*			Primary school net attendance ratio 2007–2011*			Comprehensive knowledge of HIV (%) Females 15–24 2007–2011*			Use of improved sanitation facilities (%) 2010		
	urban	rural	ratio of urban to rural	urban	rural	ratio of urban to rural	urban	rural	ratio of rural to urban	urban	rural	ratio of urban to rural	urban	rural	ratio of urban to rural	urban	rural	ratio of urban to rural	urban	rural	ratio of urban to rural
United Arab Emirates	–	–	–	–	–	–	–	–	–	–	–	–	–	–	–	–	–	–	98	95	1.0
United Kingdom	–	–	–	–	–	–	–	–	–	–	–	–	–	–	–	–	–	–	100	100	1.0
United Republic of Tanzania	44	10	4.6	83	40	2.0	11	17	1.5	44	44	1.0	91	77	1.2	55	45	1.2	20	7	2.9
United States	–	–	–	–	–	–	–	–	–	–	–	–	–	–	–	–	–	–	100	99	1.0
Uruguay	–	–	–	–	–	–	–	–	–	–	–	–	–	–	–	–	–	–	100	99	1.0
Uzbekistan	100	100	1.0	100 x	100 x	1.0 x	4 x	4 x	0.9 x	34 x	31 x	1.1 x	97 x	95 x	1.0 x	33 x	30 x	1.1 x	100	100	1.0
Vanuatu	39	23	1.7	87	72	1.2	11	11	1.0	–	–	–	85	80	1.1	23	13	1.8	64	54	1.2
Venezuela (Bolivarian Republic of)	–	–	–	–	–	–	–	–	–	–	–	–	–	–	–	–	–	–	–	–	–
Viet Nam	97	94	1.0	99	91	1.1	6	14	2.3	47	46	1.0	98	98	1.0	58	48	1.2	94	68	1.4
Yemen	38	16	2.3	62 x	26 x	2.3 x	–	–	–	30 x	34 x	0.9 x	83 x	64 x	1.3 x	4 x	1 x	6.7 x	93	34	2.7
Zambia	28	9	3.2	83	31	2.7	13	15	1.2	59	60	1.0	91	77	1.2	42	27	1.6	57	43	1.3
Zimbabwe	65	43	1.5	86	58	1.5	8	10	1.3	26	18	1.4	89	88	1.0	59	47	1.3	52	32	1.6

MEMORANDUM

Countries and areas																			urban	rural	ratio of urban to rural
Sudan and South Sudan σ	–	–	–	–	–	–	–	–	–	–	–	–	–	–	–	–	–	–	44 †	14 †	3.1 †

SUMMARY INDICATORS

Countries and areas	urban	rural	ratio	urban	rural	ratio	urban	rural	ratio	urban	rural	ratio	urban	rural	ratio	urban	rural	ratio	urban	rural	ratio
Sub-Saharan Africa	56	33	1.7	76	40	1.9	15	24	1.6	38	31	1.2	83	67	1.2	34	25	1.4	43	23	1.9
Eastern and Southern Africa	49	28	1.7	75	36	2.1	12	20	1.7	46	38	1.2	87	72	1.2	48	32	1.5	54	27	2.0
West and Central Africa	57	36	1.6	78	46	1.7	16	26	1.7	35	23	1.5	80	61	1.3	29	16	1.8	35	20	1.8
Middle East and North Africa	91	72	1.3	84	57	1.5	–	–	–	–	–	–	–	–	–	–	–	–	91	70	1.3
South Asia	52	32	1.6	73	40	1.8	31	43	1.4	39	32	1.2	–	–	–	33	14	2.3	60	28	2.1
East Asia and the Pacific	80 **	65 **	1.2 **	95	88	1.1	5	10	2.0	46 **	41 **	1.1 **	98 **	95 **	1.0 **	24 **	21 **	1.1 **	77	58	1.3
Latin America and the Caribbean	–	–	–	–	–	–	–	–	–	–	–	–	–	–	–	–	–	–	84	60	1.4
CEE/CIS	97	96	1.0	–	–	–	–	–	–	–	–	–	–	–	–	–	–	–	87	80	1.1
Least developed countries	50	31	1.6	76	40	1.9	18	27	1.5	47	41	1.1	86	73	1.2	35	24	1.4	48	30	1.6
World	65 **	41 **	1.6 **	84	53	1.6	15	28	1.9	40 **	33 **	1.2 **	–	–	–	–	18 **	–	79	47	1.7

σ Due to the cession in July 2011 of the Republic of South Sudan by the Republic of the Sudan, and its subsequent admission to the United Nations on 14 July 2011, disaggregated data for the Sudan and South Sudan as separate States are not yet available for all indicators. Aggregated data presented are for the Sudan pre-cession (see Memorandum item).

For a complete list of countries and areas in the regions, subregions and country categories, see page 98.

DEFINITIONS OF THE INDICATORS

Birth registration – Percentage of children under age 5 who were registered at the moment of the survey. This includes children whose birth certificate was seen by the interviewer or whose mother or caretaker says the birth has been registered.

Skilled attendant at birth – Percentage of births attended by skilled health personnel (doctor, nurse or midwife).

Underweight prevalence in children under 5 – Percentage of children under age 5 who are below minus two standard deviations from median weight-for-age of the World Health Organization (WHO) Child Growth Standards.

Diarrhoea treatment with oral rehydration salts (ORS) – Percentage of children under age 5 who had diarrhoea in the two weeks preceding the survey and who received oral rehydration salts (ORS packets or pre-packaged ORS fluids).

Primary school net attendance ratio – Number of children attending primary or secondary school who are of official primary school age, expressed as a percentage of the total number of children of official primary school age. Because of the inclusion of primary-school-aged children attending secondary school, this indicator can also be referred to as a primary adjusted net attendance ratio.

Comprehensive knowledge of HIV – Percentage of young women (aged 15–24) who correctly identify the two major ways of preventing the sexual transmission of HIV (using condoms and limiting sex to one faithful, uninfected partner), who reject the two most common local misconceptions about HIV transmission and who know that a healthy-looking person can be HIV-positive.

Use of improved sanitation facilities – Percentage of the population using any of the following sanitation facilities, not shared with other households: flush or pour-flush latrine connected to a piped sewerage system, septic tank or pit latrine; ventilated improved pit latrine; pit latrine with a slab; covered pit; composting toilet.

MAIN DATA SOURCES

Birth registration – Demographic and Health Surveys (DHS), Multiple Indicator Cluster Surveys (MICS), other national surveys and vital registration systems.

Skilled attendant at birth – DHS, MICS and other nationally representative sources.

Underweight prevalence in children under 5 – DHS, MICS, other national household surveys, WHO and UNICEF.

Diarrhoea treatment with oral rehydration salts (ORS) – DHS, MICS and other national household surveys.

Primary school net attendance ratio – DHS, MICS and other national household surveys.

Comprehensive knowledge of HIV – AIDS Indicator Surveys (AIS), DHS, MICS and other national household surveys; HIV/AIDS Survey Indicators Database, <www.measuredhs.com/hivdata>.

Use of improved sanitation facilities – UNICEF and WHO Joint Monitoring Programme.

Italicized disparity data are from different sources than the data for the same indicators presented elsewhere in the report: Table 2 (Nutrition – Underweight prevalence), Table 3 (Health – Diarrhoea treatment), Table 4 (HIV/AIDS – Comprehensive knowledge of HIV) and Table 8 (Women – Skilled attendant at birth).

NOTES

– Data not available.

x Data refer to years or periods other than those specified in the column heading. Such data are not included in the calculation of regional and global averages, with the exception of 2005–2006 data from India. Estimates from data years prior to 2000 are not displayed.

y Data differ from the standard definition or refer to only part of a country. If they fall within the noted reference period, such data are included in the calculation of regional and global averages.

† The WHO/UNICEF Joint Monitoring Programme For Water Supply and Sanitation (JMP) closed its databases for these estimates before the cession of the Republic of South Sudan by the Republic of the Sudan. Aggregated data presented are for the Sudan pre-cession. Disaggregated data for the Sudan and South Sudan as separate States will be published by the JMP in 2013.

* Data refer to the most recent year available during the period specified in the column heading.

** Excludes China.

TABLE 13: DISPARITIES BY HOUSEHOLD WEALTH

Countries and areas	Birth registration (%) 2005–2011* poorest 20%	richest 20%	ratio of richest to poorest	Skilled attendant at birth (%) 2007–2012* poorest 20%	richest 20%	ratio of richest to poorest	Underweight prevalence in children under 5 (%) 2007–2011* poorest 20%	richest 20%	ratio of poorest to richest	Diarrhoea treatment with oral rehydration salts (ORS) (%) 2007–2012* poorest 20%	richest 20%	ratio of richest to poorest	Primary school net attendance ratio 2007–2011* poorest 20%	richest 20%	ratio of richest to poorest	Comprehensive knowledge of HIV (%) Females 15–24 2007–2011* poorest 20%	richest 20%	ratio of richest to poorest	Comprehensive knowledge of HIV (%) Males 15–24 2007–2011* poorest 20%	richest 20%	ratio of richest to poorest
Afghanistan	31	58	1.9	16	76	4.9	–	–	–	56	52	0.9	–	–	–	–	–	–	–	–	–
Albania	98	99	1.0	98	100	1.0	8	4	2.2	–	–	–	89	91	1.0	20	60	3.0	10	38	3.8
Algeria	–	–	–	88 x	98 x	1.1 x	5x	2x	2.4	15 x	19 x	1.2 x	93 x	98 x	1.1x	5 x	20 x	3.7 x	–	–	–
Andorra	–	–	–	–	–	–	–	–	–	–	–	–	–	–	–	–	–	–	–	–	–
Angola	17 x	48 x	2.8 x	–	–	–	–	–	–	–	–	–	63	78	1.2	–	–	–	–	–	–
Antigua and Barbuda	–	–	–	–	–	–	–	–	–	–	–	–	–	–	–	–	–	–	–	–	–
Argentina	–	–	–	–	–	–	–	–	–	–	–	–	–	–	–	–	–	–	–	–	–
Armenia	100	100	1.0	99	100	1.0	8	2	5.3	–	–	–	–	–	–	–	–	–	–	–	–
Australia	–	–	–	–	–	–	–	–	–	–	–	–	–	–	–	–	–	–	–	–	–
Austria	–	–	–	–	–	–	–	–	–	–	–	–	–	–	–	–	–	–	–	–	–
Azerbaijan	92	97	1.1	76 x	100 x	1.3 x	15x	2x	7.0 x	3 x	36x	13.3x	72 x	78 x	1.1x	1 x	12 x	10.3x	2 x	14 x	6.3 x
Bahamas	–	–	–	–	–	–	–	–	–	–	–	–	–	–	–	–	–	–	–	–	–
Bahrain	–	–	–	–	–	–	–	–	–	–	–	–	–	–	–	–	–	–	–	–	–
Bangladesh	6	19	3.0	12	64	5.5	50	21	2.4	81	82	1.0	–	–	–	–	–	–	–	–	–
Barbados	–	–	–	–	–	–	–	–	–	–	–	–	–	–	–	–	–	–	–	–	–
Belarus	–	–	–	100 x	100 x	1.0 x	2x	0x	6.7 x	–	–	–	96 x	94 x	1.0x	–	–	–	–	–	–
Belgium	–	–	–	–	–	–	–	–	–	–	–	–	–	–	–	–	–	–	–	–	–
Belize	95	97	1.0	–	–	–	–	–	–	–	–	–	–	–	–	28x	55x	2.0x	–	–	–
Benin	46	75	1.6	52 x	96 x	1.9 x	25x	10x	2.4 x	15 x	32x	2.1 x	39 x	63 x	1.6x	9x	26x	3.1x	17 x	52x	3.0 x
Bhutan	100	100	1.0	34	95	2.8	16	7	2.2	60	56	0.9	85	94	1.1	7	32	4.4	–	–	–
Bolivia (Plurinational State of)	68 y	90 y	1.3 y	38	99	2.6	8	2	3.8	31	35	1.1	95	97	1.0	5	40	8.4	11	45	4.3
Bosnia and Herzegovina	99	100	1.0	99 x	100 x	1.0 x	2x	3x	0.5 x	–	–	–	99 x	98 x	1.0x	46x	49x	1.1x	–	–	–
Botswana	–	–	–	84 x	100 x	1.2 x	16	4	4.0	–	–	–	–	–	–	–	–	–	–	–	–
Brazil	–	–	–	–	–	–	–	–	–	–	–	–	–	–	–	–	–	–	–	–	–
Brunei Darussalam	–	–	–	–	–	–	–	–	–	–	–	–	–	–	–	–	–	–	–	–	–
Bulgaria	–	–	–	–	–	–	–	–	–	–	–	–	–	–	–	–	–	–	–	–	–
Burkina Faso	62	95	1.5	46	92	2.0	38x	18x	2.1 x	13	31	2.5	33 x	39 x	1.2x	8x	37x	4.4x	–	–	–
Burundi	64	87	1.4	51	81	1.6	41	17	2.4	35	42	1.2	64	87	1.4	–	–	–	–	–	–
Cambodia	48	78	1.6	49	97	2.0	35	16	2.2	32	34	1.1	79 y	86 y	1.1y	28	58	2.1	30	64	2.1
Cameroon	51	91	1.8	23 x	98 x	4.4 x	–	–	–	5 x	34x	6.8x	50 x	87 x	1.7x	12x	50x	4.0x	–	–	–
Canada	–	–	–	–	–	–	–	–	–	–	–	–	–	–	–	–	–	–	–	–	–
Cape Verde	–	–	–	–	–	–	–	–	–	–	–	–	–	–	–	–	–	–	–	–	–
Central African Republic	46	85	1.8	33	87	2.6	26	19	1.4	11	28	2.5	31 x	48 x	1.5x	14	23	1.6	19	33	1.7
Chad	5	46	9.2	8	61	7.6	33	21	1.6	5	29	5.3	–	–	–	6	18	2.9	–	–	–
Chile	–	–	–	–	–	–	–	–	–	–	–	–	–	–	–	–	–	–	–	–	–
China	–	–	–	–	–	–	–	–	–	–	–	–	–	–	–	–	–	–	–	–	–
Colombia	–	–	–	84	99	1.2	6	2	3.0	47	61	1.3	90	93	1.0	15	32	2.2	–	–	–
Comoros	72 x	93 x	1.3 x	49 x	77 x	1.6 x	–	–	–	16 x	24 x	1.5x	25 x	39 x	1.6x	–	–	–	–	–	–
Congo	69 y	91 y	1.3 y	40 x	95 x	2.4 x	16x	5x	3.1 x	13 x	18x	1.4x	–	–	–	5	12	2.4	12	27	2.3
Cook Islands	–	–	–	–	–	–	–	–	–	–	–	–	–	–	–	–	–	–	–	–	–
Costa Rica	–	–	–	–	–	–	–	–	–	–	–	–	–	–	–	–	–	–	–	–	–
Côte d'Ivoire	28	89	3.2	29 x	95 x	3.3 x	21 x,y	6x,y	3.4 x,y	6 x	12x	2.0x	35 x	55 x	1.6x	–	–	–	–	–	–
Croatia	–	–	–	–	–	–	–	–	–	–	–	–	–	–	–	–	–	–	–	–	–
Cuba	–	–	–	–	–	–	–	–	–	–	–	–	–	–	–	–	–	–	–	–	–
Cyprus	–	–	–	–	–	–	–	–	–	–	–	–	–	–	–	–	–	–	–	–	–
Czech Republic	–	–	–	–	–	–	–	–	–	–	–	–	–	–	–	–	–	–	–	–	–
Democratic People's Republic of Korea	–	–	–	–	–	–	–	–	–	–	–	–	–	–	–	–	–	–	–	–	–
Democratic Republic of the Congo	25	27	1.1	69	99	1.4	29	12	2.3	28	26	0.9	65	73	1.1	8	24	2.8	14	30	2.2
Denmark	–	–	–	–	–	–	–	–	–	–	–	–	–	–	–	–	–	–	–	–	–
Djibouti	–	–	–	–	–	–	–	–	–	–	–	–	–	–	–	–	–	–	–	–	–
Dominica	–	–	–	–	–	–	–	–	–	–	–	–	–	–	–	–	–	–	–	–	–
Dominican Republic	61	93	1.5	95	99	1.0	5	1	4.4	41	38	0.9	92	98	1.1	31	46	1.5	21	41	2.0
Ecuador	–	–	–	99 x	98 x	1.0 x	–	–	–	–	–	–	–	–	–	–	–	–	–	–	–
Egypt	99	100	1.0	55	97	1.8	8	5	1.4	34	23	0.7	81	93	1.1	2	9	4.9	9	28	3.1
El Salvador	98	99	1.0	91	98	1.1	12y	1y	12.9 y	–	–	–	–	–	–	–	–	–	–	–	–
Equatorial Guinea	–	–	–	47 x	85 x	1.8 x	–	–	–	24 x	37x	1.5x	–	–	–	–	–	–	–	–	–
Eritrea	–	–	–	7 x	81 x	12.1 x	–	–	–	–	–	–	–	–	–	–	–	–	–	–	–
Estonia	–	–	–	–	–	–	–	–	–	–	–	–	–	–	–	–	–	–	–	–	–
Ethiopia	3	18	7.0	2	46	26.8	36	15	2.4	18	45	2.5	52	86	1.7	–	–	–	–	–	–
Fiji	–	–	–	–	–	–	–	–	–	–	–	–	–	–	–	–	–	–	–	–	–
Finland	–	–	–	–	–	–	–	–	–	–	–	–	–	–	–	–	–	–	–	–	–

TABLE 13 | DISPARITIES BY HOUSEHOLD WEALTH ▶

Countries and areas	Birth registration (%) 2005–2011* poorest 20%	richest 20%	ratio of richest to poorest	Skilled attendant at birth (%) 2007–2012* poorest 20%	richest 20%	ratio of richest to poorest	Underweight prevalence in children under 5 (%) 2007–2011* poorest 20%	richest 20%	ratio of poorest to richest	Diarrhoea treatment with oral rehydration salts (ORS) (%) 2007–2012* poorest 20%	richest 20%	ratio of richest to poorest	Primary school net attendance ratio 2007–2011* poorest 20%	richest 20%	ratio of richest to poorest	Comprehensive knowledge of HIV (%) Females 15–24 2007–2011* poorest 20%	richest 20%	ratio of richest to poorest	Comprehensive knowledge of HIV (%) Males 15–24 2007–2011* poorest 20%	richest 20%	ratio of richest to poorest
France	–	–	–	–	–	–	–	–	–	–	–	–	–	–	–	–	–	–	–	–	–
Gabon	88 x	92 x	1.0 x	–	–	–	–	–	–	–	–	–	–	–	–	–	–	–	–	–	–
Gambia	46	61	1.3	34	58	1.7	24	9	2.6	*43*	*32*	0.7	28	42	1.5	20	48	2.4	–	–	–
Georgia	99	98	1.0	95 x	99 x	1.0 x	–	–	–	–	–	–	92	96	1.0	–	–	–	–	–	–
Germany	–	–	–	–	–	–	–	–	–	–	–	–	–	–	–	–	–	–	–	–	–
Ghana	47	82	1.7	39	98	2.5	19	9	2.2	45	34	0.7	61	86	1.4	17	34	2.1	23	50	2.1
Greece	–	–	–	–	–	–	–	–	–	–	–	–	–	–	–	–	–	–	–	–	–
Grenada	–	–	–	–	–	–	–	–	–	–	–	–	–	–	–	–	–	–	–	–	–
Guatemala	–	–	–	20	95	4.7	21 y	3 y	6.5 y	39	51	1.3	–	–	–	5	41	7.8	–	–	–
Guinea	21	83	4.0	26	57	2.2	24	19	1.3	18 x	59 x	3.3 x	–	–	–	–	–	–	–	–	–
Guinea-Bissau	17	35	2.0	19 x	79 x	4.0 x	22	11	2.1	16	37	2.3	52	87	1.7	6	25	4.3	–	–	–
Guyana	84	92	1.1	81	96	1.2	16	4	3.8	–	–	–	91	97	1.1	37	72	2.0	25	65	2.6
Haiti	72	92	1.3	6 x	68 x	10.5 x	22 x	6 x	3.6 x	29 x	50 x	1.7 x	–	–	–	18 x	41 x	2.2 x	28 x	52 x	1.9 x
Holy See	–	–	–	–	–	–	–	–	–	–	–	–	–	–	–	–	–	–	–	–	–
Honduras	92	96	1.0	33 x	99 x	2.9 x	16 x	2 x	8.1 x	56 x	47 x	0.8 x	80 x	90 x	1.1 x	13 x	44 x	3.4 x	–	–	–
Hungary	–	–	–	–	–	–	–	–	–	–	–	–	–	–	–	–	–	–	–	–	–
Iceland	–	–	–	–	–	–	–	–	–	–	–	–	–	–	–	–	–	–	–	–	–
India	24	72	3.0	24	85	3.6	57 x	20 x	2.9 x	19 x	43 x	2.3 x	–	–	–	4 x	45 x	11.7 x	15 x	55 x	3.8 x
Indonesia	23	84	3.7	65	86	1.3	23	10	2.2	32	27	0.9	–	–	–	3	23	7.5	2	27	12.2
Iran (Islamic Republic of)	–	–	–	–	–	–	–	–	–	–	–	–	–	–	–	–	–	–	–	–	–
Iraq	–	–	–	–	–	–	–	–	–	–	–	–	–	–	–	–	–	–	–	–	–
Ireland	–	–	–	–	–	–	–	–	–	–	–	–	–	–	–	–	–	–	–	–	–
Israel	–	–	–	–	–	–	–	–	–	–	–	–	–	–	–	–	–	–	–	–	–
Italy	–	–	–	–	–	–	–	–	–	–	–	–	–	–	–	–	–	–	–	–	–
Jamaica	96	99	1.0	97	98	1.0	–	–	–	–	–	–	–	–	–	54	69	1.3	–	–	–
Japan	–	–	–	–	–	–	–	–	–	–	–	–	–	–	–	–	–	–	–	–	–
Jordan	–	–	–	98	100	1.0	3	0	26.0	18	30	1.6	–	–	–	–	–	–	–	–	–
Kazakhstan	100	100	1.0	100 x	100 x	1.0 x	5 x	2 x	2.8 x	–	–	–	99 x	98 x	1.0 x	18 x	28 x	1.6 x	–	–	–
Kenya	48	80	1.7	20	81	4.0	25	9	2.8	40	37	0.9	58	78	1.3	29	61	2.1	42	68	1.6
Kiribati	93	94	1.0	76	93	1.2	–	–	–	–	–	–	–	–	–	42	49	1.2	38	52	1.4
Kuwait	–	–	–	–	–	–	–	–	–	–	–	–	–	–	–	–	–	–	–	–	–
Kyrgyzstan	94	95	1.0	93 x	100 x	1.1 x	2 x	2 x	0.8 x	–	–	–	94	91	1.0	17 x	29 x	1.7 x	–	–	–
Lao People's Democratic Republic	62	85	1.4	3 x	81 x	27.1 x	38 x	14 x	2.7 x	42 x	80 x	1.9 x	59 x	84 x	1.4 x	–	–	–	–	–	–
Latvia	–	–	–	–	–	–	–	–	–	–	–	–	–	–	–	–	–	–	–	–	–
Lebanon	–	–	–	–	–	–	–	–	–	–	–	–	–	–	–	–	–	–	–	–	–
Lesotho	42	49	1.2	35	90	2.6	18	9	1.9	–	–	–	83	94	1.1	26	48	1.8	14	45	3.3
Liberia	1 y	7 y	6.1 y	26	81	3.2	*21 y*	*13 y*	*1.6 y*	41	64	1.6	15	56	3.7	14	29	2.1	17	37	2.2
Libya	–	–	–	–	–	–	–	–	–	–	–	–	–	–	–	–	–	–	–	–	–
Liechtenstein	–	–	–	–	–	–	–	–	–	–	–	–	–	–	–	–	–	–	–	–	–
Lithuania	–	–	–	–	–	–	–	–	–	–	–	–	–	–	–	–	–	–	–	–	–
Luxembourg	–	–	–	–	–	–	–	–	–	–	–	–	–	–	–	–	–	–	–	–	–
Madagascar	61	93	1.5	22	90	4.1	40 x	24 x	1.7 x	12	29	2.4	59	96	1.6	10	42	4.3	8	49	6.5
Malawi	–	–	–	63	89	1.4	17	13	1.3	67	73	1.1	71 x	90 x	1.3 x	34	55	1.6	35	54	1.5
Malaysia	–	–	–	–	–	–	–	–	–	–	–	–	–	–	–	23	48	2.0	–	–	–
Maldives	92	94	1.0	89	99	1.1	24	11	2.3	–	–	–	82	82	1.0	9	19	2.0	–	–	–
Mali	65	96	1.5	35 x	86 x	2.5 x	31 x	17 x	1.8 x	8 x	29 x	3.5 x	37	56	1.5	–	–	–	–	–	–
Malta	–	–	–	–	–	–	–	–	–	–	–	–	–	–	–	–	–	–	–	–	–
Marshall Islands	92	98	1.1	*68*	*99*	*1.5*	–	–	–	–	–	–	–	–	–	12	39	3.3	37	58	1.6
Mauritania	28	83	2.9	21	95	4.6	–	–	–	10	34	3.2	41	59	1.5	0	12	29.5	4	27	6.2
Mauritius	–	–	–	–	–	–	–	–	–	–	–	–	–	–	–	–	–	–	–	–	–
Mexico	–	–	–	–	–	–	–	–	–	–	–	–	–	–	–	–	–	–	–	–	–
Micronesia (Federated States of)	–	–	–	–	–	–	–	–	–	–	–	–	–	–	–	–	–	–	–	–	–
Monaco	–	–	–	–	–	–	–	–	–	–	–	–	–	–	–	–	–	–	–	–	–
Mongolia	99	99	1.0	98	99	1.0	6	2	2.7	–	–	–	93	98	1.1	17	42	2.5	12	48	4.1
Montenegro	94	99	1.0	98 x	100 x	1.0 x	4 x	1 x	4.1 x	–	–	–	92 x	100 x	1.1 x	–	–	–	–	–	–
Morocco	–	–	–	30 x	95 x	3.2 x	–	–	–	18 x	25 x	1.4 x	77 x	95 x	1.2 x	–	–	–	–	–	–
Mozambique	20	48	2.4	37	89	2.4	–	–	–	*40*	*50*	*1.3*	72	80	1.1	41	43	1.1	16	45	2.7
Myanmar	50	96	1.9	51	96	1.9	33	14	2.5	52	75	1.4	81	94	1.2	–	–	–	–	–	–
Namibia	46	92	2.0	60	98	1.6	22	7	3.1	50	59	1.2	88	97	1.1	61	69	1.1	55	67	1.2
Nauru	71	88	1.2	97	98	1.0	7	3	2.7	–	–	–	–	–	–	13 y	10 y	0.8 y	–	25 y	–
Nepal	36	52	1.5	11	82	7.6	40	10	4.0	39	36	0.9	66 y	76 y	1.2 y	12 x	49 x	4.3 x	30 x	59 x	2.0 x
Netherlands	–	–	–	–	–	–	–	–	–	–	–	–	–	–	–	–	–	–	–	–	–

TABLE 13 | DISPARITIES BY HOUSEHOLD WEALTH ▶

Countries and areas	Birth registration (%) 2005–2011*			Skilled attendant at birth (%) 2007–2012*			Underweight prevalence in children under 5 (%) 2007–2011*			Diarrhoea treatment with oral rehydration salts (ORS) (%) 2007–2012*			Primary school net attendance ratio 2007–2011*			Comprehensive knowledge of HIV (%) Females 15–24 2007–2011*			Comprehensive knowledge of HIV (%) Males 15–24 2007–2011*		
	poorest 20%	richest 20%	ratio of richest to poorest	poorest 20%	richest 20%	ratio of richest to poorest	poorest 20%	richest 20%	ratio of poorest to richest	poorest 20%	richest 20%	ratio of richest to poorest	poorest 20%	richest 20%	ratio of richest to poorest	poorest 20%	richest 20%	ratio of richest to poorest	poorest 20%	richest 20%	ratio of richest to poorest
New Zealand	–	–	–	–	–	–	–	–	–	–	–	–	–	–	–	–	–	–	–	–	–
Nicaragua	72 y	93 y	1.3 y	42	99	2.4	9	1	6.6	53	64	1.2	–	–	–	–	–	–	–	–	–
Niger	20 y	67 y	3.3 y	5 x	59 x	11.8 x	–	–	–	14 x	32 x	2.3 x	26 x	32 x	1.2 x	5 x	30 x	6.5 x	6 x	34 x	5.8 x
Nigeria	9	62	7.0	8	86	10.3	35	10	3.5	15	53	3.5	31	72	2.4	9	34	3.6	18	41	2.2
Niue	–	–	–	–	–	–	–	–	–	–	–	–	–	–	–	–	–	–	–	–	–
Norway	–	–	–	–	–	–	–	–	–	–	–	–	–	–	–	–	–	–	–	–	–
Oman	–	–	–	–	–	–	–	–	–	–	–	–	–	–	–	–	–	–	–	–	–
Pakistan	18	38	2.1	*16*	*77*	*4.8*	–	–	–	41	44	1.1	42	74	1.8	–	–	–	–	–	–
Palau	–	–	–	–	–	–	–	–	–	–	–	–	–	–	–	–	–	–	–	–	–
Panama	–	–	–	–	–	–	–	–	–	–	–	–	–	–	–	–	–	–	–	–	–
Papua New Guinea	–	–	–	–	–	–	–	–	–	–	–	–	–	–	–	–	–	–	–	–	–
Paraguay	–	–	–	–	–	–	–	–	–	–	–	–	–	–	–	–	–	–	–	–	–
Peru	–	–	–	56	100	1.8	9	1	15.7	27	42	1.6	92	97	1.1	–	–	–	–	–	–
Philippines	–	–	–	26	94	3.7	–	–	–	37	55	1.5	–	–	–	14	26	1.8	–	–	–
Poland	–	–	–	–	–	–	–	–	–	–	–	–	–	–	–	–	–	–	–	–	–
Portugal	–	–	–	–	–	–	–	–	–	–	–	–	–	–	–	–	–	–	–	–	–
Qatar	–	–	–	–	–	–	–	–	–	–	–	–	–	–	–	–	–	–	–	–	–
Republic of Korea	–	–	–	–	–	–	–	–	–	–	–	–	–	–	–	–	–	–	–	–	–
Republic of Moldova	97 x	98 x	1.0 x	*99 x*	*100 x*	*1.0 x*	5 x	1 x	8.2 x	–	–	–	–	–	–	–	–	–	–	–	–
Romania	–	–	–	–	–	–	–	–	–	–	–	–	–	–	–	–	–	–	–	–	–
Russian Federation	–	–	–	–	–	–	–	–	–	–	–	–	–	–	–	–	–	–	–	–	–
Rwanda	58	64	1.1	61	86	1.4	16	5	3.0	22	37	1.7	80	94	1.2	–	–	–	–	–	–
Saint Kitts and Nevis	–	–	–	–	–	–	–	–	–	–	–	–	–	–	–	–	–	–	–	–	–
Saint Lucia	–	–	–	–	–	–	–	–	–	–	–	–	–	–	–	–	–	–	–	–	–
Saint Vincent and the Grenadines	–	–	–	–	–	–	–	–	–	–	–	–	–	–	–	–	–	–	–	–	–
Samoa	31	63	2.1	66	95	1.4	–	–	–	–	–	–	85 y	91 y	1.1 y	3	3	1.0	3	9	2.7
San Marino	–	–	–	–	–	–	–	–	–	–	–	–	–	–	–	–	–	–	–	–	–
Sao Tome and Principe	74	86	1.1	74	93	1.3	18	7	2.6	–	–	–	75	95	1.3	27	56	2.0	39	55	1.4
Saudi Arabia	–	–	–	–	–	–	–	–	–	–	–	–	–	–	–	–	–	–	–	–	–
Senegal	50	94	1.9	30	96	3.2	24	10	2.4	21	31	1.5	47	78	1.7	–	–	–	–	–	–
Serbia	97	100	1.0	99	100	1.0	3	2	1.4	–	–	–	96	98	1.0	28	69	2.4	28	66	2.4
Seychelles	–	–	–	–	–	–	–	–	–	–	–	–	–	–	–	–	–	–	–	–	–
Sierra Leone	74	88	1.2	44	85	1.9	22	15	1.4	75	70	0.9	59	88	1.5	14	36	2.6	–	–	–
Singapore	–	–	–	–	–	–	–	–	–	–	–	–	–	–	–	–	–	–	–	–	–
Slovakia	–	–	–	–	–	–	–	–	–	–	–	–	–	–	–	–	–	–	–	–	–
Slovenia	–	–	–	–	–	–	–	–	–	–	–	–	–	–	–	–	–	–	–	–	–
Solomon Islands	–	–	–	74	95	1.3	14	10	1.4	–	–	–	58 y	61 y	1.1 y	17	37	2.1	35	50	1.5
Somalia	1	7	6.6	11 x	77 x	7.2 x	42 x	14 x	3.0 x	7 x	31 x	4.8 x	3 x	40 x	12.5 x	1 x	8 x	13.5 x	–	–	–
South Africa	–	–	–	–	–	–	–	–	–	–	–	–	–	–	–	–	–	–	–	–	–
South Sudan⁰	21	57	2.7	8	41	5.1	32	21	1.6	27	52	1.9	12	58	4.7	3	18	6.1	–	–	–
Spain	–	–	–	–	–	–	–	–	–	–	–	–	–	–	–	–	–	–	–	–	–
Sri Lanka	97	98	1.0	97	99	1.0	29	11	2.6	–	–	–	–	–	–	–	–	–	–	–	–
State of Palestine	–	–	–	98 x	100 x	1.0 x	–	–	–	–	–	–	–	–	–	–	–	–	–	–	–
Sudan⁰	26	98	3.8	6	59	10.5	40	17	2.4	21	16	0.7	55	97	1.8	1	11	13.6	–	–	–
Suriname	94	98	1.0	81	96	1.2 x	9 x	5 x	1.8 x	–	–	–	88 x	97 x	1.1 x	23 x	54 x	2.4 x	–	–	–
Swaziland	39	73	1.9	65	94	1.4	8	4	2.3	58	60	1.0	95	99	1.0	49	72	1.5	44	64	1.5
Sweden	–	–	–	–	–	–	–	–	–	–	–	–	–	–	–	–	–	–	–	–	–
Switzerland	–	–	–	–	–	–	–	–	–	–	–	–	–	–	–	–	–	–	–	–	–
Syrian Arab Republic	92	99	1.1	*78 x*	*99 x*	*1.3 x*	*10 x*	*7 x*	*1.5 x*	45 x	59 x	1.3 x	–	–	–	4 x	10 x	2.9 x	–	–	–
Tajikistan	89	86	1.0	*90*	*90*	*1.0*	17	13	1.3	*52 x*	*50 x*	*1.0 x*	96 y	96 y	1.0 y	–	–	–	–	–	–
Thailand	99	100	1.0	*93 x*	*100 x*	*1.1 x*	11 x	3 x	3.3 x	56 x	54 x	1.0 x	97 x	98 x	1.0 x	47 x	43 x	0.9 x	–	–	–
The former Yugoslav Republic of Macedonia	99	100	1.0	98	98	1.0	2	0	–	–	–	–	97	99	1.0	9 x	45 x	5.0 x	–	–	–
Timor-Leste	50	56	1.1	10	69	6.9	49	35	1.4	70	71	1.0	60	83	1.4	9	16	1.8	11	35	3.0
Togo	59	97	1.7	28	94	3.4	21	9	2.5	8	19	2.5	80	92	1.2	18	42	2.3	20	55	2.7
Tonga	–	–	–	–	–	–	–	–	–	–	–	–	–	–	–	–	–	–	–	–	–
Trinidad and Tobago	94	98	1.0	98	100	1.0	–	–	–	–	–	–	95 x	99 x	1.0 x	48 x	62 x	1.3 x	–	–	–
Tunisia	–	–	–	–	–	–	–	–	–	–	–	–	–	–	–	–	–	–	–	–	–
Turkey	89	99	1.1	73	100	1.4	4	1	8.4	–	–	–	87 y	95 y	1.1 y	–	–	–	–	–	–
Turkmenistan	94	97	1.0	99 x	100 x	1.0 x	8 x	2 x	3.2 x	45 x	30 x	0.7 x	–	–	–	3 x	8 x	2.8 x	–	–	–
Tuvalu	39	71	1.8	99	98	1.0	1	0	–	–	–	–	–	–	–	34 y	39	1.2 y	–	67 y	–
Uganda	27	44	1.6	43	88	2.0	–	–	–	43	45	1.1	–	–	–	*20 x*	*47 x*	*2.3 x*	*28 x*	*47 x*	*1.6 x*
Ukraine	100	100	1.0	97	99	1.0	–	–	–	–	–	–	78	75	1.0	33	45	1.4	28	42	1.5

TABLE 13 | DISPARITIES BY HOUSEHOLD WEALTH

Countries and areas	Birth registration (%) 2005–2011*			Skilled attendant at birth (%) 2007–2012*			Underweight prevalence in children under 5 (%) 2007–2011*			Diarrhoea treatment with oral rehydration salts (ORS) (%) 2007–2012*			Primary school net attendance ratio 2007–2011*			Comprehensive knowledge of HIV (%) Females 15–24 2007–2011*			Comprehensive knowledge of HIV (%) Males 15–24 2007–2011*		
	poorest 20%	richest 20%	ratio of richest to poorest	poorest 20%	richest 20%	ratio of richest to poorest	poorest 20%	richest 20%	ratio of poorest to richest	poorest 20%	richest 20%	ratio of richest to poorest	poorest 20%	richest 20%	ratio of richest to poorest	poorest 20%	richest 20%	ratio of richest to poorest	poorest 20%	richest 20%	ratio of richest to poorest
United Arab Emirates	–	–	–	–	–	–	–	–	–	–	–	–	–	–	–	–	–	–	–	–	–
United Kingdom	–	–	–	–	–	–	–	–	–	–	–	–	–	–	–	–	–	–	–	–	–
United Republic of Tanzania	4	56	12.7	31	90	2.9	22	9	2.3	41	38	0.9	68	93	1.4	39	55	1.4	34	56	1.7
United States	–	–	–	–	–	–	–	–	–	–	–	–	–	–	–	–	–	–	–	–	–
Uruguay	–	–	–	–	–	–	–	–	–	–	–	–	–	–	–	–	–	–	–	–	–
Uzbekistan	100	100	1.0	100 x	100 x	1.0 x	5 x	3 x	1.5 x	–	–	–	94 x	96 x	1.0 x	25 x	33 x	1.3 x	–	–	–
Vanuatu	13	41	3.1	55	90	1.6	12	10	1.2	–	–	–	74	76	1.0	9	23	2.7	–	–	–
Venezuela (Bolivarian Republic of)	87 x	95 x	1.1 x	95 x	92 x	1.0 x	–	–	–	39 x	55 x	1.4 x	86 x	99 x	1.2 x	–	–	–	–	–	–
Viet Nam	87	98	1.1	72	99	1.4	21	3	6.6	–	–	–	95	99	1.0	38	68	1.8	–	–	–
Yemen	5	50	9.3	17 x	74 x	4.3 x	–	–	–	31 x	37 x	1.2 x	44 x	73 x	1.6 x	0 x	4 x	–	–	–	–
Zambia	5	31	5.8	27	91	3.4	16	11	1.5	61	61	1.0	73	96	1.3	24	48	2.0	24	51	2.1
Zimbabwe	35	75	2.1	48	91	1.9	–	–	–	18	28	1.6	84	91	1.1	31 x	52 x	1.7 x	37 x	51 x	1.4 x
MEMORANDUM																					
Sudan and South Sudan σ	–	–	–	–	–	–	–	–	–	–	–	–	–	–	–	–	–	–	–	–	–
SUMMARY INDICATORS #																					
Sub-Saharan Africa	25	60	2.4	27	82	3.0	30	12	2.5	27	42	1.5	53	80	1.5	16	36	2.2	22	45	2.0
Eastern and Southern Africa	23	50	2.2	28	77	2.7	26	12	2.2	34	44	1.3	62	86	1.4	–	–	–	–	–	–
West and Central Africa	26	65	2.5	28	88	3.1	31	11	2.7	21	42	2.0	43	73	1.7	10	30	3.0	17	38	2.2
Middle East and North Africa	–	–	–	–	–	–	–	–	–	–	–	–	–	–	–	–	–	–	–	–	–
South Asia	23	63	2.7	22	82	3.7	55	19	2.8	29	46	1.6	–	–	–	4	44	11.7	15	55	3.8
East Asia and the Pacific	48 **	89 **	1.9 **	54 **	92 **	1.7 **	24 **	10 **	2.5 **	36 **	41 **	1.1 **	–	–	–	14 **	35 **	2.4 **	–	–	–
Latin America and Caribbean	–	–	–	–	–	–	–	–	–	–	–	–	–	–	–	–	–	–	–	–	–
CEE/CIS	94	98	1.0	–	–	–	–	–	–	–	–	–	–	–	–	–	–	–	–	–	–
Least developed countries	25	52	2.1	30	78	2.6	33	15	2.3	40	47	1.2	61	83	1.4	–	–	–	–	–	–
World	32 **	68 **	2.1 **	31 **	85 **	2.7 **	39 **	14 **	2.7 **	29 **	44 **	1.5 **	–	–	–	–	–	–	–	–	–

σ Due to the cession in July 2011 of the Republic of South Sudan by the Republic of the Sudan, and its subsequent admission to the United Nations on 14 July 2011, disaggregated data for the Sudan and South Sudan as separate States are not yet available for all indicators. Aggregated data presented are for the Sudan pre-cession (see Memorandum item).

\# For a complete list of countries and areas in the regions, subregions and country categories, see page 98.

DEFINITIONS OF THE INDICATORS

Birth registration – Percentage of children under age 5 who were registered at the moment of the survey. This includes children whose birth certificate was seen by the interviewer or whose mother or caretaker says the birth has been registered.

Skilled attendant at birth – Percentage of births attended by skilled health personnel (doctor, nurse or midwife).

Underweight prevalence in children under 5 – Percentage of children under age 5 who are below minus two standard deviations from median weight-for-age of the World Health Organization (WHO) Child Growth Standards.

Diarrhoea treatment with oral rehydration salts (ORS) – Percentage of children under age 5 who had diarrhoea in the two weeks preceding the survey and who received oral rehydration salts (ORS packets or pre-packaged ORS fluids).

Primary school net attendance ratio – Number of children attending primary or secondary school who are of official primary school age, expressed as a percentage of the total number of children of official primary school age. Because of the inclusion of primary-school-aged children attending secondary school, this indicator can also be referred to as a primary adjusted net attendance ratio.

Comprehensive knowledge of HIV – Percentage of young men and women (aged 15–24) who correctly identify the two major ways of preventing the sexual transmission of HIV (using condoms and limiting sex to one faithful, uninfected partner), who reject the two most common local misconceptions about HIV transmission and who know that a healthy-looking person can be HIV-positive.

MAIN DATA SOURCES

Birth registration – Demographic and Health Surveys (DHS), Multiple Indicator Cluster Surveys (MICS), other national surveys and vital registration systems.

Skilled attendant at birth – DHS, MICS and other nationally representative sources.

Underweight prevalence in children under 5 – DHS, MICS, other national household surveys, WHO and UNICEF.

Diarrhoea treatment with oral rehydration salts (ORS) – DHS, MICS and other national household surveys.

Primary school attendance – DHS, MICS and other national household surveys.

Comprehensive knowledge of HIV – AIDS Indicator Surveys (AIS), DHS, MICS and other national household surveys; HIV/AIDS Survey Indicators Database, <www.measuredhs.com/hivdata>.

Italicized disparity data **are from different sources than the data for the same indicators presented elsewhere in the report: Table 2 (Nutrition – Underweight prevalence), Table 3 (Health – Diarrhoea treatment), Table 4 (HIV/AIDS – Comprehensive knowledge of HIV) and Table 8 (Women – Skilled attendant at birth).**

NOTES

– Data not available.

x Data refer to years or periods other than those specified in the column heading. Such data are not included in the calculation of regional and global averages, with the exception of 2005–2006 data from India. Estimates from data years prior to 2000 are not displayed.

y Data differ from the standard definition or refer to only part of a country. If they fall within the noted reference period, such data are included in the calculation of regional and global averages.

* Data refer to the most recent year available during the period specified in the column heading.

** Excludes China.

TABLE 14: EARLY CHILDHOOD DEVELOPMENT

Countries and areas	Attendance in early childhood education 2005–2011*					Adult support for learning ++ 2005–2011*					Father's support for learning ++ 2005–2011*	Learning materials at home 2005–2011*						Children left in inadequate care 2005–2011*				
												Children's books			Playthings++							
	total	male	female	poorest 20%	richest 20%	total	male	female	poorest 20%	richest 20%		total	poorest 20%	richest 20%	total	poorest 20%	richest 20%	total	male	female	poorest 20%	richest 20%
Afghanistan	1	1	1	0	4	73	74	73	72	80	62	2	1	5	53	52	57	40	42	39	43	27
Albania	40	39	42	26	60	86	85	87	68	96	53	32	16	52	53	57	48	13	14	11	9	16
Bangladesh	15	14	15	11	16	61	61	60	42	85	53	–	–	–	–	–	–	–	–	–	–	–
Belarus	86	87	85	–	–	97	97	96	95	98	72	–	–	–	–	–	–	–	–	–	–	–
Belize	32	30	34	16	59	86	88	83	73	94	50	40	17	73	57	55	58	2	3	2	4	1
Bhutan	10	10	10	3	27	54	52	57	40	73	51	6	1	24	52	36	60	14	13	15	17	7
Bosnia and Herzegovina	6	5	8	1	15	83	83	83	74	90	74	70	52	88	43	49	43	7	7	6	6	10
Botswana	18	–	–	–	–																	
Burkina Faso	2	3	1	0	9	14	14	14	12	26	24	–	–	–	–	–	–	–	–	–	–	–
Burundi	5	5	5	4	10	34	35	34	32	38	20	–	–	–	–	–	–	–	–	–	–	–
Cameroon	22	22	22	3	56	58	57	59	57	69	39	8	3	22	57	62	46	36	36	36	45	25
Central African Republic	5	5	6	2	17	74	74	74	70	78	42	1	0	3	49	41	51	61	60	62	58	60
Chad	5	5	4	1	16	70	69	70	64	71	29	1	0	2	43	38	50	56	57	56	58	56
Côte d'Ivoire	6	5	6	1	24	50	50	51	55	57	40	5	3	13	39	44	35	59	60	58	62	51
Democratic People's Republic of Korea	98	98	97	–	–	91	88	93	–	–	75	79	–	–	47	–	–	17	17	16	–	–
Democratic Republic of the Congo	5	5	5	2	18	61	61	62	62	76	36	1	0	2	29	21	40	60	60	60	69	39
Djibouti	14	12	16	–	–	36	36	35	–	–	23	15	–	–	24	–	–	12	11	13	–	–
Gambia	18	17	19	13	33	48	49	47	50	56	21	1	0	5	42	29	49	21	22	19	25	18
Georgia	43	44	42	17	70	93	93	93	85	99	61	72	48	91	38	41	41	8	8	8	7	6
Ghana	68	65	72	42	97	40	38	42	23	78	30	6	1	23	41	31	51	21	21	21	27	15
Guinea-Bissau	10	10	10	4	26	–	–	–	–	–	–	–	–	–	–	–	–	–	–	–	–	–
Guyana	49	48	50	33	78	89	88	89	77	99	52	54	28	86	65	67	60	11	13	10	19	6
Iraq	3	2	3	–	–	58	59	57	–	–	60	–	–	–	–	–	–	–	–	–	–	–
Jamaica	86	84	88	–	–	94	95	93	–	–	41	57	–	–	71	–	–	4	4	3	–	–
Kazakhstan	37	36	38	19	61	92	92	91	84	96	49	48	24	76	45	40	49	4	4	4	5	4
Kyrgyzstan	19	21	17	7	47	88	90	85	86	99	54	76	76	85	57	59	54	11	12	9	11	6
Lao People's Democratic Republic	7	8	7	1	44	33	33	34	20	59	24	3	1	11	57	54	40	26	26	25	33	17
Lebanon	62	63	60	–	–	56 y	58 y	54 y	–	–	74 y	29	–	–	16 y	–	–	9	8	10	–	–
Mali	10	10	10	1	40	29	27	30	28	44	14	0	0	2	40	33	49	33	33	33	33	36
Mauritania	5	5	5	2	11	48	48	47	39	64	30	–	–	–	–	–	–	–	–	–	–	–
Mongolia	60	58	61	26	83	59	56	62	44	73	41	23	6	48	68	74	62	9	9	8	10	6
Montenegro	29	28	30	6	62	97	96	98	88	100	79	77	50	92	39	49	33	6	8	5	11	3
Morocco	39	36	41	6	78	48 y	47 y	49 y	35 y	68 y	56 y	21 y	9 y	52 y	14 y	19 y	7 y	9	9	9	11	6
Mozambique	–	–	–	–	–	47	45	48	48	50	20	3	2	10	–	–	–	33	33	32	–	–
Myanmar	23	23	23	8	46	58 y	58 y	58 y	42 y	76 y	44 y	–	–	–	–	–	–	–	–	–	–	–
Nepal	30 y	29 y	31 y	14 y	61 y	–	–	–	–	–	–	–	–	–	–	–	–	–	–	–	–	–
Nigeria	32	32	32	5	70	78	78	78	68	91	38	14	2	35	35	25	42	38	38	37	41	32
Sao Tome and Principe	27	29	26	18	51	–	–	–	–	–	–	–	–	–	–	–	–	–	–	–	–	–
Senegal	22 y	23 y	21 y	7 y	43 y	–	–	–	–	–	–	–	–	–	–	–	–	–	–	–	–	–
Serbia	44	41	47	22	75	95	96	95	84	98	78	76	49	86	63	65	60	1	1	1	2	1
Sierra Leone	14	13	15	5	42	54	53	55	45	79	42	2	0	10	35	24	50	32	33	32	29	28
Somalia	2	2	2	1	6	79	80	79	76	85	48	–	–	–	–	–	–	–	–	–	–	–
South Sudan	6	6	6	2	13	–	–	–	–	–	–	–	–	–	–	–	–	–	–	–	–	–
Sudan	20	20	21	10	48	–	–	–	–	–	–	–	–	–	–	–	–	–	–	–	–	–
Suriname	39	37	40	17	63	75	75	76	61	92	31	45	20	75	64	67	63	7	6	8	13	1
Swaziland	33	32	34	36	50	50	50	50	35	71	10	4	1	12	69	64	74	15	15	15	20	9
Syrian Arab Republic	8	8	7	4	18	70	70	69	52	84	62	30	12	53	52	52	51	17	17	17	22	15
Tajikistan	10	11	10	1	29	74	73	74	56	86	23	17	4	33	46	43	44	13	13	12	15	11
Thailand	61	60	61	55	78	89	90	89	86	98	57	43	25	71	55	58	49	13	14	13	18	7
The former Yugoslav Republic of Macedonia	22	25	19	0	59	92	92	91	81	97	71	52	19	83	71	70	79	5	5	5	10	1

TABLE 14 | EARLY CHILDHOOD DEVELOPMENT

Countries and areas	Attendance in early childhood education 2005–2011*					Adult support for learning ++ 2005–2011*					Father's support for learning ++ 2005–2011*	Learning materials at home 2005–2011*						Children left in inadequate care 2005–2011*				
												Children's books			Playthings++							
	total	male	female	poorest 20%	richest 20%	total	male	female	poorest 20%	richest 20%		total	poorest 20%	richest 20%	total	poorest 20%	richest 20%	total	male	female	poorest 20%	richest 20%
Togo	29	27	31	10	52	62	61	63	55	68	38	2	0	7	31	26	41	41	42	41	45	35
Trinidad and Tobago	75	74	76	65	87	98	98	98	96	100	63	81	66	93	65	63	72	1	1	1	2	0
Ukraine	63	63	63	30	74	–	–	–	–	–	–	97	93	99	47	36	47	10	11	10	15	4
Uzbekistan	20	20	19	5	46	91	91	90	83	95	54	43	32	59	67	74	62	5	5	5	6	7
Viet Nam	72	71	73	59	91	77	74	80	63	94	61	20	3	49	49	41	54	9	10	9	17	4
Yemen	3	3	3	0	8	33	34	32	16	56	37	10	4	31	49	45	49	34	36	33	46	22
SUMMARY INDICATORS#																						
Sub-Saharan Africa	21	21	21	6	47	–	–	–	–	–	–	–	–	–	–	–	–	–	–	–	–	–
Eastern and Southern Africa	–	–	–	–	–	–	–	–	–	–	–	–	–	–	–	–	–	–	–	–	–	–
West and Central Africa	22	22	23	6	49	63	63	63	57	77	35	8	1	21	36	29	43	43	43	43	47	34
Middle East and North Africa	–	–	–	–	–	–	–	–	–	–	–	–	–	–	–	–	–	–	–	–	–	–
South Asia	–	–	–	–	–	–	–	–	–	–	–	–	–	–	–	–	–	–	–	–	–	–
East Asia and Pacific	–	–	–	–	–	–	–	–	–	–	–	–	–	–	–	–	–	–	–	–	–	–
Latin America and Caribbean	–	–	–	–	–	–	–	–	–	–	–	–	–	–	–	–	–	–	–	–	–	–
CEE/CIS	–	–	–	–	–	–	–	–	–	–	–	–	–	–	–	–	–	–	–	–	–	–
Least developed countries	11	11	12	6	24	–	–	–	–	–	–	–	–	–	–	–	–	–	–	–	–	–
World	–	–	–	–	–	–	–	–	–	–	–	–	–	–	–	–	–	–	–	–	–	–

\# For a complete list of countries and areas in the regions, subregions and country categories, see page 98.

DEFINITIONS OF THE INDICATORS

Attendance in early childhood education – Percentage of children 36–59 months old who are attending an early childhood education programme.

Adult support for learning – Percentage of children 36–59 months old with whom an adult has engaged in four or more of the following activities to promote learning and school readiness in the past three days: a) reading books to the child, b) telling stories to the child, c) singing songs to the child, d) taking the child outside the home, e) playing with the child and f) naming, counting or drawing things with the child.

Father's support for learning – Percentage of children 36–59 months old whose father has engaged in one or more of the following activities to promote learning and school readiness in the past three days: a) reading books to the child, b) telling stories to the child, c) singing songs to the child, d) taking the child outside the home, e) playing with the child and f) naming, counting or drawing things with the child.

Learning materials at home: children's books – Percentage of children 0–59 months old who have three or more children's books at home.

Learning materials at home: playthings – Percentage of children 0–59 months old with two or more of the following playthings at home: household objects or objects found outside (sticks, rocks, animals, shells, leaves, etc.), homemade toys or toys that came from a store.

Children left in inadequate care – Percentage of children 0–59 months old left alone or in the care of another child younger than 10 years of age for more than one hour at least once in the past week.

MAIN DATA SOURCES

Attendance in early childhood education – Multiple Indicator Cluster Surveys (MICS), Demographic and Health Surveys (DHS) and other national surveys.

Adult support for learning – MICS and other national surveys.

Father's support for learning – MICS and other national surveys.

Learning materials at home: children's books – MICS and other national surveys.

Learning materials at home: playthings – MICS and other national surveys.

Children left in inadequate care – MICS and other national surveys.

NOTES

– Data not available.

y Data differ from the standard definition or refer to only part of a country. If they fall within the noted reference period, such data are included in the calculation of regional and global averages.

* Data refer to the most recent year available during the period specified in the column heading.

++ Changes in the definitions of several ECD indicators were made between the third and fourth rounds of MICS (MICS3 and MICS4). In order to allow for comparability with MICS4, data from MICS3 for the adult support for learning, father's support for learning and learning materials at home (playthings) indicators were recalculated according to MICS4 indicator definitions. Therefore, the recalculated data presented here will differ from estimates reported in MICS3 national reports.

Conventions, optional protocols, signatures and ratifications

A note on terms used in this report

A **Convention** is a formal agreement between States parties. The term 'Convention' is used (rather than its synonym, 'treaty') to denote a multilateral instrument with a large number of States parties, including one open to participation by the international community as a whole and negotiated under the auspices of an international organization.

An **Optional Protocol** to a Convention is a legal instrument intended to supplement the original agreement by establishing additional rights or obligations. It may be used to address in greater detail a matter mentioned in the original agreement, to speak to a new concern relevant to any of its topics, or to add procedures for operation or enforcement. Such a protocol is optional in the sense that States parties to a Convention are not automatically bound by its provisions, but must ratify it independently. Thus, a State may be party to a Convention but not to its Optional Protocols.

The process by which a State becomes party to a Convention comprises, in most cases, two steps: signature and ratification.

By **signing a Convention**, a State indicates its intention to take steps to examine the Convention and its compatibility with domestic law. A signature does not create a legal obligation to be bound by a Convention's provisions; however, it does indicate that a State will act in good faith and will not take actions that would undermine the purpose of the Convention.

Ratification is the concrete action by which a State agrees to be legally bound by the terms of a Convention. The procedure varies according to each country's particular legislative structure. After a State has determined that a Convention is consistent with domestic laws and that steps may be taken to comply with its provisions, the appropriate national organ (e.g., a parliament) makes a formal decision to ratify. Once the instrument of ratification – a formal, sealed letter signed by the responsible authority (e.g., a president) – is deposited with the United Nations Secretary-General, the State becomes party to the Convention.

In some cases, a state will **accede** to a Convention or Optional Protocol. Essentially, **accession** is like ratifying without first having to sign.

For further information and more detailed definitions of these and related terms, see <http://treaties.un.org/Pages/Overview.aspx?path=overview/definition/page1_en.xml>.

The Convention on the Rights of Persons with Disabilities is available at <http://treaties.un.org/doc/Publication/CTC/Ch_IV_15.pdf>.
The Optional Protocol is available at <http://treaties.un.org/doc/Publication/CTC/Ch-15-a.pdf>.